GREAT VICTORIAN PICTURES

Cover: HENRY NELSON O'NEIL Eastward Ho! 1858 Private Collection

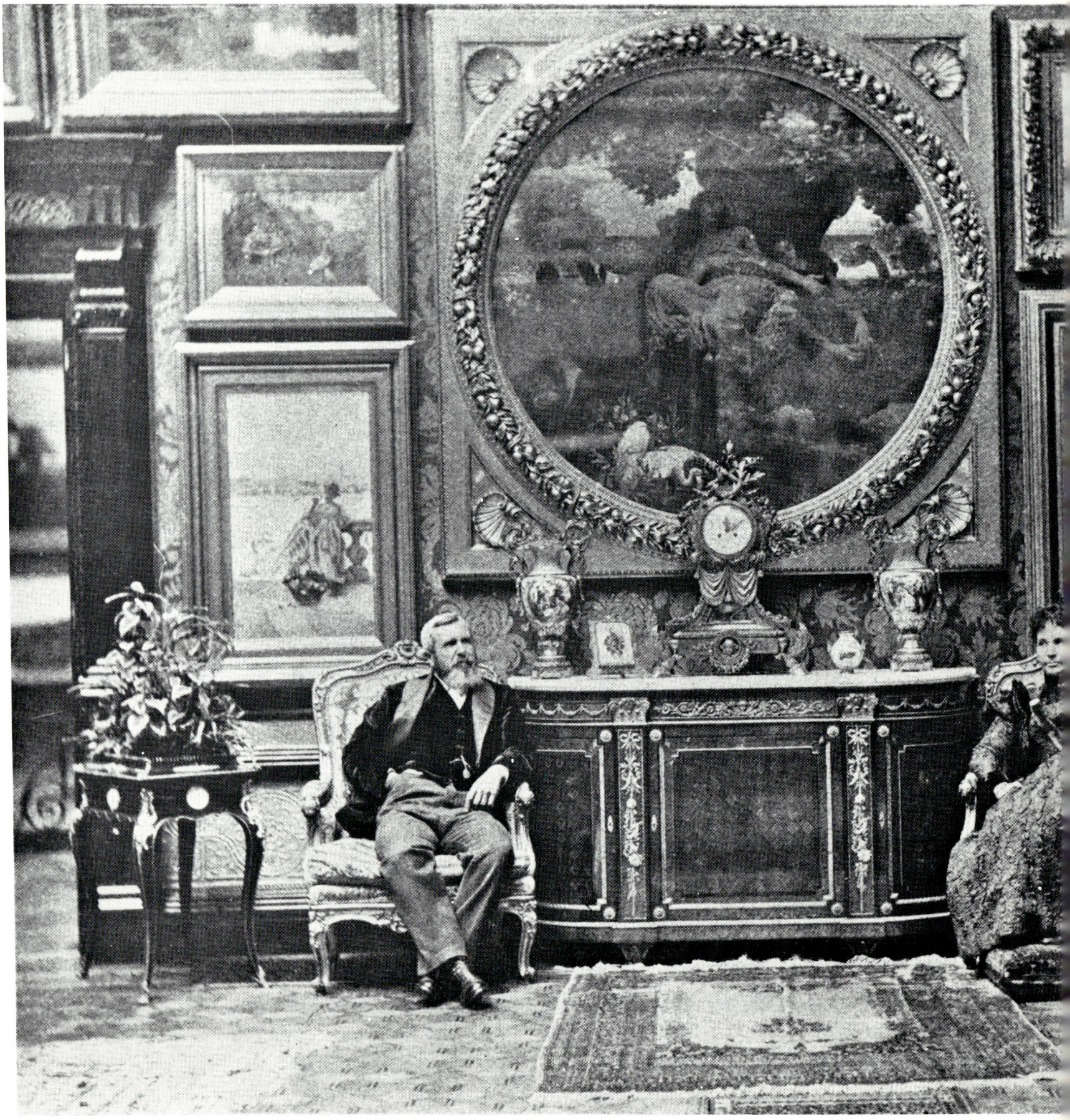

Mr and Mrs George McCulloch in their Kensington home

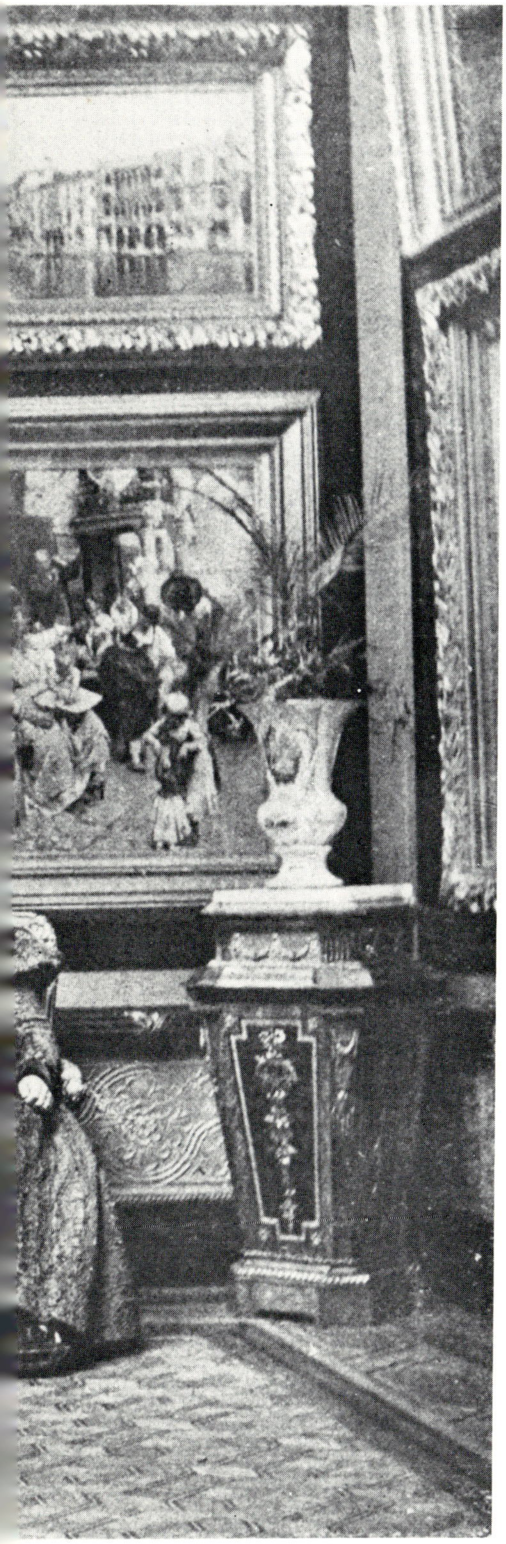

GREAT VICTORIAN PICTURES

their paths to fame

An Arts Council Exhibition 1978

Leeds City Art Gallery
in association with the University of Leeds
28 January – 11 March 1978

Leicestershire Museum and Art Gallery
25 March – 7 May

Bristol, City Art Gallery
20 May – 1 July

Royal Academy of Arts, London
July – September
(dates not confirmed at time of going to press)

Exhibition documentation designed by Ivor Heal

Catalogue designed by Roger Huggett/Sinc
Printed in England by Raithby, Lawrence and Company Ltd, Leicester and London

ISBN
Softback 0 7287 0163 4
Hardback 0 7287 0164 2

A list of all Arts Council publications
in print can be obtained from:
The Publications Department
Arts Council of Great Britain
105 Piccadilly
London W1V 0AU

Preface

Victorian painting has enjoyed and suffered each extreme of public and critical response. In the few years between Victoria's death and the First World War, the English avant-garde, led by Roger Fry, had turned their backs on the 'subject' pictures of nineteenth century Britain. Instead they looked to Cézanne and the revolution which he and other Post-Impressionists had brought to French painting. 'Significant form' – the exploration of pure line, shape and colour – became the irresistible order of the day and Victorian pictures were removed from gallery walls to become the unwieldy storage problems of museum curators throughout the country. Only the Pre-Raphaelites, themselves remote from the mainstream of Victorian art, could survive the welter of critical abuse and even they were not unscathed.

Yet throughout this century Victorian pictures have retained the affection of a large section of the public and, as concern has mounted about the increasingly isolated position of contemporary art, so historians and critics have begun to look again at the art of this unique period in which critically acclaimed pictures were genuinely popular.

'To move the heart of the million' was not always the fanciful ambition of a Victorian artist. The present exhibition brings together many of the pictures which achieved that goal and examines the reasons behind their success.

We thank Rosemary Treble who has selected the exhibition and whose researches have allowed the 'paths to fame' of each picture to be fully documented. We thank also Judith Bronkhurst who has provided valuable help in the preparation of the catalogue, and Robert Bruce-Gardner for cleaning and restoring a number of pictures so that they might be exhibited. Finally, we express our deep gratitude to the owners of the pictures for their most generous loans and interest.

Joanna Drew *Director of Exhibitions*
Michael Harrison *Exhibition Organiser*

Acknowledgements

This exhibition represents a cross-section taken through the widest practicable spectrum of Victorian art to show how an artist achieved success and what forms that success could take. As the artists range from those still famous today to those who dropped into total obscurity after the end of the Victorian era, some pictures have been harder to trace than others, and the help of many scholars, museum staffs, dealers, collectors, and fellow-students has been indispensable. There are indeed so very many people who have given generously of their time and researches, responded to endless questions, and advised and informed me at every stage in the preparation of this exhibition that it has proved impossible to name them individually in the space available. I hope they will all accept my very grateful thanks. I am also indebted to the work and example of those scholars who have pioneered the serious modern study of Victorian art, without whose published work this exhibition could not have been attempted.

At the Courtauld I owe many debts to fellow-students of the nineteenth century, and to the Book Library staff; to my colleagues in the Witt Library my thanks go for their unfailing support and practical help throughout the past year, particularly in the many moments of crisis to which they and the photographic department have responded with cheerfulness and efficiency; to Robert Bruce-Gardner for taking time in a very busy year to work on several pictures for the exhibition, and to John Sunderland who could not have been a more understanding and generous employer. Judith Bronkhurst's intensive and painstaking help during the last three months of research has been invaluable in the preparation of the catalogue; she and Malcolm Warner have contributed their special knowledge of the Pre-Raphaelite group by writing the entries for, respectively, Holman Hunt and Madox Brown, and Millais. Michael Harrison has been an expert and sympathetic exhibition organiser whose skill, patience and thoughtful interpretation have transformed the raw materials with which I presented him into an exhibition, and the supporting staff at the Arts Council and the designers have worked with exemplary speed and good humour under great pressure. Finally, my thanks to my long-suffering family and friends for their tolerance and support throughout the pangs of preparation and writing, and to my husband for infinite patience, much good advice and the shouldering of burdens.

Rosemary Treble

Introduction

Rosemary Treble

Truth, Sentiment and Health were the standards by which Victorian art was judged by its contemporaries from the very beginning of the Queen's reign through into the new century. Critical emphases shifted, both the scale of the works themselves and of spending vastly enlarged, patrons changed, international awareness of British art increased and engravings after the most successful paintings were sold throughout the world. But the constant refrain in all the writing of the period and the touchstone of every judgment was whether the work attained 'truth' generally to nature and therefore, by implication, to God's creation, whether its sentiment was appropriate and whether it was morally healthy and therefore fit for consumption.

These attitudes had their genesis in the early years of the nineteenth century. While the only modern works bought by the upper classes were, on the pattern of the eighteenth century, commissioned portraits, the emerging and newly prosperous middle classes were being supplied with cosy and jolly celebrations of village life and with illustrations from literature, all on a small domestic scale and produced by artists like Wilkie, Mulready and Collins. The Industrial Revolution had produced a new moneyed class that still felt nostalgia for the nation's rural roots, their houses were not yet palaces and the artists became businessmen themselves, gauging their market accurately and catering to it.

The standard of Victorian success was set by a painting exhibited fifteen years before Victoria came to the throne: Wilkie's *Chelsea Pensioners* shown at the 1822 RA was a sensation and had to be railed off to protect it from the crowds. What drew the crowds was the subject: it stirred patriotic memories of a recent and noble war, and bore the moral message that virtue and heroism were rewarded, for the old veterans are rejoicing at the news of the victory won by the young soldiers who have taken their places in the ranks. The common man, the humble soldier, was immortalised and a wider public than ever before could identify with the subject of the picture. It was this vein that was to be tapped so successfully throughout the Victorian era.

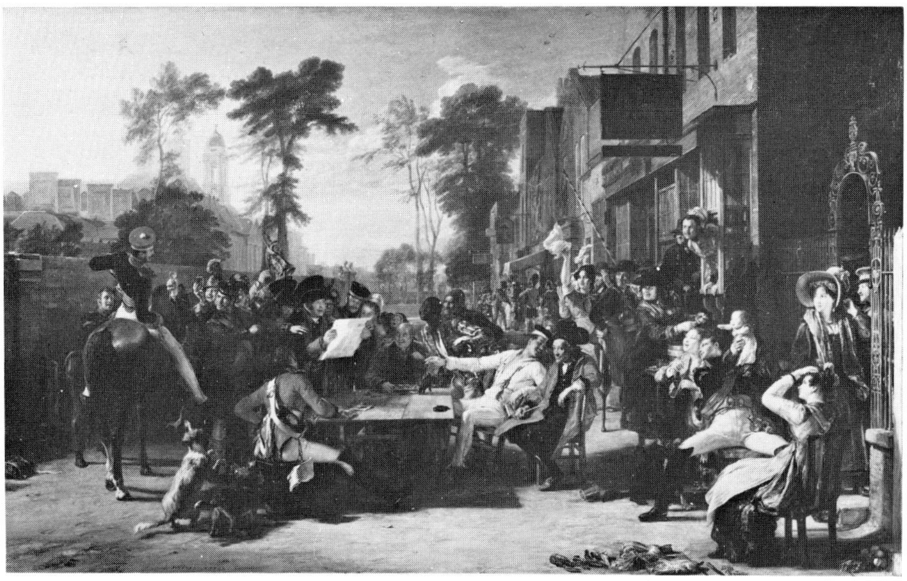

SIR DAVID WILKIE
Chelsea Pensioners reading the Gazette of the Battle of Waterloo RA 1822
Courtesy: Victoria and Albert Museum

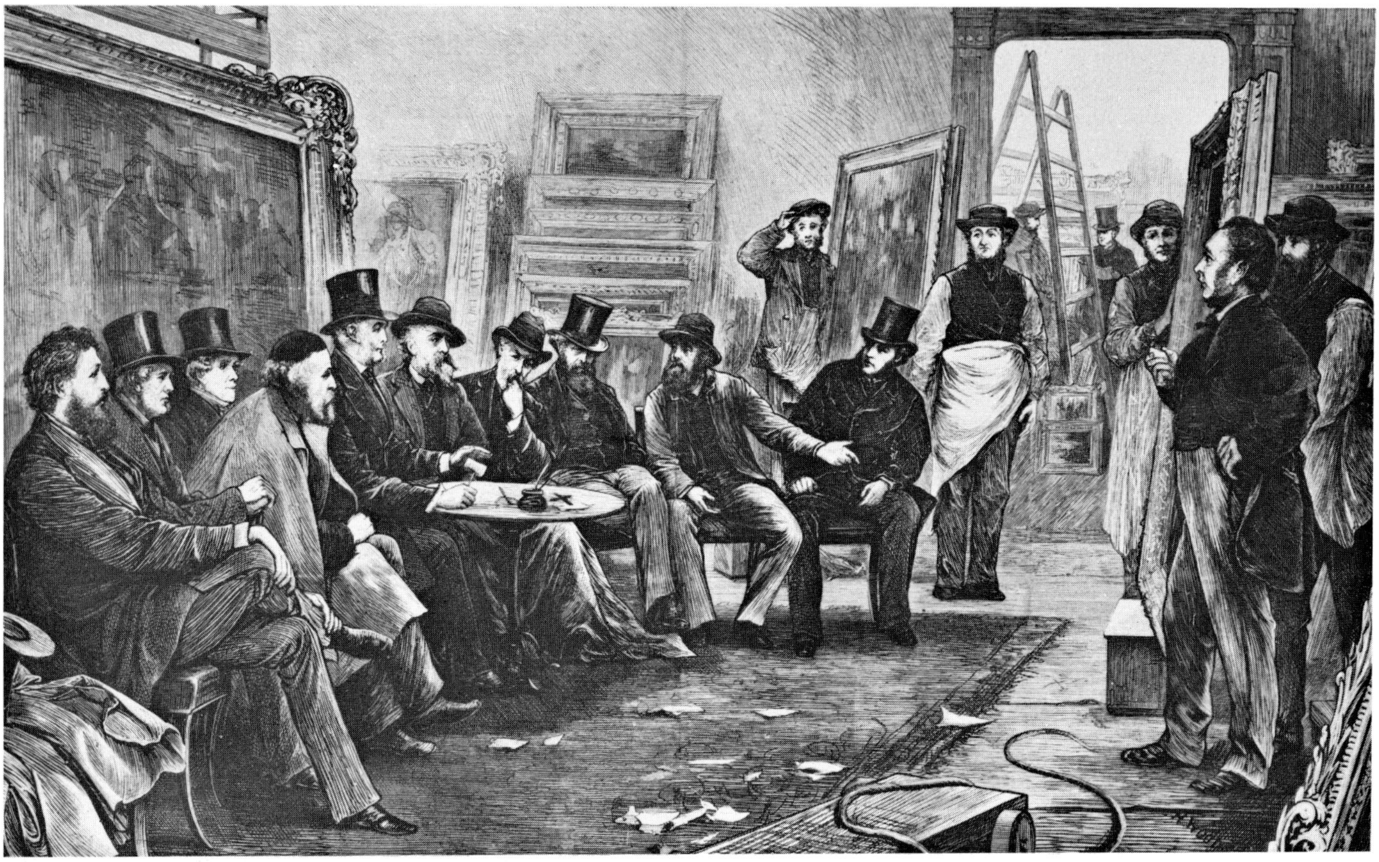

Henry Woods
The Council of Selection of the Royal Academy
The Graphic 1870

Victoria's accession in 1837 and her marriage to Prince Albert of Saxe-Coburg-Gotha in 1840 finally ended the old Whig sophistication, based on the Grand Tour and Latin culture, and replaced it with a Protestant ethos founded on domestic and public virtue. As the middle and newly-rich classes gained power, influence, respectability and self-confidence, they felt able to match the old aristocracy in the display of wealth and property; art collecting was one of the most conspicuous and prestigious means of doing this and the major early Victorian collections were formed by men like Sheepshanks, Vernon and William Wells of Redleaf. They were varied in their character, some more independent than others in their taste. Wells bought from Constable, Sheepshanks preferred literary illustration and village genre, and Vernon liked Etty nudes, large dramatic allegorical works by Landseer, and historical tableaux by Ward. Some of these patrons went directly to the artist and commissioned work without any filtering process; generally, however, the public and the majority of patrons were only able to see the work of artists who had first passed the rigorous process of selection by fellow-artists already established as Academicians. The Selection Committee for each year's Royal Academy summer exhibition was composed entirely of RAs and their selections from the vast mass of work submitted reflected what met their standards.

Sir Edwin Landseer
The Monarch of the Glen
Courtesy: John Dewar and Sons Ltd.

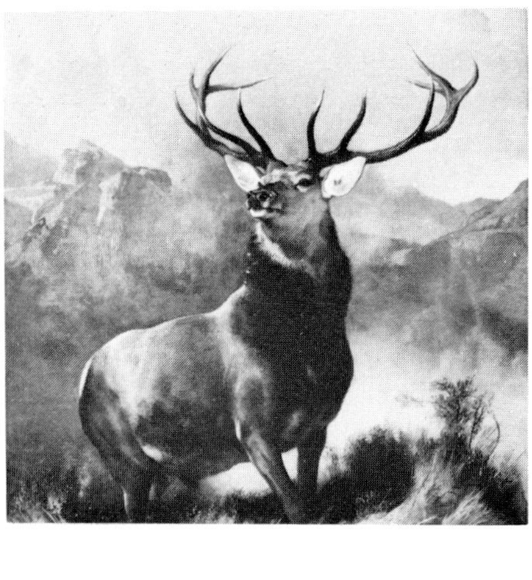

The artist whose work expressed most accurately the new values was Landseer. The animals he painted divide neatly into two groups which epitomise the qualities most admired by Victorians: sentiment, in the domestic, dependent and faithful epitomised by *The Old Shepherd's Chief Mourner* (cat. 25); and the wild, independent and brave nobility enshrined in the *Monarch of the Glen* or the *Stag at Bay* (cat. 26). Anthropomorphism not only obtained an obvious and immediate emotional response, but can also be seen as a more elaborate symbolic expression, containing an analogy of Victorian ideals of Devoted Service and the Noble Savage, faithful retainers and brave masters.

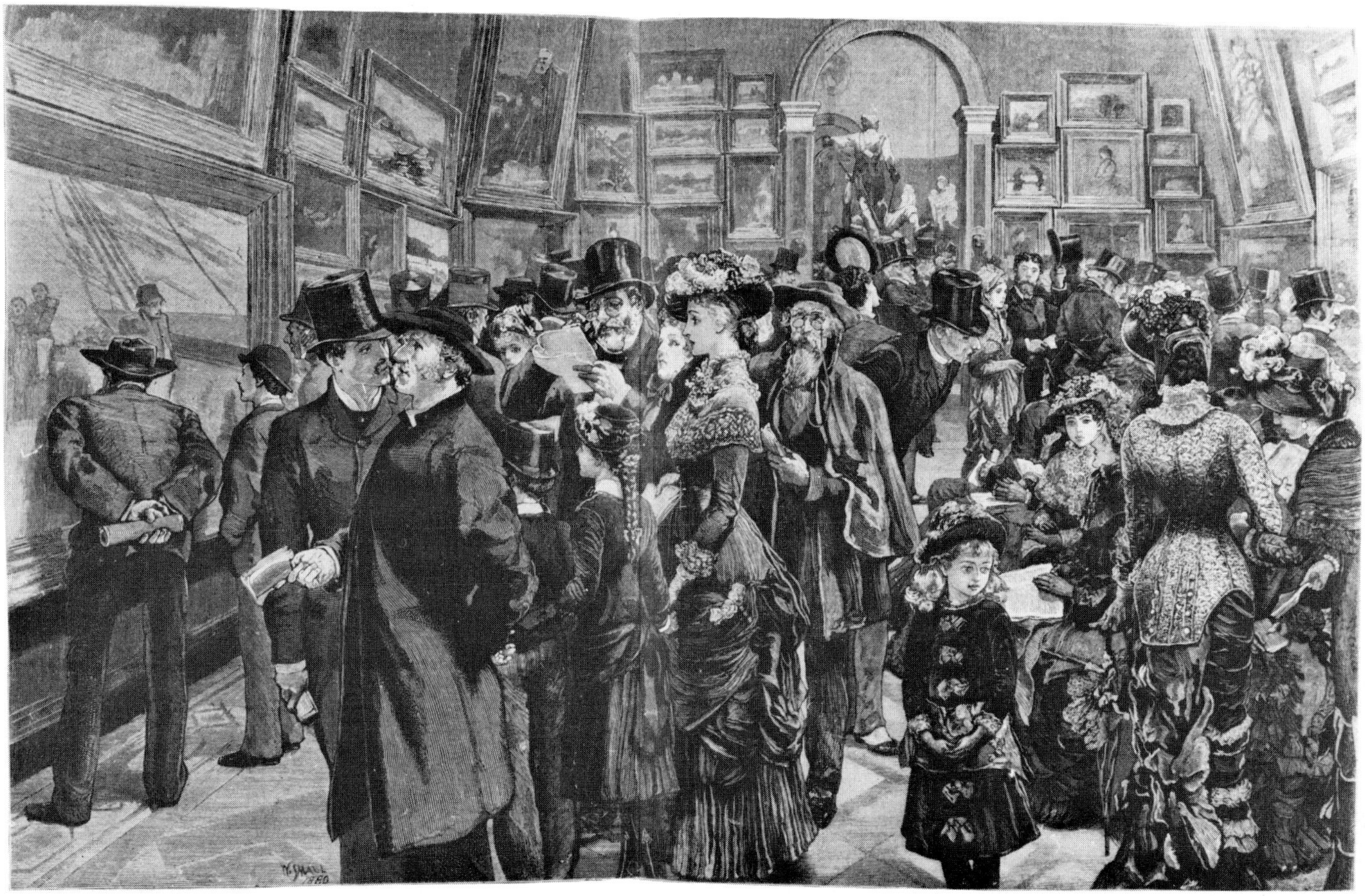

WILLIAM SMALL
At the Royal Academy
The Graphic 1880

While Landseer produced these sentimental allegories, more direct statements about the nature of contemporary life were being made in the wake of the liberal movements for social and legal reforms of the 1830s and 1840s. These were taken up by writers, most notably of course by Dickens and by Hood in his poem *The Song of the Shirt*, and by artists like Redgrave whose campaigning paintings (cat. 47) were a powerful response to the appalling conditions under which a tragically large part of the population existed. The middle-classes found the dramatic illustration of such problems moving and the first wave of social propaganda was taken up again in the 1870s by artists like Fildes, Holl and Herkomer in the short-lived social realist school.

Once audiences had been exposed to the sufferings of others it became permissible, less painful and perhaps more selfishly interesting to look at paintings dealing with aspects of their own lives. The 1850s saw a vast increase in the number of paintings about the issues that pre-occupied the middle-classes: marriage, the role of women, emigration and the drama of courtrooms, partings, and domestic tragedy. The essential elements of all these were the naturalism used to depict human emotion and the upholding of conventional morality by the visible rewarding of virtue and punishment of evil. Some critics complained of the vulgarity of some representations of modern life – Hicks and Egg were particular targets for this – but condemnation for these reasons rarely affected a work that was popular. Hicks' scenes of busy crowds in the Bank of England and The General Post Office attracted an audience who saw themselves reflected, captured in a moment of their daily lives in much the same way as people today are fascinated by television soap opera.

E.T. PARRIS
Joseph of Arimathea Converting the Britons
Lithograph after Palace of Westminster cartoon
Courtesy: Victoria and Albert Museum

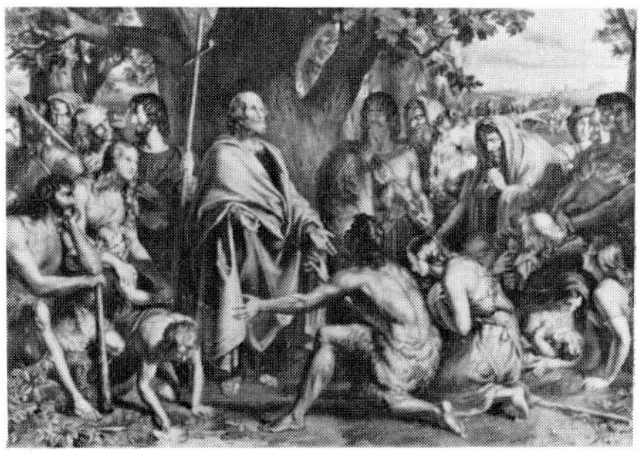

Painting of grand subjects on a large scale had been practised only by West and Haydon in the early century and had generally fallen into disfavour in the years before Victoria came to the throne, but the rebuilding of the Palace of Westminster and the need for quantities of imposing decorative painting led to a revival of grand art. The competitions held in the early 1840s for designs and fresco specimens for the proposed decorations brought forward a flurry of youthful talent eager to illustrate on an appropriate scale, and in an appropriate place, ancient British history. The scheme revived in artists' minds the splendours of large scale painting of such subjects and the 1840s saw many paintings that were direct and indirect results of this need to look back at glorious or extraordinary moments in our history, including some of a terrible nature, like Poole's *Solomon Eagle* (cat. 45). The critic of Blackwood's tried to account for the fascination which such ghastly subjects exercised on the spectator; and concluded that

> "So are we moved at tragedy: human sympathies are moved – the great natural sources of all our pleasures: pity and tenderness, and a sense of the awfulness of a great mystery, are upon us; and though pleased be too light a word, yet we are pleased; and where we are so pleased, we are made better. We feel the good flowing in upon us."

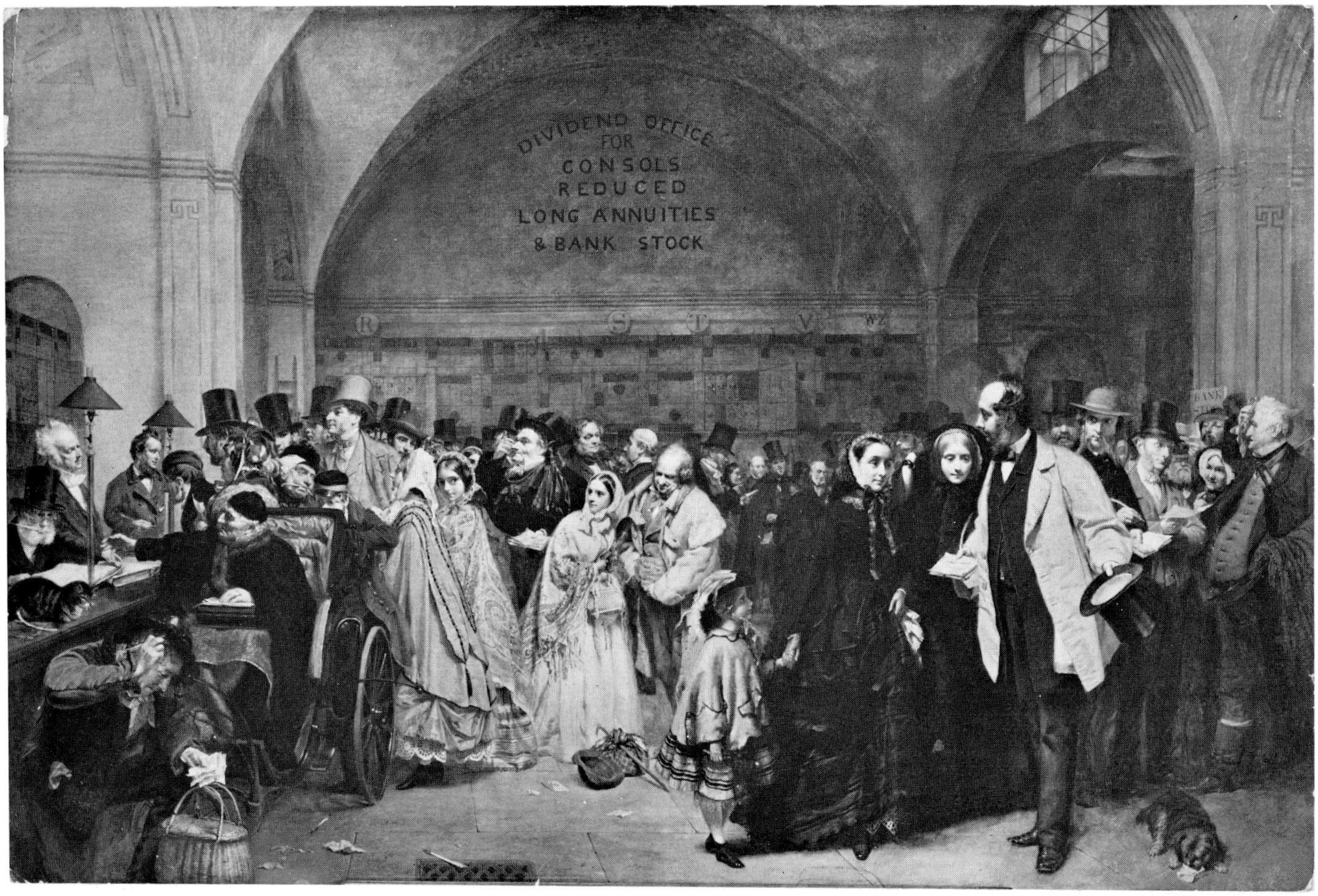

GEORGE E. HICKS
Dividend Day at the Bank of England
Courtesy: The Bank of England

Though the subsequent history of the Palace of Westminster decorations was a sad one of faulty technique and rapid decay, many public buildings later in the century had commissioned decorations in the spirit of Westminster: Ford Madox Brown's wall paintings for Manchester Town Hall in 1879–93 and the paintings carried out in the Royal Exchange in the City of London in 1900, by amongst others, Henrietta Rae and her husband Ernest Normand, are examples. Such paintings were intended to instruct, to impress and to improve those who passed through the municipal and commercial palaces which they decorated.

To paint any such subject an artist had to be equipped with at least the rudiments of classics and history; most nineteenth century artists were not from privileged backgrounds and most had therefore to educate themselves. The information explosion that took place in the nineteenth century made such knowledge accessible to people who in the previous century could not have reached any of it; the development of the great national collections and, above all, of the British Museum, the new building for which was finally completed in 1847, housed an extraordinary collection of archaeological treasures including the supreme source for Victorian classicists, the Elgin Marbles. The books that were published on history and archaeology in particular were seized upon for useful material and artists like Poynter (cat. 46), Henrietta Ward (cat. 61) and Alma-Tadema (cat. 2) made copious use of scholarly research.

The other major change brought about by modern developments in the nineteenth century was the accessibility of travel. In the eighteenth century, patrons travelled to Italy to buy Old Masters, but artists, with notable exceptions (particularly amongst water-colourists), stayed at home. In the nineteenth century, railways and steamships brought travel within the reach

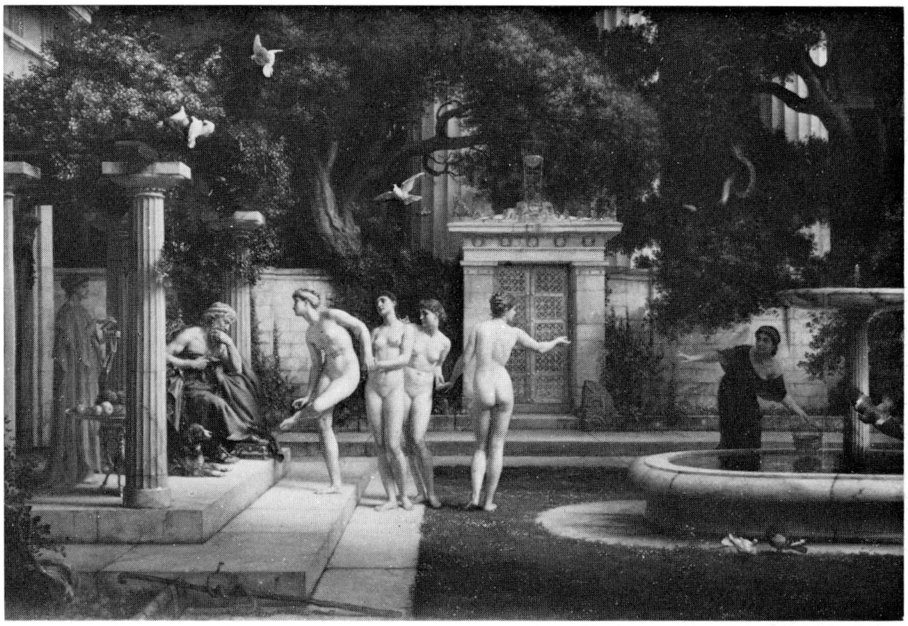

SIR EDWARD JOHN POYNTER
A Visit to Aesculapius
Courtesy: Tate Gallery, London

of many more people and artists were able to go in search of subjects in exotic countries or visit other artists and exhibitions abroad to find out what their foreign contemporaries were doing. It was the turn of the artists to do the travelling for their patrons who were now too occupied with the business of acquiring wealth to make the leisured tours enjoyed in the eighteenth century, and the artists could illustrate the Mediterranean, Middle Eastern, and Far Eastern countries from which the treasures had been taken to fill the museums in London and Western Europe. Many artists such as Lewis, Phillip and Long travelled in a country like Spain to find subjects and study the art of the country in its museums; others actually lived, worked and studied for years at a time in their chosen countries – Eastlake and Mason in Rome, and many artists in Paris. The cosmopolitanism that filtered through into their exhibited paintings may have been in some ways only a superficial veneer of foreign-ness overlaid onto a solidly Victorian outlook on life, but it was nevertheless a broadening of horizons that even at its lowest level acted as a kind of travelogue for its audience.

This new kind of awareness of other cultures, coupled with the need to impress them with British cultural superiority, commercial prowess and Imperial dominance, led to the great series of international and national

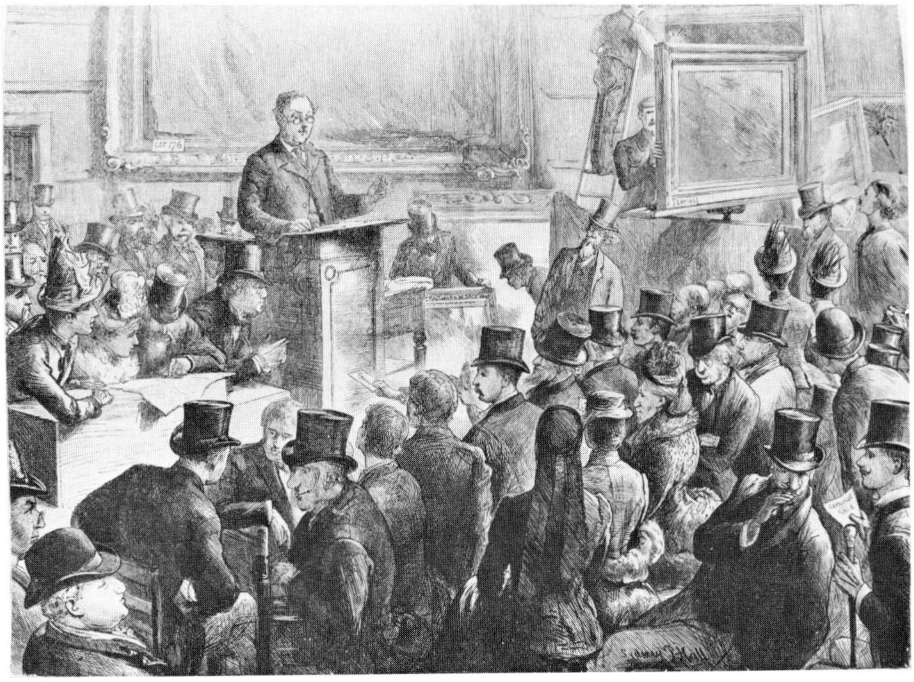

S. P. Hall
A Great Picture Sale at Christie's
The Graphic 1887

exhibitions beginning with the Great Exhibition of 1851 at the Crystal Palace. This concentrated on manufactures and the applied arts, but the French answer in 1855, with the Exposition Universelle at Paris, brought together a massive collection of international contemporary painting and set an example that was followed at intervals throughout the rest of the century. London staged further international exhibitions in 1862, when the sensation was John Gibson's painted marble sculpture, the *Tinted Venus*, and in the early 1870s, and Paris put on a major international exhibition in each decade, in 1867, 1878, 1889 and 1900. The British contingents sent to these exhibitions had mixed fortunes: the work sent to the 1867 show was severely criticised by both foreign and home critics for being of generally low quality, but in 1878 Herkomer's *Last Muster* was one of the successes of the show; and in 1889 Henry Moore and Alma-Tadema won the highest honours, though there was controversy at home over the medal distribution. Of the great national exhibitions, the two at Manchester in 1857 and 1887 were by far the most important; the 1857 Art Treasures exhibition brought together many of the most important Old Masters in British private collections, together with a major showing of contemporary art, and in 1887, to celebrate the Jubilee, over two thousand paintings, sculptures, drawings and engravings were brought together in an exhibition masterminded by the dealer William Agnew.

Agnew was probably the most influential dealer of the latter part of the century, taking over the management of the British art market from two brilliant foreigners, Flatow and Gambart who had reigned over the 1850s and 1860s. The role of the dealers became increasingly important during the century: their special exhibitions sometimes rivalled the Academy in their crowd-pulling powers, (cat. 15 and 24) and they were responsible for the generation and handling of some very large sums of money, considerable amounts of which reached the pockets of the artists themselves and indeed in several cases made substantial fortunes for artists like Millais and Hunt. It was generally the dealers who bought in the salerooms and made the market for contemporary paintings so particularly healthy: the record saleroom price for a living artist's work (Edwin Long's *Babylonian Marriage Market*, bought for Thomas Holloway) was established at £6615 in 1882 and stood until the First World War. A number of dealers also performed the valuable function of

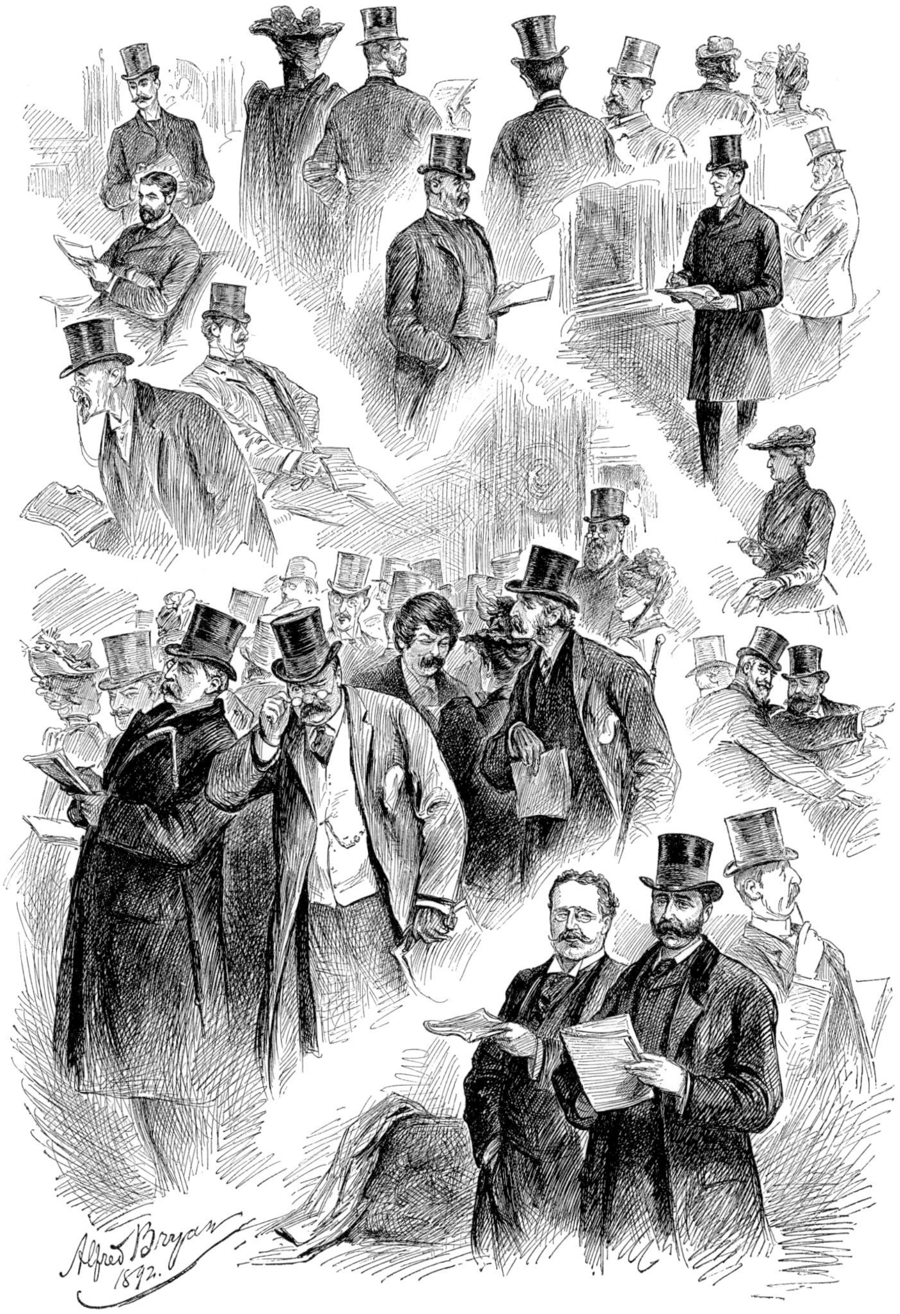

Press Day at the Royal Academy

importing foreign painting for their seasonal London exhibitions, allowing many artists who did not necessarily make regular visits to Paris and Germany to see the current established French and German successes. The revolutionary artists were not imported to London any more than they were generally shown in Paris, and English knowledge of such developments was very limited apart from the proselytising of such exceptional figures as Whistler, until the 1880s and 1890s. The Franco-Prussian war of 1870–1 forced the famous exodus of Monet and Pissarro to London, together with their dealer Durand-Ruel, but they were reluctant refugees and their stay went largely unnoticed. The dealers generally only stepped into the market when an artist had proved himself a marketable commodity and the chief means of doing that was through the reviews.

Most critics were publicists, interpreters, and filters of information and opinions on artists; some exceptional figures were also theorists, and Ruskin the most important of these, was also one of the most influential and significant

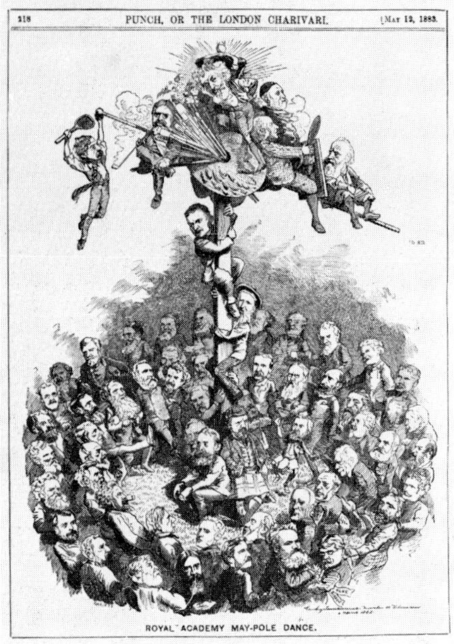

figures of the century. However, most critics were reviewers of exhibitions and as the vehicles for their writing increased and the numbers of exhibitions increased, so did their influence. During the early years of Victoria's reign the number of general periodicals multiplied as their potential readership enlarged with the coming of more leisure to greater numbers of literate people, and, as more people had both the time and ability to read, so more journals were published to supply them. Most periodicals and newspapers with any cultural pretensions carried art reviews, the appearance of the first major specialist art magazine the *Art Union* (later the *Art Journal*) in 1839 was a landmark which significantly altered and expanded the whole scene. Because much of the audience for art was very new they tended to seek guidance and the critics provided it: the influence thus gained could be used to devastating effect by a Ruskin but could also be totally disregarded when the public's interest and affection had really been engaged by an artist (as with Hicks). Ruskin's approval was enough to make an artist's reputation and this approval surprisingly often coincided with that of the other critics; although he has in the past been regarded as an isolated prophet because of his espousal of the Pre-Raphaelites at the height of their unpopularity, he was in fact often to be found in praise of many artists who, like Stanfield and Hook, were thoroughly acceptable also to the majority of reviewers. The number of critics continued to inflate until, in 1892, the RA Press Day was attended by an astonishing total of 300 journalists, all of whom would write a review of some kind; the capacity of the Victorians for consumption of opinion must surely be unsurpassed. The critics had a vital function in the dissemination of information about art outside London where much of the money in need of guidance was to be found; although a number of major provincial cities developed their own exhibiting systems around Academies and Institutes which often had autumn exhibitions showing that summer's Royal Academy and British Institution pictures, they remained generally very much in the wake of London. Lively schools of artists appeared centred particularly on Birmingham, Manchester and Liverpool, but these received little coverage in the national press and tended to be contained within their regions.

The power thus developed by critics could be played up to, but it also opened the way for conflict between those critics and any group of artists that did not wish to conform to the norms laid down. The first group of Victorian artists to dissociate themselves from the Academy establishment was The Clique, which consisted of the youthful Frith, Dadd, Egg, Phillip, Elmore, Joy and Ward, but the rapid absorption of most of them into mainstream and highly successful careers indicated that a more exceptional kind of association was needed to produce a real avant-garde. The Pre-Raphaelite Brotherhood, founded in 1848 by Millais, Hunt and Rossetti, lasted a scant five years before its members' interests had diverged too far to co-exist, but they continued to be ably defended in print by the Pre-Raphaelite partisans F.G. Stephens and W.M. Rossetti. It took the foreigners Whistler and his friend Legros to bring a fresh and revitalising influx of progressive French aesthetics to London. This, when combined with the aftermath of Pre-Raphaelitism, which had given birth to a mannered symbolism most brilliantly applied in the work of Burne-Jones, produced a grouping of the avant-garde in the 1870s most conveniently labelled the Aesthetic Movement. The addition of some social and moral earnestness by William Morris and the development of the Arts and Crafts Movement of the 1880s was made to seem perhaps more anachronistic than it was by the parallel developments in the New English Art Club led by Sickert. His contacts with the Impressionists in France enabled him to emancipate himself both from Victorian academic art and from the Aesthetes of the Grosvenor Gallery. There were however enough critics and a wide enough range of art magazines by this time to give

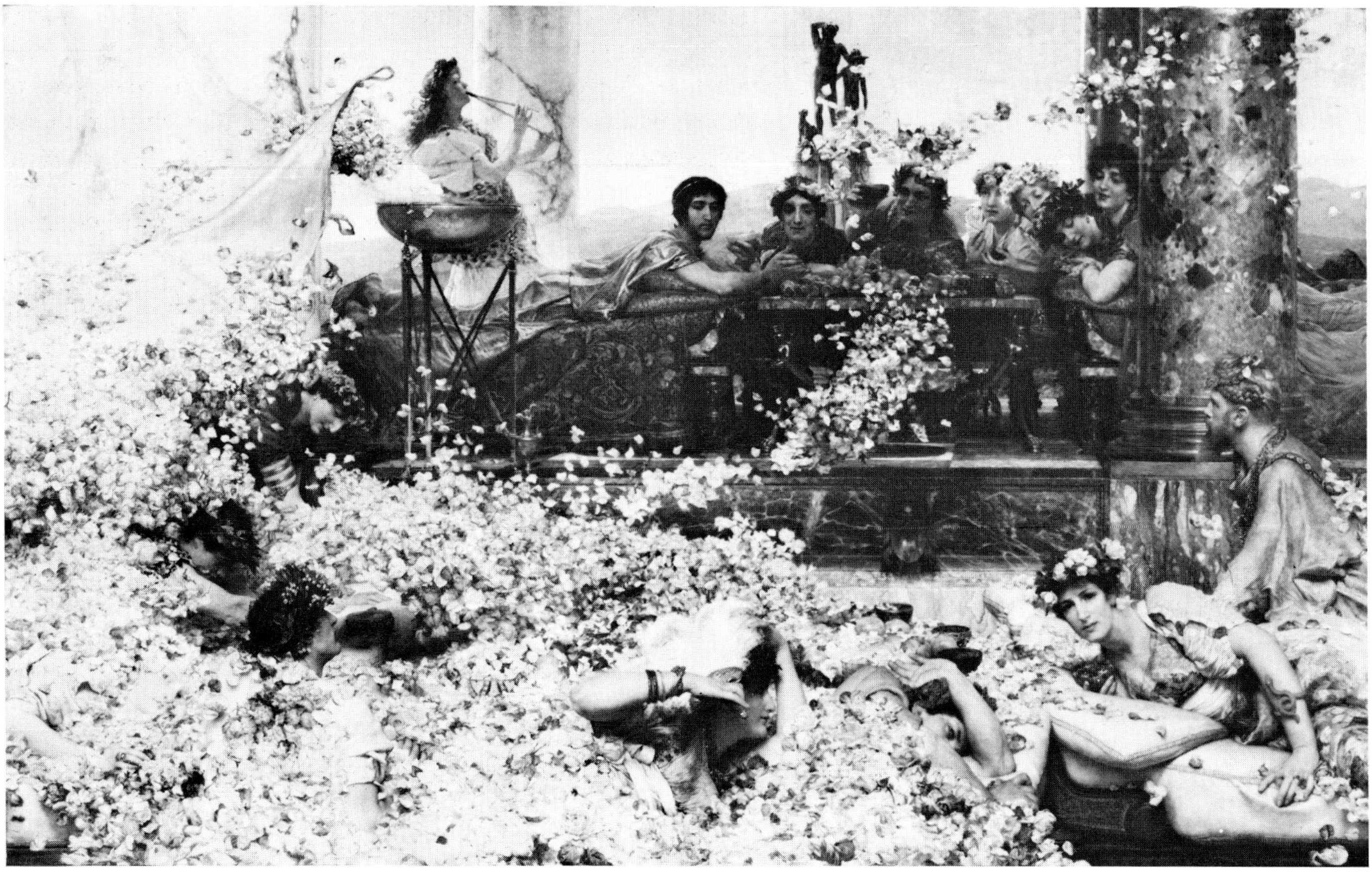

Sir Lawrence Alma-Tadema
The Roses of Heliogabalus RA 1896
Private Collection

the new groups space in print and the founding of *Studio* in 1892 gave the 90s avant-garde their ideal platform, though it also produced articles on academic stalwarts like Poynter.

The most important single factor in the development of the mainstream of Victorian art was money: it made it possible to paint big pictures for big houses at prices that could be high on commission and still higher when the picture subsequently went through the salerooms. Freak events like the theft and ransoming for £500 of T.S. ('Cow') Cooper's greatest work, *The Monarch of the Meadows*, in 1881, made news, and artists could afford to build themselves large and sometimes palatial mansions in their colonies in Kensington and St. John's Wood. Some of the artists, notably Alma-Tadema, could consume almost as conspicuously as some of their patrons: in 1888 Sir John Aird commissioned from Tadema *The Roses of Heliogabalus* for £4000 and for the four winter months it took him to paint the picture the artist had roses sent weekly from the French Riviera to ensure the truth of his representation of every one of the thousands of petals in the picture. Tadema's house was a marvel of Roman luxury and surpassed even Leighton's sumptuous Moorish recreation in Melbury Road. The badge of success for a number of artists in the 1880s was the commissioning of their own Norman Shaw house: few were so extraordinarily successful that they could emulate Holl, who made so much money from portraiture in the last eight years of his life that he had two Norman Shaw houses built in the space of four years, one in London and one in Surrey.

Many artists' fortunes were made from the sale of copyright for the engraving of their pictures and it was the great expansions of the market in engravings from the middle of the century that took art out to the widest public it had ever reached. The vast majority of these engravings were of domestic, sentimental, religious or patriotic scenes: Faed's affecting destitute poor and orphaned children, Holman Hunt's extraordinary religious images

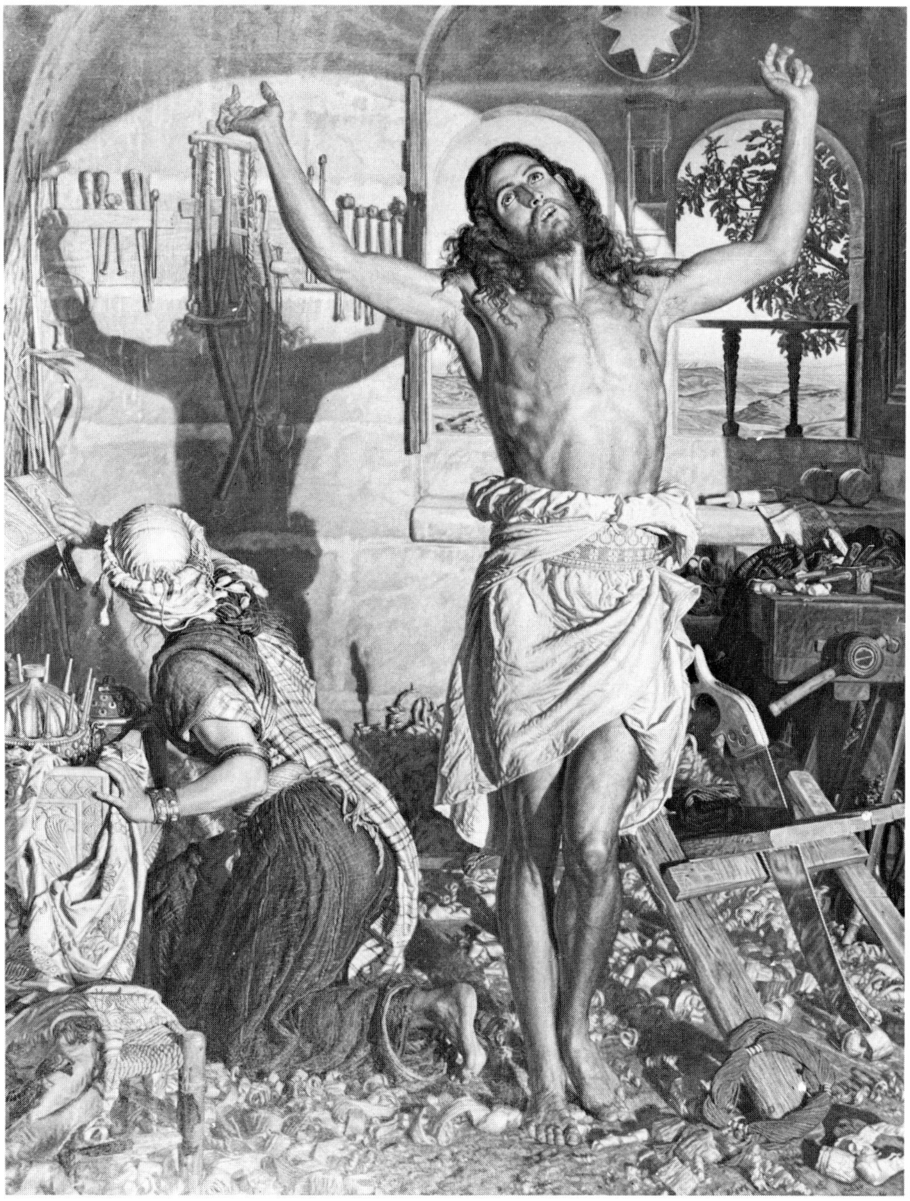

William Holman Hunt
The Shadow of Death
Courtesy: Manchester City Art Galleries

like *The Shadow of Death*, the battle scenes of Elizabeth Thompson, Ernest Crofts, and Caton Woodville, and perhaps the supreme image of Victorian duty realised, Luke Fildes' *The Doctor* (cat. 14). Steel engravings could take two years to make, but when printed were cheap and easy to distribute; once photography came into the process, photogravure made the system still easier to handle and contributed very largely to the success of some dealers which, like the Fine Art Society, made the majority of their incomes from the sale of engravings for many years. The essential criterion for engravings was the healthiness of the image, and the vast majority of engravings produced were of eminently respectable and morally improving subjects. Some artists could have their nude compositions engraved if in a sufficiently classical guise but even in the 1890s artists had difficult encounters with groups of righteous ladies who wrote letters to *The Times* signed 'The British Matron', protesting at the indecency and vice of their paintings; Henrietta Rae met considerable opposition to her classical nudes, despite the fact that she was a respectably married lady artist.

The popularity of art as a source of entertainment, recreation, and edification was unprecedented in previous centuries and has been unsurpassed in this: the statistics on attendances at some exhibitions include, for example,

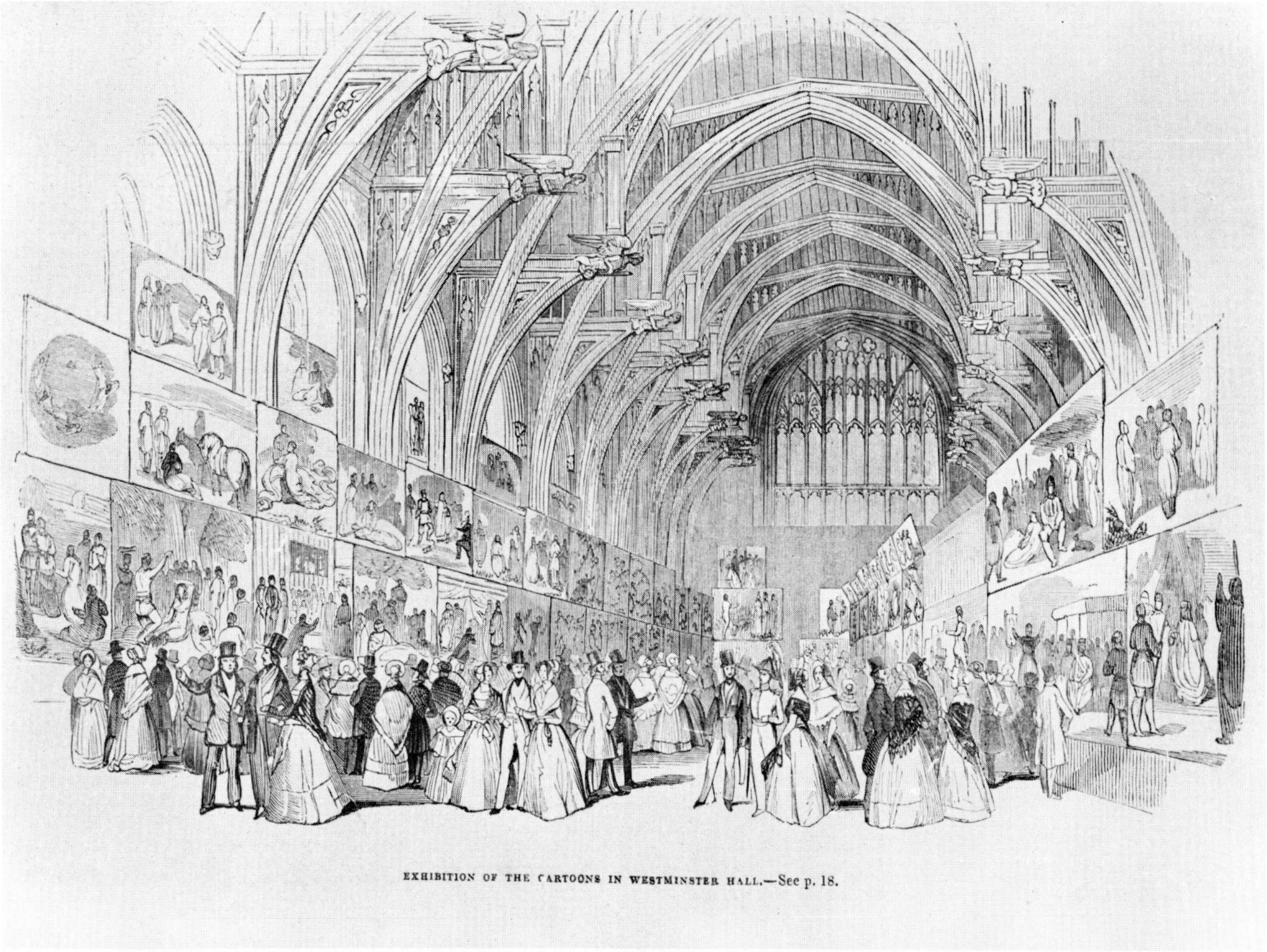

The exhibition of the Palace of Westminster cartoons

the daily thousands at the Palace of Westminster cartoon exhibition in 1843, the quarter-of-a-million people who generally visited the Royal Academy summer exhibition, and abroad the half-a-million who visited the Watts exhibition in New York in 1884–5. A number of curious ventures in integrating art with other entertainments were made like the Canterbury Music Hall at Lambeth, opened in 1858 with a picture gallery supplied by Gambart with £10,000-worth of modern paintings. In the last quarter of the century, art was very deliberately taken to the people, at least in London, in the series of exhibitions arranged in Whitechapel, beginning at St. Jude's School House and continuing at the new Whitechapel Art Gallery. In 1883, for instance, two hundred and fifty modern pictures were lent for the Easter exhibition and were seen by 36,000 East Enders in twenty days.

Perhaps the ultimate confirmation of an artist's success was to be taken up by royalty; in Prince Albert's lifetime, royal taste was guided along aesthetically approved paths, but even so Victoria's seems often to have coincided with the most popular and sentimental of public taste. A number of owners had occasion over the years to regret her interest as there are several recorded instances of the royal eye alighting on a particularly popular work which was then acquired from the unfortunate who had already bought – or in some cases even commissioned – it. This happened, for instance, over Frost's *Una* in 1848, Frith's *Ramsgate Sands* in 1854, Holl's *The Lord gave and the Lord hath taken away* in 1869, and Elizabeth Thompson's *Roll Call* in 1874; all but the Holl, whose owner stoutly resisted the exercise of the royal prerogative, were acquired. After Prince Albert's death, royal patronage ceased

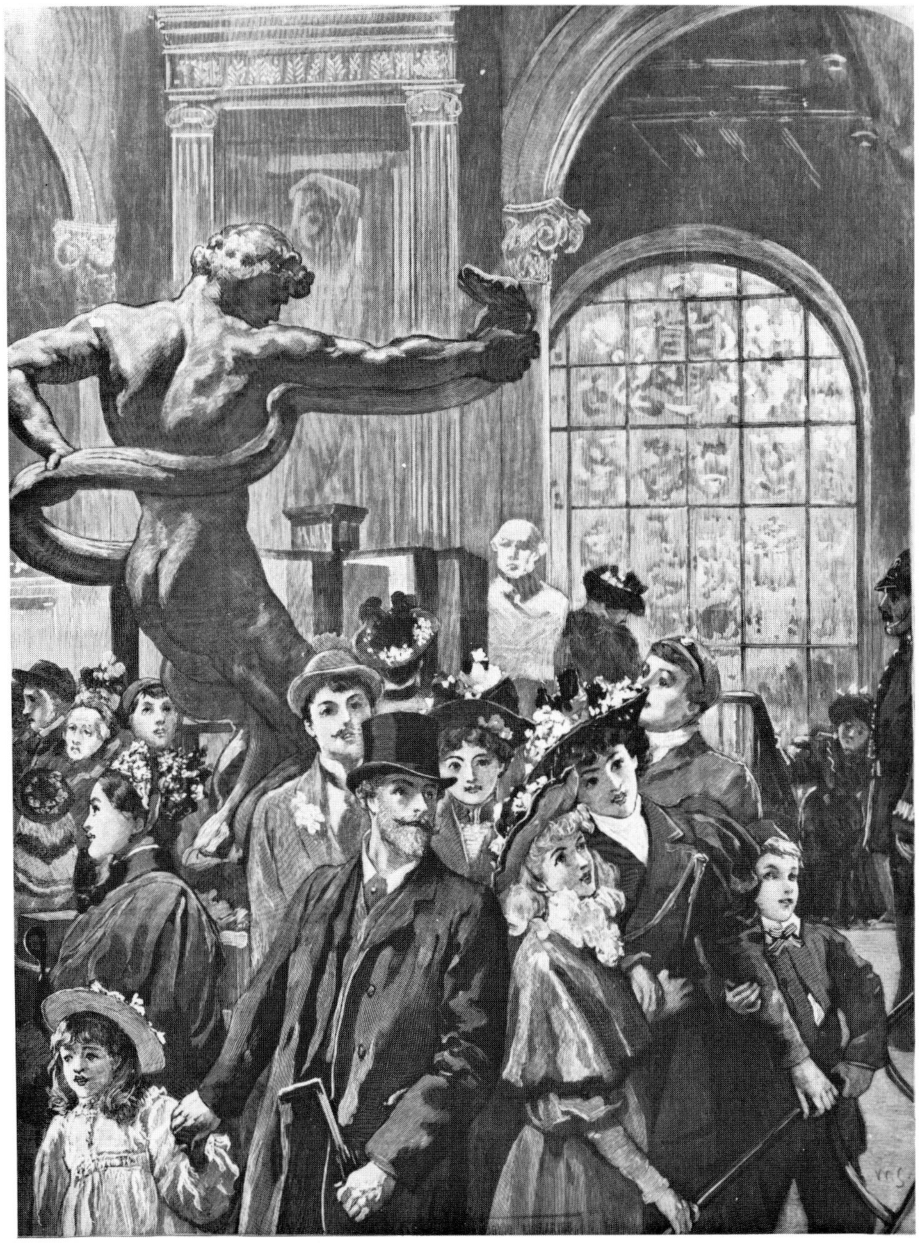

Sunday opening at the South Kensington Museum

to have any great influence on the general development of art in this country, but could still be a potent force in the making of a popular reputation. The kudos of a command to Buckingham Palace or Windsor from the RA assured immediate prestige and, if the artist was lucky, immediate popular success.

The place in the guidance of public patronage that might have been occupied by Prince Albert, if he had lived, was taken later in the century by committees administering public funds for the purchase of paintings: the most important of these was, from 1877, the Chantrey Fund, a bequest to the Royal Academy from the sculptor Sir Francis Chantrey to be used for the purchase of works from each year's RA. The other new and important element was the founding of major public art galleries, particularly those outside London, whose entry onto the art market in the 1880s made a significant impact in the salerooms. The purchase of a painting by the Chantrey Fund was an important event for an artist; if not already successful, it conferred status and consequently a guaranteed income from private commissions which followed in the wake of all public accolades. The provincial museums, on the other hand, had a less direct effect on the artists themselves; most were established during the 1880s and bought through dealers and in the salerooms, while presentations by successful

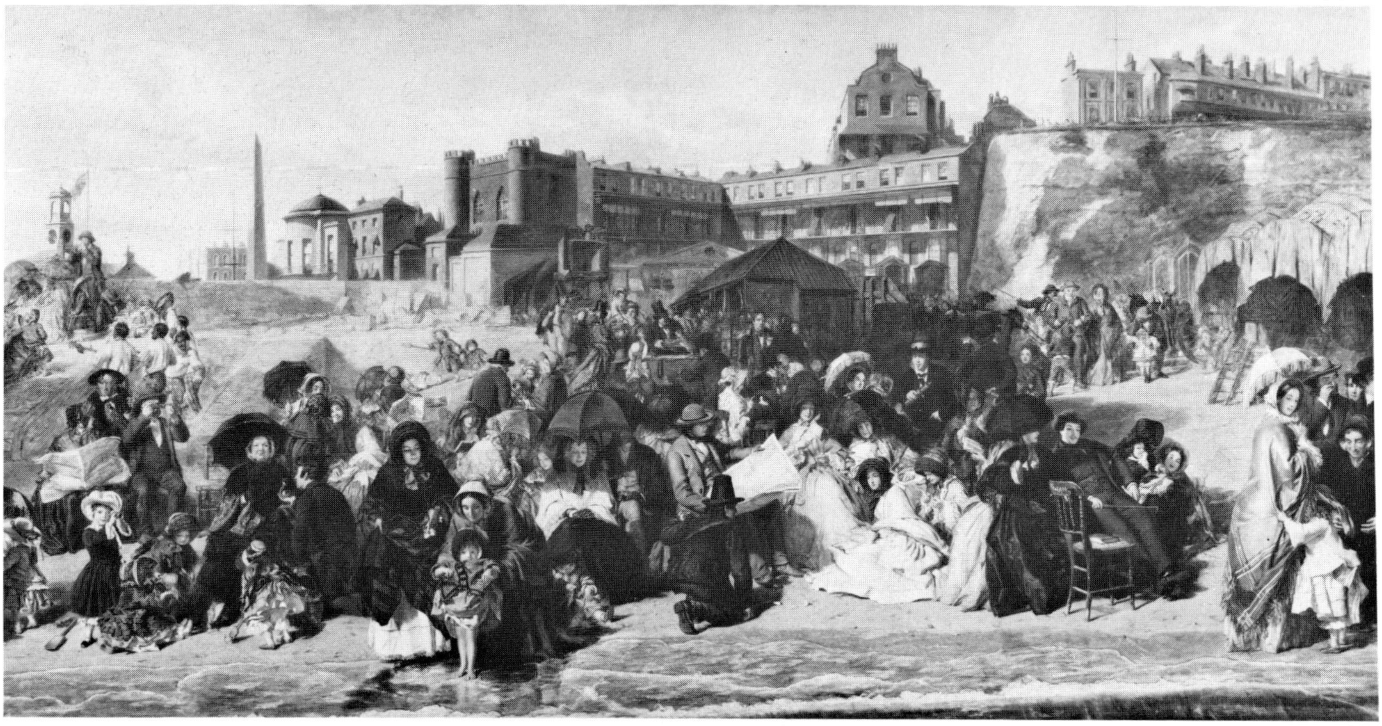

William Powell Frith
Ramsgate Sands
By Gracious Permission of Her Majesty the Queen

natives provided a vital source of works. Some more enterprising galleries like the Walker, Liverpool bought direct from the exhibitions or artists, while some galleries, like those at Sheffield and York were founded on the gift of an entire collection of contemporary art. The prestige of being represented in a provincial gallery and the quantity of modern work that was brought to a wider public became increasingly significant as the size and quality of the collections increased. The final and most important event was the gift of the Tate Collection to the nation; the Gallery was finally opened in 1897.

Victorian art ceased being Victorian in the strictest sense in 1901 on the death of the Queen and the accession of Edward VII, but the preoccupations of late Victorian art are not much distinguishable from those of early Edwardian art and many of the same concerns with narrative and symbolism continue, as well as many of the old favourites, like the landscapists, who continued to repeat exactly the same subjects in exactly the same way well into the 1920s and even 1930s. The social climate changed with the coming of the Edwardian age, but the aesthetic and intellectual climate did not change until the advent of Roger Fry and the notorious Post-Impressionist exhibition in London in 1910, which provoked first ridicule and then despair in the ranks of the Royal Academy. The achievements of Victorian art had been celebrated internationally in three great exhibitions: the St. Louis in 1904, the Franco-British in 1908, and the Rome in 1911, but the outbreak of the First World War ended all such celebrations. When peace was finally declared, society was altered beyond recognition; a few Victorians lingered on to be shown in the last great celebrations of Empire at the Wembley exhibitions of the mid-1920s, and those Victorian artists who had died were represented in the occasional Deceased Artists Winter Exhibitions at the RA but in the 1920s the oldest Academicians were compulsorily retired. In 1924 the final insult was given to Lady Butler when her submission to that year's Academy was rejected; Sir Luke Fildes' *Casual Ward* had been acclaimed in the same year as her *Roll Call*, 1874, and out of old friendship and fellow-feeling, he protested to the committee, but it was useless. The Victorian era had lasted sixty-four years, years during which hundreds of artists had worked and exhibited. They ranged from the naive to the sophisticated, from the touchingly sincere to the utterly cynical, and they reacted very differently to the popularity that came to them: Lady Butler in her *Autobiography* wrote of her reactions to success,

> "It is a curious condition of the mind between gratitude for the appreciation of one's work by those who know, and the uncomfortable sense of an exaggerated popularity with the crowd. The exaggeration is unavoidable, and, no doubt, passes, but the fact that counts is the power of touching the people's heart, . . . which remains the same through all the changing fashions in art. I remember an argument I once had with Alma-Tadema on this matter of touching the heart. He laughed at me, and didn't believe in it at all."

It was, indeed, not given to many to move the heart of the million.

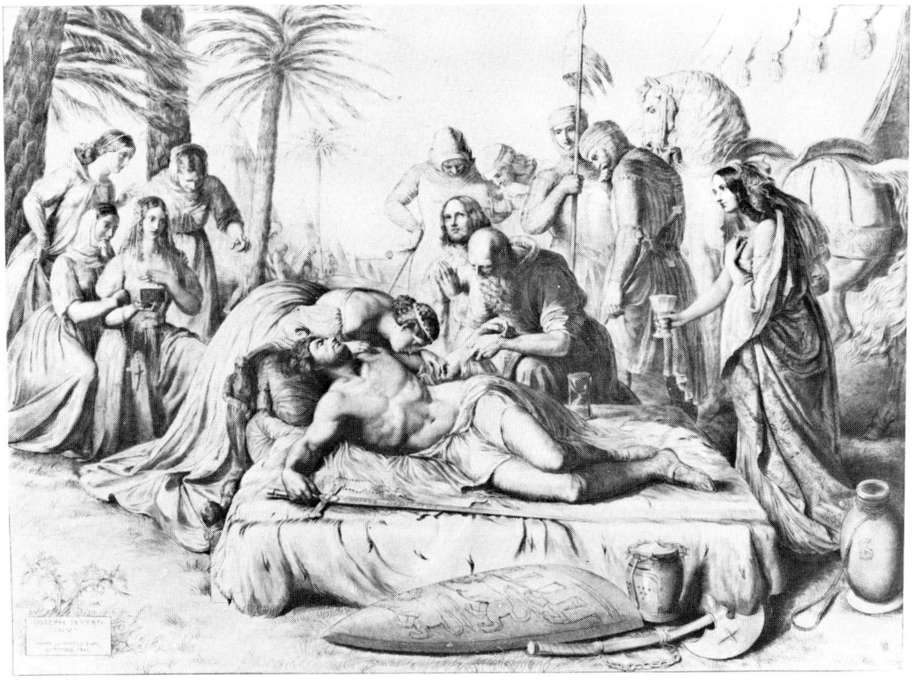

J. Severn
Queen Eleanor
Lithograph after Palace of Westminster cartoon

Lenders

Her Majesty Queen Elizabeth 56
Aberdeen Art Gallery 41
Australia, National Gallery of Victoria 11
Anonymous lenders 21, 35
Cambridge, Fitzwilliam Museum 3
Compton, The Trustees of the Watts Gallery 63
Doncaster Museum and Art Gallery 49
Glasgow Art Gallery 9
Grosvenor Estates 33
Leeds City Art Galleries 34, 57
Leicestershire Museum and Art Gallery 28, 31, 61
Lincolnshire Museums, Usher Gallery, Lincoln 4
Liverpool, Walker Art Gallery 24, 48
London, Thos. Agnew & Sons Ltd 14, 22
London, The Courtauld Institute of Art 58
London, Speaker of the House of Commons 67, 68
London, Mary Evans Picture Library 50
London, The Fine Art Society Ltd 56a
London, Guildhall Art Gallery 17, 65
London, Roy Miles Fine Paintings 8
London, A. & F. Pears Ltd 37
London, The Trustees of the Tate Gallery 10, 36, 59
London, Victoria and Albert Museum 20, 25, 29, 39, 66, 69
Lord Londonderry 2
City of Manchester Art Galleries 19, 27, 62
New York, The Forbes Magazine Collection 6, 44, 47
Nottingham, Castle Museum 5, 23, 30, 54, 64
Hon. Ranald Noel-Paton 42
T.D. Pilkington, Esq., J.P. 38
Port Sunlight, Trustees of the Lady Lever Art Gallery 12, 13
Private Collections 16, 26, 40, 51, 52
Edmund de Rothschild, Esq., T.D. 55
Royal Holloway College (University of London) 15, 32
Sheffield City Art Galleries 43, 45, 53
Tyne & Wear County Council Museums Service, Laing Art Gallery 18, 46
Vienna, Gallery Kalb 7
Yale University Art Gallery, The Edwin Austin Abbey Memorial Collection 1
York City Art Gallery 60

Abbreviations used

AJ	*The Art Journal*
Armstrong, Manchester 1887	Walter Armstrong, *Fine Art at the Royal Jubilee Exhibition*, Manchester, 1887
Beck	Hilary Beck, *Victorian Engravings*, V & A, 1973
Bell, 1967	Quentin Bell, *Victorian Artists*, 1967
BI	British Institution
Blackburn, *RA Notes*	Henry Blackburn, *Academy Notes*, with Illustrations of the Principal Pictures at Burlington House
Blackwood's	*Blackwood's Edinburgh Magazine*
Boase, 1959	T.S.R. Boase, *English Art 1800–1870*, Oxford History of English Art, 1959
Bryan's	M. Bryan, *Dictionary of Painters and Engravers*, revised ed., 1903–4
Caw, 1908	James L. Caw, *Scottish Painting Past and Present 1620–1908*, 1908
Chesneau, 1885	Ernest Chesneau, *The English School of Painting*, transl. Etherington, 2nd ed., 1885
Cunningham, 1880	Allan Cunningham, *The Lives of the Most Eminent British Painters*, revised ed., 1880
DNB	*Dictionary of National Biography*
Expo. Univ. Paris	Exposition Universelle, Paris (1855, 1867, 1878, 1889, 1900)
Franco-British, 1908	*Fine Art Section, Franco-British Exhibition*, 1908
Fraser's	*Fraser's Magazine for Town and Country*
GdBA	Gazette des Beaux-Arts, Paris
Hardie, 1968	Martin Hardie, *Water-Colour Painting in Britain, III: The Victorian Period*, 1968
Hardie, 1976	William Hardie, *Scottish Painting 1837–1939*, 1976
Hodgson, 1887	J.E. Hodgson, RA, *Fifty Years of British Art*, 1887
ILN	*The Illustrated London News*
Irwins, 1975	David and Francina Irwin, *Scottish Painters At Home and Abroad 1700–1900*, 1975
JWCI	Journal of the Warburg and Courtauld Institutes
London Internat.	International Exhibition, London (1862, 1873)
Maas, 1969	Jeremy Maas, *Victorian Painters*, 1967
Mag. of Art	*The Magazine of Art*
MAFA	Manchester Academy of Fine Arts
Manchester Jubilee, 1887	*Royal Jubilee Exhibition*, Manchester, 1887
Monkhouse, 1899	Cosmo Monkhouse, *British Contemporary Artists*, 1899
OWS	Old Water-Colour Society
Palgrave, *Essays*, 1866	F.T. Palgrave, *Essays on Art*, 1866
Pall Mall	*The Pall Mall Gazette*
Phythian, 1908	J.E. Phythian, *Fifty Years of Modern Painting*, 1908
RA Pictures	*Royal Academy Pictures*
RA Winter 1901	*Exhibition of Works by British Artists deceased since 1850*, Royal Academy, Winter, 1901
RA Winter 1911	*Exhibition of Works by Five Deceased British Artists* (Orchardson, Frith, Macbeth, Swan, D. Farquharson), Royal Academy, Winter, 1911
RA Winter, 1922	*Exhibition of Works by Recently Deceased Members of the Royal Academy*, Royal Academy, Winter, 1922
RA Winter, 1933	*Commemorative Exhibition of Works by Late Members*, Royal Academy, Winter 1933
RCambA	Royal Cambrian Academy, Conwy
Redgrave, 1890	Richard and Samuel Redgrave, *A Century of British Painters*, 1890, republ., 1947
Reynolds, 1953	Graham Reynolds, *Painters of the Victorian Scene*, 1953
Reynolds, 1966	Graham Reynolds, *Victorian Painting*, 1966
Rome, 1911	*International Fine Arts Exhibition*, Rome, 1911
RSA	Royal Scottish Academy, Edinburgh
Ruskin, *Works*	E.T. Cook and A. Wedderburn, *The Works of John Ruskin*, Library Edition, 1903–12
St Louis Internat.	*International Exhibition*, St Louis, USA, 1904
Sandby, 1862	W. Sandby, *The History of the Royal Academy of Arts*, 1862
Temple, 1897	A.G. Temple, *The Art of Painting in the Queen's Reign*, 1897
Wembley, 1924, 1925	British Empire Exhibition, Wembley, 1924 and 1925
Wood, *Dictionary*, 1971	Christopher Wood, *A Dictionary of Victorian Painters*, 1971
Wood, *Panorama*, 1976	Christopher Wood, *Victorian Panorama – Paintings of Victorian Life*, 1976

Catalogue

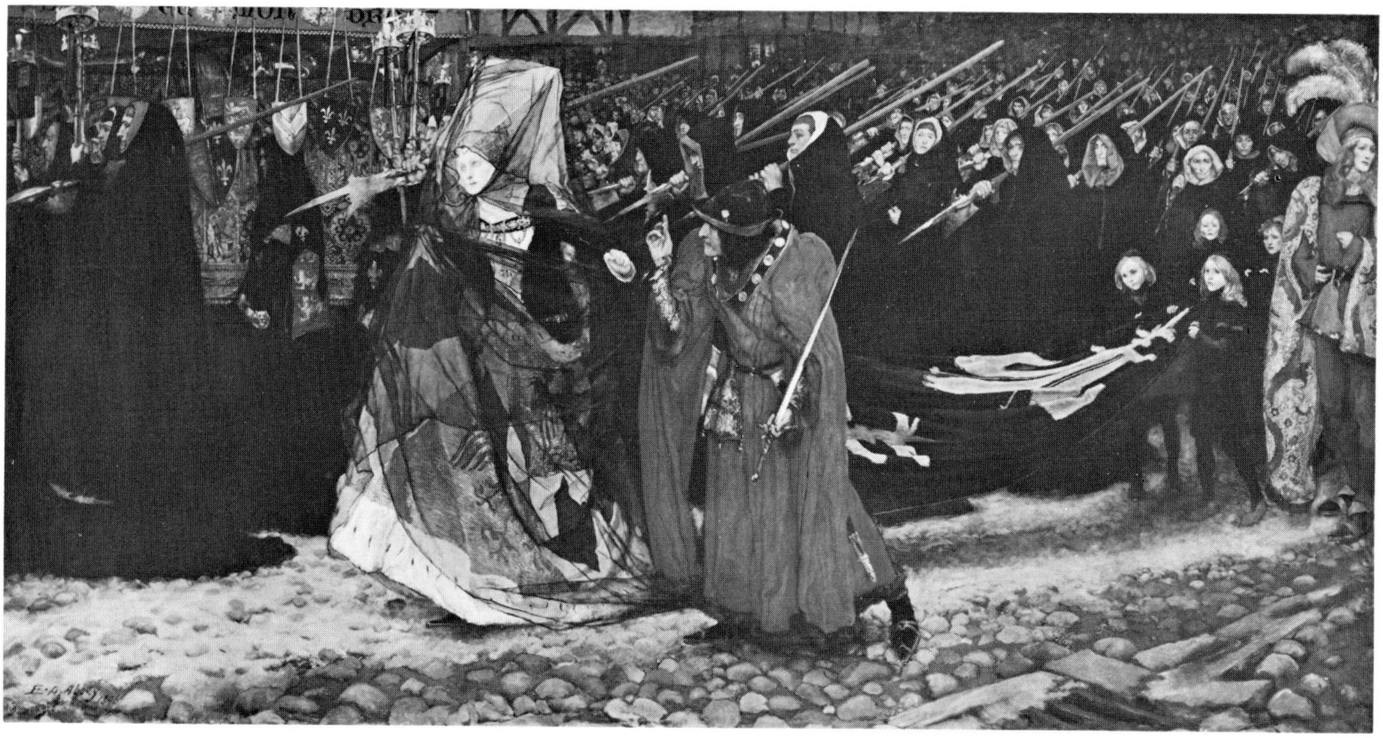

EDWIN AUSTIN ABBEY, 1852–1911,
ARA 1896, RA 1898

1 Richard Duke of Gloucester and the Lady Anne 1896

oil on canvas, 52½ × 104¼ in
INSCR. E.A. Abbey / 1896

PROV: George McCulloch, purch. fr. artist; Mrs. J. Coutts Michie; McCulloch sale, Christie's, 29 May 1913 (107) bt. Brown & Phillips; Mrs. E.A. Abbey (by 1921), by whom pres. to Yale, 1937.
EXH: RA 1896 (616); Jubilee Exh. Guildhall 1897 (54b); Salon, Soc. Nat. des Beaux-Arts, Paris 1908 (1); RA Winter 1909 (50); Rome 1911 (115); *Coll. of Pictures & Drawings by Edwin Austin Abbey*, RA Winter 1912 (466); *Anglo-American Exh.*, Bourlet & Sons, London 1914 (502); *Jubilee Autumn Exh.*, Liverpool 1922 (851); *Memorial Exh. of the Work of Edwin Austin Abbey*, American Academy of Arts & Letters, New York 1928–9 (24); *Paintings, Drawings & Pastels by E.A. Abbey*, Yale, 1939 (62); *Edwin Austin Abbey*, Yale/Philadelphia/New York 1974 (2 – see for other American showings).
LIT: *AJ*, June 1896 p171; *Athenaeum* 6 June 1896 p753; Blackburn *RA Notes* 1896 p21 (not repr.); *Graphic* 2 May p523 & 16 May 1896 p.591; *Mag. of Art* 1896 p357; *Punch* 9 May 1896 pp217, 226–7; *Studio* July 1896 p111; *Times* 1 June 1896 p12; M.H. Spielman, 'Edwin Austin Abbey, RA, III', *Mag. of Art* 1899 pp150, 193, repr. p145; E. V. Lucas, *The Life and works of Edwin Austin Abbey, RA*, London & New York, 1921, II, pp290, 292, 294–7, 307–8, 318, repr. fp296; *Edwin Austin Abbey* cat., Yale 1974 pp9–10 etc., repr. cover, detail p37 (see for further repr. refs.).
ENGR: Leopold Flameng, etching, Art Union of London, 1897 (Beck 61).
STUDIES: study for Richard, charcoal, 24⅝ × 18⅞ in, s & d 1895, exh. Yale 1939 (44).

> "Mr. Abbey is one of the artistic surprises of this century, an artist who has the faculty of coming suddenly to the front in all sorts of new branches of Art. He has made, this Spring, an astonishing success with his picture . . . of the wooing of the Duke of Gloucester and the Lady Anne, a success for which he has worked honestly and devotedly. As a piece of composition, of colour arrangement, of dramatic, as opposed to theatrical effect, for qualities of earnest observation and careful painting, this canvas deserves praise that can scarcely be exaggerated. In drawing and movement it is admirable, and the audacity of the contrast between the deep, luminous blacks and the vivid reds of the colour scheme is delightful. The picture ranks distinctly as one of the greatest of its year, a welcome relief to the commonplaces which too plentifully surround it." (*AJ*).

For the *Athenaeum* it was "the most powerful *spectacle* in the Academy" and it is clear that for critics and public alike, Abbey had produced the picture of the year. It illustrates the moment in Richard III (Act I, sc. 2) when Richard proffers his ring to the Lady Anne as she walks beside the coffin of her father-in-law King Henry VI, murdered by Richard, also the murderer of her husband, Edward, Prince of Wales. She has just reviled him for his crimes, but Richard's protestations of innocence shake her resolve:

> *Glo.* Say, then, my peace is made.
> *Anne* That shalt thou know hereafter.
> *Glo.* But shall I live in hope?
> *Anne* All men, I hope, live so.
> *Glo.* Vouchsafe to wear this ring.
> *Anne* To take is not to give. (*Puts on the ring.*)
> *Glo.* Look how my ring encompasseth thy finger,
> Even so thy breast encloseth my poor heart;
> Wear both of them, for both of them are thine.

Abbey chose to publish in the RA catalogue Richard's first lines spoken alone after the funeral procession has moved on:

> Was ever woman in this humour woo'd?
> Was ever woman in this humour won?

The acclamation that greeted the painting was joined in by many artists; a letter quoted by Lucas (p297) from Gilbert, the sculptor, expressed the general feeling:

> "Dear Mrs. Abbey, You should be the proudest woman on earth, for your dear little husband has made all his little brethren proud of him – and justly so. Our 'Black and White' American cousin has proved himself a great colourist, a great realist, and an idealist second to none. His picture is beautiful and all are proud of it, but no one delights in it more than – Yours very sincerely, Alfred Gilbert."

Abbey was born and brought up in Philadelphia, training there as a wood engraver and at the Academy until he found employment with Harper's, publishers of the most famous of the American illustrated journals, for whom he continued to work for twenty years. At the age of 26, Abbey settled in England, dividing his time between London and Gloucestershire, and rapidly achieved a considerable reputation as an illustrator and watercolourist, much influenced by the Pre-Raphaelites and the English masters of 1860s illustration, but bringing his own intense, decorative manner to it. After showing only three paintings at the RA, Abbey was astonishingly rapidly elected to ARA, an achievement that owed much to his work on the Boston Public Library murals (with John Singer Sargent and Puvis de Chavannes). He was as painstaking in his researches on English 15th and 18th century life as were Poynter and Alma-Tadema on classical Rome and visitors to his immense, purpose-built studio, Henry James and Spielmann among them, testify to the extraordinary lengths to which Abbey was prepared to go, here, for instance, over the costumes for his pictures:

> ". . . the amazing wardrobe – an interior building constructed at one end of the studio (where), hung in due order, classified with such care, love, and pride as an entomologist might display in the arrangement of his specimens, is the vast collection of garments of all periods and styles which Mr. Abbey has collected or had devised, and to which additions are continuously being made. Here they hang, on right and on left, in diminishing perspective . . ." (Spielmann, p196).

When Abbey discovered that he had painted the coat-of-arms for the wrong branch of the family on the Lady Anne's dress, he repainted

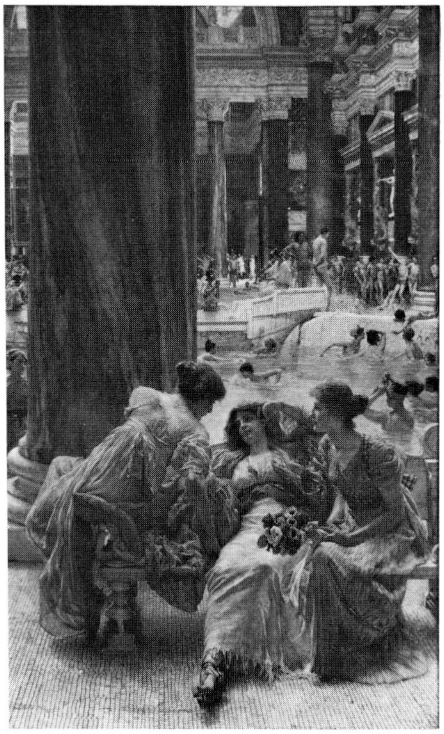

the entire area; similarly, having painted the halberds point up, he discovered they were always carried inverted for funerals and every one was repainted. It was Spielmann again who drew attention to Abbey's debt in the painting of the ranks of halberds to similar treatments in Velasquez's *Surrender of Breda*, Rembrandt's *Night Watch* and Uccello's *San Romano* battles, though Baron Leys was also mentioned.

Though Abbey was dissatisfied with the quality of Flameng's etching of the *Richard* (Lucas p308), its publication by the Art Union was a tribute not only to the success of the painting itself but to Abbey as a master in his chosen decorative style and the last of an extraordinary line of Anglo-Americans that began with Haydon and C.R. Leslie and reached its zenith with Whistler and Henry James. As if to confirm his adoption, Abbey and his picture dominated *Punch's* view of that year's RA, with the Lady Anne at the centre of 'A Royal Academy Soirée'; for *Punch*

"This is *the* picture of the year, . . . A marvellous work . . . This will be the talk of the public" – as it proved to be, despite the puns on the setting of the scene, probably at Westminster, which:

> "will entitle the American artist to be remembered ever after as 'Westminster Abbey' . . . Most certainly it is the very Abbeyest of 'Abbey Thoughts'."

Yale University Art Gallery, The Edwin Austin Abbey Memorial Collection

Sir Lawrence Alma-Tadema, 1836–1912, ARA 1876, RA 1879, KT. 1899, OM 1905

2 Thermae Antoninianae (Baths of Caracalla) 1899

oil on canvas, $60 \times 37\frac{1}{2}$ in
INSCR: L. Alma-Tadema OP CCCLVI

PROV: Judge Samuel Lathrop Bronson, New Haven, Connecticut; his sale, Art Association, New York, 15 Mar 1907 (73) A. Tooth & Sons; Scott & Fowles; Leon Mandel, his sale, Art Association, New York, 17 Jan 1917 (171); Cleve Bonner, Beverley Hills, California; purchased by Allen Funt, New York, 1973; his sale, Sotheby's Belgravia, 6 Nov 1973 (28) bt. Charles Jerdein, from whom purchased by Lord Londonderry.
EXH. RA 1899 (238); *Victorians in Togas: Paintings by Sir Lawrence Alma-Tadema from the Collection of Allen Funt*, Metropolitan Museum of Art, New York 1973 (28).
LIT: *AJ*, June 1899, pp162, 164; *Athenaeum*, 28 Jan, p119, 1 Apr, p408, 29 Apr 1899, p536; *Mag. of Art*, 1899, p388; *Times*, 29 Apr 1899, p14; Rudolf Dircks, 'The Later Work of Sir L. Alma-Tadema', *Art Annual*, Christmas 1910, p32; Vern G. Swanson, *Sir Lawrence Alma-Tadema: The Painter of the Victorian Vision of the Ancient World*, 1977, pp38, 44, 141, pl.24.
REPR: Blackburn, *RA Notes*, 1899, sketch of principal figures, p81.
ENGR: photogravure, publ. Arthur Tooth & Sons, London, New York and Berlin, 1900, $33\frac{1}{4} \times 21\frac{1}{8}$ in (Beck 56); a print was lot 726 in the sale of the contents of the artist's house, 34 Grove End Road, London NW, Hampton's, 9 June 1913.

In the year of Alma-Tadema's knighthood, *The Baths of Caracalla*, his principal picture of the 1899 RA, was captured for the New England collection of Judge Samuel Bronson. Americans had increasingly been buying Tadema's recreations of Roman life, but this was a major prize to take back across the Atlantic; it was joined in 1901 by *Spring* (RA 1895), bought by the famous American collector Charles Yerkes for £7500 (and now, entirely appropriately, in the Getty Museum, California – see Burton B. Fredericksen, *Alma-Tadema's Spring*, Getty Museum, 1976). Both pictures, amongst many minor works, circulated on the American art market in the early years of this century and there can be no doubt that they were an essential source for the films of D.W. Griffith and Cecil B. de Mille (see Mario Amaya, 'The Painter who inspired Hollywood', *Sunday Times Mag.*, 18 Feb 1968). Until the later 19th century, the transatlantic traffic had consisted chiefly of American artists coming to Europe to study in the art capitals of London, Paris, Munich and Berlin, visiting Italy, Brittany and the Low Countries, and returning to capitalise on their European sophistication. Many stayed (see Abbey and Merritt, cat. nos. 1, 36), but it was not until relatively late in the century that some American collectors had the confidence to invest in the art of their British contemporaries.

Tadema's fame in Europe was immense and honours had showered on him from every country; he had been made a Chevalier of the Légion d'Honneur with Henry Moore in 1889, but it was not until 1899 that he was knighted in the Queen's eightieth birthday honours. That November he was fêted with a magnificent banquet attended by virtually every member of the Art Establishment; the Chairman's address by Onslow Ford expressed exactly what Alma-Tadema meant to people at the end of the century:

> "he expressed our British satisfaction that Holland had given him to us; and he bore witness to Sir Lawrence's powers, his activity, his influence; to his merit as an artist, which is increasing with his years; to his research, his invention, his exquisite grace in drawing and colour, and his unerring taste; and, lastly, to his diligence, which has produced 273 pictures since he took up his residence within our borders." (M.H. Spielmann, 'The Alma-Tadema Celebration', *Mag. of Art*, Jan 1900, (p138).

Comyns Carr expressed similar sentiments more informally in some verses entitled 'The *Car*-men *Tademare*', sung by George Henschel at the banquet: the refrain achieved such fame that the last three lines could still be chanted by art students well into this century:

Who knows him well he best can tell
That a stouter friend hath no man
Than this lusty knight, who for our delight
Hath painted Greek and Roman.
Then here let every citizen,
Who holds a brush or wields a pen,
Drink deep as his Zuyder Zee
To Alma Tad —
Of the Royal Acad —
Of the Royal Academee.

Alma-Tadema dazzled his viewers with archaeological expertise, a wealth of brilliantly painted detail and a willingness to go to extraordinary lengths to ensure the faithful rendering of his chosen subject: when painting *The Roses of Heliogabalus* (RA 1888, private collection) commissioned by Sir John Aird for a princely £4000, Tadema ordered roses every week for four months from the French Riviera to make sure that every petal of the thousands in the painting was painted from the life. In the case of *The Baths of Caracalla*, the girls sit on Tadema's famous schizophrenic couch – one side Egyptian and the other Roman, visible here. It was in the sale of Tadema's extraordinary house in St John's Wood, on 9 June 1913, and is now in the V & A (see Sheffield 1976 (41)). *The Times* review assured the reader that in 'this jewel-like work'

> ". . . let nobody imagine that Mr. Tadema has invented the marble boat to gratify his own taste for painting those surfaces: it is absolutely correct according to the latest conclusions of Signor Lanciani . . ."

a reference to the work of the archaeologist Rodolfo Lanciani, whose researches had been made accessible in his *The Ruins and Excavations of Ancient Rome: A Companion Book for Students and Travellers*, 1897; precise details of the Baths of Caracalla are given on pp533–540, including diagrams and a photograph of a composite capital which Tadema seems to have incorporated in the largest column visible in the background of his picture, as well as the marble ship placed in the middle of the swimming pond. Tadema openly acknowledged the use he made of photographs and made a remarkable collection contained in 168 folios now at Birmingham University (see introduction by Anne Goodchild to Alma-Tadema exh., Sheffield 1976), amplifying these with his own watercolour studies made most importantly at Pompeii, all of which were used repeatedly in his paintings; indeed, so extensive was Tadema's knowledge that he delivered a paper, 'Marbles: Their Ancient Application', to the Royal Institute of British Architects in 1907, with the heartfelt conclusion that "marble is beautiful stuff to deal with".

Lord Londonderry

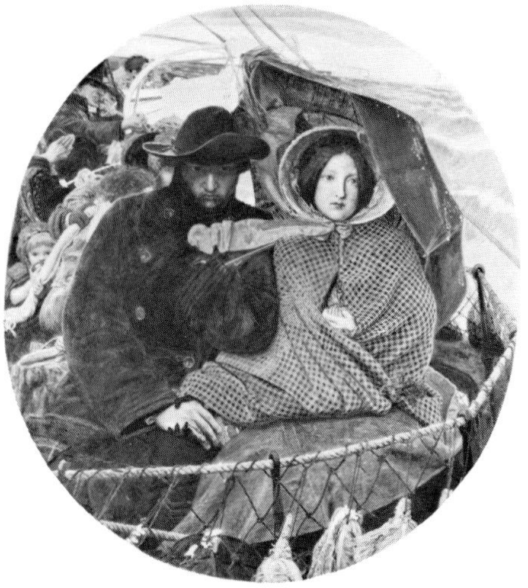

FORD MADOX BROWN, 1821–1893

3 The Last of England 1860

oil on canvas, oval, $18\frac{1}{4} \times 16\frac{5}{8}$ in
INSCR: F Madox Brown 1860

PROV: Bought from the artist by Col. W.J. Gillum 1860 for £157 10s; Miss Mary Slater by 1909; bought from Miss Slater, under the terms of the Marlay Bequest, by the Fitzwilliam Museum, 1924.
EXH: *Collected Works by Ford Madox Brown*, Leicester Galleries 1909 (4, repr); *Art and the Industrial Revolution*, Manchester 1968 (11).
LIT: Ford Madox Hueffer, *Ford Madox Brown: A Record of his Life and Work*, 1896, pp169, 438; *Catalogue of Pictures in the Marlay Bequest, Fitzwilliam Museum, Cambridge*, compiled by W.G. Constable, Cambridge U.P., 1927, p60 and pl.XXX; Mary Bennett, *Catalogue of the Exhibition Ford Madox Brown*, Liverpool 1964, p21.
VERSIONS: 1. Birmingham City Art Gallery. The original painting of 1852–55, oil on panel, oval, $32\frac{1}{2} \times 29\frac{1}{2}$ in.
2. Tate Gallery. Watercolour of 1864–66, circular, 13 in diameter.

The Last of England was Brown's first picture to be generally praised, and is still considered by many to be his masterpiece. His ideal – "Absolutely without regard to the art of any period or country, I have tried to render this scene as it would appear" (*Catalogue notes to Brown's 1865 one-man show at 191 Piccadilly*, p9) – may seem naive to an age which has rejected the concept of the innocent eye; nevertheless the heroism of such an attempt resulted in an image of desolation which, though related specifically to a mid-Victorian social issue, greatly moves the twentieth-century spectator. The method employed, that of the hard-edged Pre-Raphaelite style, was justified by Brown as being the objective correlative of the theme: "The minuteness of detail which would be visible under such conditions of broad day-light, I have thought necessary to imitate, as bringing the pathos of the subject more home to the beholder" (*1865 Catalogue*, p9).

The immediate impulse behind the genesis of the picture was the emigration of the sculptor Thomas Woolner (1825–92) to Australia in July 1852. Emigration from the United Kingdom reached its nineteenth-century peak in that year: 369,000 Britons left for abroad, a tremendous number considering that the total population in 1851 was 27,370,629. Brown was not the first mid-Victorian artist to take up the subject, but his is the most memorable treatment of it.

Brown has chosen a dull, cold day for the picture as befits both the theme and also the artist's own depressed state at a time when he was himself contemplating emigrating to India. The fact that the main couple are painted from the artist and his wife Emma adds poignancy, as Madox Brown explained in 1865:

> "I have, therefore, in order to present the parting scene in its fullest tragic development, singled out a couple from the middle classes, high enough, through education and refinement, to appreciate all they are now giving up, and yet depressed enough in means to have to put up with the discomforts and humiliations incident to a vessel 'all one class'." (*1865 Catalogue*, p9).

The constriction of space is emphasised by the oval format, which also suggests, on a psychological plane, both the circumstances hemming the couple in and necessitating their departure and "the circle of love" (*1865 Catalogue*, p9) which enabled many Victorians to cope with the buffetings of fortune.

Nothing in the picture is extraneous to the theme, from the receding white cliffs of Dover in the right background to the name "Eldorado" on the lifeboat and the cabbages attached to the stern of the ship indicating a long voyage. Brown made clear in his 1865 Catalogue notes that the other passengers represented a typical cross-section of British emigrants:

> ". . . an honest family of the green-grocer kind, father (mother lost), elder daughter, and younger children, makes the best of things with tobacco-pipe and apples, &c., &c. Still further back a reprobate shakes his fist with curses at the land of his birth, as though that were answerable for *his* want of success; his old mother reproves him for his foul-mouthed profanity, while a boon companion, with flushed countenance, and got up in nautical togs for the voyage, signifies drunken approbation." (*Ibid* p9).

These figures are so crowded together that they serve to throw into relief the static central couple and baby, with hands clenched for love, protection and comfort. The fact that the detail of the figures does not lessen towards the background results in a flattening of the picture plane which gives the effect of vertigo caused by the roughness of the Channel on a dull day.

The description of the other passengers recalls Carlyle's proposal, in *Past and Present* (1843), for an emigration service to ship off superfluous and potentially troublesome workers to less populated countries. The sage was much in Brown's mind in the early 1850s, for *Work*, the important painting on which he was working at the same time as *The Last of England*, not only included a portrait of Carlyle but can be seen as embodying his philosophy.

Brown's diary contains a fascinating account of the progress on both pictures. In *The Last of England* as much as possible was painted outdoors, even at the risk of ruining the artist's health, and this – added to financial difficulties – accounted for the length of time Brown took over the work, for the climatic conditions had to be of a certain kind before the painting could be advanced. The sort of dedication which he brought to the task shines through the diary entries; for example, we find him writing on 2 September 1855, two days before the original painting was finally completed:

> "It has been intensely cold – no sun, no rain, a high wind. But this seemed the sweetest weather possible, for it was the weather for my picture, and made my hand look blue with the cold, as I require it in the work." (*Præraphaelite Diaries and Letters*, 1900, pp192–93)

The version in the exhibition, undertaken largely for financial reasons, differs from the original only in the treatment of the female emigrant's shawl. Brown had pondered deeply the choice of this garment which, justifiably, considering the area it takes up, he thought "a serious affair" (*Ibid*, p130).

Brown was never a popular artist but, when the conservative *Art Journal* engraved the original oil of *The Last of England*, then in the collection of John Crossley of Halifax, in 1870, the accompanying text is a useful indicator of his standing in the eyes of a more general public than that which attended his show at the Egyptian Hall in 1865.

> "The works of Mr. Madox Brown are but little known beyond that comparatively limited circle, the Art-world; this, however, includes the artists' patrons as well as the painters themselves, and of course must be added to both, the Art-critics. It is many years since we remember to have seen a picture by him at the Royal Academy or elsewhere; in fact, he is now altogether unknown in our picture-galleries, though held in high esteem, and deservedly so, by competent judges and connoisseurs, who can see even in what is called 'Pre-Raffaelism' of a certain order much to admire . . . (but) those who were wise enough to visit (the 1865 exhibition) could scarcely fail of being impressed by what they saw . . .
>
> Whatever diversity of opinion may prevail among critics as to the merits or demerits of his style and usual treatment, there can be none in recognising the artist as a man of original genius, showing high development of thought; a hard worker, following no leader, and indefatigable in research towards the attainment of accuracy. His pictures are as far removed from all prettiness as it is possible for a work of Art to be, and therefore are most unlikely to catch, and retain, the eye of the general public; but they are works to be studied, and the lessons they teach, *as examples of painting*, are such as cannot be lost on an unprejudiced mind." (*AJ*, Aug 1870, p236).

Mary Bennett, of the Walker Art Gallery, is preparing a Catalogue of the works of Ford Madox Brown, and Deborah Cherry has edited his letters and unpublished diaries in preparation for her forthcoming biography of the artist.

J.E.B.

Fitzwilliam Museum, Cambridge

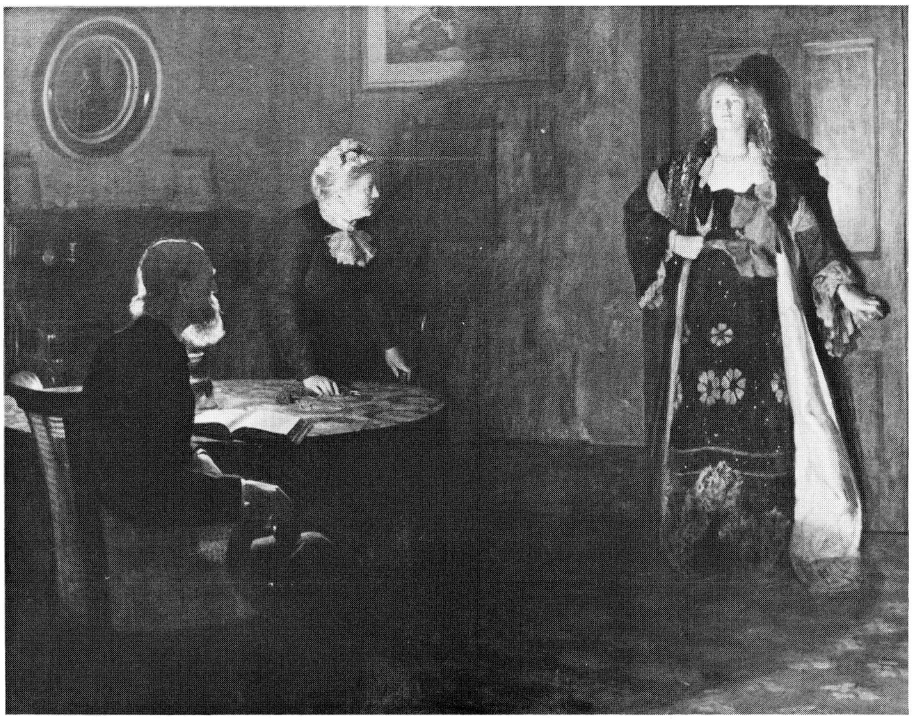

HON. JOHN COLLIER, 1850–1934

4 The Prodigal Daughter 1903

oil on canvas, 63 × 85 in
INSCR: John Collier 1903

PROV: The artist; presented to the Usher Gallery, Lincoln, by the Hon. Mrs. Collier, 1935.
EXH: RA 1903 (427); Walker, Liverpool, Autumn 1903 (5); Rome 1911 (147); *Paintings by the Hon. John Collier*, Plymouth 1924 (33); *Paintings by the Honble. John Collier*, Lincoln 1930 (6); *Memorial Exh. of Paintings by the late The Honourable John Collier*, Plymouth, Birkenhead, Lincoln, Darlington, Burton-upon-Trent, Leamington, Wolverhampton, December 1934–November 1935 (variously numbered).
LIT: *AJ*, 1903, p175; *Mag. of Art*, 1903, p387, repr, p385; *The Times*, 2 May 1903, p13; Blackburn, *RA Notes* 1903, p26, repr. p101; *RA Pictures*, 1903, p.iii, repr. p103; Walter Herries Pollock, The Art of the Hon. John Collier, *Art Annual*, London, 1914, pp6, 29, repr. in colour facing p22; obit., *The Times*, 12 April 1934, p17.
REPR: *ILN* suppl. 30 May 1903, p.viii; *The Pictures of 1903*, Pall Mall Magazine "Extra", May 1903, p61; *Souvenir*, Rome, 1911, p197.

Collier had his greatest popular success as the painter of so-called "problem pictures" like *Trouble* (1898), *The Cheat* (1905), *Mariage de Convenance* (1907), and *Sentence of Death* (1908), and *The Prodigal Daughter* was generally considered one of his most important:

> "startlingly successful . . . perhaps the best picture he has ever painted. The old man's head, haloed by the lamp it eclipses, is finely conceived, with force and daring, and the whole composition, seen in a white light, marks a considerable advance alike in artistic accomplishment and in tone and dramatic power." (*Mag. of Art*, 1903)

and, in the *Art Journal:*

> "Perhaps the largest measure of popularity will be accorded to the large picture by the Hon. John Collier . . . in which he has presented a scene from some drama in modern life. The setting of his scene is plainly suburban and middle-class, a commonplace, shabby-genteel room in which the prodigal daughter, dressed in showy finery, seems strangely out of place. Mr. Collier has not, however, depended simply upon the assertion of everyday facts to give interest to his work; he has made the subject an excuse for painting an admirable effect of artificial light and for securing clever differentiation in types of human character. The picture is a curious commentary on heredity; it seems almost impossible that such a type of woman as the daughter who has gone defiantly her own way, could have sprung from surroundings so conventional and narrowly respectable. The artist, indeed, suggests a problem which offers scope for wide discussion."

Collier's skilful deployment of the dramatic conventions of theatrical tableaux may owe something to his friendships with (and portraits of) the leading actors and actresses of the day – Lewis Waller, Mrs. Kendall, Ellen Terry, and Beerbohm Tree. The use of a print hanging on the wall, designed to emphasise the poignant message of the narrative, also owes a debt to earlier use of the device by artists like Augustus Egg in the first scene of *Past and Present* (see cat. no. 10); here, the print is that published in 1847 after *The Combat*, (RA 1847), a scene of two stags locked in violent struggle, by Richard Ansdell (1815–85, a Liverpool artist, contemporary and rival of Landseer). The painting was in the Naylor Collection when it was shown at the 1890 Grosvenor Gallery Winter Exhibition.

Speculation on the subject reached a crescendo in the review in *The Times*, which called the picture:

> "the popular attraction, and to a certain extent the popular puzzle . . . This is an English Magda – the runaway daughter of a quiet old couple, returning in her finery to her simple home. The details of the dramatic moment are a little difficult to understand; has she just entered the room, or is she leaving it, repelled? Is she telling a story, or has she told it, unforgiven, and is she about to pass out again into the night? These things want explaining, for a narrative picture ought to have no ambiguity; but meantime we can unreservedly admire the fine, upright figure of the girl, the tragedy of her face, the painting of her dress, and the old father's head seen against the lamp.
>
> On the whole, the picture is a marked success for Mr. Collier."

It was this kind of categorisation, still being made in 1920, that provoked Collier's exasperated reply, quoted in *The Times* obituary, that the problem pictures:

> "are nothing of the kind. The ones that have been so termed merely depict little tragedies of modern life, and I have always endeavoured to make their meaning perfectly plain. If I ever again paint a picture of modern life, which is doubtful, I shall give it a title a yard long, setting forth the life history of the characters, and, if necessary, their names and addresses."

Collier's training was in Munich and Paris, at the Slade and finally at the elbow of Alma-Tadema and Millais which, coupled with his family background, ensured his success as a society portrait painter in the tradition of Frank Holl and Dicksee. He published three volumes on painting: *A Primer of Art* (1882), *A Manual of Oil Painting* (1886) and *The Art of Portrait Painting* (1905), following the didactic tradition set by earlier artists like O'Neil, Redgrave and Poynter. In addition to his regular appearances at the Academy, the Grosvenor Gallery and the New Gallery, the Leicester Galleries showed 52 landscape studies in 1915, the Sunderland Art Gallery mounted a full-scale retrospective of all aspects of his art in 1922, and *The Times* obituary records another show of his landscape studies in 1931 at the Museum Galleries, Haymarket. The artist's widow arranged the memorial exhibition of Collier's paintings, which toured the country in 1934–35, and presented many of the pictures to public galleries.

Usher Gallery, Lincoln

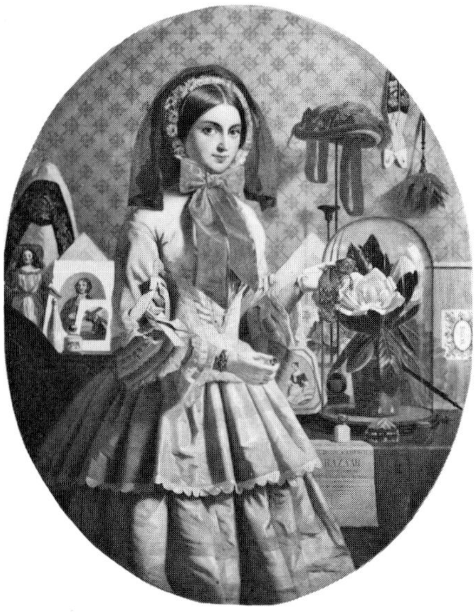

JAMES COLLINSON, 1825–1881

5 **For Sale** 1857

oil on canvas, oval, 23 × 18 in

PROV: Professor Thomas Bodkin, by 1925; his sale, Sotheby's, 11 Nov 1959 (97) bt. Agnew for Nottingham.
EXH: RA 1857 (115); Dublin Municipal Art Gallery 1920; *Pictures of "Victorian Life" by Artists of the Period (1837–1901)*, Leicester Galleries 1937 (96); *An Exhibition of Victorian Paintings*, Birmingham 1937 (25); *The Pre-Raphaelite Brotherhood*, Birmingham 1947 (16); *The Pre-Raphaelites*, Port Sunlight 1948 (100); *Pre-Raphaelites and their Followers*, Bournemouth 1951 (22); *Some Pre-Raphaelite Paintings and Drawings*, Welsh Arts Council 1955 (22); Nottingham 1959 (13).
LIT: *Literary Gazette*, 23 May 1857, p499; *DNB*, 1908, IV, p838; Thomas Bodkin, 'James Collinson', *Apollo*, May 1940, pp132–3, repr. p130; S.R., 'James Collinson of Mansfield', *Nottingham Guardian*, 11 Nov 1952 (Witt cutting); *Country Life*, 3 Dec 1959, pp1028–9; William E. Fredeman, *Pre-Raphaelitism: A Bibliocritical Study*, Cambridge, Mass. 1965, pp132–3; Forbes, *RA Revisited*, p30, repr, p30.
Castle Museum, Nottingham

6 **To Let** 1857

oil on canvas, oval, 23 × 18 in

PROV: Professor Thomas Bodkin, by 1925; his sale, Sotheby's, 11 Nov 1959 (98) bt. Fine Art Society.
EXH: RA 1857 (102); Birmingham 1919; Dublin 1920; Leicester Galleries 1937 (98); Birmingham 1937 (98) and 1947 (17); Port Sunlight 1948 (99); Bournemouth 1951 (24); Welsh Arts Council 1955 (21); Nottingham 1959 (12); *Victorian Paintings*, Charles Keyser Gallery, London 1971; *Victorian Art*, Hofstra University, New York 1972 (66); Metropolitan Museum, New York 1974–5; *The Pre-Raphaelite Era 1848–1914*, Delaware 1976 (2–2).
LIT: *AJ*, June 1857, p167; and see above.
ENGR: W.T. Davey, 1 Feb 1858.
The Forbes Magazine Collection

VERSIONS: 1. *At the Bazaar*, s & d 1857, and *The Landlady*, s & d 1856; both oil on canvas laid down on panel, oval; 24 × 18 in. Prov: Frost; J.G. Graves, before 1910; Graves Gift to Sheffield City Art Galleries, 1929. Exh: RA *1st 100 Years* 1951–2 (286, 284); Sheffield 1968 (36, 35).

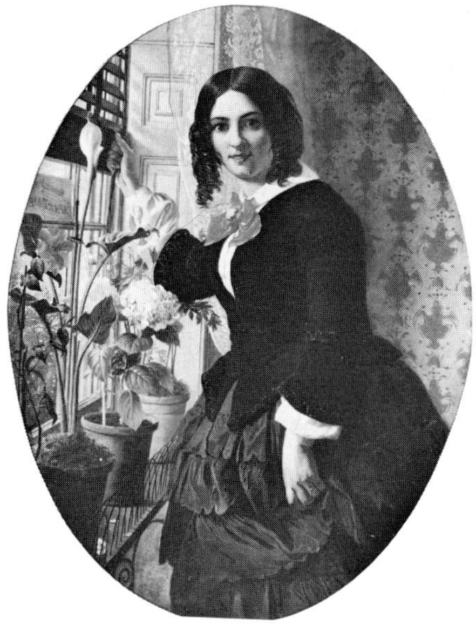

2. *The Empty Purse* (version of *For Sale/At the Bazaar*) oil on canvas, 24 × 19⅜ in. Prov: Presented anonymously to the Tate, 1917. Repr: Bell, 1967, pl.28; Maas, 1969, p140.

Collinson's two exhibits at the 1857 RA, *To Let* and *For Sale*, passed unnoticed by all but two of the reviewers; that of the *Literary Gazette* explains, at least partially, why:

> "A pair of subjects . . . representing . . . two specimens of vulgarity in the shape of a showy landlady and a lively saleswoman, are attractive at a distance from their smart drawing and bright colour; but are hung too high to allow of any certain estimate being formed of their merits."

The *Art Journal* was puzzled but complimentary about *To Let*:

> "The point of the title is not very clear; the picture shows a lady in a dark dress, in the act of drawing up her Venetian blind, at a window well furnished with flowers. The figure is round and well drawn."

He had missed the point that the woman has placed a notice in her window reading 'Furnished Apartments'; her left hand proclaims her married respectability, but she is plumply attractive and her crimson bow matches the camellia flowering in its pot on the windowsill beside a Bleeding Heart, a lily and a hydrangea. The companion picture, *For Sale*, shows a slighter, and therefore in the convention of the day, younger girl, dressed to the nines, in front of a table laden with goods for sale; the yellow leaflet announces it as St. Bride's Church Bazaar and the objects ranged behind her reveal a similar attention to significant detail. For instance, the doll at the far left, dressed in eighteenth century finery, is probably a comment on the superficial nature of fashion and its followers. Next to it is a small coloured print, typical of those published by the Religious Tract Society, of Christ bearing the Cross: the Tate version of the picture, *The Empty Purse*, shows the print inscribed 'Follow Me'.

The existence of the replicas and of Davey's engraving of *To Let* is reasonable evidence that, despite being ignored by the critics, these pictures gave Collinson the chief success of his career. He was one of the original seven Pre-Raphaelite Brothers, introduced to the group by Dante Gabriel Rossetti and became engaged to his sister Christina. Pre-Raphaelitism had little effect on his genre paintings until 1850 when, according to W.M. Rossetti, Collinson decided 'to cut the Wilkie style of art for the Early Christian' and painted his one fully Pre-Raphaelite work, *The Renunciation of Queen Elizabeth of Hungary* (Portland Gallery 1851, now at Johannesburg; see Alastair Grieve, *Burlington*, May 1969, p293). The religious subject was symptomatic of Collinson's state of mind for he soon after reverted to the Catholicism which he had given up on his engagement to Christina. He resigned from the PRB as he felt unable to associate as an artist with those who did not share his faith. William Bell Scott gives a characteristically prejudiced account of the episode after criticising the *St. Elizabeth* for flaccid and weak drawing, he continued

> "In all respects the picture resembled the *feckless* dilettanteism of the converts who were then dropping out of their places in Oxford and Cambridge into Mariolatry and Jesuitism. In fact, this James Collinson actually did become a Romanist, wanted to be a priest, painted no more, but entered a seminary [Stonyhurst], where they set him to clean the boots as an apprenticeship in humility and obedience. They did not want him as a priest, they were already getting tired of that species of convert; so he left, turned to painting again, and disappeared." (*Autobiographical Notes of the Life of William Bell Scott*, 1902, I, p281).

His disappearance was not complete, though his obituarist in the *Athenaeum* was hard pressed to find anything to note from the years after *St. Elizabeth* other than a list of his showings at the RA, BI and Suffolk Street. These do, however, represent a fairly steady output of apparently small-scale cabinet and genre paintings, of which the two here exhibited were clearly the most important subjects. The Sheffield versions, respectably retitled (whether by Collinson or a later owner it is impossible to say) *At the Bazaar* and *The Landlady* are dated respectively 1857 and 1856 which would be correct for the 1857 RA, the Nottingham/Forbes pair are undated but bear the correct RA titles. The identity of the exhibited pictures will remain unsolved unless it proves possible to discover more of the provenances of the two-and-a-half sets of pictures. Professor Bodkin's papers are deposited in Dublin at the National Gallery and Trinity College. Future investigation of these may provide information which it has proved impossible to obtain elsewhere. Copies of the Birmingham 1919 and the Dublin 1920 exhibition catalogues are so far untraceable, so we do not know whether Bodkin already owned the pictures when they were shown there. The *Country Life* article of 1959, at the time of Bodkin's sale at Sotheby's, states that Bodkin bought all his pictures but one (a Netscher) very cheaply in Dublin before 1925. The Tate's *Empty Purse* was presented in 1917, and Graves bought the pair now at Sheffield before 1910. The article in the *Nottingham Guardian* of 1952, evidently well-researched by a local historian and very useful on Collinson's Mansfield origins, points out that the Johannesburg picture 'reappeared during the First World War'. It seems, therefore, that all the major Collinsons now known to us emerged onto the market over a period of probably rather less than twenty years in the first quarter of this century.

Collinson the man was remembered by his Pre-Raphaelite friends chiefly for being amiable 'but in his own person tame and sleepy . . . he could but rarely see the fun of anything, although he sometimes laughed in a lachrymose manner, and I fear our attempts to enliven him were but futile.' (W. Holman Hunt, *Pre-Raphaelitism and the Pre-Raphaelite Brotherhood*, 1905, II, pp161–2). Anecdotes about Collinson so persistently refer to his chronic sleepiness that the poor man may indeed have suffered from a form of narcolepsy. It is tempting to connect him with the Dormouse at the Mad Hatter's Tea Party; *Alice* was not published until 1865 but Carroll knew all the Rossettis and William Michael's *Reminiscences* (1906) record his theory that the Dormouse was modelled on Dante Gabriel's pet wombat which habitually slept on the table, in a manner not dissimilar to Collinson's.

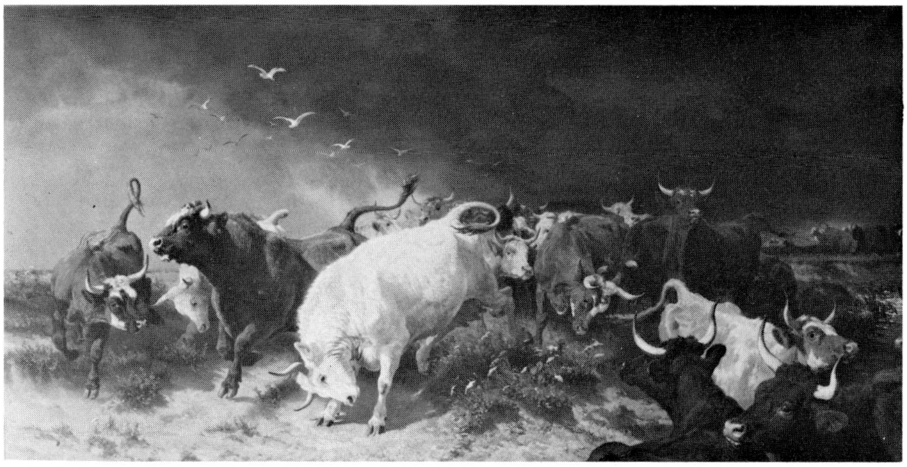

Henry Williams Banks Davis, 1833–1914, ARA 1873, RA 1877

7 A Panic 1872

oil on canvas, 48 × 96¼ in
INSCR: H.W.B. Davis 1872

PROV: W.E.J. Roffey; his sale, Christie's, 9/10 July 1875 (275) bt. Tooth (£488 5s); Kaye Knowles, Warrington Crescent, London; his sale, Christie's, 14 May 1887 (81) bt. Agnew (£735) for Andrew Knowles; Pawsey & Payne Ltd, by 1976; Bonham's, 3 Mar 1977 (59).
LIT: (all references are to the exhibited picture) *AJ*, June 1872, p152; *Athenaeum*, 4 May 1873, p566; *ILN*, 18 May 1872, p5; *Times*, 4 May 1872, p5; M. Phipps Jackson, 'Henry William Banks Davis, RA', *Mag. of Art*, 1881, p127; Davis entry, Thieme-Becker.
VERSION: *A Panic*, original exhibited work; oil on canvas, 96 × 192 in. Prov: Morrison Coll., Fonthill House, Wiltshire, in 1872 (see Thieme-Becker); J.E. Champney, by whom presented to Beverley, Yorkshire (now Humberside), 1921. Exh: RA 1872 (124).
ENGR: Charles G. Lewis; line and stipple engraving, 21 × 41⅞ in, publ G. Ramage & Son, 1874.

Davis's painting for the 1872 RA (a reduced version of which is here exhibited) was enormous: it measures 8 × 16 ft, dimensions rarely exceeded in Victorian art by any painter except Leighton. It was clearly, therefore, a major bid for attention and recognition, and as such was entirely successful: the painting was well received and the following year Davis was elected ARA. He had been showing at the RA for twenty years, but was still not yet forty; the artist who had established an invincible position as the country's leading painter of cattle, Thomas Sidney Cooper, was his senior by thirty years and Davis was making a dramatic bid not only for his ARA but for a place as Cooper's successor. The older artist aware perhaps of pressure, exhibited his largest picture, *The Monarch of the Meadows* (private collection), in the 1873 RA.

A Panic excited considerable attention: the *Art Journal* called it:

> "the most spirited cattle-piece that has appeared among us for years . . . [it] represents a herd of oxen driven in wild terror by an approaching thunderstorm. In comparison with the very tame cattle-subjects commonly painted [a reference to Cooper], this must be regarded as leaving all of them far behind; and it not only takes rank with the finest representations of bovine form and nature ever seen, but surpasses all in life and action. The animals appear to be of the size of life, and consequently suggest to the remembrance every similar representation from the infancy of Art to our own day, but only to enhance the estimation of this work."

The most obvious comparisons for contemporaries to make were with the French animal painters Constant Troyon and Rosa Bonheur. Davis's picture was only slightly smaller than Rosa Bonheur's most famous painting, *The Horse Fair*, Paris Salon 1853, (Metropolitan Museum, New York) which he would probably have seen when it was toured round England by Gambart, as well as its quarter-size replica in the National Gallery (bequeathed 1859, delivered 1865). Bonheur also painted cattle stampedes such as *La route de Poissy*.

Continental scale and spectator-involving effects had educated the eye of the *ILN* reviewer who described the violent action and went on:

> "The composition, drawing, foreshortening and knowledge of animal character which the subject has brought into play are of a very high order; and if the painting had been equally good, the picture would have been one of the greatest masterpieces of its kind in our school. But the execution is somewhat hard. The beasts are too smooth and clean, in proportion to the large dimension of the canvas, the textures of the hides are wanting in the richness of *pleine pâte* they would have received at the hands of a Troyon or De Haas."

These complaints were echoed by the *Athenaeum* and it may be this that decided Davis to produce a reduced version of much greater vivacity and vigour, the version exhibited here. It is precisely quarter-sized, but whether it is a large sketch, elaborated and finished, or an entirely separate replica is not clear. Its early provenance from W.E.J. Roffey's sale, the catalogue of which included no measurements, is confirmed by Agnew's copy of the catalogue; lot 275 was catalogued as 'Exh. at the RA, 1872', but in Agnew's copy this is crossed out and annotated 'smaller picture'. The original RA picture survives in relatively good condition, given its size, at Beverley.

Davis had begun his career much influenced by Pre-Raphaelite landscape, but a love of France and frequent stays there throughout his life, together with friendships with a number of French artists, finally changed his direction in the late 1860s to a broader and more dramatic treatment of animals in landscape. His principal patrons were Lord and Lady Middleton, at whose houses in Yorkshire and Ross-shire Davis frequently stayed from the early 1880s. From then on his work alternated northern moorland scenes with deer, like *Approach to the Bealloch-na-ba, Applecross* (RA 1888, private collection), and sunny prospects of Picardy, such as *A gleamy day, Picardy* (RA 1891, Cardiff), all of which were generally well-received. Graves's *Art Sales* shows that his work only twice topped £1000 in the salerooms between 1875 and 1910, and sold fairly steadily in the low hundreds, but he was a consistently popular and successful artist, whose paintings figured in good collections like those of Humphrey Roberts, J.P. Heseltine, and W.Y. Baker, as well as in the huge collection of George McCulloch. Replicas of his largest works were commissioned on several occasions.

Information on Davis is currently being collected by the artist's grandson, Harry I. Lee, to whom we are indebted for biographical details.

Gallery Kalb, Vienna

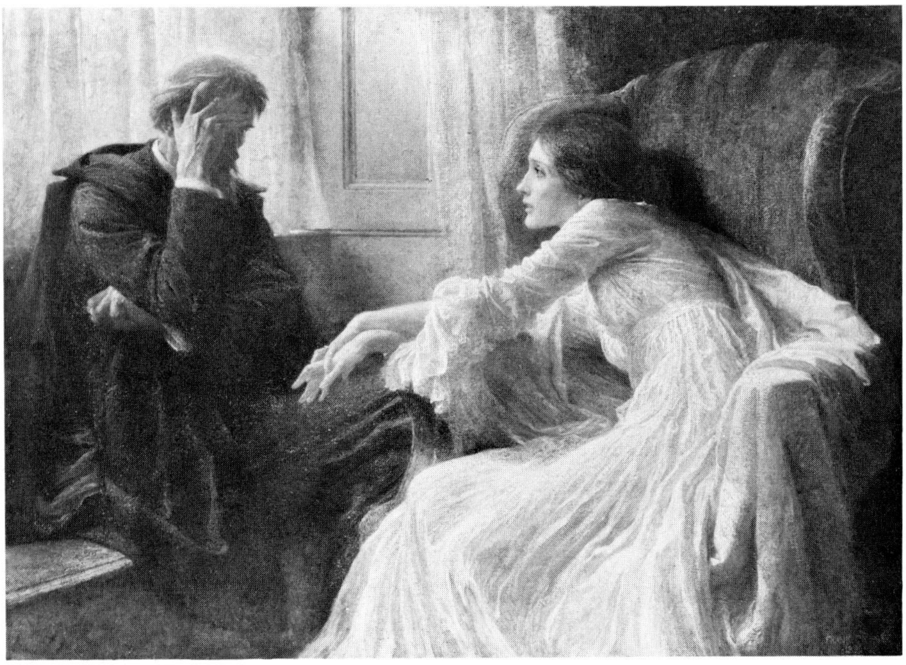

Sir Frank Dicksee, 1853–1928, ara 1881, ra 1891, pra 1924, kt. 1925, kcvo 1927

8 The Confession 1896

oil on canvas, 45 × 63 in
INSCR: Frank Dicksee 1896

PROV: Lord and Lady Wantage; Christie's, 16 July 1976 (79) & 13 May 1977 (126) bt. Miles.
EXH: RA 1896 (340); Expo. Universelle Paris 1900 (67); Whitechapel, Spring 1903 (102); *The Victorian Era*, Roy Miles Fine Paintings, 1977.
LIT: *AJ*, June 1896, pp171–172, repr. p163; *Athenaeum*, 23 May 1896, p688; Blackburn, *RA Notes*, 1896, pp13–14, repr. p72; *Graphic*, 2 May, p523 and 9 May 1896, p562; *Mag. of Art*, 1896, p298; *RA Pictures*, 1896, p.ii, repr. p131; *Studio*, July 1896, p111; *Times*, 2 May 1896, p15; Jules Comte, ed., *L'Art a l'Exposition Universelle de 1900*, p195; E. Rimbault Dibdin, 'The Art of Frank Dicksee, RA', *Art Annual*, Christmas 1905, pp14–15, repr. p2; A. G. Temple, *Wantage Coll. Cat.*, 1902 & 1905 (57).

The Confession, though sent as an afterthought, made such an impression at the Paris Exposition of 1900 that it was awarded a Silver Medal. Four years earlier, the only reviewer of the '96 RA who spoke of Dicksee's 'true painter's talent', dismissing worries about the precise nature of the subject – 'After all, it matters very little, for the painting suffices, apart from the subject' – was Aman-Jean, the French Symbolist painter invited by *Studio* to review that year's RA. The other critics, all English, found the subject too 'needlessly painful' (*Times*) to be acceptable – a reaction identical to the one that greeted Egg's *Past and Present* (cat. no. 10) in the 1858 RA, nearly forty years before.

The *Art Journal* pointed out that Dicksee 'seems to alternate between rather morbid suggestion and a certain sumptuousness of detail painting': The '96 RA contained an example of each extreme and most critics vastly preferred *The Mirror* (202) repr. Dibdin 1905, p13. Despite its exotic narcissicism – an 'Eastern' woman on a sumptuously-draped seat gazes into a hand-mirror – it was considered to have a 'much more healthy feeling' than *The Confession*. *The Art Journal* complained of the latter's

> "somewhat painful subject, treated in a manner which, without being realistic in the ordinary sense, accentuates the melancholy motive. A wan, emaciated woman, in the last stage apparently of illness, is telling her story to a saddened man, who is sitting with his face in shadow, and his head resting in his hand. The picture is in a scheme of pale colours, greys and greens, and its curious indefiniteness of effect seems somehow to add to the hopelessness of the whole subject."

The *Athenaeum*, while preferring *The Mirror*, labelled both too clever, but damned *The Confession* as 'tragedy of a stagey kind. Like other productions of Mr. Dicksee, it is rather accomplished than sound . . .' Spielmann, in his introduction to *RA Pictures 1896*, also objected to the 'not wholly pleasant, if sympathetic, greenish-grey tone of colour', but found in the picture 'a kind of sad fascination'. Nine years later, when Dibdin produced the *Art Annual* on Dicksee, the genre had become familiar, Collier's 'Problem Picture' was an established feature of each year's RA, and Dibdin's description of the 'agonised woman, writhing like Paula Tanqueray' was able to revel in Dicksee's 'strongly dramatic effect . . . and characteristic subtlety'.

Dicksee came of a family of artists and learned from his father, Thomas Dicksee, before entering the RA Schools; he achieved his first and, in some ways greatest, success with only his second exhibit at the RA. *Harmony* (RA 1877, Tate) was a Chantrey purchase and made his name: it was a successful blend of what the *AJ* later called 'Venetian colouring and medieval mysticism', owing much both to his work in stained glass design for Henry Holiday and to a detailed knowledge of Millais. The mediaeval pictures continued and, with only five RA exhibited pictures and aged only 27, Dicksee was made ARA in 1881. Five years later, the first of his scenes of emotional intensity was shown, *Memories* (RA 1886, repr. Dibdin p18), and these continued with pictures like *A Reverie* (RA 1895, Liverpool) and *The Confession*. The second Chantrey purchase of a Dicksee, *The Two Crowns* (RA 1900, Tate) was a great popular success, the Picture of the Year in a *Daily News* poll. The last twenty-five years of his life saw a gradual decline in his critical reputation (even in 1905 a defensive tone can be detected in Dibdin's writing) to the point where his election as President of the Academy in 1924 was regarded as an unfortunate inevitability of seniority. Dicksee used his position as PRA to make speeches in which he:

> "denounced certain morbid and unwholesome tendencies in modern art, which he attributed partly to the reaction against mere prettiness partly to the heresy that hard work was not needed for the production of anything of permanent value . . . he deplored what he called the cult of ugliness, and said that art could be retained on sound and wholesome lines in two ways, by knowledge and by the exercise of the feeling of sincerity." (obit., *Times*, 18 Oct 1928, p21).

His sad decline into the stereotype of the old inveighing against the new in his last years does no justice to his own accomplishments at the turn of the century in dealing with essentially Victorian subjects, such as that of *The Confession*, with great sophistication of design, delicacy of colour and brilliant technique; it is not difficult to understand how a Silver Medal could be awarded in Paris, it is perhaps harder to understand why in the London of the 1890s critics were still reacting like mid-Victorians to subject-matter and allowing that to destroy their awareness of the painting. The painting was bought by Lord and Lady Wantage whose connoisseurship and distinguished collection of Old Masters seems to have informed their buying of contemporary work (see cat. 35).

Roy Miles Fine Paintings, London

SIR CHARLES LOCK EASTLAKE, 1793–1865, ARA 1827, RA 1830, PRA 1850, KB 1850

9 Christ lamenting over Jerusalem (1841)

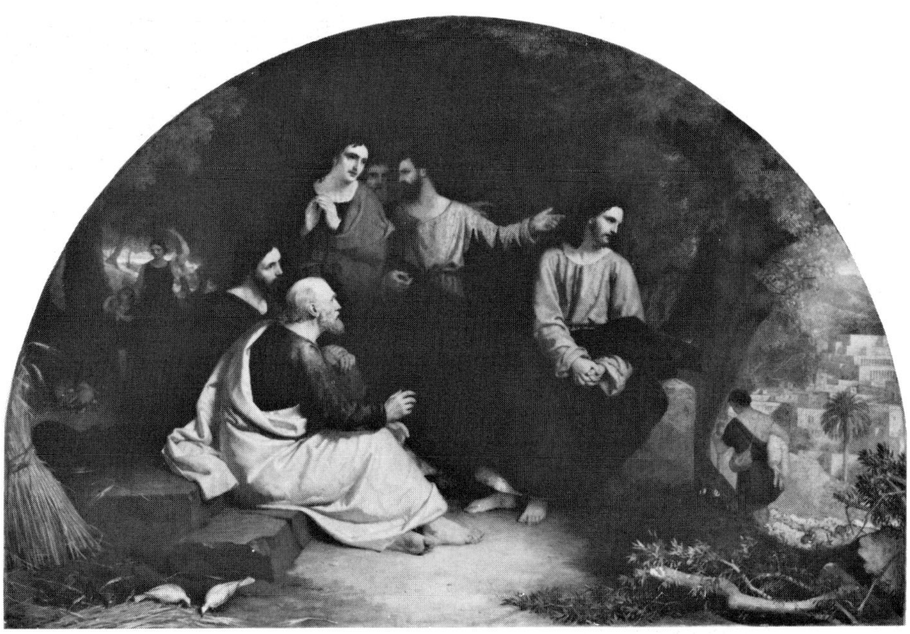

39 × 59 in
INSCR: C.L. Eastlake, 1855

PROV: Drake's Little Gallery, 13 St Mary Axe, Leadenhall St, London EC3, n.d., from whom bt. by John Weir; presented to Glasgow by Weir, 1928.
EXH: *Three World-Famous Pictures*, Drake's Little Gallery, n.d. (V & A annot. *c.*1925), cat. p2; *Narrative Paintings*, Glasgow 1940 (54); *Sir Charles Lock Eastlake*, Plymouth 1965 (23); Sheffield 1968 (115).
LIT: (selected bibl., all refer to the exhibited picture or the Vernon version) *Art Union*, 15 May 1841, p76; *Athenaeum*, 8 May 1841, p367; *Blackwood's*, Sept 1841, p349; *Gentleman's Mag.*, June 1841, p630; *Literary Gazette*, 15 May 1841, p314; *Times*, 4 May 1841, p5; 'The Vernon Gallery: Christ lamenting over Jerusalem', *AJ*, Apr 1854, p107, engr. facing; 'British Artists IX: Sir Charles Lock Eastlake', *AJ*, Oct 1855, p278; obit., *AJ*, Feb 1866, p60; Lady Eastlake, ed., *Contributions to the Literature of the Fine Arts by Sir Charles Lock Eastlake* with a Memoir, 1870, p196; W. Cosmo Monkhouse, *Pictures by Sir Charles Eastlake*, 1875, pp49, 64, engr.; Cunningham, 1880, III, p320; Patrick Conner, *Ruskin*, in preparation; David Robertson, *Sir Charles Eastlake and the Victorian Art World*, to be published in 1978.
VERSIONS: 1. exhibited picture, RA 1841 (75); commissioned by Smith Child, Bt. 1868, of Stallington Hall, Staffs.; untraced.
2. repetition painted for Robert Vernon, *c.*1842; Vernon Bequest to the nation, 1847, now Tate (397); engr: Samuel Cousins, 1847; J. Outrim, *AJ* 1854; W.H. Simmons, 1861.
3. repetition, coll. John Naylor by 1854 (see Waagen, III, p241), Naylor sale, Christie's, 19 Jan 1923 (29) bt. Sampson (£22 1s); exh. Manchester Art Treasures 1857 (359).

> "We cannot find words to express our admiration of this work – as near perfection as was ever a production of genius."

So began the *Art Union's* review of Eastlake's painting and so it continued for over a column:

> "It is, beyond doubt, the gem of the collection; one that may stand without prejudice beside the most famous productions of the great old masters . . . This picture is one for the nation to be proud of – one that will be invariably referred to in every discussion that may arise hereafter as to the rank which British Art is entitled to hold. It is impossible for us to exaggerate in any terms we may apply to it. It is the emanation of a mind nobly, gracefully, and beautifully constructed, the production of a pencil possessing a combination of the rarest powers; and finished with a deep and thorough knowledge of all the qualities of which the art is capable. If we class it immeasurably above any work – either of the painter or the poet – that our age has given birth to, as a lesson in practical wisdom, virtue, and beauty, we shall scarcely do justice to the genius that produced it . . ."

The picture was acclaimed as a didactic vehicle for religious teaching and moral uplift as much as for its 'exquisite' composition, the characterisation, the symbolic detail, the finish, colouring, and light and shade.

> ". . . In a word, the work is PERFECT. It is worth a pilgrimage to examine it, and a fortune to possess it. There are few who would not gladly sacrifice the produce of years of labour to acquire so glorious, beautiful, and instructive a companion. It will dwell with our happiest memories for life."

The *Athenaeum* began its RA review for that year with a long paragraph on the picture that was scarcely less eulogistic, and the *Literary Gazette* and the *Times* matched them in quality if not in quantity of praise, leaving the *Gentleman's Magazine* alone in the opinion that Collins, Allan and Eastlake 'are all inferior to themselves'. The public evidently shared the rapture of the critics, to the considerable disadvantage of the *Blackwood's* man who was forced to admit that he could say little of Mr. Eastlake's 'universally admired' picture as 'it was so difficult of access'; the crowds that pressed around it may not have equalled those around Wilkie's *Chelsea Pensioners* in 1822, but it was undoubtedly thought to be a masterpiece.

The subsequent history of the original painting has so far defied all attempts at research and the painting is no longer in the possession of Sir Smith Child's descendants. So successful was the painting, however, that at least two, and possibly three, replicas were commissioned, all of very similar measurements and amongst which is the picture dated 1855 now at Glasgow and exhibited here. The best-known version is that painted by Eastlake for Vernon probably in 1842; this was engraved by the *Art Journal* in 1854 and discussed by Waagen as the exhibited work but by 1877 Blackburn's *Pictorial Notes in the National Gallery* was referring to it as a repetition. The version recorded by Waagen in the Naylor Collection by 1854 was finally sold at Christie's in 1923, bought by Sampson, dealers whose turnover was usually brisk. Drake's Little Gallery exhibited what is now the Glasgow version, publishing a brochure advertising Three World-Famous Pictures (the others were John Martin's *Belshazzar's Feast* and Ary Scheffer's *Christ the Consoler*). A copy of this catalogue is in the V & A Library, dated on the index card at *c.*1925, the only indication of a date so far known. Weir subsequently bought the picture and presented it to Glasgow in 1928. The extraordinary coincidence of two different versions of the same Eastlake painting appearing on the London art market within two years of each other would be easy to resolve by joining the two provenances together were it not for the fact that the Naylor picture is recorded in 1854, while the Glasgow picture is dated 1855. There are several possible explanations for this discrepancy but, in the absence of further evidence, the count of replicas must for the time being remain at three.

Eastlake's earlier successes had been with Italianate subjects of peasants in the Campagna, the result of his fourteen years in Rome 1816–30; the only other painting of his that approached the level of popular success enjoyed by *Christ lamenting* was his 1839 RA exhibit *Christ blessing little children* (Manchester). Twenty years later, the *Art Journal* was still able to publish a twelve-verse panegyric, 'written on viewing the admirable engraving by J.H. Watt' after Eastlake's painting (engr. exh. RA 1859, see Beck (1)), secure in the knowledge that its popularity had endured. The lines ended:

> *Art* is the world's interpreter!
> It speaks to every land the same;
> And Art can higher fame confer,
> And wider spread the painter's name,
> Than all the poetry of mind
> To land and language strict confin'd!
>
> Then, on the eloquence of truth,
> How grand to fix a nation's gaze;
> And robe in everlasting youth
> The images of perished days!
> More glorious, Eastlake, such renown
> Than hero's wreath – or monarch's crown!

Within twenty years, Cunningham was calling Eastlake's two great popular pictures 'feeble conventional renderings of Scripture subjects', an echo of Thackeray's scorn when in 1838 the Michael Angelo Titmarsh of *Fraser's Magazine* dubbed the artist 'Archbishop Eastlake'. Eastlake's absolute achievement must be reckoned as an arts administrator of vital importance to the art of the mid-century, the lynch-pin of the Palace of Westminster decoration planning, and a Director of the National Gallery who transformed the quality of the collection, but to the vast mass of his contemporaries he remained the painter of *Christ blessing* and, above all, of *Christ lamenting*.

Glasgow Art Gallery

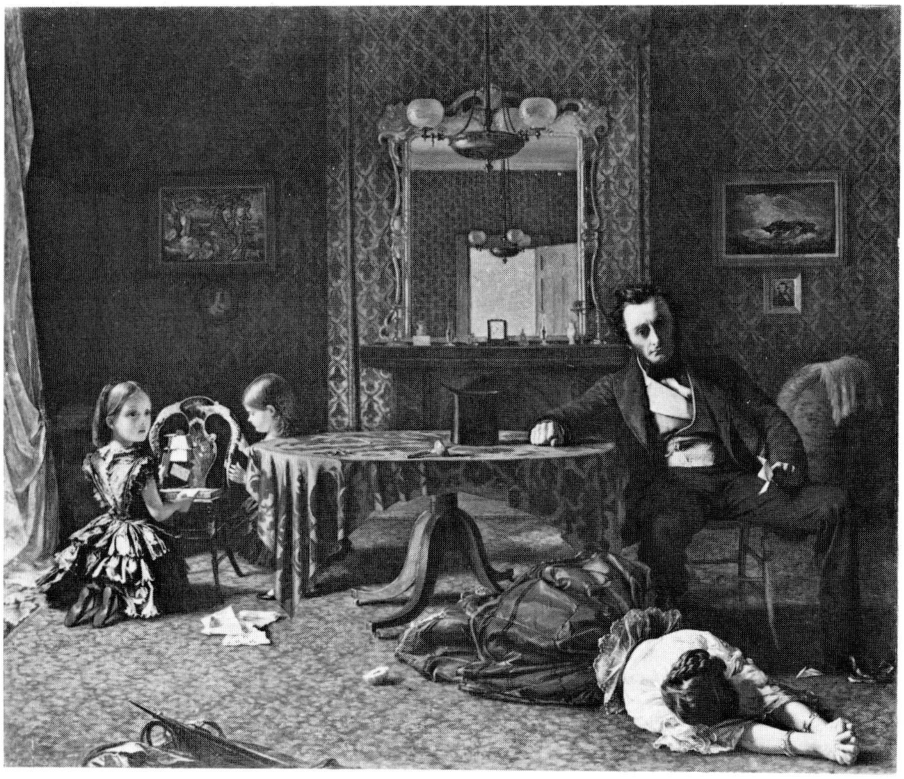

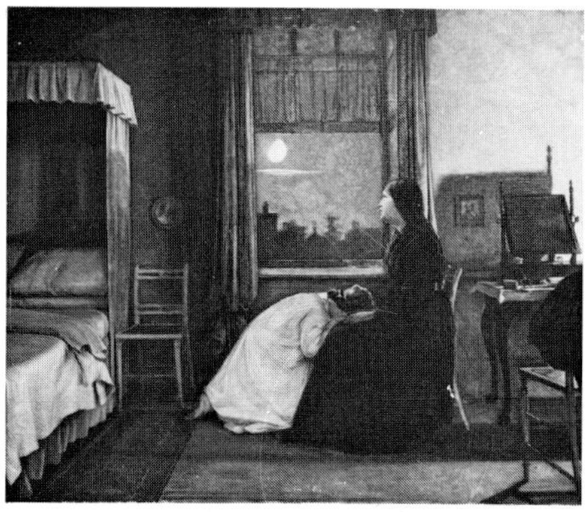

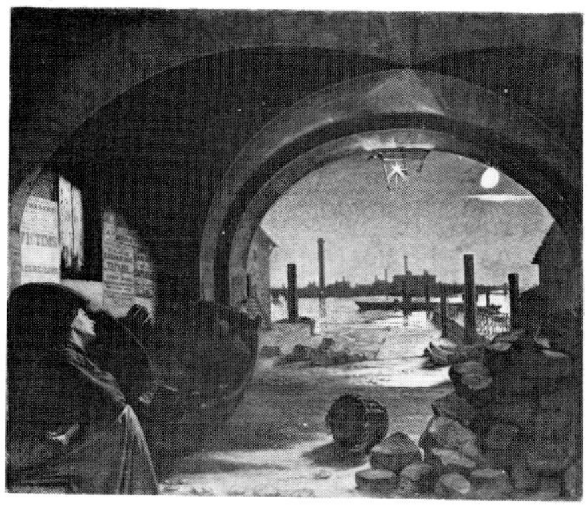

AUGUSTUS LEOPOLD EGG, 1816–1863, ARA 1848, RA 1860

10 "August the 4th. Have just heard that B— has been dead more than a fortnight, so his poor children have now lost both parents. I hear *she* was seen on Friday last near the Strand, evidently without a place to lay her head. What a fall hers has been!" (known as **Past and Present)** 1858

Three, separately framed, oil on canvas, each 25 × 30 in
EACH INSCR: Augst. Egg 1858

PROV: the artist; his sale, Christie's, 18 May 1863 (124) bt. Agnew (£346 10s), sold to J.G. Robinson;
Sir Alec and Lady Martin, presented to the Tate in memory of their daughter, 1918.
EXH: RA 1858 (372); London Internat. 1862 (638); *British Narrative Painting*, CEMA 1944 (8–10).
LIT: *AJ*, June 1858, pp167–8; *Athenaeum*, 1 May 1858, pp565–6; *Critic*, 15 May 1858, p235; *Literary Gazette*, 15 May 1858, p475; Ruskin, *RA Notes 1858*, *Works*, XIV, p166; *Times*, 1 May, p5, 22 May 1858, p9; *AJ*, July 1862, p150; *Athenaeum*, 3 May 1862, p598; F.T. Palgrave, *Descriptive Handbook to the Fine Art Collection*, (London Internat. Exh.), 1862, pp53–4; Sandby, 1862, p311; obit., *AJ*, May 1863, p87; obit., *Athenaeum*, 11 Apr 1863, pp491–2; Holman Hunt, 'Notes on the Life of Augustus L. Egg – VII', *Reader*, 9 Jan 1864, p57; Reynolds, 1953, p78, pls 48–50; John Lewis Bradley, 'An Unpublished Ruskin Letter', *Burlington*, Jan 1858, pp25–6; Anne d'Harnoncourt, *The Awakening Conscience*, Courtauld Institute MA Report, 1967 (unpublished), pp38–40 & cat.; Reynolds, 1966, pp30, 95, 109, 117; Wood, *Panorama*, 1976, p141, repr p140.
STUDIES: 'Studies for the past and present, &c, – in oils 4', Egg sale, Christie's, 18 May 1863 (124) bt. Rowbottom (10s 6d).
VERSIONS: *Past and Present*: *Misfortune*, *Prayer* and *Despair*; each 19 × 16 in. Gambart sale, Christie's, 3/4 May 1861 (134) bt. respectively Earle (£53 11s), Agnew (£73 10s and £63).

"Mr. Egg's unnamed picture is divided into three compartments, each more ghastly and terrible than the other, till in the last we come to such a sink of misery and loathsomeness, painted with such an unhealthy determination to dissect horror and to catalogue the dissecting-room that we turn from what is a real and possible terror as from an impure thing that seems out of place in a gallery of laughing brightness, where young, unstained, unpainted and happy faces come to chat and trifle. There must be a line drawn as to where the horrors that should not be painted for public and innocent sight begin, and we think Mr. Egg has put one foot at least beyond this line."

The *Athenaeum's* hysterical reaction probably contributed to the notoriety which Egg's triptych rapidly acquired; Frith's *Derby Day* undisputedly reigned over the 1858 RA, but Egg's pictures attracted crowds of sensation-seekers eager to be outraged. There was also some confusion over the subject, which *The Times* thought added to their attraction, and Ruskin was forced to explain it precisely:

"In the central piece the husband discovers his wife's infidelity: he dies five years afterwards. The two lateral pictures represent the same moment of night a fortnight after his death. The same little cloud is under the moon. The two children see it from the chamber in which they are praying for their lost mother; and their mother, from behind a boat under a vault on the river shore."

Egg was a great friend of Holman Hunt, and Hunt's *The Awakening Conscience* (RA 1854, Tate) might almost be a preliminary episode in Egg's tragedy. Egg's central scene of the discovery of infidelity includes numerous symbolic elements in Hunt's manner. Most of these were spotted by *The Times*:

"[the wife] lies prostrate before her heart-stricken partner, who holds the letter, the evidence of her treachery, in his hand. Their two children look up from their amusement of card castle-building at the sound of her fall. Their card castle has a French novel [by Balzac] for its foundation – a Hogarthian indication of the source of their mother's perversion, a mode of pointing a moral carried still further by the 'goodly apple rotten at the core' on the table [half on the floor], and the pictures of Adam and Eve driven out of Paradise and Stanfield's '*Abandoned*' on the walls."

The prints are specifically identified with the wife and husband by being hung on either side of the fireplace over their respective portraits. Over the fire is a large mirror in which is the reflection of the open door through which the erring wife will soon go. The lover's portrait is ground under the husband's foot near the wife's outstretched arms which are braceletted in such a way as to appear shackled. Ruskin enlarged on his interpretation of the picture in a letter to Mrs. John Simon (see *Burlington*, 1958):

"The picture does not pretend to represent a pretty story – but a piece of very common-place vice – an ordinary husband – employed at some house in the city – an ordinary wife – who can't read French well enough to understand the least bit of de Balzac's subtlety or Sand's nobleness but who reads Bulwer, or James, and Harrison Ainsworth; who has been seduced by a sham count, with a moustache – and who has mixed his lost letter with unexpected Christmas bills. Of course that is all the picture ever was meant to represent, and I don't believe that much of the world's vice is far above that standard – but when it really comes to its own wretched and appropriate catastrophe, and is finally stoned or crushed into putrescence – it becomes – for all its commonness, 'impressive' – just as that wretched vault of Waterloo bridge is impressive in the ghostly moonlight – I don't mean to say the vault is impressive as Rouen Cathedral porch would be – nor that the poor woman is impressive as your heroine would be – but in her own small muddy and shaky[?] way, she *is*, and there's no other word for it."

The flanking scenes the *Athenaeum* described:

"The destitute wife under the dark grave-vault shadow of an Adelphi arch, – last refuge of the homeless sin, vice and beggary of London: the thin, starved legs of a bastard child – perhaps dead at her breast – protrude from her rags. There was never such moonlight painted as from that loathsome sewer arch you see mantling the yellow river with liquid gold."

The *Art Journal*, having begun its review by castigating Egg –

"Although the domestic wreck illustrated in these pictures . . . may be in real life of daily occurrence, it is a subject too poignant for a series of paintings. We are saturated by the public prints with the details of such incidents, and would rather fall back upon the consoling influences of Art . . ."

called this scene an

"unexampled success – we use the term in its most literal sense. We congratulate the painter on his utilisation of the *inferno* of the Adelphi arches; they are the lowest of all the profound deeps of human abandonment in this metropolis; but he has forgotten the rats which meet in hungry hundreds on the vantage-ground left by the retiring tide, – those inhabitants of lower London would have assisted the desolation of the place."

Other Victorian treatments of such themes proliferated in the mid-century; discussed in some detail by d'Honancourt and Wood they include Redgrave's *The Outcast* (1851, RA Diploma Gallery), Watts's *Found Drowned* and *Under a Dry Arch* (*c* 1848–50, Watts Gallery) and Rossetti's unfinished *Found* (1854–82, Delaware). Egg's pictures continued to excite a kind of fascinated horror when they were shown at the London International Exhibition in 1862, and he was clearly unable to find a buyer for them as they were still on his hands when he died. A number of titles have been applied to them: 'London Trilogy' (*Times* 1858), 'The Adulteress and her fate' (*Athenaeum* 1862), 'A Tale of Terror' (Palgrave 1862), 'Fate of a Faithless Wife' (*DNB*), but they soon acquired a label 'Past and Present'. D'Honancourt suggests this came from a misreading of Ruskin whose review of Anna Blunden's *Past and Present* (RA 1858 (428)) immediately preceded that on Egg. Wood suggests a debt to Hood's poem of the same title, and it is worth noting that Carlyle's essay on morality and economics, *Past and Present*, had made the phrase famous since its publication in 1843.

The fullest explanation of the painting was given by Hunt in his long memorial series of articles on Egg in the *Reader* in 1863–4. He states that Egg deliberately set out to paint a morality in all the starkness necessary, despite his previous predilection for 'elegant and rich accompaniments' brilliantly finished (see, for instance, his Shakespearean pictures such as *Launce's Substitute for Proteus' Dog*, RA 1849, now at Leicester) and in the knowledge that it would not find popular favour, because of his belief in the need for such morally didactic images. Hunt's only quibble was that, faced everywhere with evidence that sinners reap greater rewards than the virtuous, this woman should have suffered so directly.

"Hogarth left no gap in his histories. Egg leaves us to wonder whether the erring wife was more overcome by her conscience, and so sought voluntarily a place of repentance, or was more imprudent than those who in daily life gather honours and worship by their wickedness. Whatever its shortcomings, however, the invention was free from the false sentimentality of many modern novel-writers, who dwell upon vice with prurient unction, and make its votaries the only intellectual and poetic characters of their book . . ."

The Trustees of the Tate Gallery
Shown at the Royal Academy only

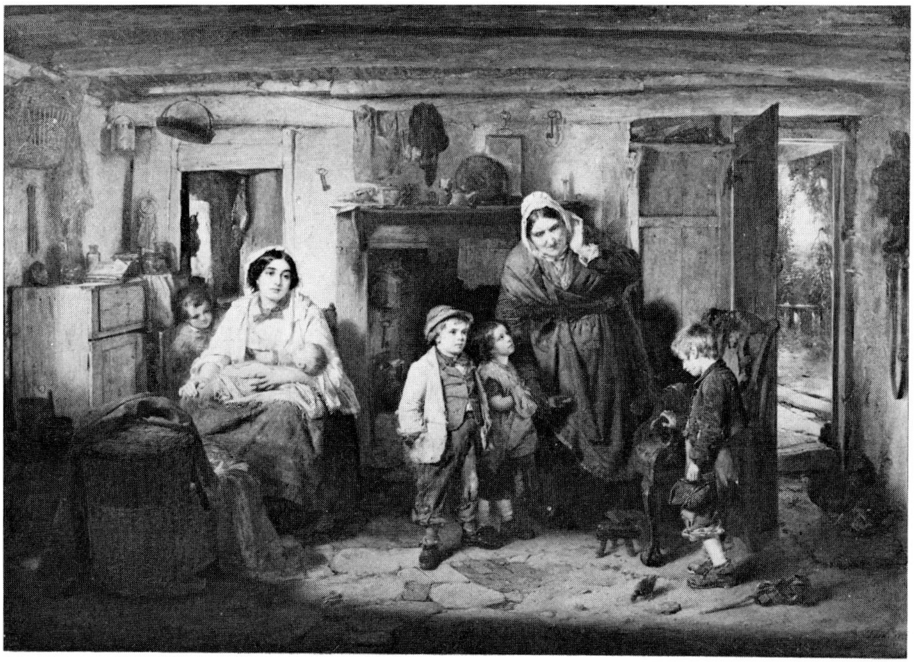

THOMAS FAED, 1826–1900, ARSA 1849, HRSA 1862, ARA 1861, RA 1864–93

11 The Mitherless Bairn 1855

oil on panel, $25 \times 35\frac{5}{8}$ in
INSCR: Faed 1855 London

PROV: Calvert Toulmin, Bayswater, London, by 1871; his sale, Christie's, 26 June 1886 (45) bt. Agnew; purchased by Melbourne, on the advice of A. Taddy Thomson, 1886.

EXH: RA 1855 (141); *Thomas Faed Exh.*, Agnew's 1860; London Internat. Exh. 1871 (407); *Victorian Social Conscience*, Sydney 1976 (18).

LIT: *AJ*, 1 June 1855, p172; *Athenaeum*, 2 June 1855, p649; *ILN*, 9 June 1855, p564, engr. p565; *Literary Gazette*, 12 May 1855, p299; Ruskin, *RA Notes 1855*, *Works*, XIV, p15, *Times*, 7 May 1855, p10; Sandby, 1862, p340; *AJ*, 1 Jan 1866, p4, engr. facing; *Zeitschrift für Bildende Kunst*, 1871, p380; James Dafforne, 'Thomas Faed, RA, HRSA', *AJ*, Jan 1871, p2; *AJ*, Aug 1872, p220; 'Our Living Artists: Thomas Faed, RA', *Mag. of Art*, 1878, p95; R. Walker, 'Thomas Faed, RA', *Good Words*, 1885, p307; Marion Hepworth Dixon, 'Thomas Faed, RA', *Mag. of Art*, 1893, p272–3; *Illustrated Cat. of the National Gallery*, Melbourne, 1894 (3); obit. *Times*, 23 Aug 1900, p7; *Bryan's*, II, p142; *DNB* 1909, XXII, p623; Caw, 1908, p165; Reynolds, 1966, pp112, 115, pl. 70, Irwins, 1975, pp301–2.

ENGR: 1. unsigned, wood engraving, publ. *ILN*, 9 June 1855, p565.
2. Samuel Cousins, mezzotint, $25\frac{3}{4} \times 33\frac{1}{4}$ in, publ. Henry Graves & Co., 1860.
3. Richard Josey, mezzotint, $14\frac{3}{4} \times 21$ in, publ. Henry Graves & Co., 1880.

VERSION: reduced replica; oil on canvas; $13\frac{7}{8} \times 24\frac{1}{4}$ in; inscr: Thomas Faed. Prov: John W. Leather, Leeds, by 1866; his sale, Christie's, 9 Feb 1867 (59) bt. Johnson; James Fallow, Manchester; his sale, Christie's, 23 May 1868 (114) bt. Mouncey; Simpkins, beq. to Brighton Art Gallery and Museums, 1916. Exh: Wembley, 1925 (W. 48). Engr: P. Lightfoot, steel engraving, publ. *AJ*, 1 Jan 1866, facing p4.

The Mitherless Bairn was universally acknowledged by Faed's contemporaries and by his posthumous biographers as his first great success in 1855, 'and from that time almost to the end of his career he was one of the most popular of British painters' (*DNB*) because, thought the *Magazine of Art*, it 'struck a note which appealed to the learned and the unlearned'. Eleven years after it was first exhibited, The *Art Journal* published an engraving, taken from the replica, accompanied by extravagant praise:

"No description, whether in prose or poetry, could surpass the efforts of the painter in the recital of the subject set forth in this admirable picture . . . It is one of those pictorial compositions which takes its place legitimately within the range of poetical art – not, however, of romance, but fact; and in it we see how far the painter's art may transcend that of the poet in the expression of a single idea . . ."

Faed had in fact exhibited the picture with the last two verses from 'The Mitherless Bairn' by the Scottish poet William Thom (*c*1798–1848); published in a volume of Thom's collected work, *Rhymes and Recollections of a Hand-Loom Weaver*, 1844 (pp104–5). Faed had already used subjects from Lady Anne Lindsay's *Auld Robin Gray*, Goldsmith's *The Vicar of Wakefield* and was later to use Ballantyne and Tennyson but it was Burns, always the principal literary source for Scottish painters, who dominated Faed's subjects. *Good Words* claimed that the story of *The Mitherless Bairn* was based on:

"an incident – idealised – of (Faed's) own childhood . . . When the artist was about eight years of age, a little vagrant, on the plea that he had no father or mother, imposed upon the children of Burley Mill (Faed's Kirkcudbright home), who coaxed him to stay in the house, and fed and petted him until he 'waxed fat and kicked', and grew so insolent that he had to be turned away. It afterwards came out that he was not an orphan at all, but the son of two sturdy tramps who were the terror of the district!"

Whether this was so or not, Faed focused on the sentiment in his picture and it was this that captivated reviewers and public alike. Such was its success that he followed it with a pendant, *Home and the Homeless* (RA 1856), commissioned by Baroness Burdett-Coutts, the philanthropist and patron of art (her sale, Christie's, 4 May 1922 (184) bt. Starmer), and continued to produce subjects in the same vein for the rest of his exhibiting life, which ended only when he was forced by failing sight to resign his RA in 1893.

Virtually the only voice of dissent was, inevitably, that of Ruskin, who dismissed *The Mitherless Bairn* as 'the most commonplace

Wilkieism – white spots everywhere'; Ruskin was correct in spotting Wilkie as Faed's mentor, and it was inevitable that he should have disliked Faed's prosaic and cosy little sentimental genre scenes during the very years when his defence of the Pre-Raphaelites was at its height, but Faed himself must have been puzzled by the attack. He was quoted by Dixon in 1893 in full Ruskinian vein:

> "I never see a picture or read a poem that impresses me deeply, that I do not notice everywhere the presence of the real. So-called imagination is nothing more or less than a superior capacity for observation."

A measure of Faed's popularity was the most unusual one-man show of his work that Agnew's put on in 1860, and the exceptional number of magazine articles devoted to him, all of which analysed at length his later successes: these included *Sunday in the backwoods* (RA 1859, Montreal), *The poor, the poor man's friend* (RA 1867, V & A) and *Worn out* (RA 1868, Daniel Thwaites in 1900, sold Christie's 27 Oct 1950 (74) bt. Newman). It was observed that he had heavily influenced both Scottish and English artists. Though none were named, the Cranbrook Colony artists were probably at the head of the list, and Dixon noted:

> "The bare record of the fraudulent imitations of the artist's work would go to fill a chapter. In sooth, so many imitations of the painter's famous 'Mitherless Bairn' exist, that the original was like to be discountenanced only the other day at Christie's. It fetched, in consequence of the untoward rumour that the initial canvas had crossed to America, something under a thousand pounds. A goodly sum, perhaps, in many eyes, but one inadequate enough, if we consider the painter's usual rate of trafficking."

Though written in 1893, this must refer to the sale of the picture bought by Melbourne in 1886 and exhibited here. Faed's main income probably came from the sale of copyrights on his pictures and a letter of 1855 to Henry Graves (BM Add. Mss 46140) shows how quickly he learnt to negotiate favourable terms and control the choice of engraver of his pictures, playing Graves off against the Art Union of Edinburgh who were also bidding for the rights on the picture.

Though Faed had slipped from favour in the later century, Caw's epitaph sums up the opinions of all the turn of the century commentators:

> ". . . He treated the primary affections with simplicity and respect, and the pure atmosphere of home sanctifies his cottage hearths . . . Simple and sincere, it is worthy of respect, if not of high admiration."

National Gallery of Victoria, Melbourne, Australia

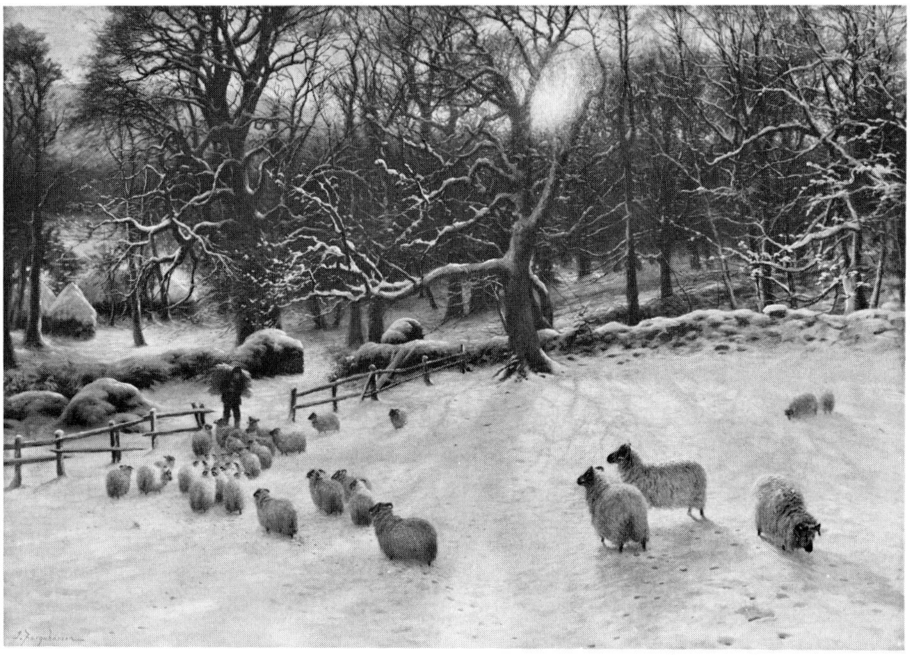

Courtesy: Frost and Reed Ltd.

JOSEPH FARQUHARSON, 1846–1935, ARA 1900, RA 1915

12 'The shortening winter's day is near a close' 1903

oil on canvas, 46 × 66¼ in

PROV: purchased from Thos. Agnew & Sons, 30 Mar 1903.
EXH: RA 1903 (174); Liverpool 1904 (8); Glasgow 1905; Franco-British 1908 (291).
LIT: *AJ*, June 1903, p177; *Academy*, 9 May 1903, p467; *Mag. of Art*, 1903, p426; *Studio*, June 1903, p51; William Macdonald Sinclair, 'The Art of Joseph Farquharson', *Art Annual*, 1912, repr p17; Caw, 1908, p306.
REPR: Blackburn, *RA Notes*, 1903, p58; *RA Pictures*, 1903, p116; *Souvenir*, Franco-British, 1908, facing p153.

The Farquharson landscapes each year at the Academy were instantly recognisable: there was almost always a chilly expanse of snow, dotted with sheep, often with a shepherd, crows, or a fox included, all underlined by a title like '*When snow the pasture sheets*', '*And winter's breath came cold and chill*', '*Cauld blaws the wind frae east to west*', '*Over snowfields waste and pathless*', or '*The weary waste of snows*'. They were perennial favourites with the public and most of the later Victorian and Edwardian collections with any pretensions to landscape included at least one Farquharson snow scene. The Levers bought '*The shortening winter's day*' from Agnew's before the RA show opened, a measure of their confidence and taste. It was hung on the line in the large room at the RA and it was clearly, as far as the reviewers were concerned, the principal picture of the four exhibited by Farquharson that year – satisfactory confirmations that they had secured an entirely typical and particularly good Farquharson. The *Academy* called it "A notable landscape", and went on:

> "It has not the impulse of the pictures of the La Thangue school [members of the New English Art Club]: it is, if I may say so, a constructed landscape, but for ingenuity of painting, and for the power to convey the illusion of sunlight on snow, darkened by the shadows and the leafless trees behind which the winter sun is setting, this landscape is a *tour de force*. Mr. Farquharson's vision of nature is always interesting, and he is one of the few members of the Academy who resist the shackles of conventionalism."

Several reviewers were so struck by the sunset effect that the picture was referred to simply as 'Mr. Joseph Farquharson's '*Winter Sunset*' (*Studio*) or his 'best picture, a sunset over snow' (*AJ*), and in the *Magazine of Art*,

> ". . . another of his striking snow pictures, lighted with prismatic colours by the sun."

The landscapes that year were considered strong and David Farquharson's *Winter* was generally considered the most distinguished of its kind in the exhibition, but M.H. Spielmann, in the *Magazine of Art*, took the opportunity to criticise:

> "A certain school of painters, [which] succeeds in turning out year after year what seem to be stereotyped repetitions of old effects, encouraged thereto by their own inadequacy, and by the applause and admirers of the obvious and the commonplace . . ."

He conceded, however, that "there is enough here to mark an advance in the English School of Landscape" and Farquharson was amongst those exempted from the strictures.

Farquharson was a junior member of that Edinburgh school of landscape painters led by MacWhirter and Tom and Peter Graham; the latter was a friend of Farquharson's father and taught the boy in his teens, until he went to the Edinburgh Trustees' Academy. He exhibited at the RA for the first time in 1873 and seven years later spent the first of several winters in the Paris studio of the French academic artist Carolus-Duran, a great advocate of copying from Velasquez. The lessons learned there may have stood him in good stead in his first notable success, '*The joyless winter day*', bought with the Chantrey Fund in 1883. Probably his most extreme expression of winter bleakness, it made an ideal vehicle for a whole-hearted academic exercise in the manipulation of tonal values in an almost monochrome painting. It was described by M. Phipps Jackson in his article on Farquharson in the *Art Journal* (May 1893, pp153–7):

> "On a bleak and barren snow-covered Scotch moor, a shepherd is driving home his flock. Muffled in his plaid the man seeks to save himself from the swirl of the eddying snowflakes, whilst the sheep, half blind by the darkened atmosphere, yield ready obedience to his guidance. There is powerful, almost painful force, in the realisation of this scene." (p154).

Landseer's treatment of similar themes must have been known to Farquharson, but the younger artist does not seem to have intended the religious symbolism deliberately applied by Landseer to some of his paintings such as *The Lost Sheep* (RA 1850), which was exhibited with the Christ the Good Shepherd text from *Luke*, XV, 4. Farquharson's other 1883 painting was a grim scene of a destitute family in a country lane entitled *Where next?* (repr. *AJ*, 1893, p155) but the success of his snowbound sheep seems to have persuaded him to abandon this brief flirtation with social realism. A visit to Egypt in 1885 resulted in the succeeding years in some bazaar and desert scenes in the manner of Frederick Goodall, but northern winters dominated the rest of his work. As late as 1926, Sickert was still able to cite Farquharson as the admirable antithesis to Courbet, whose 'palette-knife paintings' he attacked in an article in the *Daily Telegraph* (reprinted in *A Free House!*, ed. Osbert Sitwell, 1947, pp204–6). Sickert considered that:

> "Farquharson's extraordinary virtuosity has been developed by experience, but it arises certainly from the fact that he is thinking of telling his story. The arrest of the fox in the snow of the picture called *Supper Time* is a breathless moment. The subject is the very *raison d'etre* of the picture. Bloomsbury will perhaps tell you that it is wrong to paint a live fox. Fortunately the writ of Bloomsbury does not run in the North of Scotland."

'*The shortening winter's day*' remains to this day one of the most popular paintings in the Lady Lever Art Gallery.

The Trustees of the Lady Lever Art Gallery, Port Sunlight

Sir (Samuel) Luke Fildes, 1843–1927, ARA 1879, RA 1887, KB 1906, KCVO 1918

13 An Al-fresco Toilette 1889

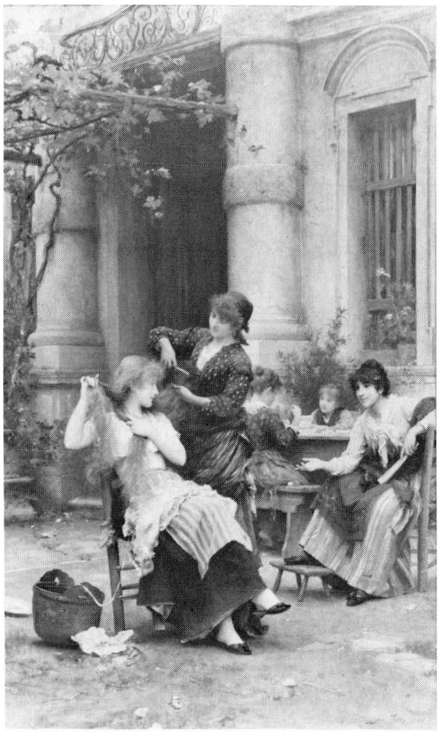

oil on canvas, 68 × 42½ in
INSCR: Luke Fildes 1889

PROV: commissioned by Arthur Anderson, Wimpole Street; his sale, Christie's, 19 May 1894 (32) bt. Tooth (£1365); George McCulloch; his sale, Christie's, 29 May 1913 (135) bt. Gooden & Fox (£1575).
EXH: RA 1889 (307); Guildhall 1892 (33); *McCulloch Coll.*, RA Winter 1909 (32); RA Winter 1928 (282).
LIT: *AJ*, July 1889, p217; *Academy*, 25 May 1889, p365; *Athenaeum*, 6 Apr, pp446–7, 18 May 1889, p636; *Graphic*, 4 May, p467, 18 May 1889, p539; *ILN*, 11 May 1889, p590; *Portfolio*, June 1889, p118; *Spectator*, 25 May 1889, p712; *Times*, 22 May 1889, p15; David Croal Thomson, 'Luke Fildes, RA', *Art Annual*, 1895, pp17–18, engr. facing p16; *DNB*, Suppl. 193, p304; L.V. Fildes, *Luke Fildes, RA, A Victorian Painter*, 1968, p113, repr. facing p114.
STUDY: sketch for seated girl at left, combing her hair; pencil. Repr. *Art Annual*, 1895, p17; Bell, 1967, pl.96.

> "One of the most successful of his Italian pictures, *An Al-fresco Toilette* . . . gives the high-water mark of the Italian series, and it must be acknowledged that it is a very beautiful picture." (*Art Annual*, p17).

D.C. Thomson's unconsciously appropriate metaphor emphasises that Fildes's Italian scenes were all Venetian, studied and begun there on visits between 1874 and 1889 and finished in London.

The foundations of Fildes's reputation had been laid with the success of his *Applicants for Admission to a Casual Ward* at the 1874 RA (Royal Holloway College); up till then he had been making a living as a black-and-white illustrator for the late '60s magazines. The subject was initially published as a wood engraving in the first number of the *Graphic* on 4 December 1869; the destitute people huddled against the wall of a police station on a bitter winter evening are waiting their turn for a ticket giving them admission to a workhouse for the night. Its success made the *Graphic*, and Fildes determined to turn it into a large picture for the RA. Fildes and Frank Holl (see cat. 22) were established as the leaders of the new Social Realist school, but, though Holl continued with social documents like *Newgate: Committed for Trial* (also Royal Holloway College) until the end of the '70s, Fildes's first visit to Venice in 1874 deflected him away from realism and back to sentiment.

Most Victorians associated Venetian subjects with Turner and Ruskin; Fildes was seen as the leader of the Neo-Venetian school which changed this and his extremely pretty Venetian genre scenes of "those gay groups of girls . . . which he paints with so much aplomb" (*Portfolio*) at canal sides, on balconies, selling flowers, or simply combing their hair, enjoyed a great vogue with the exhibition-going public, illustrated magazines and with collectors. His brother-in-law Henry Woods followed his example and the two artists were the English counterparts of the two most successful continental purveyors of Italian prettiness, Eugen von Blaas and Carl van Haanen, both of whom Woods had got to know well while living in Venice. Van Haanen was a particular friend and correspondence between them survives in the Fildes collection given recently to the V & A. Von Blaas figured frequently in private collections and his scenes of Latin ladies on balconies sold very well in northern Europe.

Fildes's most important Venetian subject to date was a large and successful composition of young Venetian women doing their washing on the steps leading down to the canal, titled simply *Venetians* (RA 1885, Manchester). An *Al-fresco Toilette* was seen as both the best painting of the series and as evidence of the need for a change in Fildes's work. The reviews were impressed by its charm, colour, finish, and the prettiness of the girls; and the *Art Journal* pointed out that the building was Henry Woods's studio. The *Athenaeum* had already run a piece on the picture using its original title, *The Morning of the Festa*, at the beginning of April, describing in detail the colour and composition, but it ended by advising Fildes that he had perhaps exhausted the Venetian theme and should return to his English subjects. *The Times* agreed and the *Academy* suggested that

> "Mr. Fildes is, to our mind, never at his best save when his own mother-earth invigorates, and his own people inspire him."

They may perhaps have detected the artifice in the so-called Venetian girls – the main figure of the girl combing her hair was, according to their son, Mrs. Fildes.

The Trustees of the Lady Lever Art Gallery, Port Sunlight

Sir (Samuel) Luke Fildes

14 The Doctor 1891

photogravure, $20\frac{1}{4} \times 29\frac{1}{2}$ in

PUBL: Thos. Agnew & Sons Ltd., 1892.
LIT: (all references are to the exhibited picture) *AJ*, June 1891, p195; *Academy*, 9 May 1891, p448; *Athenaeum*, 2 May 1891, p574; *Graphic*, 2 May 1891, p486; *ILN*, 2 May 1891, p573; *Mag. of Art*, 1891, pp220, 253; *Portfolio*, June 1891, p.xi; *Times*, 2 May 1891, p14; Walter Armstrong, 'The Henry Tate Collection. II', *AJ*, Apr 1893, pp11–12; *Art Annual*, 1895, pp12–13, repr. frontisp.; Geoffrey Agnew, *Agnew's 1817–1967*, p66 engr. repr. p66; Fildes, 1968, pp46, 103, 108–9, 118–23, 135, 157, 211, 223–4.

> "... what will universally be admitted to be 'the picture of the year'. This is the remarkable work on which Mr. Fildes has been so long engaged, and which now comes before the world under the title of '*The Doctor*'. Mr. Fildes has tried many different themes and styles of late years, and has succeeded in all, though in a varying degree; he has been bright and interesting in English subject pictures, almost too pretty in his rendering of Venetian workgirls, and brilliantly accomplished in portraits of ladies. But he has never done anything nearly so considerable as this picture of an English workman's home, seen at the tragical moment when a child's life is in imminent danger. The child lies upon pillows, placed upon a couple of chairs; close by sits the doctor, with keen and kindly face, his eyes bent upon the silent sufferer, and his mind at watch for the moment when, if nature is but kind, it may be possible for his science to do something to help. His figure and that of the little patient are lit by a lamp, which is shaded from the spectator; through a window to the right the first streaks of dawn are beginning to penetrate and fall upon the figure of the mother, who sits with head bent down upon a little table, her husband, a stalwart workman, standing by, grave and scarcely hoping ..."

Thus *The Times* received what immediately became one of the great popular pictures of the century.

At some time in the mid-1880s, Henry Tate first asked Fildes to paint an English subject picture for him and in 1887 Fildes undertook formally to paint one at a cost to Tate of £3000. *The Doctor* was completed four years later and shown at the 1891 RA. Fildes had sketched cottages all over England and Scotland, but finally constructed in his studio a life-size mock-up, a composite of several Devonshire fishermen's cottages; it can be seen in the background of the drawing published by the *Graphic* of Fildes at work on *The Doctor*. Fildes had himself photographed, dressed and posed for the figure of the doctor; this was then used for the guidance of the models from whom he painted. His son relates how, once the news of Fildes's progress on the painting got around London, his medical friends came to his studio 'in relays' to sit for the figure so that they could afterwards claim involvement with the noble picture; in fact, most of the work was done from a professional model. One preparatory oil sketch was made for the composition (repr. *Art Annual*, p13) showing the doctor on the right. The critics particularly appreciated the interesting technical problem he had posed by combining the warm yellow lamplight shining on the doctor and sick child with the cold grey dawn light showing through the window on the right, but the public response was, unequivocally, to the sentiment.

Fildes had followed the success of *The Casuals* in 1874 with *The Widower* of 1876 (Sydney), a Faed-style scene of a man nursing a sick child. According to his son, Fildes based *The Doctor* on his memory of the family doctor's devotion when his first child died in 1877; when the painting finally appeared, the medical profession was so flattered that in 1892 newly-qualified doctors were being told:

> "A library of books written in your honour would not do what this picture has done and will do for the medical profession in making the hearts of our fellow men warm to us with confidence and affection ... Above everything, whatever may be the rank in your profession to which you may attain, remember always to hold before you the ideal figure of Luke Fildes' picture, and be at once gentle men and gentle doctors." (quoted Fildes, 1968, p118).

It was also adopted by religious writers and was used in, for instance, Thomas Lund's *The Religion of Art in Three Pictures*, published in 1891, which based its preaching on *An Idyll* by M. Greiffenhagen, *St. Elizabeth's Renunciation* by P.H. Calderon, and Fildes's *The Doctor*.

The photogravure, exhibited here, was published by Agnew's in 1892 and became the most popular single print ever issued by the firm. The copyright was pirated in America where its success was, if anything, still greater: the picture even appeared on a postage stamp. *The Doctor* was the last social subject picture of Fildes's career; he spent the rest of his life painting the society portraits which he had taken up in the late 1880s and confirmed his place as one of the most financially successful artists in the century. But it was *The Doctor* which ensured Fildes's place in the popular memory, and the painting became one of the chief attractions of the newly-opened Tate Gallery.

Thos. Agnew & Sons Ltd.

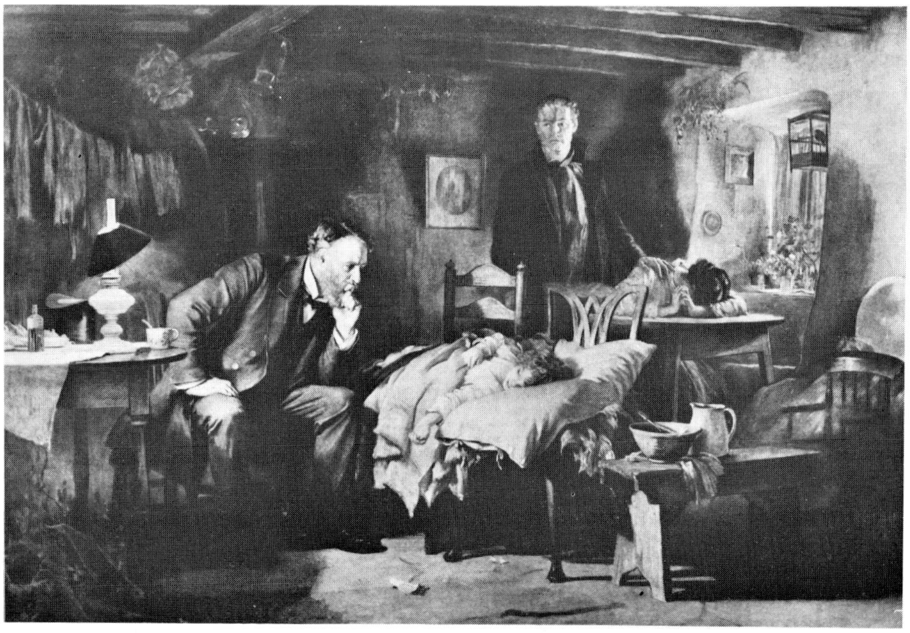

William Powell Frith, 1819–1909, ARA 1845, RA 1853–90, CVO 1908

15 The Railway Station 1862

oil on canvas, 46×101 in
INSCR: W.P. Frith fect 1862

PROV: commissioned by L.V. Flatow for £4500, 1860; sold to Henry Graves & Co with copyright for £16,000, 1865; purchased from Graves by Thomas Holloway for £2000, 16 Apr 1883.
EXH: Flatow's Gallery 1862; London Internat. Exh. 1872 (73); Philadelphia 1876; Expo Univ Paris 1878 (78); RA Winter 1911 (37); Wembley 1924 (W.21); RA Winter 1934 (626).
LIT (selected): *AJ*, May 1862, pp122–3; *Athenaeum*, 12 Apr 1862, pp502–4; *Critic* 19 Apr 1862, pp397–8; *ILN*, 3 May 1862, p457; *Times*, 19 Apr 1862; Tom Taylor, *The Railway Station, painted by W.P. Frith, Esq., RA*, 1862, and see for further reviews from *Daily News*, *Daily Telegraph*, *Observer*, *Morning Post*, *Globe*, *Evening Standard*, *Era*, *Builder*, *Queen*, *Plymouth & Devonport Journal*; W.W. Fenn, 'William Powell Frith, RA', *Mag. of Art*, 1880, p82; W.P. Frith, *My Autobiography and Reminiscences*, 1887, II, pp327–35; Chesneau, 1885, p286; Walter Shaw Sparrow, 'The Royal Holloway College Picture-Gallery, I', *Mag. of Art*, 1891, p241; C.W. Carey, *Royal Holloway College, Egham, Catalogue of Pictures*, 3rd ed., 1896 (20), pp21–3, 90–1; C.W. Carey, 'The Royal Holloway College Collection – I', *AJ*, May 1897, pp132–3, repr. facing p132; Wood, *Panorama*, 1976, pp207–11, repr. pp208–9; Jeannie Chapel, forthcoming article on the College and its collection, *Connoisseur*, 1978.
ENGR: Francis Holl, mixed mezzotint, $25\frac{1}{2} \times 48$ in, publ. Henry Graves & Co., 1866.
VERSIONS: the best known of the numerous versions is at Leicester.

The sensational success of *The Derby Day* at the 1858 RA impelled Frith to embark on a still larger and more ambitious epic of modern life, *The Railway Station*. He painted an oil sketch for the composition in 1860 which he showed to the dealer, L.V. Flatow, who immediately commissioned the finished picture, oil sketch and copyright for the total of £4500, leaving Frith the right to exhibit the painting later at the RA, a right which he afterwards resigned 'for a consideration in the shape of seven hundred and fifty pounds' (*Autobiography*, p328). In 1860, when Frith began the sketch, Holman Hunt had asked Gambart

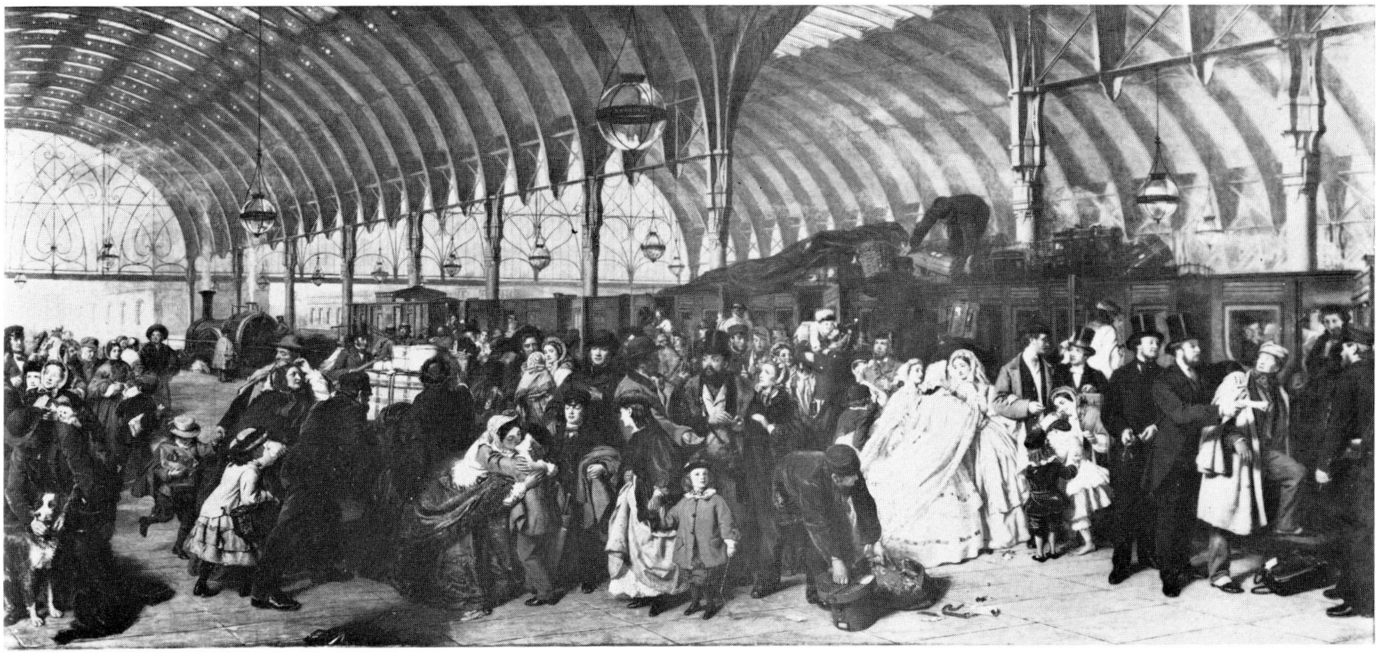

for 5500 guineas (see cat 24), so Frith's price was not a record, though vastly inflated figures for Flatow's price were quoted in the press, ranging from 8000 guineas (*AJ*) to £8700 (*Critic*) and £8750 (*Times* and *ILN*), in their eagerness to sensationalise an already exceptional transaction.

Louis Victor Flatow (often mistakenly spelt as Flatou, see Maas, *Gambart*, 1975, pp45–7) was, like Gambart, an immigrant from the continent and their rivalry was one of the most financially fruitful factors in the mid-century London art world. Frith was uncertain of himself when working on *The Railway Station* but Flatow's enthusiasm was vindicated when the completed painting was finally shown at his gallery in the Haymarket in the spring of 1862: Frith's *Autobiography* records:

> "a great success. I find that 21,150 people paid for admission in seven weeks, and the subscription for the engraving was equally surprising and satisfactory. The critics contradicted one another as usual, without doing good or harm to me or the picture. Flatow was triumphant; coaxing, wheedling, and almost bullying, his unhappy visitors. Many of them, I verily believe, subscribed for the engraving to get rid of his importunity." (p334)

The lengthy reviews in the newspapers and journals explained the subject in the greatest detail. The picture was pronounced

> "a work of immense power, not only in the variety and interest of its incident – in its fidelity of individual character – in its admirable grouping and colour – but in its conscientious elaboration of finish." (*AJ*).

The narration of the incidents in what the *Art Journal* called 'this painted volume' took up most of the reviews.

Frith included portraits of himself and his family in the group just to left of centre: a mother says a fond farewell to her younger son while the older boy, about to escort his brother away to school for the first time, looks on, his father's hand on his shoulder. At the extreme right is the most-discussed incident in the picture; a criminal identified in most reviews as a bankrupt or forger on the run, is arrested as he climbs into the carriage where his wife is already waiting. The two policemen were portraits of two famous detectives whose exploits in solving some notorious cases had made them public figures. The bridal party next to this group was seen as "an extreme contrast, both moral and pictorial" (*ILN*) which to Tom Taylor intensified both. Other groups show a scarlet-coated recruiting sergeant holding up his baby to be kissed farewell, an opulent-looking foreigner in the centre arguing with a cabby, a family rushing from the left, late for the train, while in the background the luggage is loaded onto the roof of the train. The horizontal composition is unified by the imposing ironwork arches of the vaulted roof of Paddington station; for this, Frith had enlisted the help of the architectural draughtsman and decorative artist, W. Scott Morton, in much the same way as he had obtained the expert help of J.F. Herring to draw the horses on the distant racecourse in *Derby Day*.

The *ILN* summed up contemporary reactions:

> "If subjects of a religious, poetical, or historical character demand higher powers of imagination, the illustration of contemporary life is nevertheless one of the most valuable functions of art. As a painter of his own time Mr. Frith is only equalled by Hogarth, and in all the more technical qualities of art the living artist is certainly the superior. The painter has deserved well of his own country and still more of posterity. The conception of this remarkable picture is throughout admirable. It is comprehensive and epical in the suggestiveness of its range, yet true to literal nature and even the most trivial matter of fact. A more characteristic illustration of the age could not have been selected..."

The painting was one of the principal treasures of the collection formed by Thomas Holloway and presented to his university college for young ladies at Egham in Surrey. The building of the Holloway College was begun in 1879 and it was formally declared open by the Queen in 1886. Holloway began his picture collection in 1881, only two years before his death, buying mostly contemporary and some older English paintings, with a few contemporary continental paintings, almost entirely at Christie's sales. Carey, curator and cataloguer of the collection, explained in 1896,

> "The present Picture Gallery was originally designed for the purpose of a Recreation Hall, the gift of pictures having been an after-thought on the part of Mr. Holloway, when it was too late to alter and improve the lighting of the Gallery."

The paintings were undoubtedly intended to be morally as well as aesthetically uplifting to the young ladies of the college; Holloway's most notable and, in this context, most pointed, purchase was Edwin Long's *The Babylonian Marriage Market* (RA 1875) for which he paid the then record saleroom price (£6615) for a living artist's work. The collection will be fully discussed in the detailed catalogue now being prepared for the College by Jeannie Chapel.

Royal Holloway College (*University of London*)

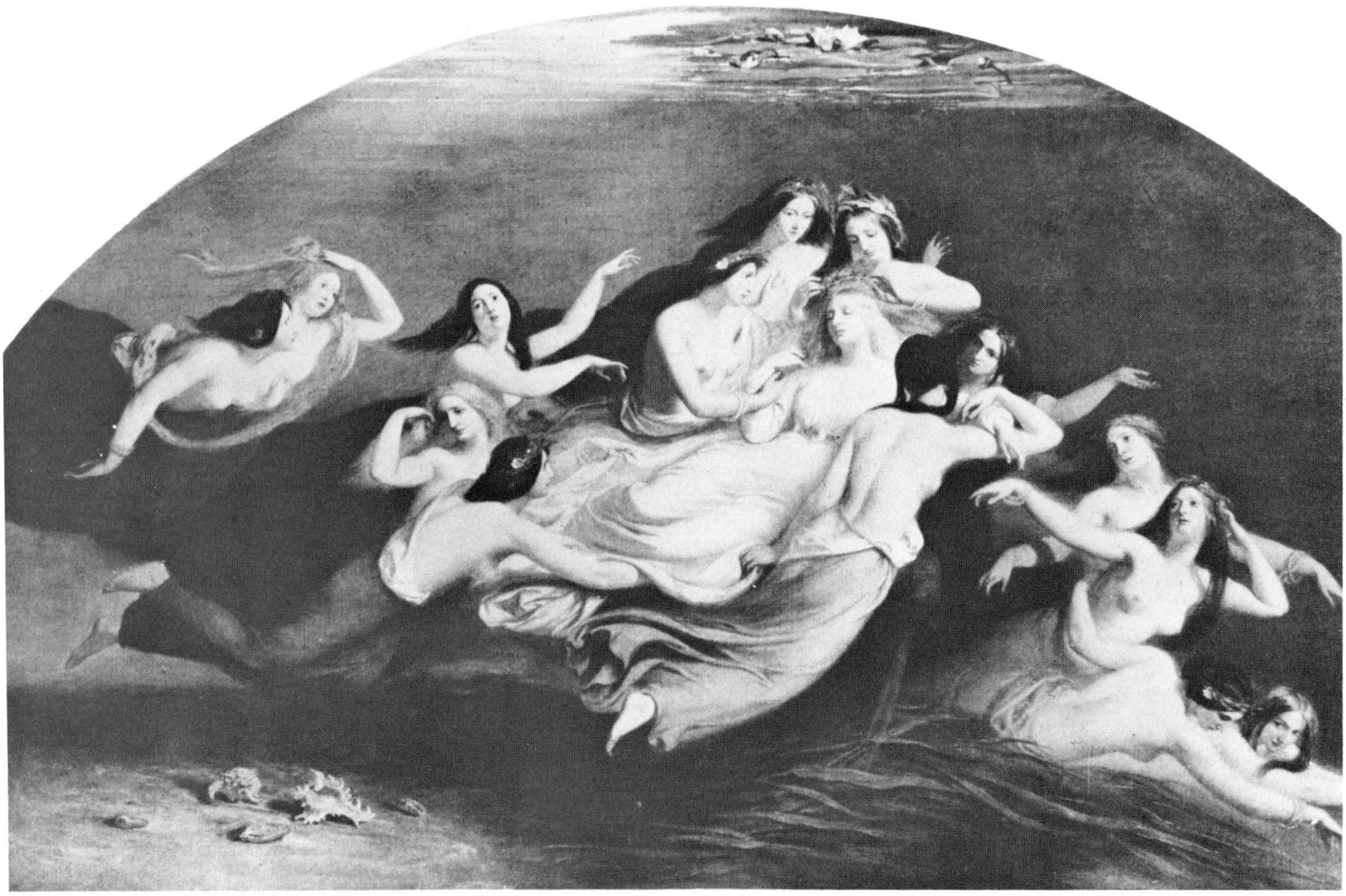

WILLIAM EDWARD FROST, 1810–1877, ARA 1846, RA 1870–76

16 Sabrina 1845

oil on canvas, 44 × 72 in; arched top

PROV: (?)Art Union of London; Lord Northwick, Thirlestane House, Cheltenham; sale at Thirlestane, Phillips, 26 July–23 Aug 1859, fourth day (328) bt. Gambart (206 gns); E. Saunders, by 1873; Christie's, 21 June 1875 (107) bt. Carfini (£157 10s); purchased from a private collection by M. Newman Ltd. 1965; by whom sold to present owner.
EXH: RA 1845 (325); London Internat. 1873 (999); M. Newman Ltd. 1966.
LIT: *Art Union*, June 1845, p186; *Athenaeum*, 17 May 1845, p495; *Fraser's*, June 1845, p718; *ILN*, 10 May 1845, p294; *Literary Gazette*, 24 May 1845, p330; 'British Artists XXI: William Edward Frost, *AJ* Jan 1857, p6, engr. p7; Northwick Sale, *AJ*, Sept 1859, p286, and *GdBA*, Oct 1859, p54; Sandby, 1862, p220; obit., *Athenaeum*, 9 June 1877, p744; Bryan's 1903; *DNB*, 1908, p279.
ENGR: 1. Peter Lightfoot; engraving; 18⅝ × 26¾ in; publ. Art Union of London, 1849; Beck (13). Four proofs, presumably of this engraving, were lot 202 in Frost's studio sale, Christie's, 14–16 Mar 1878.
2. J. & G.P. Nicholls; wood engraving; 4⅜ × 7⅛ in; publ. *AJ*, Jan 1857, p7.

Sabrina, shown at the RA in 1845, was decisive in securing for Frost the two most important advancements in his career: election to ARA in 1846 and the patronage of the Queen and Prince Albert. He had been a medal-winning student at the RA, exhibiting from 1836, won the RA Gold Medal for Painting in 1839, and third prize in the Palace of Westminster Cartoon Exhibition in 1843 for a subject from Spenser and it was with this last subject that Frost found his metier, the admiration of fellow artists and public success. The *Athenaeum* obituary recalled,

> "So considerable was the charm of Mr. Frost's productions, that the Queen bought 'Una and the Wood Nymphs', and he obtained extensive patronage from the Prince Consort, the Court, and amateurs in general. His pictures were engraved over and over again; they were repeated; they became the subjects of prizes, and even of lectures and poems, and excited an enthusiasm of the intensity of which our younger contemporaries have but faint idea."

The Queen and Albert between them bought at least three important Frosts: Victoria bought *Una and the Wood Nymphs* (RA 1847), and commissioned a version of the central group from *Euphrosyne* (RA 1848) as a gift to the Prince Consort, this is known as *L'Allegro* and still hangs at Osborne; Albert commissioned *The Disarming of Cupid* (RA 1850). These were the years of his greatest fame but sadly for Frost the revolutionary effect of Pre-Raphaelitism and the influence of Ruskin conspired against him. The full reversal of taste during the next thirty years is expressed most trenchantly in the *Academy* obituary: Frost painted

> "... works of the 'nymph' ideal, in which every leg, every finger, and every curve of impossible drapery – not to speak of every face and every 'bosom' – had to be 'graceful', 'classical', and what not – and of course also 'chaste' and proper for the eyes of the British matron in her dining room. After some years of enervating correctness, and having illustrated, in the rapture of art-union purchasers, all those qualities of aesthetic beauty which are 'most tolerable and not to be endured,' the star of this praiseworthy and well-equipped artist declined: Pre-Raphaelitism, beginning in 1849, struck rapid and paralysing blows at the Frost style of painting, as at some others still worthier of extinction." (16 June 1877, pp543–4).

Frost was recognised as a follower of Etty, Hilton and Howard, and was generally associated with his friend Pickersgill, in this style of nude figure scene using literary and mythological subjects as a vehicle. The gulf that lay between the taste of the 1840s and the 1860s can be seen by comparing William Michael Rossetti's comments on the British paintings in the London International Exhibition of 1862 and those of Thackeray reviewing Sabrina in 1845. Rossetti thought that the influence of Etty:

> "might at one time have produced a marked effect upon the [British] school; but, coming to be taken up, divorced from its greatness in colour, by a conventionalist like Frost, its arch-disciple, it has fallen into mere foppery and premature senility, and by this time into deserved disrepute. F.R. Pickersgill has sometimes a similar aim, with no small reality of colourist power, but he cannot be said to have carried it far." (repr. in W.M. Rossetti, *Fine Art, Chiefly Contemporary*, 1867, p158)

For Thackeray in 1845:

> "(Frost's) picture is like a mixture of very good Hilton and Howard raised to a state of genius. There is sameness in the heads, but great grace and beauty, a fine sweeping movement in the composition of the beautiful fairy figures, undulating gracefully through the stream while lilies lie gracefully overhead." (*Fraser's*)

The *ILN* shared this view, though it felt that Frost, while successfully wearing the mantle of Henry Howard, should emancipate himself from a potentially debilitating influence. Nevertheless, the *Sabrina* 'is a fine conception of Milton's meaning in his Masque; well grouped, full of fine feeling, and in parts very delicately painted.' *The Art Union* described 'this valuable picture' as 'masterly', the drawing as evidence of great learning, the heads 'perfectly qualified to illustrate the moving verse.'

Thackeray and the *Athenaeum* referred *Sabrina*, an illustration to lines from Milton's

Comus, to the frescoes commissioned by Prince Albert in 1843 for the small garden pavilion in the grounds of Buckingham Palace, an experimental rehearsal for the use of fresco on a large scale in the decoration of the Palace of Westminster. The focus of the decoration was to be in the Octagon Room, whose eight lunettes were to feature scenes from *Comus*; by 1845 Stanfield, Uwins, Leslie, Ross, Maclise, Landseer, Dyce and Eastlake had completed their frescoes. Etty had been amongst the original group of artists commissioned, but both his designs were rejected and he was replaced by Dyce. Etty showed oil versions of his failed designs at the Academy (*Hesperus*, his second attempt, in 1844, now at Port Sunlight, and *Circe and the Sirens Three*, the first design, in 1846, now at Perth, Western Australia; see Dennis Farr, *William Etty*, 1958, pp95–8); Maclise and Leslie showed oil versions of their designs at the RA in 1844. Frost's choice of a Comus subject for the 1845 RA could not have been coincidental: Etty had painted two versions of the same Sabrina subject, one RA 1831 (Christie's 1946, untraced) and a variant now at Leicester, dated 1841, and as Etty's disciple he was on the fringes of the garden pavilion group and may even have nourished hopes of a commission for himself. Whether this *Sabrina* was an oil version of a hopeful design for a lunette, a demonstration of what he could have done if he had been asked, or merely the result of his involvement and identification with Etty, is impossible to say. The measurements and shape are very close to those of the oil versions of the lunettes by the commissioned artists, but Frost is not mentioned in Mrs. Jameson's introduction to Lewis Gruner's coloured engravings of the designs (publ. 1846). Thackeray, in the 1845 *Fraser's* review, was outspokenly rude about the low fees paid for the pavilion designs and hoped for Frost's sake that he was not involved in the venture. Frost's studio sale in 1878 included two groups of watercolours made at the Sketching Club by Pickersgill and Hook: of these, four by Pickersgill and one by Hook were named subjects from *Comus*.

Private Collection

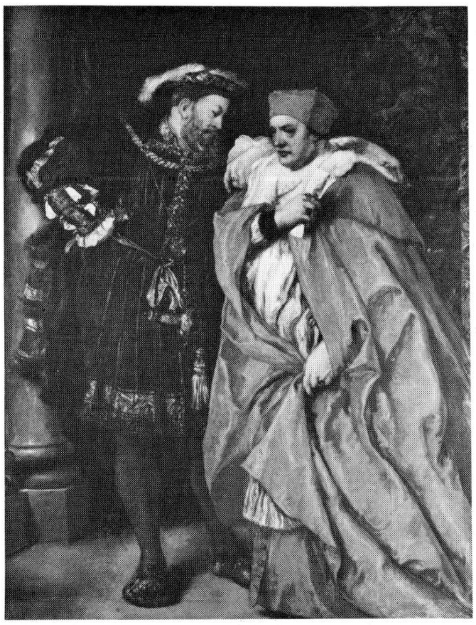

SIR JOHN GILBERT, 1817–1897, ARWS 1852, RWS 1854, PRWS 1871, KT. 1872, ARA 1872, RA 1876

17 **Ego et Rex Meus** 1889

oil on canvas, 63 × 41 in
INSCR: J.G. 1888

PROV: Presented by the artist to the City of London, 1893.
EXH: RA 1889 (293); Leeds 1890; People's Palace 1897; Glasgow 1899; Expo. Univ. Paris 1900 (92); RA Winter 1901 (37); Glasgow Internat. 1901 (302); Whitechapel 1909 (62).
LIT: *Athenaeum*, 1 June 1889, p701; Blackburn, *RA Notes*, 1889, p.xi, repr, p31; A.G. Temple, 'Sir John Gilbert's Gift to the City of London'. *AJ*, July 1893, pp199–200; 'Sir John Gilbert's Gift to the City of London', *Mag. of Art*, 1893, pp320–1, 355–8, xxix, repr. p320; obit. *Times*, 7 Oct 1897, p4; M.H. Spielmann, 'Sir John Gilbert, RA, PRWS: A Memorial Sketch', *Mag. of Art*, 1898, p64, repr. p59.
REPR: *ILN*, 11 May 1889, engr. p585; A.G. Temple, *Reproductions by the Collotype Process of the Pictures presented to the Art Gallery of the Corporation of the City of London by Sir John Gilbert, RA, PRWS, &c*, with descriptive and biographical letterpress, 1893, facing p10.

In May 1893 the *Magazine of Art* announced:

> "The generous distribution by Sir John Gilbert, RA, PRWS, of his works among the Corporations of London, Liverpool, Birmingham, and Manchester, is one of those acts of patriotic munificence of which Mr. G.F. Watts has set so fine an example. It has for some years been known that Sir John did intend to leave his works to the nation. His first thought was to build a gallery for their reception, but his more recent decision is a far wiser one, by reason of its greater utility to the greater number. The recipients have shown their appreciation by a haste that under other circumstances might be called indecent. Members of the London Corporation called at once upon Sir John and secured for the Guildhall the cream of the collection. This consists of about twenty oil and watercolours, of a market value, it is believed, of more than £15,000. Half-an-hour later came the Liverpool representatives, post haste, and were also permitted to make their choice."

Gilbert was given the Freedom of the City of London, the first artist to be so honoured; he was then 76 and near the end of a life whose greatest achievement in both popular fame and in terms of sheer volume had been his wood engraved drawings for the illustrated magazines and for books. Latterly it was estimated that he had made some 30,000 illustrations for the *ILN* alone, and although Spielmann thought this probably exaggerated, it was close enough to the truth to indicate Gilbert's extraordinary industry and the degree to which he was in demand. He was almost entirely self-taught, failed to enter the RA Schools and resorted to black-and-white illustration to earn his living. He had aspirations from the beginning, however, to the more aesthetically respectable media of watercolour and oil, the ambition of every Victorian illustrator, and exhibited at the British Institution from 1837 and at the RA from 1838. From 1852 he showed yearly at the Old Water Colour Society, becoming its President in 1871; this resulted in his knighthood and his election the following year to ARA. Randall Davies's *OWS* article on Gilbert's career as a watercolourist (*OWS*, X, 1933, pp20–43) points out that though his contemporaries called him 'the English Rubens', Gilbert's watercolour compositions had more in common with the historical figures scenes of the very English George Cattermole, who generally painted monastic scenes (though in limited and sombrely brown soup tones) than with the physical and technical vigour of Rubens. Nevertheless, Gilbert's often crowded historical scenes are warm-toned and lively in colour and he delighted in the massing of colourfully uniformed and costumed figures in battle tableaux and in grand royal or ecclesiastical scenes. Almost all his subjects were taken from the fifteenth and sixteenth centuries and scenes involving Henry VIII and his court were amongst his favourite.

Ego et Rex Meus illustrates the opening of Act I, sc. 2 in Shakespeare's *Henry VIII* when the King thanks Cardinal Wolsey for revealing the Duke of Buckingham's supposedly treacherous plot; Wolsey's duplicity, the magnificence of the robes, the figures filling the picture space are all skilfully treated by Gilbert, and, though the picture was not much commented on when it was first shown at the RA in 1889, it became on its arrival at the Guildhall one of the most frequently lent and most popular pictures in the gallery.

In 1966 Richard Ormond published details from Gilbert's diaries and account books (*Country Life*, 18 and 25 Aug 1966) which revealed that in the last twenty years of his life his popularity declined and with it his prices: this may be the practical, if unglamorous, reason for his decision in 1885 to sell no more of his pictures 'with a view to presenting a collection of them to the nation' (*DNB*). When the time came they were in fact distributed to London, Birmingham, Blackburn, Liverpool and Manchester; the Guildhall finally received five oils and eleven watercolours.

Guildhall Art Gallery

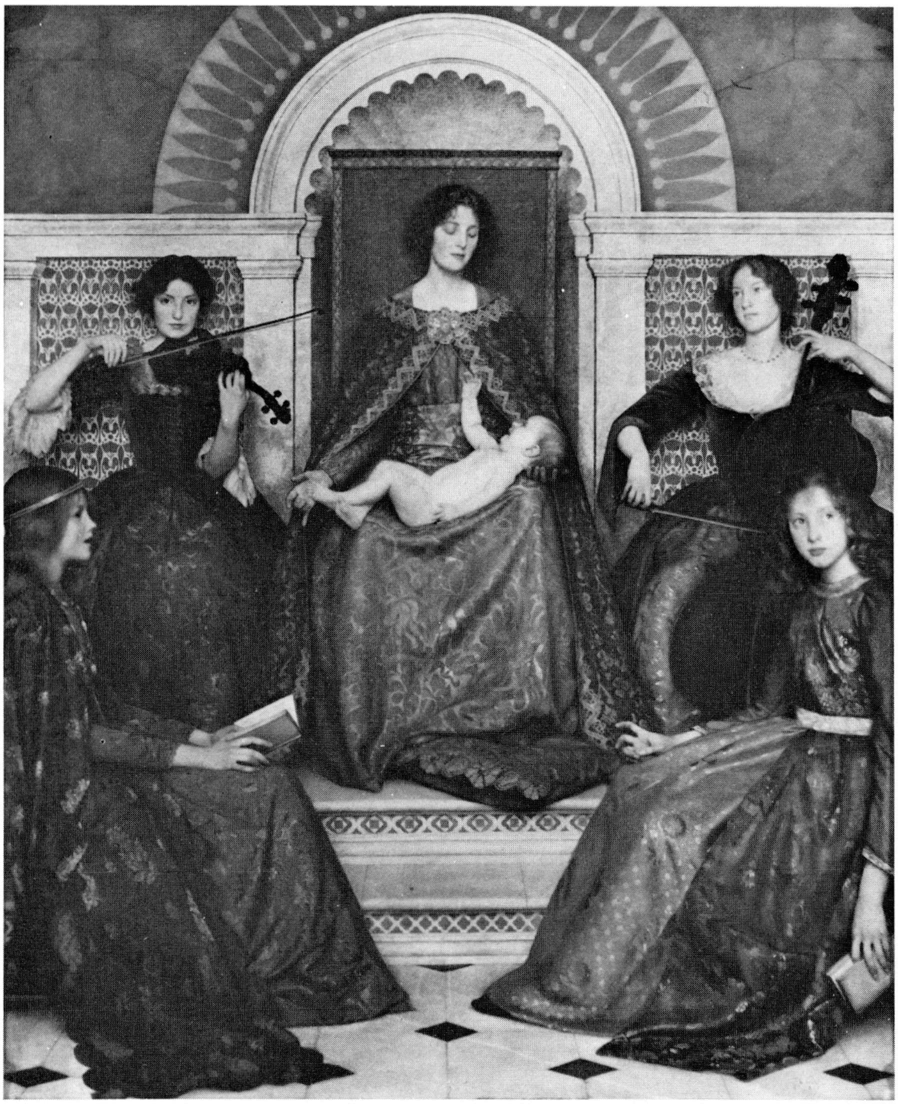

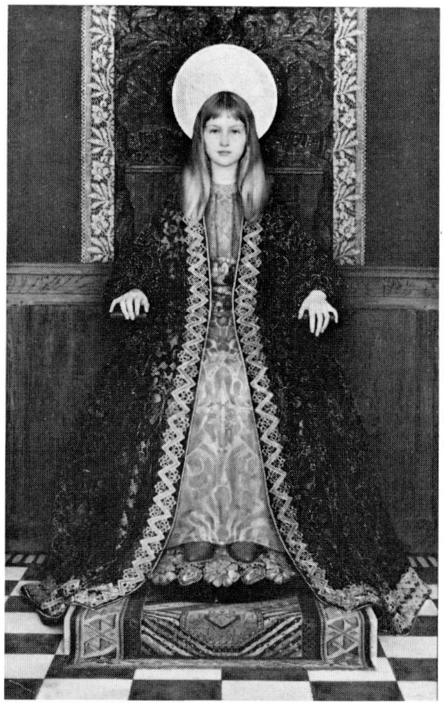

The Child Enthroned *Courtesy: The Fine Art Society*

THOMAS COOPER GOTCH, 1854–1931, NEAC 1886, RBA 1885, RI 1912, PRBC 1913

18 Holy Motherhood 1902

oil on canvas, 72 × 66 in
INSCR: T.C. Gotch

PROV: purchased by Newcastle from the artist, 1910.
EXH: RA 1902 (249); St. Louis Internat. 1904 (96); *Children's Portraits and Child Pictures by T.C. Gotch, RBC*, Newcastle 1910 (33); *Victorian Paintings*, Newcastle 1967–8 (10) repr.
LIT: *AJ*, June 1902, p216, repr. p211; *Mag. of Art*, 1902, p395; *Studio*, June 1902, p38; Marion Hepworth Dixon, 'A Painter of Womanhood', *The Lady's Realm*, Dec 1904, repr. p175; Charles H. Caffin, 'A Painter of Childhood and Girlhood', *Harper's Monthly Magazine*, May 1910, p932, repr. p928.
REPR: *RA Pictures*, 1902, p72.

Gotch spent the winter of 1891–2 in Florence. He was a member of the New English Art Club, one of the original Newlyn School artists and a fully-fledged practitioner of the new style along with Stanhope Forbes, Tuke and Walter Langley. His experience in Florence of Quattrocento artists like Fra Angelico and Benozzo Gozzoli transformed his ideas and he abandoned his plein-air principles for the hermetic and intensely stylised decorative symbolism that occupied the rest of his life. The change was first seen in *My Crown and Sceptre* (RA 1892, Sydney), but two years later *The Child Enthroned*

> "very emphatically defined his new creed, and asserted the nature of the principles to which he had decided to conform for the future. Story was abandoned, incident set aside, and even the touch of personality which marked *My Crown and Sceptre* was entirely eliminated. What remained was a delightfully pure type of art, something that, by its novelty of form, attracted general attention, and yet by its observation of the highest canons of technical practice was able to satisfy the most exacting demand for efficiency of execution. Realistically, the picture was as complete as it was possible to make it: nothing in the rendering of textures or the treatment of details was neglected or left unexplained . . . yet all through the charm of a dainty and poetic idea made itself felt." (Alfred Lys Baldry, 'The Work of T.C. Gotch', *Studio*, Mar 1898, pp78, 81).

Baldry's article, the first on the artist, reproduces some of the most important Newlyn paintings, like *The Story of the Money-Pig* (Cape Town) and *Twixt Life and Death* (RA 1890, ex McCulloch Coll.), and goes on to detail Gotch's progress towards symbolism. *My Crown and Sceptre* is a still relatively naturalistic portrait of his daughter, in a pink dress, seated on an imposing chair backed by a curtain – she has a posy, a wreath of flowers and a be-ribboned cornstalk and has evidently just played the Queen of the May in a pageant.

The Child Enthroned (RA 1894, private collection, exh. Fine Art Society 1977) was a far more sophisticated interpretation of the Early Renaissance: the child who was, with intentional significance a girl (again Hester), sits on a throne in magnificent red and blue robes, behind is panelling, and a dossal and wall of intense vermilion. The halo, the absolute symmetry, the purity and intensity of the colour, and the precision and finish of the execution give the painting an extraordinary quality and made a profound impression on its audience.

> ". . . among the younger men it is Mr. Gotch who succeeds in impressing the spectator most with his sincerity and intensity of feeling. It may well be objected that 'The Child Enthroned' is too obviously a girl; but the refinement of the drawing, the almost Gothic conviction of feeling carries it in triumph over the dangers that always threaten such conventions as these." (*Mag. of Art*, 1894, p273).

The subject was in fact mistaken for the Christ Child when it was shown at the 1896 Paris Salon, but it was intended as an ideal of young, virginal womanhood and as such was the mainspring of his new philosophy. Caffin's article in *Harper's* explains the artist's progressive ideas on the status of women (the fact that Gotch's wife was a practising artist may have had some bearing on this) and elaborates at length, and to somewhat counter-productive extremes, Gotch's ideas on the sanctity of childhood and the supremacy of the feminine ideal, but fails to explain whether these are his own observations or whether they come first-hand from Gotch.

Holy Motherhood is Gotch's most complete expression of his idea of the adult female experience; when it was reproduced by Marion Hepworth Dixon in, appropriately enough, *The Lady's Realm*, Dixon wrote (p64),

> ". . . the serene and the virginal attract the artist to the exclusion of nearly every other quality, and it is to this love of purity and what for want of a better word I must call 'detachment' in his allegorical figures that Mr. Gotch owes his hold on the public."

This hold on the public had been greatly strengthened by the Chantrey Purchase of his 1896 RA picture, *Alleluia*, a highly decorative vision of a choir of angelic (but still modern) young girls, brilliantly coloured, haloed and ranged in carefully designed ranks. The Newcastle picture now exhibited and *Alleluia* are probably the clearest expressions of his interpretation of the compositional devices of, in particular, Benozzo Gozzoli and Bellini, but the atmosphere is entirely that of the late nineteenth century. He had already demonstrated a knowledge of French Symbolism in its more decadent forms (acquired during his student days in Paris and on subsequent visits) in pictures like *Death the Bride* (RA 1895, Kettering) and continued to produce paintings like *The Awakening* (RA 1898, Bristol) that are somewhat too vulnerable to modern interpretative psychology. However, the very fact that so many of his paintings are in public galleries indicates the degree of his popularity; a number are in the former Dominions, the result of his work for the Royal British Colonial Society of Artists, of which he was President for many years. The 1910 exhibition of his work at the Laing, Newcastle, resulted in the gallery's purchase of *Holy Motherhood* and a much later version of the same idea, *The Mother Enthroned* (RA 1919, 86 × 114 in) is at Sheffield. Kettering, the artist's home town, organised a Memorial Exhibition of Gotch's work in 1932.

Laing Art Gallery, Tyne & Wear County Council Museums Service

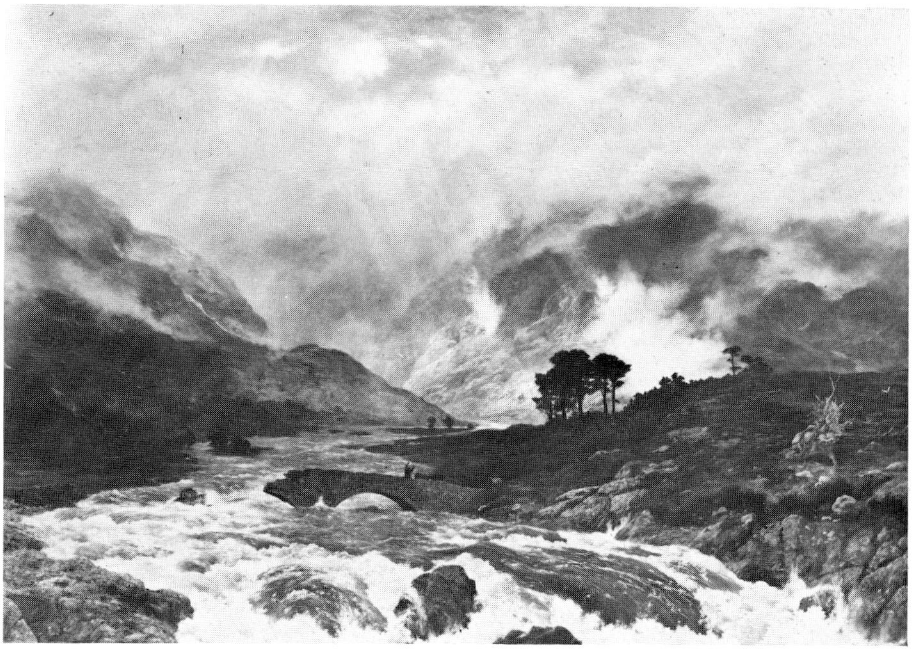

PETER GRAHAM, 1836–1921, ARSA 1859–77, ARA 1877, RA 1881

19 A Spate in the Highlands 1866

oil on canvas, $47\frac{1}{4} \times 69\frac{5}{8}$ in
INSCR: P. Graham / 1866

PROV: Frederick Somes, Beech Hill Park, Loughton, Essex, by 1867; anon. sale, Christie's, 8 May 1869 (109) bt. Gambart (£1071); Sir William Cunliffe Brooks, Bt., MP, by 1887; by whom bequeathed to Manchester, 1901.

EXH: RA 1866 (373); Expo. Univ. Paris 1867 (41); Manchester Jubilee 1887 (169); Guildhall 1892 (2); Blackburn 1894 (82); *Scottish Exh.*, Glasgow 1911 (477); RA Winter 1922 (105); RSA 1922; Accrington 1928; Blackburn 1931; Blackpool 1935–6; Oldham 1938; Cardiff 1939–45; Mansfield 1949.

LIT: *AJ*, June 1866, p170; *Athenaeum*, 2 June 1866, pp742–3; *Blackwood's*, Aug 1866, p193; *GdBA*, July 1866, p88; *ILN*, 26 May 1866, p518; *Times*, 5 May, p9, 12 June 1866, p6; W.W. Fenn, 'Peter Graham, ARA', *Mag. of Art*, 1879, p144; P.G. Hamerton, *Landscape*, 1885, pp251–2, repr. betw. pp68 & 69, and *Thoughts about Art*, 1889, p34; Hodgson, 1887, p89; Armstrong, Manchester 1887, p20; Walter Armstrong, 'Scottish Painters IX', *Portfolio*, Nov 1887, pp211–12; Temple, 1897, pp263–4; W. Matthews Gilbert, 'Peter Graham, RA', *The Art Annual*, 1899, pp11–12, repr. p12; Caw, 1908, p255; *Manchester Cat.*, 1910 (173); Irwins, 1975, p363.

ENGR: Photogravures and collotypes, Arthur Tooth & Son, publ. 1892, etc.

VERSIONS OR STUDIES: Graves *Sales* lists nine occasions between 1882 and 1909 when pictures with variations on the same title have appeared at Christie's; from the measurements given, it seems likely that there were at least four different paintings, ranging in size from 12 × 9 in to 30 × 43 in, any one of which may have been a study for, or version of, the exhibited painting. One of these may be identifiable with *Spate in the Highlands;* oil; $19\frac{1}{2} \times 29\frac{1}{2}$ in, beq. to Aberdeen by Mrs. Leslie, Nethermuir 1902. In 1885, Hamerton refers to Graham's 'first sketch of the subject', of which he had a photograph (guard page facing repr.).

> "To how few artists is it given to take the town, literally, by storm, with the first picture they exhibit at the Royal Academy?" (Gilbert).

Peter Graham, the latest in a long line of mid-century Scottish immigrants had indeed successfully stormed the Academy: the RA 1866 reviews all acclaimed *A Spate in the Highlands* for its power and dramatic force, while its popularity with the public was apparently so great that the *Athenaeum* records it was 'constantly fronted by a crowd of persons'. It was catalogued with two lines of Burns (from the first verse of 'Winter: A Dirge'); most Scottish landscape artists, like the earlier generation of genre painters, gave a literary polish to their work with atmospheric quotations. After describing the mist-shrouded valley containing the foaming stream in spate, *The Times* went on:

> "Desolation, the power of storm, and the struggle of the elements are the leading ideas of this picture, which is of the finest order of literal workmanship; if, indeed, it be not fairly entitled to be called ideal, by virtue of its subordination of parts to the whole and the predominance throughout of a prevailing sentiment. Everybody can understand why we describe Mr. Mason's landscapes as idealized. Where there is so little of impressiveness or beauty in the mere details of subjects which yet affect us so powerfully, we cannot doubt that their strong hold of the mind and the memory must be due to something peculiar and indescribable in the mind of the painter. But Mr. Graham's subject is itself stern and soul-subduing enough to account for all we feel before it."

This echo of Ruskin's views, expressed for instance on Stanfield's *The Abandoned* (cat. Untraced Pictures), is interesting coming from *The Times*; F.G. Stephens, in the *Athenaeum* adopted a more critical Ruskinian stance when, after praising the incident in 'this remarkable picture' (the drover has noticed the washed-away bridge just in time to drive his herd back to safety), and Graham's understanding of colour and accurate observation of nature, he complained about the 'treacly' execution of the foreground which he identified as caused by 'his shiny, gum-laden Scotch vehicle' (paint medium). The same point was made in the *Art Journal*, but there is no doubt that, these quibbles aside, Graham's picture was a resounding success, and recognised as such even by the French.

Unfortunately for Graham, success on that scale was almost impossible to cap and, though the picture continued to attract superlatives throughout the century, it was recognised that Graham's later efforts never quite achieved the same quality. Hamerton, twenty years after it was first shown, called it 'One of the best landscapes of the last thirty years' – something of a modification of his comment in 1873 (quoted in Hamerton, 1889) that Graham was 'one of the most thoroughly accomplished landscape-painters the world has ever seen'. The latter statement should however, be seen in its context – Hamerton was discussing the benefits of the French method of studying by making numerous oil-sketches, and quoted Graham approvingly on the dangers for the novice of attempting study from nature.

> "He believes, and so do I, that the shortest road to good landscape-painting is an indirect road, and that he himself got his first initiation into the mysteries of landscape effect through constant observation of the delicate play of light and shade in a gallery of statues. He earnestly recommends the practice of portraiture as the best preliminary training. It is a complete mistake to go to landscape under the impression that it is easy. The naked figure, difficult as that also is, is a simple object in comparison with a forest or a mountain. We ought to proceed, in study, from simplicity to intricacy, and the great difficulty in landscape is to find anything that is simple enough for early study."

A pupil of Lauder's at Edinburgh and a contemporary of Orchardson, MacWhirter and Pettie, Graham had abandoned his sculpture gallery in 1859 and adopted his lifelong practice of making studies from nature. He was prepared to go to extraordinary lengths to obtain them; from 1872 he showed large paintings of bleak storm-lashed northern cliffs, covered with seabirds, and Gilbert describes how Graham spent days in a boat off an unpopulated island near Cape Wrath to make the necessary studies. This spartan research produced works like *Where gannets build* (RA 1896), and "*Ribbed and paled in with rocks unscaleable and roaring water.*" (RA 1885). Graham's other line was in highland landscapes swathed in mists out of which generally peered two or more highland cattle; typical examples are *Caledonia, Stern and Wild* (McCulloch sale 1913 (144)) and the Newcastle *Landscape with Cattle*, and these seem generally to have been painted in more comfortable circumstances as Gilbert reveals that for many years, up until 1891, Graham had a country house in Buckinghamshire – 'Attached to it were a park and paddock, where were kept half a dozen Highland cattle, which as occasion required did duty as artist's models.' So successful were both lines that a waiting list was operated and Graham's studio only ever contained, according to Gilbert, the picture on which the artist was working. He was allotted a paragraph – as much as Linnell, Leader and Wyllie – in Phythian's 'Fifty Years of Modern Painting':

> "His vigorous, realistic pictures of the moors and glens of the Scottish Highlands, and the shaggy cattle that inhabit them, and of the haunts of the wild fowl on the rock-bound northern coasts, have become very familiar, even to the man in the street, through the reproductions so often exhibited in the print-sellers' windows. Grey misty skies, with, perhaps, fitful gleams of sunlight breaking through the clouds, and lighting up the otherwise cold green grass, grey rock, or grey-green sea, have been painted by him with minor variations year after year until we have been ready to take them as looked at." (1910, pp343–4).

An artist in this fortunate position, backed by Agnew, and unable to keep up with the demand from collectors for his paintings could happily afford to ignore the critics.

City of Manchester Art Galleries

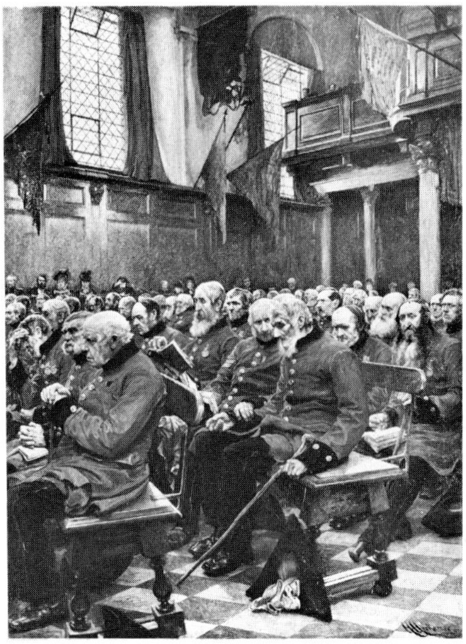

The Last Muster – painting
Courtesy: Lady Lever Art Gallery

SIR HUBERT VON HERKOMER, 1849–1914, ARA 1879, RA 1890, KT. 1907

20 The Last Muster 1871/1875/1909

lithograph, $24 \times 18\frac{1}{2}$ in
INSCR: H.v.H. 1909; Hubert von Herkomer

PROV: presented by the artist, 1910.
LIT: (selected references to the exhibited picture unless otherwise stated). *AJ*, Aug 1875, p252; *Academy*, 23 May 1875, p537–8; *Athenaeum*, 1 May 1875, p591; *Graphic*, 1 May, p415, 15 May 1875; *ILN*, 8 May 1875, p446; Ruskin, *RA Notes 1875*, *Works*, XIV, p291; *Times*, 1 May 1875, p12; Edmond Duranty, *GdBA*, 1878, p304; E. Bergerat, *Les Chefs-d'Oeuvre d'Art a l'Exposition Universelle*, Paris, 1878, II, pp14–16; *L'Art*, 1879, p179; Chesneau, 1885, p295–6; '"The Last Muster" by Professor Hubert Herkomer, ARA', *Mag. of Art*, Oct 1889, p16 & photogravure; *Autobiography of Hubert Herkomer*, privately printed, 1890, pp43–7; Harry Quilter, *Preferences in Art, Life and Literature*, 1892, p317; W.L. Courtney, 'Hubert Herkomer, RA. The Story of his Life', *Art Annual*, 1892, pp9–10, engr. frontisp.; Sir Hubert von Herkomer, *The Herkomers*, 1910–11, I, pp150ff; J. Saxon Mills, *Life and Letters of Sir Hubert Herkomer, CVO, RA, A Study in Struggle and Success*, 1923, pp58–9, pp77–93, repr facing p82, (ref lithograph) p300.
VERSIONS (oil and engr): 1. *Sunday at Chelsea Hospital;* wood engraving: publ. *Graphic*, 18 Feb 1871, p152. Lit: *Graphic*, 18 Feb 1871, p151; *The Complete Letters of Vincent van Gogh*, 1959, No's 238, 263, 280, R20, R24; cat. *English Influences on Vincent van Gogh*, Arts Council 1974/5.
2. Watercolour version of *Graphic* wood engraving, commissioned by the editor, W.L. Thomas, winter 1870–1. Lit: Mills, *op. cit.*, pp62, 77.
3. *The Last Muster;* oil on canvas; 82×61 in. Prov: Sir Cuthbert Quilter, Christie's, 9 July 1908 (57) bt. Agnew (£3255); Hague sale, Christie's, 22 June 1923 (152); Lady Lever Art Gallery, Port Sunlight. Exh: RA 1875; Expo. Univ. Paris 1878 (Médaille d'honneur); Manchester Jubilee 1887; Birmingham 1887; Chicago 1893; Guildhall 1894; West Ham 1897; Dublin 1907; Franco-British 1908; Rome 1911; and at Munich, Berlin (Herkomer Exh.), Bristol, etc.
4. *Sketch of the Last Muster* (detail of the dead pensioner and his comrade); wood engraving; publ. *Graphic*, 15 May 1875, betw. pp470–1.
5. Engr. A. Turrell.

At the Paris Exposition Universelle of 1878 the two Médailles d'honneur for English artists went to Millais and Herkomer; the latter was not yet even an ARA while Millais had long emancipated himself from the commitments of Pre-Raphaelitism and was securely established as a hugely successful society and popular artist. *The Last Muster* attracted so much attention in Paris that the *Graphic* published an engraving of the scene, and commented:

> "The collection is most distinctly national, and on the walls, at every turn, he finds old favourites which bring back to his mind strange reminiscences of past times, as he remembers the successive years in which he first saw the various Millaises (sic), Friths, and Poynters, which surround him. Not, however, that the human occupants of the rooms are mainly English, for the undoubtedly fine collection has attracted great attention, not only in art, but in many other French circles, and a motley crowd frequently encircles certain pictures of which the subjects attract the popular taste. Such a one is Mr. Hubert Herkomer's *Last Muster* . . . The military taste of the French is proverbial, and that this picture, so essentially military in its tone, should be a general favourite is hardly to be wondered at." (29 June 1878, p634).

The picture had already achieved marked success in its first incarnation as a wood engraved illustration for the *Graphic* in 1871; encouraged, Herkomer had set about enlarging the subject in oil and it was finally exhibited at the 1875 RA to considerable applause. Herkomer tried to create a fresco-like surface by painting without a ground straight onto sized canvas; the paint immediately started chipping and despite his efforts then and those of others since, the paint surface is now very fragile. He also had no training in perspective drawing and arrived at the structure by his own practical inventions. The reviewers recognised a new and vigorous talent and were particularly touched by its representation of the moment of death:

> "The great power with which the wide range of types in the congregation of pensioners that fill the canvas is rendered; the grasp of the character of each; the pathos of the deep marks of time and service and hardship in the rows of aged heads, telling the life-story of each man; and the force and truth of the painting of those heads are worthy of the highest praise. One pale, emaciated figure, sitting on a bench in the immediate foreground, gives point to the first section of the title, and at the same time strikes the keynote of the pathetic composition. His head is drooping, his eyes are closed, he does not respond to the friendly challenge of the grip at his wrist of the old companion-in-arms at his side – it is verily the 'last muster' for him. Few things in painting have struck us as more touching than this incident . . ." (*ILN*).

From a rough tally kept of the exhibiting histories of the major Victorian paintings, *The Last Muster* comes out a clear winner in both the sheer number of exhibitions to which it was lent up to the First War and in the importance of those exhibitions, and its popularity appears to have lasted undimmed until at least the 1920s. Herkomer was clearly still very proud of his most famous picture when, in 1909, he decided to make a lithographic version of it. By this time his reputation was as established as Millais' had been in 1878: his art school at Bushey in Hertfordshire was opened in 1883 (and is described in minute detail in *My School and My Gospel*, 1908); he exhibited regularly and achieved a new reputation in the 1880s as a Society portrait painter; he wrote copiously and pompously about his family (he was by birth

Bavarian and his family had settled in England when he was eight), his art and his theories, and spent much of his later years experimenting with various graphic media. Lithography was the last to be tried, and his conclusions were collected in a lecture delivered at Lululand (his house in Bushey) to an invited audience of artists, published as *A Certain Phase of Lithography* in 1910. He was trying to avoid producing lithographs that merely resembled original chalk drawings and resorted much to the example of Rembrandt's etching experiments and to Menzel in an attempt to find a new and totally individual graphic technique. *The Last Muster* was perhaps a fitting vehicle; Herkomer's greatest success, that had first been seen thirty-six years before, was now wheeled out again and emerges remarkably freshly in the new medium.

Victoria and Albert Museum

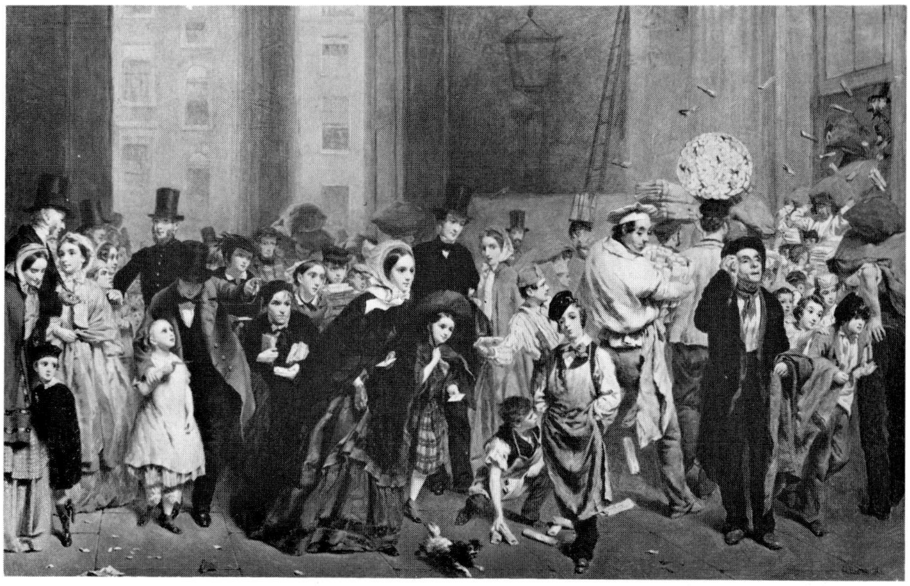

George Elgar Hicks, 1824–1914

21 The General Post Office – 1 minute to 6 1860

oil on canvas, 35 × 53 in
INSCR: GE Hicks 1860

PROV: M. Bernard Ltd., by 1948; Sotheby's Belgravia, 19 Oct 1971 (61) bt. Richard Green Ltd.
EXH: RA 1860 (367); *British Life*, Arts Council 1953 (30); *Victorian Painting 1837–1887*, Agnew 1961 (81).
LIT: *AJ*, June 1860, p170; *Athenaeum*, 19 May 1860, p688; *Blackwood's*, July 1860, p68; *Fraser's*, June 1860, p878; *Literary Gazette* 19 May 1860, p615; *Punch*, 16 June 1860, p247; Walter Thornbury, *The May Exhibition: A Guide to the Pictures in the Royal Academy*, 1860, pp40–1; *Times*, 17 May 1860, p11; James Dafforne, 'British Artists CIV: George Elgar Hicks', *AJ*, Apr 1872, p98; Reynolds, 1953, pp13–14, 89, fig 73; Maas, 1969, p117; Wood, *Panorama*, 1976, p168, fig 180 & cover.
REPR: advertisements in *Connoisseur*, 1948 (colour), Dec 1971 (colour), June 1975.
VERSION: oil on panel; 14¼ × 22 in; inscr verso GE Hicks 1860. Prov: commissioned by Mr. Vokins (£70); Sotheby's Belgravia, 22 Feb 1972 (50) bt. R. Green; Sotheby's Belgravia, 9 July 1974 (70).
STUDY: *Study of a boy in an apron stooping to pick up packages from the ground*, on the same sheet three slight sketches of the same subject; pencil, heightened with white; 11⅝ × 7⅝ in; inscr GE Hicks 1860. Bequeathed by H.H. Harrod to the V & A (E.832–1948).

Hicks's essays on modern urban life in the manner of Frith were loved by the RA visitors and greatly disapproved of by most of the critics. His first success in the genre was with *Dividend Day at the Bank* (RA 1859, Bank of England) which *The Times* thought degenerated 'into that excessive characterisation which borders on caricature . . . these subjects bring out whatever vulgarity is in a man.' The *Literary Gazette* felt that Hicks had chosen a subject beyond his talents and, while it appreciated the fidelity of the characterisation, the end result lacked vitality. Stephens, in the *Athenaeum* sounded the sternest warning, as might be expected of a Pre-Raphaelite partisan:

> "Mr. Hicks, exquisite in drawing-room idylls, must now forsooth attempt Frithisms and the humours of London life. [This] is an unreal, laboured piece of unsuccessful humour, with here and there a pretty face. The subject is too much for Mr. Hicks. Let him get back to his violet banks and silk gowns – there he is at home. Why will serious men attempt funny subjects and funny men serious ones?" (21 May 1859, p682).

What the 1859 critics did not reveal was that *Dividend Day* was one of the popular successes of the exhibition and, as Dafforne points out, established a completely new style for the artist. Frith's *Derby Day* had been the sensation of the decade at the 1858 RA, and Hicks very smartly seized on the idea and embarked on a series of analogous subjects like the *Dividend Day* (the City equivalent of a racecourse payout) and immediately followed up his success with the *General Post Office* of 1860.

The subject was topical as public and parliamentary debates were in progress on the conduct of the postal services which were severely overburdened by what Dickens described in 1850 as 'waterspouts of newspapers' (*Household Words*, 30 March 1850). The excited and hurrying crowd in its literally last-minute dash to catch the post is arranged in a flowing and easily readable composition, very dependent on Frith but with a looser and more dashing stroke. Thornbury's concluding remark in his review may explain at least part of the picture's appeal. In his opinion,

> "The last moment of posting time is a scene expressing the ardour and abundance of our national life, and well worth perpetuating."

Whatever its attraction, *Punch* found himself 'pushed and hustled' in front of it,

> "the crush represented in Mr. Hicks's picture gives only a faint idea of the crowd around it. The glimpses which you catch of it between hats, over shoulders, and under arms, increase the reality of the scene."

Even allowing for some satirical exaggeration, *Punch's* report of crowds is confirmed by *Fraser's* and by the *Literary Gazette*, though both have mixed feelings about the quality of the painting. It was left to the *Times* and the *Athenaeum* to deliver the swingeing criticisms. *The Times*:

> "If Mr. Hicks is ever to take the place he is manfully striving for, he must learn to respect the line which separates expression from exaggeration. In his large and elaborate work . . . we have the rush and struggle . . . represented with no lack of industry, or cleverness, or humour. But let Mr. Hicks go back and view the scene again . . . He will learn two lessons – first, that he has attempted too much; next, that he has missed some essential truths. The picture is wearisome from the excess of its crowded and unvarying incidents. A very little of it would have sufficed. Then there is untruth in the impossible cleanness of these faces and white jackets. If we must have a mob of newsboys, let us have them with all their grime and printers' ink, their threadbare garments and shapeless headgear. Let us have such newsboys as Mr. Leech sketches for us. His broadest work never degenerates into caricature, however rampant in its humour or careless in its execution. Mr. Hicks's elaborate painting, executed in perfect good faith, and with Hogarthian seriousness of intention, suggests caricature throughout. It is not given to many to handle common contemporary life. Happy those who can. To do so with success requires the most genuine appreciation of the human comedy going on about us, united with the nicest taste and the most consummate judgment."

None of which, in Stephens's opinion, Hicks had:

> "There is hardly a more hopeless and meretricious picture in the RA than that by . . . Hicks; indeed, but for its prominent position, we should pass over it in silence, content that mere mechanism could do no harm. Placed as this work is, we have no other choice than to point out the poor and machine-like character of a picture which, by its showy and pretentious execution, is sure to find observers."

Stephens did not object to the subject, worthy indeed of Hogarth, but found the figures lifeless, their gazes fixed inexplicably on vague points, the faces too 'painted up to the pink of doll-like perfection, and not to the dingy reality of London life' and concluded,

> "There are crowds of incident, but no character; and plenty of faces, but little interesting and vital expression."

Stephens's principles were undoubtedly offended, but the gulf that yawned between the other critics and the public was almost as wide. Hicks's case is perhaps the most extreme occurrence of this in Victorian painting and it seems likely that the determined opposition of the critics (with the exception of the *Art Journal*) discouraged him so much that he soon abandoned his modern life series and returned to the Keepsake beauties, sentimental genre and portraiture that he continued to show at the Academy well into the new century. His other principal modern life pictures were *Billingsgate* (RA 1861, M. Bernard in 1953, repr Reynolds, 1953, pl.74) and *Infant Orphan Election at the London Tavern – Polling* (RA 1865, Alexander Gallery 1976). The Dafforne article, itself very brief, is the only significant contemporary source for Hicks, an artist who never achieved Academy distinctions and who seems to have remained outside all the usual Victorian artistic circles.

Anonymous Loan

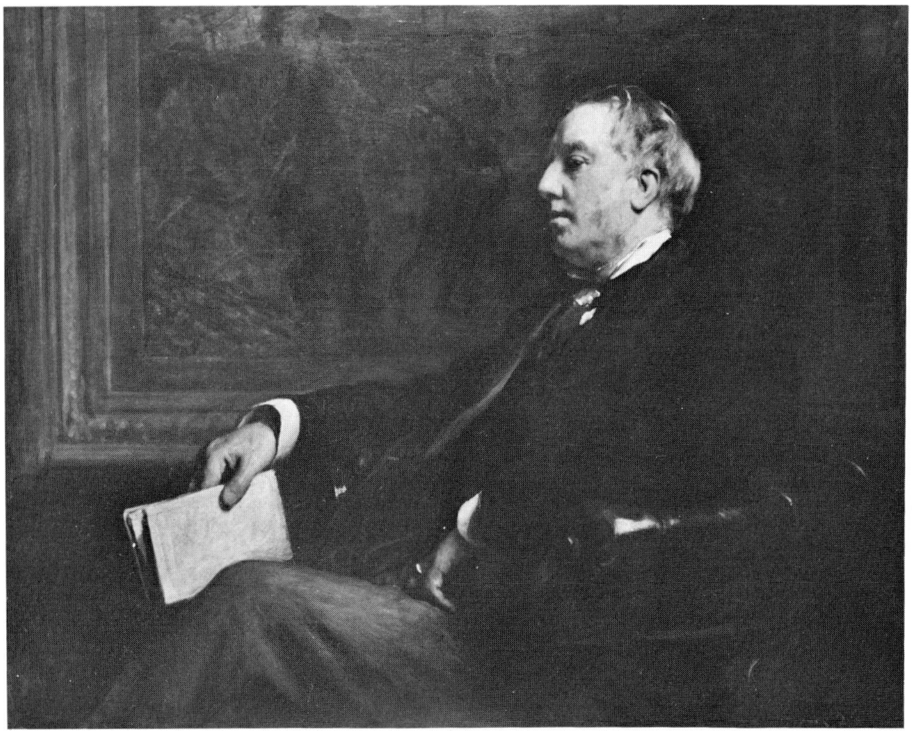

FRANK HOLL, 1845–1888, ARA 1878, RA 1883

22 William Agnew, Esq., MP 1883

oil on canvas, 40 × 50 in
INSCR: Frank Holl, 1883

PROV: commissioned by William Agnew.
EXH: RA 1883 (1433); *A Special Selection from the Works of Frank Holl, RA*, RA Winter 1889 (218).
LIT: *AJ*, July 1883, p217; *Athenaeum*, 16 June 1883, p770; A.M. Reynolds, *The Life and Work of Frank Holl*, 1912, pp226–7 & see 283–4, 289–90, 294; see Geoffrey Agnew, *Agnew's 1817–1967*, pp23–38.
STUDY: Study of head and shoulders; oil on canvas, 23 × 20 in; Thos. Agnew & Sons. Repr: *Country Life*, 16 June 1966, p1577; *Agnew's*, 1967, p31.

Holl's success as a portrait painter was so great that the pressure of commissions finally killed him. When he died, he was, in the words of Harry Quilter's obituary notice, "beyond all comparison the most popular of our living portrait-painters", with a reputation that challenged and held its own in portraiture with those of Millais and Watts. His portrait of the veteran engraver *Samuel Cousins* at the 1879 RA (now Tate), made an extraordinary impression on the critics, the public and, most importantly, on potential patrons and, as Holl's daughter wrote in her biography, "commissions literally rained in" on the artist. He had shown one portrait in 1878, and another besides the Cousins in 1879; between then and his death nine years later in 1888, he painted the phenomenal total of 198 portraits, 61 of which were shown at the Academy, and a further 24 at the Grosvenor Gallery. Only two were of women; all the rest were imposing formal portraits of the great men of the day. *The Times*, writing of Holl's portraits in the 1883 RA, said:

> "The characteristic of his portraits is their strength and generally their truth. He seems to seize and grasp the character of his sitter, and to stamp it on the canvas in a way which shows that unmistakeable mastery. There is nothing poetical in his portraits, as there is so often in those of Mr. Watts; they depend for their success on sheer forcible painting, together with their dramatic suggestiveness." (5 May 1883, p12).

Amongst the portraits most admired after the Cousins were those of *John Bright* (RA 1883, Birmingham), the *Duke of Cleveland* (RA 1886, private collection, Mass., USA), *Gladstone* (RA 1888, Hawarden) and what was acclaimed as his masterpiece, the *Earl Spencer* (RA 1888, Althorp). Of the latter, M.H. Spielmann wrote in Holl's obituary in the *Magazine of Art*:

> "... it is one of the most truthful, the most manly, vigorous, and subtle of all his portraits; being wanting, moreover, in that rather exaggerated contrast of light and shade with which – studio-lighting aiding – he often invested the faces of his sitters. It constitutes, in short, the nearest approach in point of conception, execution, and feeling, to the works of his idol, Velasquez; retaining always his own unmistakeable individuality of style and method."

Holl recorded in his journal that he conceived it in "my Rembrandt effect", it was anyway acclaimed at the RA in the summer of his death as his greatest work to date.

It was William Agnew who had been instrumental in the commission, and he had himself already sat to Holl for a portrait, exhibited here, which, though it had excited no particular attention when shown at the 1883 RA along with seven other Holl portraits, was pronounced 'Natural and easy in pose' (*AJ*) and 'a first-rate likeness' (*Athenaeum*). William Agnew was a hugely influential figure in the Victorian art world and dominated three decades from 1861, when he and his brother formally took over on the retirement of their father Thomas Agnew, the founder. As dealers, the fortunes of Agnew's were founded on the elder Thomas Agnew's inspired decision to deal in contemporary art; William pursued this policy, and became the pivot of many artists' careers, organising commissions and sales with extraordinary energy. In the background of this portrait can be seen *The Wayfarers*, an important painting by Fred Walker, a particular protegé of Agnew's. William Agnew had an exceptionally acute perception of what made a good – and saleable – picture: the stories in artists' autobiographies of the period are legion describing his swift moves to secure paintings in the teeth of competition. One of his unsuccessful but typical bids was for Elizabeth Thompson's *Roll Call* (cat. 56) at the 1874 RA; she records that Thomas Agnew had offered the then owner of the picture anything he asked and was refused; William Agnew came through the melée of admirers at the Private View and, wrote the artist:

> "for enthusiasm . . . beat them all . . . [he] spoke in such expressions of admiration that his voice positively shook, and he said that, having missed purchasing this work, he would feel 'proud and happy' if I would paint him one, the time, subject and price, whatever it might be, being left entirely to me." (Lady Butler, *An Autobiography*, 1922, p109).

The secret of Agnew's success seems to have been his genuine and very Victorian capacity for absolute emotional involvement in the work from which he made his living. Holl's journal records his reaction on seeing the completed portrait of Gladstone:

> "Agnew afterwards was *truly*, quite hysterical, and real tears came into his eyes, and rolled down his cheeks, as he spoke of the impression this head made upon him."

Despite his hard-headed and brilliant business abilities which put the firm at the head of Victorian art dealers in both contemporary painting and Old Masters, Agnew was clearly also a sympathetic and imaginative individual with whom both artists and collectors could establish a successful and fruitful working relationship.

Holl's success in portraiture completely overwhelmed his earlier work which, along with that of Fildes and Herkomer, had led the new wave of social realism in the 1870s, founded on their work for the *Graphic* and other illustrated magazines. The best known of these were *No Tidings from the Sea* (RA 1870, Royal Collection), commissioned by Queen Victoria when she failed to buy from the owner Holl's 1869 RA success. *The Lord gave and the Lord hath taken away*, and further tragic subjects like '*I am the resurrection and the life*' (RA 1872, Leeds), *Her Firstborn* (RA 1876, Dundee), and *Newgate: committed for trial* (RA 1878, Royal Holloway College). Though often criticised by reviewers for their morbid subject-matter, the paintings, and the engravings after them, made Holl's reputation with the public.

Thos. Agnew & Sons Ltd.

James Clarke Hook, 1819–1907,
ARA 1850, RA 1860–1907

23 **Hearts of Oak** 1875

oil on canvas, $37\frac{1}{2} \times 56\frac{1}{2}$ in
INSCR: J.C.H. (monogram) 1875

PROV: George Orme, The Manor House, Sutton, Surrey; his sale, Christie's, 25 May 1895 (31) bt. Tooth (£777); George McCulloch, his sale, Christie's, 29 May 1913 (150) bt. Wallis (£357); purchased by Nottingham, 1913.
EXH: RA 1875 (47); McCulloch Coll., RA Winter 1909 (239).
LIT: *AJ*, July 1875, p217; *Athenaeum*, 9 Jan, p59, 1 May 1875, p591; Blackburn, *RA Notes*, 1875, p8; *Graphic*, 15 May 1875, p474; *ILN*, 22 May 1875, p486; Ruskin, *RA Notes 1875*, *Works*, 1903–12, XIV, pp265, 281; *Times*, 1 May 1875, p12; F.G. Stephens, 'J.C. Hook, RA: His Life and Work', *Art Annual*, 1888, p30; A.L. Baldry, 'The Collection of George McCulloch, Esq.', *AJ*, July, 1897, p219, repr. p218; *Nottingham Cat.*, 1926 (124), repr. facing p14; A.J. Hook, *Life of James Clarke Hook, RA*, 1929–32, III, Appendix C; Denise Bethel, *James Clarke Hook, RA, 1819–1907*, Courtauld Institute of Art Unpublished MA Report, 1975.

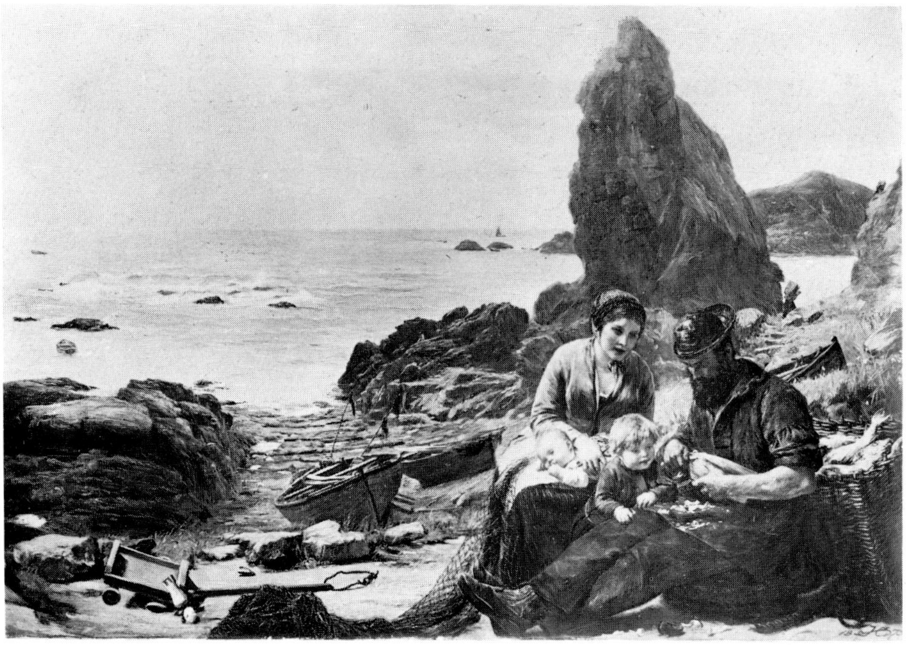

Every summer for half-a-century the public could rely on finding the statutory three or four Hooks in the Academy: his work was of a consistently reliable quality and was, from '*Luff, boy*' in 1859, absolutely recognisable. The coast scenes, populated with sturdy fisherfolk picturesquely at work, were to be found in most private collections of any size and went through the salerooms at prices that often approached those of Stanfield in his heyday. F.G. Stephens considered his popularity lay in the opportunities for escapism that his apparently realist, but in fact much idealised, scenes offered the audience:

> "This is he, who, if the giving of abundant delight be a source of happiness to men, must needs be one of the most richly blessed of his generation. Apart from all artistic and technical considerations, this has been pre-eminently Hook's good fortune. Thousands of townsmen, jaded of eye, of heart, of spirit, have, like myself stood before his pictures and seemed to hear the far-off sea grow louder day by day, and thanked him in their thoughts for those splendid previsions of the sunlight and the coast." (F.G. Dumas, *Illustrated biographies of modern artists*, 1882, James Clarke Hook by F.G. Stephens, p222).

Hearts of Oak was one of the four Hooks at the 1875 RA: it was a good year with Elizabeth Thompson's *Quatre Bras*, Herkomer's *Last Muster* (cat. 20) and Long's *Babylonian Marriage Market* (Royal Holloway College), so it was hardly surprising that the picture attracted only averagely complimentary notices. It had, however, the signal virtue of being one of the four pictures whose presence so delighted Ruskin that he was persuaded to take up his RA Notes once more:

> "I thought I should be able to write an entirely good-humoured, and therefore, in all likelihood, practically useful, sketch of the socially pleasant qualities of modern English painting, which were not enough acknowledged in my former essays." (*Works*, XIV, p265).

But he was driven back to criticism by the more important paintings and dealt querulously with the picture:

> "Beautiful, but incomplete; the painter wants more heart of oak himself. If he had let all his other canvases alone and finished this, the year's work would have been a treasure for all the centuries; while now it is only 'the Hook of the season'.
>
> "It looks right and harmonious in its subdued sunshine. But it isn't. Why should mussel-shells cast a shadow, but boats and hats none! Why should toy-carts and small stones have light and dark sides, and tall rocks none! I fancy all the pictures this year must have been painted in the sunless east wind; and only a bit of sunshine put in here and there out of the painter's head, where he thought it would do nobody any harm." (*Works*, XIV, p281).

The other critics found it typical, and admired the family group, while F.G. Stephens, a close friend of the artist, gave his usual generous support in the *Athenaeum*:

> "Everybody turns with satisfaction to Mr. Hook's pictures. Indeed, they satisfy at once the technical critic and those who love art for the pleasure that art affords. In the famous RA's pictures we have Venetian art, in one of its freshest and most original forms, translated into forcible English; the art of Bonifazio, crisp, wholesome, *riant*, and pure as it could be, brought at once, and independently, to illustrate the ways and moods of British fishermen and country people . . ."

Most of the reviews mentioned that the scene was taken on the Aberdeenshire coast, a piece of information stored away from January that year when Stephens published his regular announcement of Hook's RA pictures for the year; it was, effectively, a press-release system in operation and had been practised most successfully in the previous decade by the *Art Journal* for Mr. and Mrs. Ward.

Hearts of Oak was never considered to be amongst Hook's greatest pictures – it was not, for instance, included with the nineteen Hooks shown after the artists's death at the 1908 Winter RA. It was a well-received, typical Hook, with the advantage of a good title – it was exhibited with the lines from *King John* (Act II, sc1):

> ". . . that England, hedged in with the main,
> that water-walled bulwark, still secure
> And confident from foreign purposes."

The appeal to national sentiment was calculated and successful, as were the many other uses of the phrase by authors of verses, popular songs and plays. Dictionaries of quotations offer, for example, David Garrick's play 'Hearts of Oak', and S.J. Arnold's 'Death of Nelson', amongst others all recycling lines about ships of British oak and men with hearts of oak.

The first great success of Hook's career came with '*Luff Boy*' (RA 1859, private collection, USA); it was always the title offered as an identity badge after Hook's name. It looks, from reproductions, awkwardly drawn, with some problems in foreshortening, but it has a dramatic viewpoint – the spectator is placed in the boat itself and the horizon-line is near the top of the canvas – giving it great immediacy and a vivid documentary quality that was probably responsible for winning critics and public alike.

Hook was a committed socialist, a fiercely anti-clerical Nonconformist, and farmed his own land in Surrey so expertly that he and his family were virtually self-sufficient. G.D. Leslie gives some delightful anecdotes about the artist while very full accounts of his career to 1888 are given in the Art Annual by Stephens and A.H. Palmer's five long *Portfolio* articles. The three privately-printed volumes by his son are biographical but are uninformative on the paintings.

Castle Museum, Nottingham

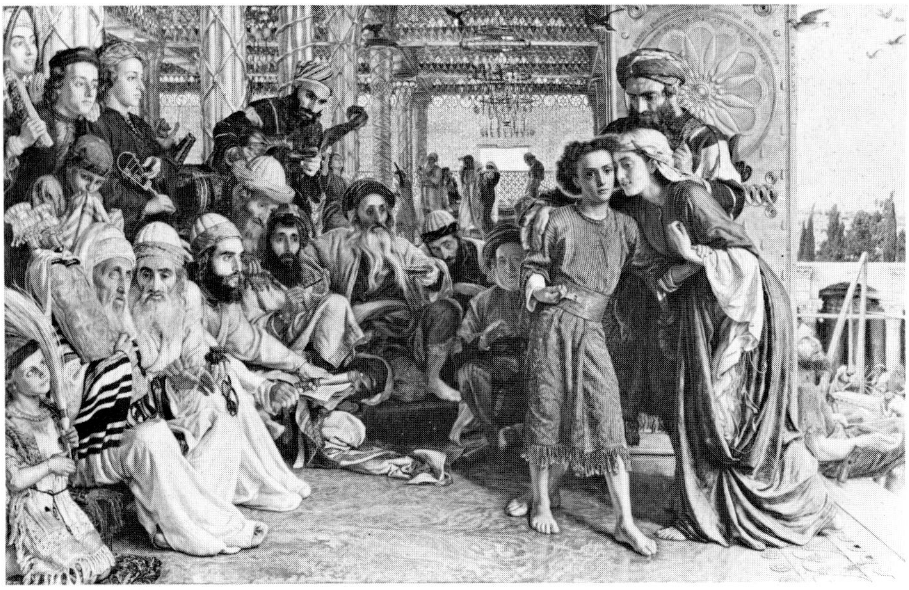

William Holman Hunt, 1827–1910, om (1905), dcl (1905)

24 The Finding of the Saviour in the Temple

line engraving by Auguste Blanchard
$20\frac{3}{4} \times 29\frac{1}{4}$ in
publ. Gambart & Co., November 1867.

lit: William Holman Hunt, *Pre-Raphaelitism and the Pre-Raphaelite Brotherhood*, 1905, II, pp187–97; Mary Bennett, Catalogue of the *William Holman Hunt Exhibition*, Liverpool and London, 1969 (31); Jeremy Maas, *Gambart: Prince of the Victorian Art World*, 1975, pp114–22, 126–27, 131–32, 176, 204–05.

Two-and-a-half years before the publication of the engraving of *The Finding of the Saviour in the Temple* was first announced on 2 April 1863, Gambart, the most powerful art dealer of the day, had orders for it amounting to 10,000 guineas. This gives some idea of the popularity the picture had gained during its exhibition, and of the press and advertising coverage it had received. By the time the engraving went on sale in November 1867 the number of subscribers had greatly increased. Even so, the amount of prints issued was prodigious, even by Victorian standards: 10,000 prints at 5 and 3 guineas each, 1,000 artist's proofs at 15 guineas, 1,000 before letters proofs at 12 guineas and 1,000 lettered proofs at 8 guineas. It is thought that Gambart made a profit from the sale of the engravings of £5,000.

The picture, as well as the engraving, was a sensation in the mid-Victorian art scene, and not in monetary terms alone. It was the first major work Hunt undertook in the Middle East, where he had gone in order to apply Pre-Raphaelite principles of truth to nature to scriptural subjects. Syria had not vastly changed since Biblical times, and Hunt therefore felt that by studying the country and its inhabitants he could create a sacred art relevant to his age, in which realism and symbolism were inextricably woven. He told Egg before his departure in January 1854 that "my desire is very strong to make more tangible Jesus Christ's history and teaching" (Hunt, I, p349).

The picture presented many more difficulties than he had envisaged when he arrived in Jerusalem in June 1854; and it was not finally completed until April 1860, in England. With the didactic and religious streak in Hunt went a shrewd business brain, and he calculated that a sum of not less than 5,500 guineas would recover his outlay and enable him to return to the East to paint another scriptural subject. This was an unheard of sale price at the time, but Hunt was confident that the purchaser would recoup it from exhibition fees and the sale of the engraving. Dickens advised Hunt to hold out for his price, but suggested that Gambart pay him in instalments. As William Michael Rossetti made clear in a letter to William Bell Scott of 14 May 1860, this was in fact done; the initial instalment of £3,000 was to be followed by "the remainder in bills at eighteen months" (W. Bell Scott, *Autobiographical Notes*, 1902, II, p58). Gambart's reputation was greatly enhanced by the purchase of both the picture and copyright; he made £4,000 from exhibition fees alone. The showing of the work on its own – then an unusual and daring undertaking – commenced at the German Gallery in April 1860, and soon attracted 800 to 1,000 visitors a day, each paying a shilling entry fee (the same as for the Royal Academy).

The number of visitors was more than double Hunt's expectations, but still more money was to be made from the sale of the engraving, as both he and Gambart realised. Years of toil had produced the picture, and the importance of obtaining a first-class engraving was not to be underestimated. Hunt stated that, "Gambart (in November 1860) employed Signor Morelli to make a drawing of the picture in black and white for the use of his engraver, and it was a wondrously exact and elaborate transcript of the original. To make the tracing for him, which I could not leave to other hands, I often was at the gallery at half-past five in the morning". (Hunt, II, pp193–94).

The engraver, Auguste Blanchard, was paid 2,000 guineas and Gambart expected him to take four years to produce the proofs. It was not until the autumn of 1867, that Hunt, returning to England from Florence via Paris, went with Gambart to see Blanchard and the engraving with which the artist was greatly satisfied. A key plate was issued to accompany the print; this elucidated the elaborate symbolism and emphasised the care taken by Hunt to obtain accuracy of detail in the architecture and costumes. The more educated of the purchasers, and especially those of the Evangelical persuasion, would have connected the scene in the courtyard of the builders selecting the cornerstone of the Temple with the figure of Christ himself, the cornerstone of the New Dispensation. Though largely forgotten today, the practice of studying the Bible for types of the Saviour was extremely common at the time. Hunt, through his reading of *Modern Painters*, volume II (1846), with its analysis of Tintoretto's *Annunciation* in the Scuola di San Rocco, had realised that prefigurative, or typological, symbolism could be used in painting to obtain a unique and indissoluble blend of realism and symbolism. The elaborate frame, upon which Hunt was working in February 1859, continued the symbolism within the picture: for instance, on the left, the serpent of the Mosaic law is intertwined with the Cross.

The popularity of both picture and engraving was surely due to this way of treating a sacred subject, which could thus appeal to the spectator on different levels. It could be accepted simply as an attempt on an historical or archaeological plane to show what the finding of the Saviour in the Temple was actually like at the time, and therefore to deepen the spectator's empathy with the life of Christ; while on another level, the use of typological symbolism added a further dimension for those able to understand.

J.E.B.

Walker Art Gallery, Liverpool

SIR EDWIN LANDSEER, 1802–1873, ARA 1826, RA 1831, KT. 1850

25 The Old Shepherd's Chief Mourner 1837

oil on canvas, 18 × 24 in

PROV: John Sheepshanks, 1837, by whom presented to the South Kensington Museum, 1857.
EXH: RA 1837 (112); International Exh. Dublin 1865 (19); RA Bicentenary 1968–9 (231); *British Romantic Painting*, Paris 1972 (155).
LIT: *Blackwood's*, Sept 1837, p337; *Literary Gazette*, 13 May 1837, p306; Ruskin, *Modern Painters I, Works*, III, pp88–9; *The Early Works of Sir Edwin Landseer, RA. A brief sketch of the life of the artist, illustrated by sixteen of his most popular works*, 1869, pp57–8, pl.XIII; *Landseer Gallery*, 1871, pl.14; James Dafforne, *Pictures by Sir Edwin Landseer RA, with descriptions and a biographical sketch of the painter*, 1873, pp16–18; Algernon Graves, *Catalogue of the Works of the late Sir Edwin Landseer, RA*, 1876, pp20, 47; C.S. Mann, *Landseer*, 1877, p110 & repr; Cosmo Monkhouse, *The Studies of Sir Edwin Landseer, RA, with a history of his art-life*, 1877, pp66–8; M.F. Sweetser, *Landseer*, Boston, 1879, pp68–70; Cunningham, 1880, III, p386; F.G. Stephens, *Sir Edwin Landseer*, 3rd ed., 1881, p77, repr facing p48; *English Art in the Public Galleries of London*, 1888, II, p165 & repr; Redgrave, 1890, p381; James A. Manson, *Sir Edwin Landseer, RA*, 1902, pp89–91, repr betw. pp80–1; Bryan's, p171, repr facing p172; Reynolds, 1966, pp15, 27, pl.8; etc.
STUDIES: *Sketch-book with sketch of the Shepherd's Chief Mourner*, &c, 1825 (sic) – 16 pages, Landseer sale, Christie's, 8 May 1874 (1001). *Sketch for Chief Mourner*, coll. Marchioness of Londonderry, sold Christie's, 20 Apr 1885 (55) bt. Nathan (£1 18s).
ENGR: by B.P. Gibbon, 1838, Jacob Bell (two sizes, one with embellishments), F. Hollyer, 1869 (Beck (18)), S.G. Hunt, 1884.

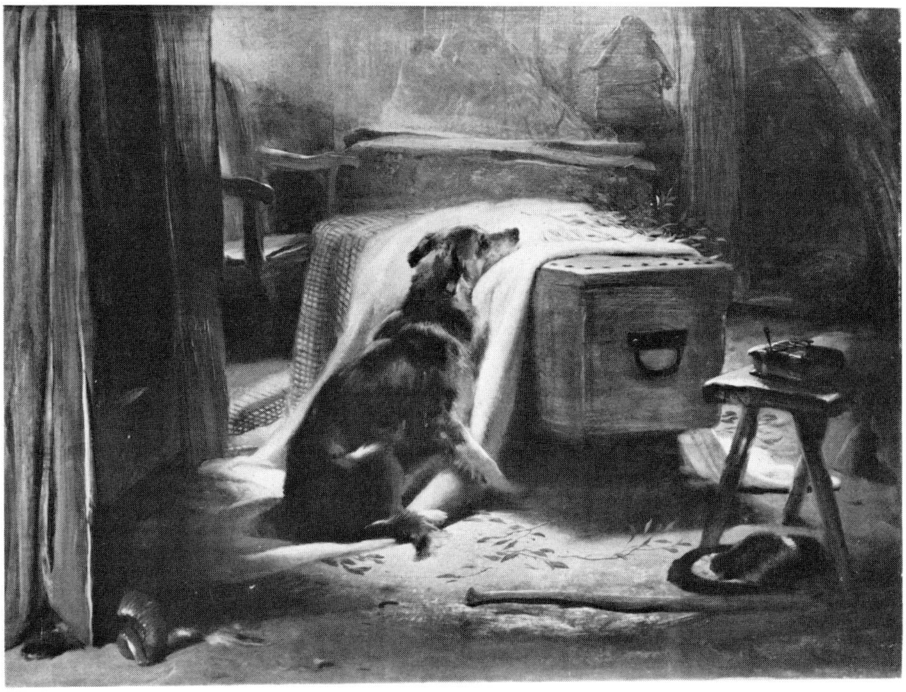

The 1837 RA opened as usual at the beginning of May; on 20 June Victoria succeeded to the throne and Landseer's first great popular success was, appropriately, his first properly Victorian picture. *The Old Shepherd's Chief Mourner* was well received by the critics:

> "No stronger appeal to the feelings of humanity in favour of the brute creature, more especially of that faithful creature the dog, can be made than will be found in this touching performance. As a work of art, it claims our admiration; as an expression of sentiment, our sympathy."

wrote the *Literary Gazette*, and the *Athenaeum*, though it began its description by calling it the least of Landseer's animal pictures, felt especially for:

> "the patient mournful dog, who crouches beside [the coffin], with a love strong as death. This is one of the most simply pathetic things in the Exhibition – though nothing more than an animal and 'still life' – and we looked upon it long and sadly."

Blackwood's was perhaps the most fanciful:

> "We wish [Landseer] were chiefly the painter of fables. His animals, especially his dogs, are of the fabulous days of Aesop, when they could speak, and in this he is poetical. How pathetically beautiful [it] is . . . There is honest grief. What a tale of bygone familiarity, duty, and mutual affection, does that creature's head exhibit, watching at the coffin of his master . . ."

This last came nearest to anticipating the tenor of Ruskin's argument when, in a famous passage in the first volume of *Modern Painters* (1843), he used *The Old Shepherd's Chief Mourner* as an example of a great and poetic picture. The description appears in his 'definition of Greatness in Art', in which he declared that as grammar and language are to poetry so are technical painting skills to art; what transforms a painting into a work of art is its content, thus producing the simple formula:

> "the greatest picture is that which conveys to the mind of the spectator the greatest number of the greatest ideas." (*Works*, III, p92).

Although Rubens, Rembrandt, Cimabue and Giotto, amongst others, are quoted as great artists, only the Landseer is treated at length. He called it

> "one of the most perfect poems or pictures (I use the words as synonymous) which modern times have seen: . . . Here the exquisite execution of the glossy and crisp hair of the dog, the bright sharp touching of the green bough beside it, the clear painting of the wood of the coffin and the folds of the blanket, are language – language clear and expressive in the highest degree. But the close pressure of the dog's breast against the wood, the convulsive clinging of the paws, which has dragged the blanket off the trestle, the total powerlessness of the head laid, close and motionless, upon its folds, the fixed and tearful fall of the eye in its utter hopelessness, the rigidity of repose which marks that there has been no motion nor change in the trance of agony since the last blow was struck on the coffin-lid, the quietness and gloom of the chamber, the spectacles marking the place where the Bible was last closed, indicating how lonely has been the life, how unwatched the departure, of him who is now laid solitary in his sleep; – these are all thoughts – thoughts by which the picture is separated at once from hundreds of equal merit, as far as mere painting goes, by which it ranks as a work of high art, and stamps its author, not as the neat imitator of the texture of a skin, or the fold of a drapery, but as the Man of Mind."

Almost every book on Landseer in the nineteenth century quotes at least part of this passage and its influence on Landseer's reputation and on the success of the picture itself was clearly most significant. *The Old Shepherd's Chief Mourner* was first engraved in 1838 and repeatedly later and became one of the best-loved prints of the century. It established Landseer as the leading animal painter in direct succession to James Ward, whose popularity he far exceeded, earning him such titles as 'the Shakespeare of the World of Dogs'. Dafforne in 1873 accounted for this popularity:

> "Animal-painters there have been, and are, both in England and on the Continent – artists whose works are held in high estimation, and deservedly so; but their pictures want the peculiar charm which is characteristic of him – the elevation of the animal, and especially of the dog, into something that closely approximates to human nature in its generous sympathies . . . [Landseer's] pictures, independent of their merits as works of art, appeal to the tastes of thousands of our countrymen and countrywomen: nationally, we love the race of domestic animals, and are interested in everything that relates to them, and Landseer has presented them to us in their most attractive aspects." (p3).

The pendant to the *Old Shepherd's Chief Mourner*, *The Shepherd's Grave*, was also painted in 1837 but was not shown until the Manchester Art Treasures in 1857; it belonged to William Wells of Redleaf, Landseer's principal early patron, whose famous collection was at least as well known as Sheepshanks'.

Landseer painted most of the rest of his subsequently famous and hugely popular doggy pictures in the years immediately after the *Old Shepherd's Chief Mourner*. Amongst these, two of the best-known are now in the Tate: *A Distinguished Member of the Humane Society* (RA 1838) a Newfoundland dog, and *Dignity and Impudence* (1839) a noble bloodhound and a small white Scotch terrier at the entrance of their kennel. It was these, together with his first successful dog picture, *Suspense* (BI 1834), a bloodhound waiting outside a door for his master, a knight whose mailed gloves are on the table, that provided the prototypes for later Victorian animal painters like Briton Riviere (Landseer's chief successor), John Charles Dollman, and many others.

Victoria and Albert Museum

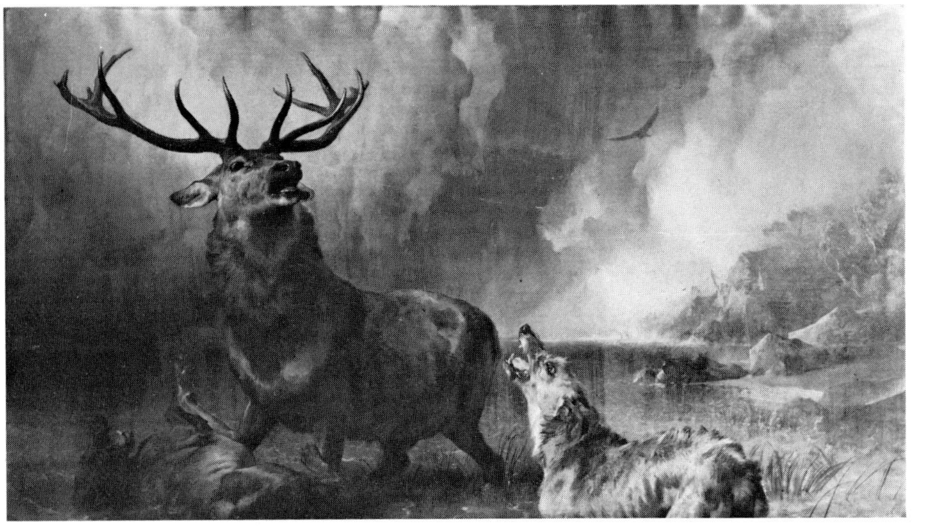

Sir Edwin Landseer

26 Stag at Bay 1846

oil on canvas, $60\frac{1}{4} \times 106\frac{1}{2}$ in

PROV: commissioned by the Marquess of Breadalbane (1796–1862); Lady E. Pringle, by 1874; Edward Cecil Guinness, 1st Earl of Iveagh.
EXH: RA 1846 (165); Manchester Art Treasures 1857 (435); *Landseer Exh.*, RA Winter 1874 (234); RA Winter 1901 (77).
LIT: *Art Union*, June 1846, p176; *Athenaeum*, 9 May 1846, p479; *ILN*, 9 May, p311, 16 May 1846, p319; *Literary Gazette*, 9 May 1846, p432; *Times*, 6 May 1846, p5; Dafforne, 1873, p62, pl.19; Graves, 1876, pp28, 49; Monkhouse, 1877, p80; Sweetser, 1879, pp101–2; Cunningham, 1880, III, p387; Stephens, 1881, p90, repr facing p84; Manson, 1902, p138; *DNB*; Reynolds, 1966, p14.
ENGR: by Thomas Landseer, 1848, Charles Mottram, 1853, George Zobel, 1866, etc.
STUDY: *Stag at Bay*, chalk [study for the large picture?], Lady Cosmo Russell sale, Christie's, 14 June 1884 (28) bt. Agnew (£30 9s).

Stag at Bay and *The Monarch of the Glen* were Landseer's two most famous later paintings; they appealed to the national sporting instinct, with overtones in the case of stag-hunting of vast Scottish baronial estates, and a royal, if not positively mediaeval, way of life. Landseer understood the psychology of it all very well; in a letter to the Earl of Ellesmere in 1837 he wrote,

> ". . . There is something in the toil and trouble, the wild weather and savage scenery that makes butchers of us all. Who does not glory in the death of a fine stag? on the spot – when in truth he ought to be ashamed of the assassination. I quite agree with your Lordship, there are many people one could shoot with greater pleasure and greater justice. Still, with all my respect for the animal's inoffensive character – my love of him *as a subject for the pencil* gets the better of such tenderness – a creature always picturesque and *never* ungraceful is too great a property to sacrifice to common feelings of humanity . . ." (whole letter quoted in cat. of *Landseer Exh.*, RA 1961 (152)).

Most of the reviewers and Landseer's biographers responded to the depiction of the stag as the noble victim of man's inhumanity:

> ". . . Landseer . . . again astonishes by the marvels of his manipulation, dashing in more truth and nature with one bold sweep of his brush than some minute artist will produce (or, perchance, prevent) with a score or two. What a tale of sorrow is written in the countenance of the *Stag at Bay*! It is the perfection of brute-eloquence, which calls on the most unfeeling of hunters to sympathise. Then with what vigour does the strong hair grow from the back of the dog! The dark watery sky, all pregnant with rain, hangs in gloomy accompaniment to the expression of animal grief. One may almost hear the drops begin to patter upon the water in the background, so lowly, blackly, and intensely does the weight of vapour press down upon it." (*Times*).

The picture represented the opposite type of Landseer's work to the dog-pictures: ever since the early pictures epitomised by the unpleasant *The Cat's Paw* (BI 1824), Landseer had had great success with scenes of sporting carnage, with works like *The Hunting of Chevy Chase* (RA 1826, Birmingham) and *The Otter Speared* (RA 1844, Newcastle). The Queen's first commission was given in 1839 and Landseer became the chronicler of the royal family's sporting and holiday activities (see cat. *This Brilliant Year*, RA 1977). His position was thus secured and he remained the most popular artist in this country until his death in 1873, despite a depressive illness which increasingly restricted and sometimes halted the work of his later years. Homage from abroad was led by Rosa Bonheur and Landseer's reputation, helped by the wide sale of engravings (many of them by his brother) after his works. As early as 1846, the *Art Union* annotated its complimentary review of *Stag at Bay* with some impressive figures:

> "It is worthy of remark, as a circumstance to excite no little surprise in England, and perfect astonishment on the Continent, that for the four pictures painted by Mr. Edwin Landseer this year, he received nearly seven thousand pounds – i.e., £2400 for the paintings, and £4450 for the "copyrights": the copyrights of the *Peace* and *War* [both Tate, destroyed in flood, 1928] were purchased for £2650, by Mr. Alderman Moon; that of the *Refreshment*, for £1000, by Messrs. Henry Graves and Co; and that of *The Stag at Bay*, for £800 (with a share of the profits), by Mr. M'Lean. It is, we imagine, utterly impossible that the sale of the engravings can be such as to return so prodigious an outlay. But, in order to effect this purpose, immense exertions will be made by the publishers; whose attention, and whose capital, will thus be drawn off from the issue of works of loftier motive and worthier purpose."

The publishers more than recouped their initial outlay and Landseer's fortune was founded on the sale of copyrights: his estate was declared at £200,000 in 1876 (see Reitlinger, 1961, pp93–5, 105–7) and Landseers going through the salerooms during the artist's lifetime achieved large prices from 1860 onwards, with major works fetching £3000–£4000. In 1881, for instance, Holloway bought *Man Proposes, God Disposes* (RA 1864, Royal Holloway College) for £6615, and *The Monarch of the Glen* (RA 1851, John Dewar & Sons Ltd) was sold by Agnew's to Mr. Barratt of Pear's Soap for £8000. The record, however, was held by the *Otter Speared* (also known as *The Otter Hunt*, Newcastle, see above) for which Baron Albert Grant was said to have paid £10,000; according to the *DNB*, though it gives no details, £10,000 was also paid for *Stag at Bay*.

The first modern showing of Landseer's work was at the RA in 1961; and another exhibition, *Landseer and his world*, was at Sheffield in 1972; a general biography by Campbell Lennie was recently published, and a catalogue is currently being prepared by Richard Ormond.

Private Collection

BENJAMIN WILLIAMS LEADER. 1831–1923, ARA 1883, RA 1898

27 February Fill Dyke 1881

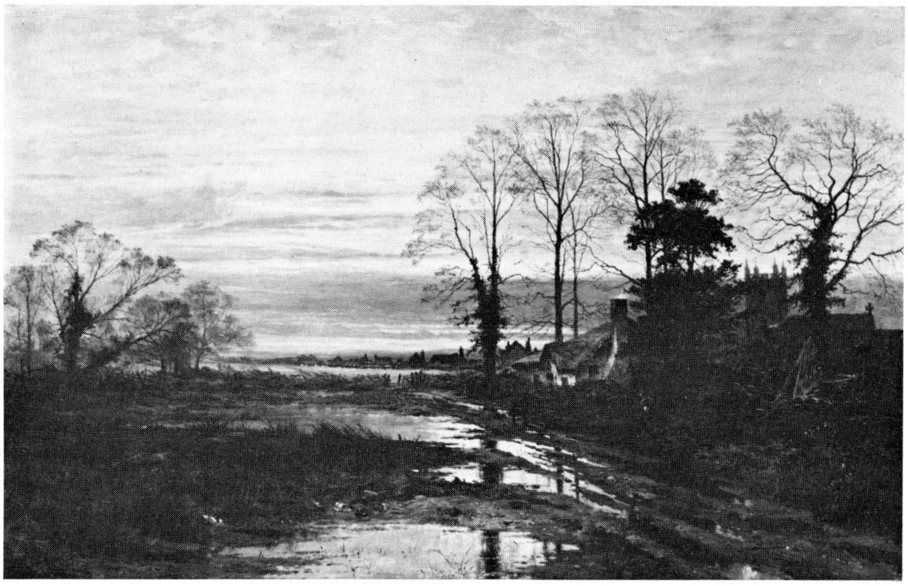

oil on canvas, 30¼ × 48¼ in
INSCR: B.W. Leader. 1881

PROV: (?) Walter Towne, by 1882; (?) Alexander Young, by 1883; John E. Yates, by whom bequeathed to Manchester, 1934.
EXH: (?) Worcester 1882 (111); (?) Whitechapel 1883 (72); Cardiff 1939–45; Mansfield 1949.
LIT: (all references are to the RA 1881 picture unless otherwise stated). *AJ*, June 1881, p186; *Athenaeum*, 14 June 1881, p754; *Graphic*, 21 May 1881, p503; *ILN*, 11 June 1881, p579; *Mag. of Art*, 1881, p398; *Times*, 24 May 1881, p5; Armstrong, Manchester, 1887, p14; *AJ*, July 1887, p250; Hodgson, 1887, pp89–90; Lewis Lusk, 'The Life and Work of B.W. Leader, RA', *Art Annual*, 1901, p6, repr; *DNB*, 1937; Kenneth Clark, *Landscape into Art*, 1949, pp89–90, pl.79; *Reynolds*, 1966, pp155, 177, pl.11; Bell, 1967, pp59, 79, pl.92; Maas, 1969, p228; *Manchester Concise Catalogue*, 1976, I, p114, repr.
VERSION: exhibited picture; oil on canvas, 47 × 71½ in. Prov: J.E. Wilson; bequeathed by Mrs. Wilson to Birmingham, 1914. Exh: RA 1881 (42); Manchester Jubilee 1887 (23).
ENGR: (after the RA 1881 picture) Théophile Chauvel, etching, 17¼ × 23⅝ in, publ. Arthur Tooth & Sons, 1884.

By the end of the century Leader's *February Fill Dyke* had achieved the kind of popular immortality that in British landscape art had previously only been granted to Constable. The title is taken from the old country rhyme in which white of course is snow and rain is black, rendered by James Orchard Halliwell in 1849 (*Popular Rhymes & Nursery Tales of England*, republ. 1970) as:

> February fill the dyke,
> Be it black or be it white;
> But if it be white,
> It's the better to like.

Leader stated (Lusk, p6) that the scene is of a November evening after rain. The painting, now in Birmingham (of which the picture shown here is a reduced version) was received at the 1881 RA with no more than a paragraph of praise from each reviewer, but almost all were agreed that it was the artist's best picture to date. The *Graphic* thought he had

> "produced nothing so artistically complete . . . It is remarkable not less for its comprehensive truth of effect than for the fidelity with which the individual facts of nature are rendered."

The *Art Journal*, too, commended its truth in the rendering of 'a thoroughly English landscape' after rain, and the *Athenaeum* thought it far more ambitious and stronger than a neighbouring picture by Hale but also 'far less refined and artistic'. It found:

> "The illumination, which is the subject, is very happy indeed. The execution is more dexterous than searching, and would bear refining."

The Times too was double-edged:

> ". . . a large, fine landscape in Mr. Leader's usual style – very fine in general atmospheric effect and in its rendering of the wet sky and road, but rather poor in its tree-drawing, and certainly too much varnished."

The *Magazine of Art* was in revolt against what it saw as extreme forms of Ruskinian observation; it thought a landscape by Naish had

> "an intensity of brilliant detail which is no doubt apparent in nature to any exceptionally strong and long eyesight, but which to ordinary vision seems somewhat more insistent than the natural fact. Also to the literal school belongs Mr. Leader, whose *February Fill Dyke* is an exceedingly real rainy landscape with a quite illusory perspective of wet road stretching flatly away; all here is fresh in execution and exceedingly honest, the homeliness of this scene being more attractive as the subject of this artist's treatment than is the somewhat ambitious effect of his *Glyder Vawr*."

In these fairly cursory reviews intimations can already be found of the sort of criticisms that would be levelled against the painting and its type in the twentieth century by writers like Fry, Bell, and later on, Clark, but there is little to explain the particular quality in it which should have made it so captivating. When the large painting was shown at the great Manchester Jubilee exhibition in 1887, it was greeted by the *Art Journal* as already an old favourite that needed no description. To Armstrong it was simply Leader's best landscape, while Hodgson waxed lyrical:

> "B.W. Leader loves a flooded country in late November, with the dark land and the leafless trees defined against a golden sky. He paints effects which we only see occasionally; they burst upon us sometimes when we are jogging home after a day's hunting, and then we pull up suddenly and gaze as if spellbound."

Between its two showings, the subject had been handsomely etched by Chauvel in 1884; though it was published in London, Paris and in America, this alone cannot have been responsible for so much of the picture's familiarity. Lewis Lusk, in 1901, attributes Leader's election to ARA in 1883 to the showing of *February Fill Dyke* in 1881, which was capped by what he regarded as Leader's best painting, *In the evening there shall be light* of 1882. Lusk writes of the sentiment in his famous landscapes of 'rain-filled rutty roads', and of

> "His careful retention of the picturesque, his style of arranging his masses, his selection of cloud effects, his peculiarly poetic strain of the lyric order . . . there is sufficient likelihood that these qualities of his work will always ensure respect and study from many a maturing mind. They are all inherent in the national character."

This interpretation of Leader seems to have been unique to Lusk, but he does go on to write perceptively of Leader's ties to the landscape of the West Midlands derived from his boyhood by the Severn:

> ". . . he exhales the grey opalescence and soft sweet colour of Western Britain, and that in a manner which is his own . . ."

and on the amber luminosity of that landscape, perhaps the most potent factor in Leader's appeal:

> ". . . having perceived the Amber Note, even cold reason decides that it is Mr. Leader's fidelity to that quality which has given to his work much of that charm which has given, and will continue to give, him fame . . ."

Leader capitalised on a successfully realised idea and spent the rest of his career producing increasingly florid but always immediately recognisable Welsh and Worcestershire landscapes. In 1908, Phythian dismissed him in a paragraph but nevertheless allowed that his popularity was great:

> "Mr. Leader is one of the most conspicuous examples of the artist who, having made a reputation for a particular kind of work, finds himself able to repeat it year after year, even though manner becomes mannerism, and art, artificiality . . . His pleasantly composed and agreeably coloured landscapes have long made him one of the most popular of our landscape painters. He is a dexterously rapid worker, with an eye for the picturesque view. There is no sign in his works of a deep love of nature. He records something of her superficial beauty, but interprets little or nothing of her innermost spirit. His earlier work was much more subtle than his later work has been, and it was stronger in colour and fuller in tone." (p342).

In recent years *February Fill Dyke* has been called the equivalent, in landscape art, to Holman Hunt's *The Light of the World* in religious art or Millais's *Bubbles*, and there is no doubt that to a modern audience it remains one of the most famous of Victorian paintings.

City of Manchester Art Galleries

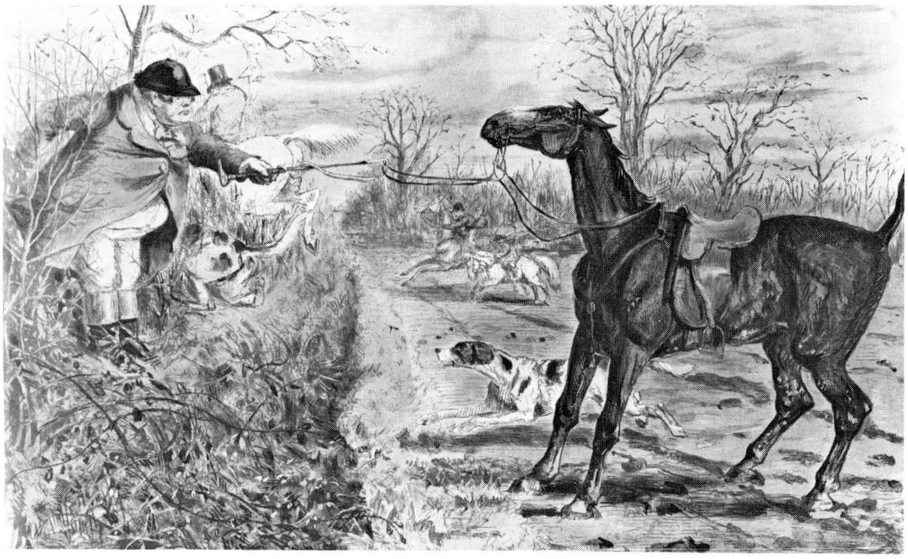

John Leech, 1817–1864

28 Mr Jorrocks (loq) "Come hup! I say – You ugly brute!" 1866
1 of set of 13, 'John Leech – His Celebrated Hunting Subjects'

chromolithograph, 14⅜ × 23½ in
Publ. Thos. Agnew & Sons, 1865.

EXH: *Ben Marshall, John Leech: a commemorative exh.*, Leicester 1967 (88).
LIT: *AJ*, Oct 1862, p211, Dec 1865, p383; L.M. Lamont, ed., *Thomas Armstrong, CB, A Memoir, 1832–1911*, 1912, pp12–14; Henry Stacy Marks, *Pen and Pencil Sketches*, 1894, I, p190; Thomas Bodkin, *The Noble Science: John Leech in the Hunting Field*, 1948, pp16–17, pl.12 & facing p.

John Leech, the great *Punch* cartoonist and illustrator of Jorrocks, died in October 1864, and the nation went into mourning:

> "It was as if something personal to every one was gone; as if a fruit we all ate and rejoiced in had vanished for ever; a something good and cheery, and to be thankful for, which came every week as sure as Thursday – never to come again." (John Brown, *North British Review*, May 1865, p216).
>
> "Suddenly there is a great blank among us, and the shadow of a great darkness . . . The death of Garrick was said to have eclipsed the gaiety of nations, and the death of Mr. Leech will touch many more hearts, both of this and other nations, than Garrick ever reached." (*Times*, 31 Oct 1864, p10).

The *Times* obituary went on to speak of the value of his drawings as social documents 'of certain phases of this Victorian era' which also reflected Leech's own personality, his love of beauty and truth in nature as well as of the ridiculous. Other obituaries in the *Cornhill* and the *Athenaeum* were equally long and genuine expressions of the extraordinary affection in which the artist was held by both his freinds and by the public. Thackeray in 1854 had remarked,

> "There is no blinking the fact that in Mr. Punch's cabinet John Leech is the right-hand man . . . The truth, the strength, the free vigour, the kind humour, the John Bull pluck and spirit of that hand are approached by no competitor." (*Quarterly Review*, Dec 1854, p82).

To all intents and purposes, Leech was *Punch* and as the magazine had a wide continental circulation, achieved international fame; the French and German satirical and comic magazines on his death produced drawings in homage to his memory and his galaxy of continental admirers included Manet, who dedicated a drawing to Leech in the early 1860s (now Williamstown, USA), Mendelssohn (see J.C. Horsley's autobiography, 1903), and, later, Van Gogh.

Leech was chronically in need of money to meet the demands of his rapacious family and, like most illustrators of the century, was also ambitious for recognition in the more elevated medium of oil. He therefore embarked on a series of oil sketches based on an ingeniously improvised method by which a lithographic enlargement of his original small drawings could be printed onto canvases and then, with the advice of Millais, painted over in oil by Leech. These hybrid creations could be as large as 24 × 34 in, and a number have survived (see, for instance, *A Brilliant Idea*, V & A). Leech showed sixty-seven of them at the Egyptian Hall, Piccadilly, in 1862; the *Art Journal* review noted that it was likely to be a profitable venture, and went on:

> "How much soever these quaint and racy conceits are relished in the pages to which they so pithily contribute, they are even yet more enjoyable by enlargement – the point of the jokes gains pungency from expansion . . . Their character and unflagging excellence has raised Mr. Leech to an eminence which he is likely to enjoy alone . . . [he] is not a caricaturist, yet he deals with the weaknesses of humanity, although rarely or never offensive to the most refined sensibility."

His drawings were commended for avoiding the 'hideous exaggerations' of Rowlandson and Hogarth, whose excellence could not disguise their coarseness, and no subsequent cartoonists 'have met all tastes, as do Mr. Leech's sketches'. The lengthy, amusing and flattering review of the exhibition in the *Times* was by Thackeray, a great friend and ally of Leech's; the prestige of writer and newspaper were great and the artist is said to have exclaimed, on reading the review, 'That's like putting a thousand pounds into my pocket! (W.P. Frith, *John Leech: His Life and Work*, 1891, II, p258). Frith records that the exhibition was indeed a great success and 'visited by thousands of admiring spectators, who left several thousand pounds behind them, . . . the room . . . was filled all day long with a laughing crowd.'

Agnew's immediately began preparing a selection of the lithographs (over which Leech had made the oil sketches) for publication. The *Art Journal* published an enthusiastic progress report on them in October 1862:

> ". . . it is . . . due to our readers that we should prepare them for the appearance of a series of engravings which certainly must command the widest popularity, as, without question, they will prove to be without rival amongst the countless productions of the lithographer's art."

They were finally published on 5 January 1865 just over two months after Leech's death, in two series: ten scenes from *Punch* entitled '*John Leech's Social Subjects, Sports and Pastimes*' and ten scenes entitled '*John Leech – His Celebrated Hunting Subjects*', at ten guineas a set. A further three hunting scenes were added in October 1866. Most of the hunting subjects were from *Punch*, whose pages had seen many such cartoons, the product of Leech's passion for hunting, but two were taken from Leech's illustrations for the sporting novels of R.S. Surtees, illustrations which had made Jorrocks a national character: *One of Multum in Parvo's 'going' days*, from *Mr. Sponge's Sporting Tour*, first published with thirteen etchings and eighty-nine woodcuts by Leech in 1853, and the lithograph exhibited here, taken from Handley Cross. The original etching for *Come hup!* is only 4¼ × 6 in, but the designs seem to have been strong enough to withstand quadrupling of the measurements. The oil sketch of this subject was No. 2 in the 1862 exhibition, and was one of the three hunting scenes added in 1866. According to Bodkin, whose 1948 volume reproduces the entire set, *Come hup!* was so popular that though Agnew's sold them singly and in sets, it was no longer available in the 1912 Agnew's catalogue. There are many Victorian recollections, like those of Stacy Marks, and, here, Thomas Armstrong that recall 'the enlarged versions of his sporting cuts, printed in colours, which were to be seen forty years ago in billiard-rooms all over the country'. Frith's biography of Leech stimulated a renewed spate of articles on the artist, all still as affectionate and fulsome as those of the 1860s. Leicester, appropriately for the hunting county, has a complete set.

Leicestershire Museums and Art Gallery

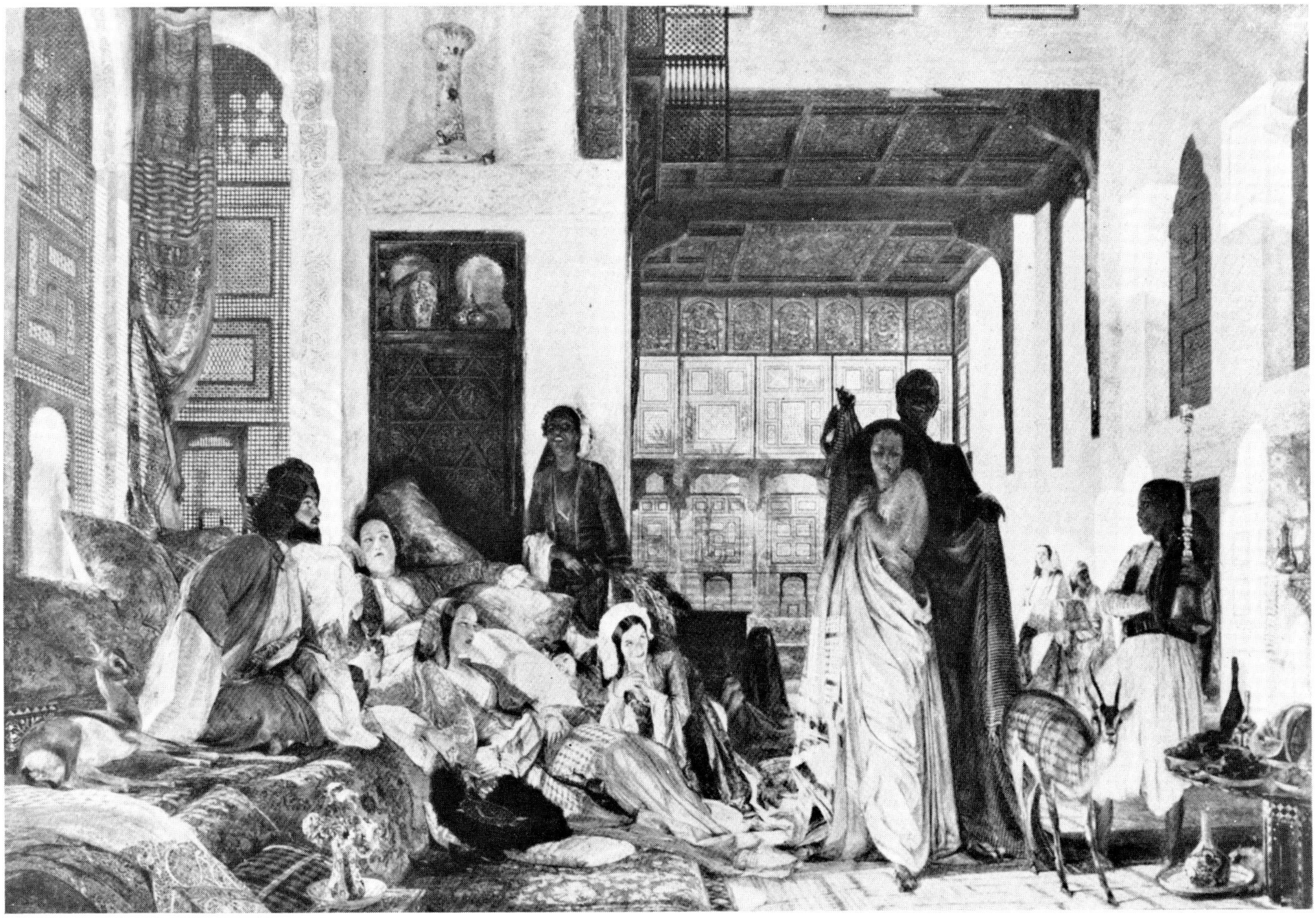

The Hhareem – the originally exhibited picture, whereabouts unknown

JOHN FREDERICK LEWIS, 1805–1876,
ARWS 1827, RWS 1829, PRWS 1855–8,
ARA 1859, RA 1865–76

29 The Hhareem 1850

watercolour and bodycolour, 18½ × 26½ in

PROV: Birket Foster, by 1891; his sale, Christie's, 28 Apr 1894 (25) bt. Strong (£183 15s); Victor Rienaecker; his sale, Christie's, 30 Nov 1923 (67) bt. Agnew (£94 5s); anon sale, Christie's, 16 July 1948 (69) bt. Agnew for V & A.
EXH: RA Winter 1891 (watercolours 144); Agnew 1922 (63); Ottawa 1965 (81); *J.F. Lewis, RA*, Newcastle 1971 (71); *John Frederick Lewis*, Guildford House Gallery, Guildford 1977 (104).
LIT: (all pre-1900 references are to the OWS 1850 exhibited original), *AJ*, June 1850, p179; *Athenaeum*, 23 Feb, p210, 4 May 1850, p480; *Critic*, 15 May 1850, p253; *ILN*, 4 May 1850, p299–300; *Times*, 1 May 1850, p8; Ruskin, letter, *Times*, 30 May 1851, *Works*, XII, p326; Edmond About, *Voyage à travers l'Exposition des Beaux-Arts*, Paris, 1855, p32; Maxime du Camp, *Les Beaux-Arts à l'Exposition Universelle de 1855*, Paris, 1855, pp317–18; Théophile Gautier, *Les Beaux-Arts en Europe, 1855*, Paris, 1857; 'British Artists XXXII: John Frederick Lewis', *AJ*, Feb 1858, pp42–3; Claude Phillips, 'John Frederick Lewis, RA', *Portfolio*, 1892, pp94–6; H.M. Cundall, 'Early Water-Colour Drawings at Messrs. Agnew's', *Studio*, May 1922, p240 & repr; Randall Davies & Basil S. Long, 'John Frederick Lewis, RA (1805–1876)', *The Old Water-Colour Society's Club Annual Vol.*, 1926, pp34–5, pl. VIII; Hugh Stokes, '*John Frederick Lewis RA*', *Walker's Quarterly*, 1929,

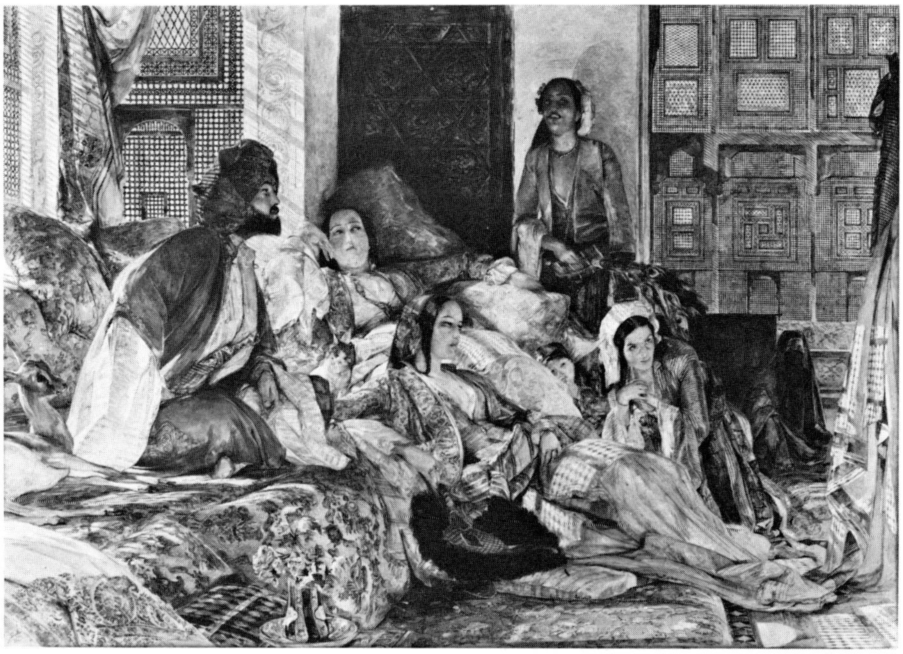

pp29, 31–3; Reynolds, 1966, pp143–4, 156; Hardie, 1968, III, p52; Maas, 1969, p92; Michael Kitson, review of Newcastle exh., *Burlington*, Dec 1971, pp761–2, pl.75.
ORIGINAL EXHIBITED VERSION: *The Hhareem*, watercolour, 35½ × 53 in; inscr. Cairo, 1849. Prov: commissioned by Joseph Arden in Cairo before 1850; his sale, Christie's, 26 Apr 1879 (84) bt. Birch (£724 10s); J.W. Birch in 1896; Mrs. Birch (anon) sale, Christie's, 11 June 1909 (195) bt. Merton (£525); untraced. Exh: Griffith's Gallery, Pall Mall, Feb 1850; OWS 1850 (147); RSA 1853 (494); Expo. Univ. Paris 1855 (1047); Guildhall 1896 (48); Franco-British 1908 (471). Repr: *Souvenir*, Franco-British, 1908.

The showing of *The Hhareem* in 1850 gave the Old Water-Colour Society what was probably its greatest popular and critical success to date. Most reviews devoted many column-inches to the picture which dominated everything else in the show. The subject was a Turkish pasha reclining on cushions, a pet gazelle at his side, his three wives to his left, a servant behind them, all looking to the right where a new African recruit to the hareem is being unveiled by a Nubian eunuch.

Recent writers on Lewis have favoured the theory that the V & A watercolour is the original exhibited work, cut down at the behest of some morally outraged Victorian, but the original work is reproduced in the *Souvenir* of the Franco-British exhibition of 1908 and there are enough minute differences (particularly in the background) between it and the V & A watercolour to confirm that the latter is a quite separate version of the left half of the original composition.

The original exhibited work was in watercolour and bodycolour and measured 35½ × 53 in. It was commissioned in Cairo by Joseph Arden, shown by him at the 1855 Paris Exposition Universelle, and bought from his collection at Christie's in 1879 by J.W. Birch in whose family it survived intact until it was sold at Christie's in 1909, still measuring the full 35½ × 53 in. It has not been seen since, but the watercolour now shown, and bought by the V & A in 1948, is apparently traceable to the watercolour owned by Birket Foster. When it was shown at the RA in the Winter of 1891 it was described as 'Interior of a room in which a pasha is seated on a divan, surrounded by his family; a slave stands behind', and was recorded as measuring 18¾ × 26¼ in. (at Birket Foster's sale in 1894 it was given as 18 × 26 in.); it was possibly a commissioned version of the respectable half of the composition, or indeed part of a version of the whole (the robes of the new hareem girl are visible at the right-hand edge and could suggest that it has been cut down). There is no apparent reason why the original exhibited picture, last seen at Christie's in 1909, should not still be in existence although it has so far proved impossible to trace.

The critical reception of the painting in 1850 rapturously articulated in print what the crowds at the exhibition were saying: the *Critic* and the *Art Journal* called it the greatest and most extraordinary watercolour they had ever seen and proceeded to detail with the greatest admiration every element in the composition save what the *Critic* and the *Athenaeum* thought were the ineptly drawn feet (of figures in the right-hand half of the composition). Once the figures had been described the greatest praise was reserved for the setting. The *Athenaeum*:

> "The apartment . . . is plain; the walls being white, with beams and supports of dark wood. The only objects within it on which the riches and taste of the owner have been lavished are the windows – one of which possesses a gorgeous enrichment of coloured glass – and the exquisitely designed and elaborated reticulations of lattice work by which they are covered to protect the room from the direct rays of the sun. Perhaps the most remarkable novelty in the conduct of the whole work is the almost miraculous perfection with which this background is designed and completed. No interior of Neefs or Steenwyk surpasses the skill with which it is wrought. The variety of delicate tones and tints spread over and ramifying all its parts – is a marvel. One of the defects in the former works of Mr. Lewis was a certain husky darkness and opacity, the consequence of his imperfect management of the 'body colour' which he has always used in profusion. No such defect is found here: – though the drawing is for the most part made up of light and silvery grey tones, all is transparent and harmonious in effect . . ."

The *Athenaeum* had already previewed the picture when it was shown in February at Griffith's in Pall Mall and tried to forestall the anticipated complaints at the risqué nature of the subject by stating their satisfaction at how

> "completely the painter has triumphed in his treatment over his elements – how he has banished everything like grossness and sensuality."

It was unqualified in its praise of Lewis' technical skill and detailing and pronounced it an unparalleled phenomenon.

The *Critic* made many of the same points and commented finally,

> "The love of precision in detail is gaining ground in England, and in no instance, perhaps, has the public yet seen it carried so far as here. The colour is harmonious and of a subdued richness: the hand has dared, and dared with success, whatsoever the eye saw, and the picture is altogether unique. May it not remain so long!"

Evidently a reference to the Pre-Raphaelites, the *Critic* here anticipates Ruskin's inclusion of Lewis as a Pre-Raphaelite in his 1851 pamphlet on the group (a view he later retracted). What was probably the most lavish and overheated praise of Ruskin's career was reserved for Lewis' *A Frank Encampment in the Desert of Mount Sinai, 1842*, (OWS 1856), Yale Center for British Art), which he ranked with the work of Veronese.

Lewis had already made a reputation as a watercolourist of mostly Spanish subjects in the late 1820s and 1830s, until he left England in 1837, reaching Egypt in 1840. He lived there in what Thackeray in 1844 described as 'the most complete Oriental fashion' (Thackeray (as the editor Fitz-Boodle), *Notes of a Journey from Cornhill to Grand Cairo by Mr. M.A. Titmarsh*, 1844). After 1841 Lewis showed no further pictures at the OWS until, under threat of having his membership withdrawn, he finally sent *The Hhareem* to London; he followed his picture home from Cairo in 1851. He was elected President of the OWS in 1855 but resigned in 1858, pleading the poverty caused by his slow and painstaking output of watercolours, in order to concentrate on the more lucrative and stable medium of oil.

Curiously enough, *The Times* review (which incidentally took a swipe at the Pre-Raphaelites' 'missal-manner . . . the flatness of Catholicism') linked Lewis' style (as opposed to subject-matter) with the Oriental, though it fixes on the Chinese rather than anything Middle-Eastern:

> ". . . The accuracy in depicting the minutest details of costume and still life, the absence of human rotundity, the dubious perspective which belong to the screens from the Celestial Empire, seem to have been taken by Mr. Lewis for his model. He has succeeded to a wonder, and the Oriental treatment is in a sort of harmony with the Oriental subject; but is this sort of thing likely to conduce to a progress in art?"

The French answer to that in 1855 was a resounding no; About, the rudest, and du Camp were agreed on the pointlessness of such laborious work. Only Gautier, an Anglophile, devoted pages of eulogistic description (the most informative published) to the picture, echoing the Chinese analogy and adding his own references to the Persian. None of the French critics mention the possibility of Lewis' indebtedness to Delacroix, though Lewis spent the winter of 1837 in Paris when he may have seen the fruits of Delacroix's first visit to North Africa, and in particular his *Les Algeriennes* of 1834 (Louvre). Lewis was, however, a very consistent artist and re-used types and subjects throughout his career: there are many later hareem scenes and it is already possible to detect the type of his pasha in his drawing for the title page of his *Sketches and Drawings of the Alhambra*, 1835.

Victoria and Albert Museum

SIR JAMES DROMGOLE LINTON, ANWS 1867, RI 1870, PRI 1884–98 AND 1909–16, Kt. 1885

30 The Banquet 1882

oil on canvas, 50 × 99 in
INSCR: J.D. Linton 1882

PROV: commissioned by Charles J. Jacoby, Nottingham; his sale, Christie's, 20 Mar 1911 (77) bt. Shepherd (£115 10s); purchased by Nottingham, 1911.
EXH: RA 1882 (609); *A Series of Pictures illustrating The Life of a Soldier in the Sixteenth Century and a collection of dawings by J.D. Linton, PRI*, Fine Art Society 1884 (50); Manchester Jubilee 1887 (521); Glasgow 1888 (106).
LIT: *AJ*, June 1882, p212; *Academy*, 29 Apr 1882, pp308–9; *Athenaeum*, 27 May 1882, p673; *Portfolio*, June 1882, p131; *Times*, 3 June 1882, p5; Walter Armstrong, 'Mr. Linton's Pictures', cat. intro. to *The Life of a Soldier*, FAS 1884, pp5–12, sketch p9; *Athenaeum*, 20 Dec 1884, p811; *Portfolio*, 1885, p43; *Times*, 15 Dec 1884, p4; Frederick Wedmore, 'Sir James D. Linton, PRI', *AJ*, 1891, p62, repr p61; F.G. Stephens, 'Sir James D. Linton, PRI', *Portfolio*, 1893, pp224–31; *Nottingham Catalogue*, 1926 (144).
REPR: Blackburn, *RA Notes*, 1882, p54.
VERSION: *The Banquet*; oil, 28½ × 48½ in; Dr. Dyce Brown, sold Christie's, 3 Apr 1911 (99) bt. Barrett (£120 15s).
STUDY: for the whole composition, oil on panel, 8 × 16 in; coll. Mrs. D. Skillington.

Linton was the classic example of the Victorian artist who, despite his success in other fields, still hankered after, sought, and failed to win, Academy status. *The Life of a Soldier in the Sixteenth Century*, the series of five very large paintings commissioned by Charles Jacoby for the decoration of his drawing room, was Linton's great assault on the ramparts of the RA; by common consent, *The Banquet* was the best of the series but the critics generally felt Linton had over-reached himself. Linton had shown the first of the series, *Victorious*, at the Grosvenor Gallery in 1880, but the other four were shown in successive years at the RA 1881–4; Armstrong's introduction to the catalogue of

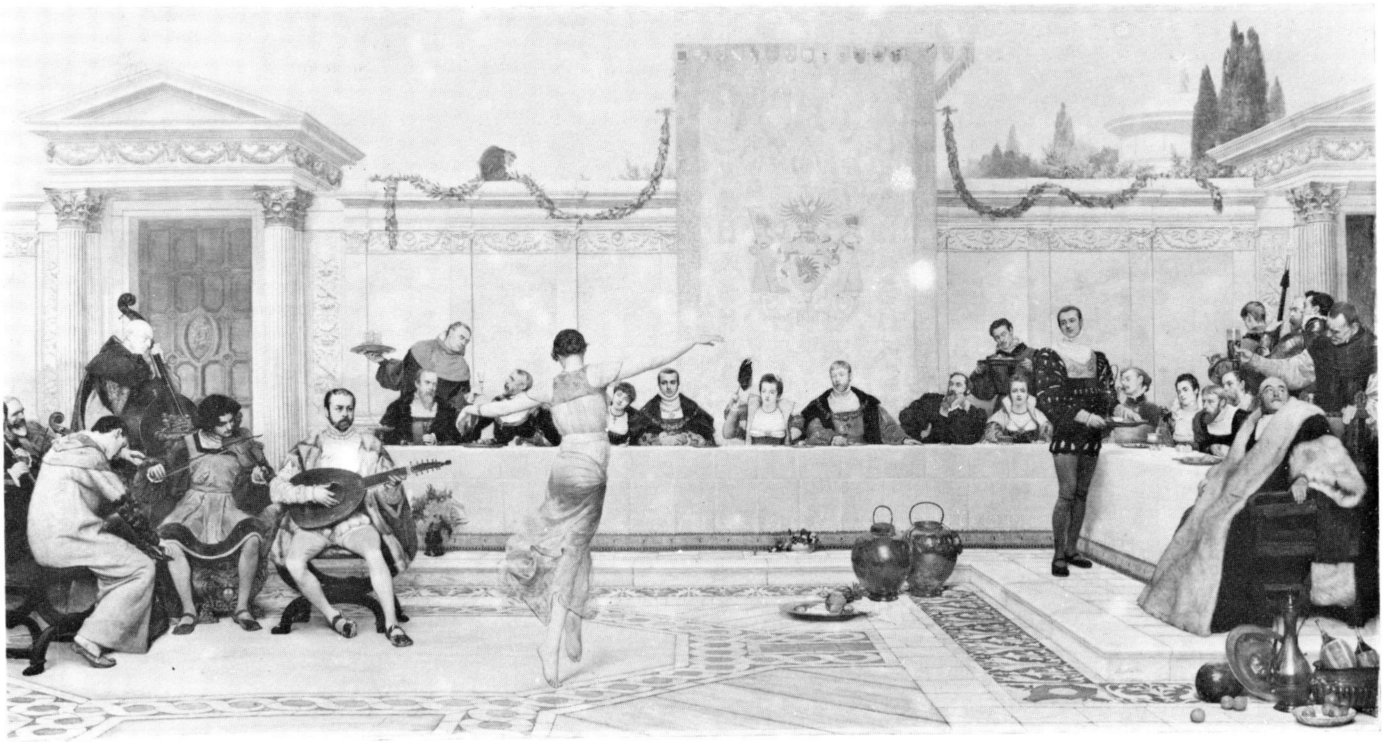

the complete set, shown at the Fine Art Society in a special exhibition in 1884, expresses much of what the reviewers had been saying.

He observed that Linton was attempting to marry a Venetian conception of the world with a Dutch technique – Titian, Veronese and Tintoretto painted by Terburg and Metzu, and it was 'this divided allegiance' that accounted for the final deficiencies in Linton's great series.

> "There is, on the one hand, the copiousness, the fullness of colour, and the decorative splendour of Venice; on the other, the elaborate textures, the illusive modelling and chiaroscuro, the absolute precision of touch of the masters of Leyden and Deventer; but between the two some of the energetic vitality which should distinguish such scenes . . . has in part disappeared. In saying this, I have frankly acknowledged what I believe to be the one serious shortcoming in Mr. Linton's art. It is a defect into which all who base themselves upon 'the masters' rather than upon constant deference to nature are apt to slip; and it may well be doubted whether it is not, after all, a cheap price to pay for such quality and infinity of colour, for such truth of form and texture, for such grace in movement, in the fall of drapery, in the carriage of the head and limbs, as we meet with again and again in these pictures."

The Banquet was the third in the series to be painted; Armstrong described it thus:

> "The sovereign entertains his general in the open air, at a feast where eyes and ears can be delighted at the same time as a grosser sense. In point of colour and movement this may be considered the best of the set. The high tones are managed with consummate skill, while the twirling dancer in the foreground really conveys an idea of trained lightness and of the elastic grace which comes of complete suppleness of muscle."

It contains Linton's strongest allusions to Veronese: he would have known Veronese's *The Family of Darius before Alexander* well as it had been in the National Gallery since 1857, but *The Marriage of Cana* in the Louvre would have been a more direct compositional source for the backgrounds of classical architecture, the disposition of figures, in this case along the far side of a banqueting table that stretches almost the width of the picture, modified by Linton with a curious combination of the conventions of the *Last Supper* with the *Dance of Salome*. Many of his artist friends sat for the figures, including Luke Fildes, Edwin Hayes, G.G. Kilburne, E.J. Gregory and H.J. Stock.

The *Athenaeum* review of 1882 detected a debt to Yriate's recently published history of the Malatestas, but both *The Times* and Armstrong point out that it is 'an imaginary' Prince or Duke of the Adriatic shore' whose army is led against the forces of Islam by a soldier of fortune. The others in the series were *Victorious*, the fourth episode in the story, shown at the Grosvenor Gallery in 1880 (Jacoby sale (75) bt. Sampson (£110 5s)), *The Benediction*, second in the sequence and shown at the RA 1881 Jacoby sale (76) bt. Sampson (£110 5s), *The Surrender*, third in sequence and shown at the RA 1883 (Jacoby sale (78) bt. Sampson (£157 10s)), and *The Declaration of War*, the first episode, shown at the RA 1884 (Jacoby sale (79) bt. Barrett (£220 10s)). *The Surrender* was resold by Sampson at Christie's later that year (18 Nov 1911 (69) bt. Morrison (£115 10s)), but there is no further trace of any of the rest of the series. Linton appears to have made replicas of at least two of the scenes, which were sold by Dr. Dyce Brown at Christie's in the same year (3 Apr 1911 (99 & 100), both $28\frac{1}{2} \times 48\frac{1}{2}$ in, bt. Barrett and Sampson).

In his other work Linton achieved the highest distinctions, becoming President of the Institute of Oil Painters in 1883 and President of the Royal Institute of Painters in Water-Colours in 1884; he held both offices until 1897 and 1898 respectively and resumed as PRI on Gregory's death in 1909. He was highly regarded and two lengthy articles in the early 1890s document his very busy career in some detail. F.G. Stephens opened his *Portfolio* article on Linton with some perceptive observations, calling him:

> "a faultless executant, a draughtsman of flawless skill, and a designer of unusual dramatic power. It has long been a notion of mine that if [Linton] had been less accomplished, his popularity would have been even wider, if not higher, than we know it to be, and I have convinced myself that it is no paradox which avers that mankind resents nothing more thoroughly than such faultlessness as his. Especially is this true . . . of the artistic variety of man, which always seeks, and often secures, comfort in fault-finding . . ."

Stephens compared him favourably with Leighton and Hunt in his ability to fulfill his own standards of excellence.

Castle Museum, Nottingham

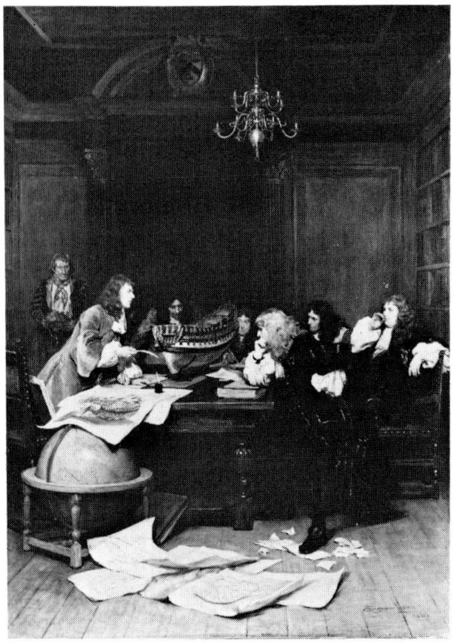

JOHN SEYMOUR LUCAS, 1849–1923, ARA 1886, RA 1898

31 A "Whip" for Van Tromp: the Admiralty, 1652 1883

oil on canvas, 64½×47¾in
INSCR: Seymour Lucas 1883

PROV: Messrs. Murietta, sold Christie's, 2 May 1892 (118) bt. Agnew (£525) for Leicester, out of the Billings Bequest.
EXH: RA 1883 (653); *Historical & Pageant Exh.*, Whitechapel 1909 (Upper gallery 27); Rome 1911 (252): *Special Autumn Exh. ... Also Works by J. Seymour Lucas, RA*, Wolverhampton 1912 (14); Wembley 1925 (W.19).
LIT: *AJ*, July 1883, p220; *Athenaeum*, 16 June 1883, p768; Blackburn, *RA Notes*, 1883, p58; *Graphic*, 26 May 1883, p538; *Mag. of Art*, 1883, p351; *Times*, 11 May 1883, p4; 'Seymour Lucas, ARA', *AJ*, Mar 1887, p69; Edmund Gosse, 'Seymour Lucas, ARA', *Mag. of Art*, 1888, p6, engr. p4; *Leicester Cat.*, 1899 (92); Allan Fea, 'Seymour Lucas, RA', *AJ*, Christmas No. 1908, p9, repr. p26; F. Gordon Roe, obit., *Connoisseur*, July 1923, p115; Adrian Bury, 'John Seymour Lucas, RA', *Connoisseur*, Dec 1953, p176.
REPR: *The Nation's Pictures*, 1902, 17; *Illustrated Selection of Pictures in the Leicester Art Gallery*, 1906, p6; *Souvenir*, Rome 1911, p243; *Souvenir*, Wembley 1925, p39.
VERSION: *A New Whip for the Dutch;* oil on canvas; 27×38¾ in; inscr: Seymour Lucas 1883; Prov: Charles Wells sale, Christie's 4 June 1887 (76) bt. Perman; Henry L. Florence bequest to the V & A, 1917.

In the 1870s and 1880s, decades that saw a great reaction against the historical tableaux of artists like Edward Matthew Ward, Gosse remarked that

> "In the severe scrutiny now applied to historical painting, there can be little that survives except the fittest."

Seymour Lucas was one of the fittest and, in a year in which (in the opinion of the *Magazine of Art*) 'the picture of the year is not in the Academy, but at Messrs. Goupil's and is signed, not "Millais", nor "Holl", nor "Leighton", but "Theodore Rousseau"', Lucas still managed to elicit considerable praise from less progressive journals. *The Times* went so far as to call it 'the strongest work of the artist', and the *Graphic*, in the longest notice given to Lucas that year, examined it closely for historical accuracy in the portraits, costumes and characters involved.

The subject appealed to the large streak of chauvinism in the Empire-building Victorians: in a period which saw more colonial and European wars than there were years in Victoria's reign, a picture showing the planning of the defeat of the Dutch navy in the 17th century would have been interpreted as the liveliest and most patriotic comment on Britain's foreign policy. Discussions in the Admiralty are going on between John Evelyn, Pepys and the Earl of Sandwich over a new ship, forty of which were built specifically to use against the Dutch navy, led by the brilliantly successful Admiral Van Tromp in the first Anglo-Dutch War, 1652–4. The 'whip' refers to the dispute between the Dutch and the English over whether the Dutch ships in the Channel should salute the English flag: Van Tromp

> "had hoisted a broom at the masthead of his ship as a menace that he would sweep the English from the seas; the English Admiral had replied by hoisting a whip at his masthead (said to be the origin of the Royal pennant.)" (Leicester, 1899, p30).

Lucas's debt to Ernest Meissonier (1812–1891) is easy to recognise and was noted in his day, but he was only one of a number of English artists, including Pettie, Crofts, Gow and Lady Butler, who learnt much from Meissonier's characteristic dash, his swaggering seventeenth century figures, and his massed groupings of troops. Napoleon III's presentation of *La Rixe* to Prince Albert in 1855 (see Pettie, cat. 43) began a fashion for the artist in this country that was most faithfully followed by the Marquess of Hertford and his son Sir Richard Wallace. Between them, they bought 16 Meissoniers between 1857 and 1872; all but one of these were shown together with the rest of the Wallace Collection at the Bethnal Green Museum, 1872–5, where, though mostly very small, they contributed greatly to Meissonier's reputation in England. London dealers were showing quantities of French Salon art, and many English artists travelled regularly to Paris and, less often, the French provinces to go round the galleries. Meissonnier was undoubtedly one of the most successful French artists of the day and this was confirmed when the Galerie Georges Petit in Paris put on a major retrospective, accompanied by a massive and handsomely-bound volume, in 1884. The same gallery staged another large show in 1893, this time a memorial exhibition, and Tooth's brought the whole collection to London – 'his third apotheosis' as Claude Phillips put it. Phillips' article in the *Magazine of Art* about this exhibition (1893, pp280–5) followed only two years after Walter Armstrong's long obituary article on the artist in the same magazine (1891, pp199–204), but probably the most important work published in this country on Meissonnier before his death was Lionel Robinson's 1887 *Art Annual* volume. Art Annuals, published by J.S. Virtue, the owner of the *Art Journal*, were sure signals of an artist's arrival in the pantheon – uniform with the Meissonier volume were those on Leighton, Millais and Alma Tadema. The final important English salute to the artist came in 1897 with the publication of the translation of Vallery C.O. Gréard's *Meissonier, His Life and his Art*.

Seymour Lucas's other important works include *After Culloden: rebel hunting* (RA 1884, Tate), bought for the Chantrey Bequest for £700 and *St Paul's – the King's visit to Wren* (RA 1888, Newcastle). Like other artists of the period, Lucas had a small collection of Old Masters, not all of which were necessarily bad copies. These were sold some months before he died at Christie's (15 Dec 1922, lot 1–17); they included a so-called Van Goyen, Hogarth, Poussin, Van Dycks, Opie, and a Zoffany, the latter being probably of the most interest to his own work – it was of a gentleman, seated by a writing table, holding a staff and letter. Zoffany's characteristic dramatic line may have been Lucas's chief English inspiration.

Though the 1880s were the period of Lucas's greatest success, he was resourceful enough to turn almost completely to portraiture when he recognised the signs of fashion turning against his history pictures. He still, however, occasionally produced a history picture: *The King of Spain's Navy is Abroad*, for instance, of 1912 (untraced) shows a very similar format to that of *A 'Whip' for Van Tromp*, right down to the globe, though here it is on a circular-based stand.

Leicestershire Museums and Art Gallery

JOHN MACWHIRTER, 1839–1911, ARSA 1867, ARA 1879, HRSA 1880, RA 1893

32 Spindrift 1876

oil on canvas, 32 × 56 in
INSCR: MacWhirter

PROV: Edward Hermon, MP, Wyfold Court; his sale, Christie's, 13 May 1882 (70) bt. Martin (£215) for Thomas Holloway.
EXH: RA 1876 (427); Guildhall 1897 (45); RA Winter 1922 (104).
LIT: *AJ*, Sept 1876, p262; *ILN*, 20 May 1876, p498; *Times*, 31 May 1876, p5; James Dafforne, 'The Works of John MacWhirter, ARSA', *AJ*, Jan 1879, p11; Walter Shaw Sparrow, 'The Royal Holloway College Picture-Gallery II', *Mag. of Art*, 1891, p271, repr p273; C.W. Carey, *Royal Holloway College, Egham, Catalogue of Pictures*, 1896, 3rd ed (56); C.W. Carey, 'The Royal Holloway College Collection – II', *AJ*, July 1897, pp202–3; Dr. William Macdonald Sinclair, 'John MacWhirter RA', *Art Annual*, Christmas 1903,, pp11, 30, repr p10.
VERSION: *A Seaweed Collector*; oil on canvas, 20 × 32 in; signed with initials; sold Sotheby's, Belgravia, 30 Aug 1974 (231).

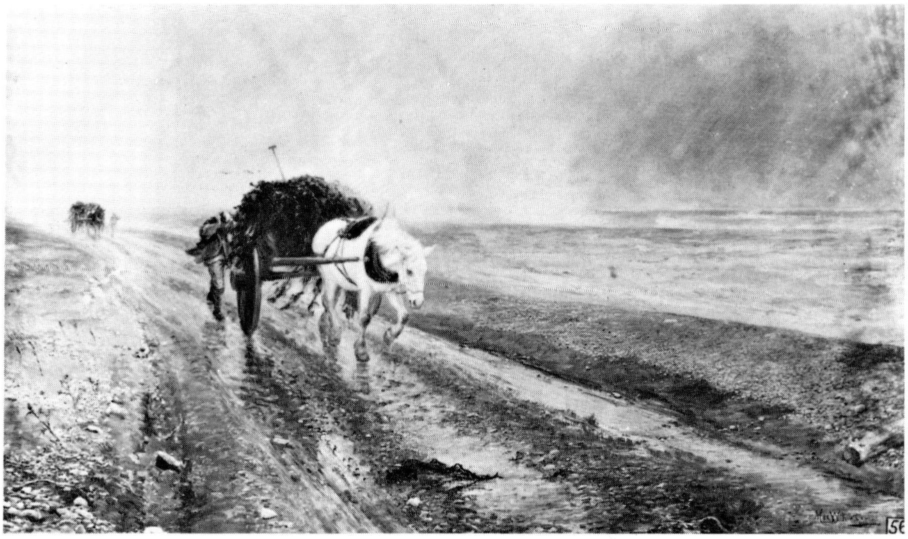

Walter Shaw Sparrow's article on the Royal Holloway College Picture Gallery may be taken as a fairly accurate gauge of the attitude of a conventional writer of the early '90s to the art of the previous fifty years represented in the Holloway collection. His treatment of MacWhirter's *Spindrift* demonstrates that the artist's reputation was probably at its peak towards the turn of the century; he was finally elected RA in 1893 and ten years later two monographs on him were published within a year of each other. Shaw Sparrow wrote:

> "The atmospheric effect of [the picture] is beyond praise. Notice, too, the straining attitude of the old white horse. Facing the rough and boisterous revelling of the wind, he, with an almost pathetic determination, takes what steps he can, but without any unnecessary ado. In short, truth and poetry are happily united in this picture . . ."

The picture had attracted only brief, though complimentary reviews, when it appeared at the 1876 RA; the *Art Journal* had called it a masterly transcript from nature, while the *Times* felt moved to dissociate itself somewhat from the chauvinism of recent criticisms of the Scottish landscapists.

> ". . . passing from Scottish sea to land, we [cannot] join in the unmeasured depreciation often heaped on painters like M'Whirter, Smart, Docharty, and their fellows, though we may say of them as of the Scottish sea painters, that the family likeness is sometimes fatiguing, if not irritating."

It found *Spindrift* a sincere expression by MacWhirter of a sad scene, while to the *ILN* it was 'spirited'.

MacWhirter had trained under Lauder at Edinburgh, along with Pettie, Orchardson and the Grahams, and after considerable early success in Scotland had settled in London in 1869. He won favour with Ruskin in 1870 for some minutely-detailed botanical studies which Ruskin compared with Dürer buying twenty-five in 1870 for use in his teaching at Oxford. MacWhirter was a lifelong follower of Ruskin's theories on Contemplative Landscape, as defined in *Modern Painters* and exemplified by Turner, and they were applied throughout his work. This was divided by Sinclair into seven classes:

> "I, The Highland; II, The Generally Scottish; III, The Italian; IV, Pictures from other Countries; V, Domestic and Subject; VI, Trees; VII, Flowers."

MacWhirter did indeed travel a great deal from boyhood and the lists of his exhibited pictures reveal that he went as far afield as Turkey and North America, as well as all over Europe. According to Konody in the *DNB*, MacWhirter

> "owed his popularity largely to the tinge of sentiment which invested his otherwise naturalistic landscapes with a certain literary significance, and which is reflected in the fanciful titles he gave to his landscapes and studies of trees."

Sinclair ascribes much of this literary influence to MacWhirter's friendship with the popular 'poetic novelist of the West Highlands', William Black, whose romantic Highland novels added much to the already potent mixture in the Victorian idea of Scotland (see Irwins, 1975, pp364–5). As MacWhirter also used a great many themes from poetry, it seems possible that *Spindrift*, which was exhibited without any literary references, may have had some connection with the collection of poems by his friend Noel Paton published in 1867 and called *Spindrift;* the title is taken from the poem to his wife, prefacing the volume and includes the lines:

> Mere Spindrift, by the gusts of fancy blown
> From the deep, clear, and silent sea of Life, . . .

MacWhirter himself was determinedly prosaic in a letter to the Holloway College in 1887 recalling how he had come to the subject:

> " 'Spindrift' means the spray of the sea caught up and whirled away by the wind. I saw the seaweed cart coming along when I was walking on a stormy day, and made a note of it in my sketch-book. I afterwards made careful studies of the wet road, gravel, &c. The scene is near Loch Range, Arran." (see cat. 1896).

Apparently in this case he relied less on his memory than in later years when he became a dedicated advocate of training the memory, aided by the briefest of notes. In his short book of instruction published in 1900, *Landscape Painting in Water-Colour*, MacWhirter chose Turner and Millais for his highest praise in their treatment of landscape:

> "You cannot study these painters too much. Turner, for light and atmosphere, and the drawing of mountains and clouds; Millais, for everything. *All* his work is healthy and loveable. His landscapes, *Chill October*, etc., are all poetical in feeling, while at the same time they are faithful, unconventional studies direct from nature. I think, however, that his finest landscape work is to be found in the background to his figure subjects, . . ." (pp12–13).

He urged the development of the memory to the point where "a *distinct* impression" could be retained from which to paint the scene – advice which recalls that of Lecoq de Boisbaudran, the teacher of Whistler, Rodin, Tissot, Fantin-Latour, Legros and many others and author of *The Training of the Memory in Art*, first published in Paris in one volume in 1877 (first complete translation into English, 1911).

Amongst MacWhirter's other well-known paintings were *The Track of a Hurricane* (RA 1885, Forbes Magazine Collection), with symbolic overtones in the savagely uprooted trees and broken landscape, and its complete antithesis, an idyllic alpine pasture, *June in the Austrian Tyrol* (RA 1892, Chantrey Purchase, Tate). Although his individual saleroom prices were never high, MacWhirter was so consistently popular that he was able to build himself a Renaissance palace at 1 Abbey Road, St John's Wood, an impressive monument to his taste and income.

Royal Holloway College

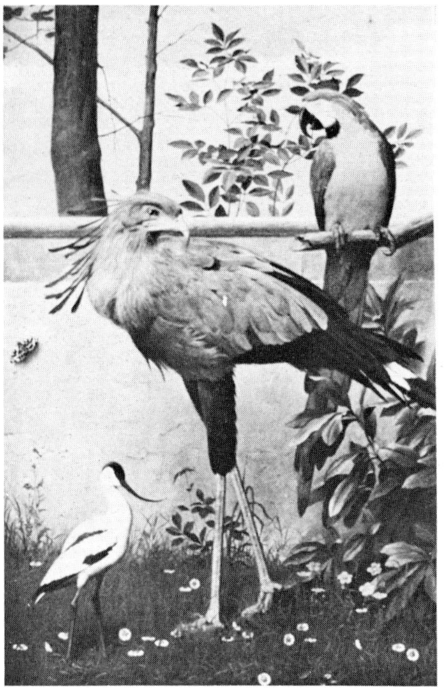

HENRY STACY MARKS, 1829–1898, ARA 1871, RA 1878–96

33 Secretary Bird, blue and orange Macaw, Avocet 1880

oil on canvas, 49 × 22 in

PROV: commissioned by the 1st Duke of Westminster for Eaton Hall, Cheshire.
EXH: *Twelve Panels of Birds painted by H.S. Marks, R.A., for the ante-drawing room at Eaton, Cheshire*, Agnew, May 1880 (9).
LIT: *Academy*, 8 May 1880, p350; 'Sketches by H.S. Marks, RA', *The Architect*, 5 June 1880, p389, repr. betw. pp388–9; *Athenaeum*, 1 May 1880, p575; *Portfolio*, June 1880, p105; *Times*, 10 May, p5, leader, 18 May 1880, p9; Arthur Griffiths, 'Birds in Decoration', *Mag. of Art*, 1881, pp138–140; Henry Stacy Marks, *Pen and Pencil Sketches*, 1894, I, pp212–19, II, pp177–8; obit., *Times*, 11 Jan 1898, p4; George D. Leslie, 'In Memoriam: Henry Stacy Marks RA', *Mag. of Art*, Mar 1898, p240; Ruskin, Letters, *Works*, XXXVII, pp229, 301–2; *DNB*, XXII, p1013.

On 18 May 1880, *The Times* leader took as its subject the principles of decorative art, prompted by the current exhibitions in London of two decorative painters – the Austrian Makart, and Stacy Marks. Marks' bird panels were discussed with approval for he had, *The Times* thought, achieved the ideal:

> ". . . The decorative painter must keep always burning the lamp of sacrifice. He should paint not to concentrate thought on his work, but that his work may carry thought on and beyond, till the work itself be forgotten in the thought. He need not be careful to observe the rigid reality of nature or history; not that he should not have studied, and be able to observe it if he would, but that his purpose requires its violation. The guests at Eaton do not want to have studies in natural history collected for their instruction, but to find on the walls, when they choose to look, a sort of pictorial accompaniment to their prevailing mood, from grave to gay, from the overpowering wisdom of a pelican to the mocking irony of some of its companions."

For *The Times* to carry a long and discursive leader on such a subject was probably unprecedented, but the occasion was exceptional – the exhibition at Agnew's of the twelve decorative panels of birds commissioned from Stacy Marks by the Duke of Westminster for his great new house, then being completed to the designs of Alfred Waterhouse. Waterhouse had introduced his patron to Marks in 1874, and the Duke had promptly invited the artist to Cheshire, on the strength of his decorative panels showing in that year's RA; he commissioned two immense decorations for the saloon, the subject, chosen by Marks, was to be the Canterbury Pilgrims. This took four years to complete and the bird panels were commissioned towards the end of that time, in November 1877. Marks, in his autobiography *Pen and Pencil Sketches*, describes how he, the Duke and Waterhouse chose one of the smaller drawing-rooms, and decided on twelve panels in groups of three. He goes on:

> "As I wished to include birds of all shapes and sizes, of different climes and conditions, from the Indian adjutant to the humble English wagtail, the cockatoo from Australia, the macaw from South America, the African crane, and the European stork, I imagined them in a fairy garden, an ornithological Walhalla, where no bird quarrels with another, but is content with the climate, conditions, and surroundings of its present abode – an abode where food is always present without the trouble of seeking for it, into which bands of yelling schoolchildren are not permitted to enter, those terrors of the actual 'Zoo'; where pinioning is forbidden, and wing-hacking unknown." (p218).

The 'ornithological Walhalla' was described by the *Portfolio*:

> "A stone wall is represented running through the twelve panels three-quarters the height of the picture, enclosing a paddock thick with grass and buttercups and daisies, in which are flamingoes, crowned cranes, Stanley and Demoiselle cranes, Mantchurian cranes, scarlet ibis, blue and scarlet macaws, pelicans, cockatoos, adjutants, herons, secretary birds, storks, boatbills, American egrets, parrots, &c, in all their variety and beauty of plumage. The grouping, positions, and actions of the different birds are full of grace and meaning and denote an eye and hand well versed in the observation and recording of birdlife. The rich and delicate hues of the plumage in the limpid atmosphere about them form a delightful harmony."

As the *Academy* said,

> "The world of birds Mr. Marks has made his own, in pictures painted year after year, and now in these twelve decorative panels he has completed his right to be considered the king of that division of animated nature."

Marks had been painting more or less peculiar birds since he scored a major success with his *St. Francis* (RA 1870, repr. *Mag. of Art*, 1879, p100): his earlier pictures were mediaeval- or Shakespearean-comic, with titles like *Toothache in the middle ages*, much appreciated by both authors of biographical articles on him in the 1870s (Dafforne, *AJ*, 1870, pp361–3 and Fenn, *Mag. of Art*, 1879, pp97–100), and by the public, though it was the *St. Francis* which secured his ARA. He was one of the most successful of the members of the St. John's Wood Clique (see Storey, cat. 55) and the only one to earn the admiration and friendship of Ruskin. Marks had first met Ruskin in 1856, but renewed their acquaintance in 1876 when he asked Ruskin to write on the memorial exhibition of his friend Fred Walker; they quickly established a friendship based on Ruskin's admiration for Marks's studies of birds and Marks's help in such matters as buying Bewicks on Ruskin's behalf. Ruskin was one of the first to receive news of the Eaton Hall commission, which Marks sent him along with some drawings of vultures. Ruskin replied:

> "I jumped all about the room when I got your letter. I've been gloating like a good vulture over those vultures ever since I got them, and have got wilder and wilder about them every day; and I'm just going to show them in my lecture here on Tuesday as examples of true natural history drawing; and all you tell me of your feelings about them, and your work, at least the issue of it in the bird-room at the Duke of Westminster's, is wholly delightful to me . . ." (*Works*, XXXVII, p229).

More admiration, with much idiosyncratic advice, followed in November 1879, on completion of the panels:

> "My dear Marco . . . I must . . . say how entirely glad I am to see the strength of a good painter set upon natural history, and this intense fact and abstract of animal character used as a principal element in decoration. The effort is so unexampled, that you cannot hope to satisfy yourself, or satisfy all conditions of success at the first trial. But you have, at all events done, and the Duke is happy, more than any patron of art in these times, in having induced you to do, what will be the beginning of a most noble and vital school of natural history, and useful, no less than charming art. I think you will have ultimately to keep the foliage darker and flatter – and for my own share *I* should like some blue sky and flying birdies behind. But I'm such a lover of blue (except in beards, stockings, and devils) that I'm no safe counsellor." (*Works*, XXXVII, pp301–2).

Clearly Marks had achieved a great success with a major private patron, with Ruskin, with the critics in general, and in the eyes of the major dealer of the day. His work in decoration and book illustration was recognised by his contemporaries as innovatory and lively – Walter Crane particularly admired the 'bold outlines and flat tints' of some nursery rhyme illustrations by Marks (Crane, *Of the Decorative Illustration of Books Old and New*, 1896, p128), but a full understanding of his significance awaits the results of Helen Smith's study of the history of decorative art in the period, currently in preparation.

Marion Spielmann, the editor of the *Magazine of Art*, was undoubtedly an admirer of Marks: he published a three-page article on the Agnew show, with wood engravings of two of the panels, and, for the second of Marks's three shows at the Fine Art Society (in 1889, 1890 and 1895) published Marks's own discussion of his drawings, with a dozen reproductions. On his death, Spielmann published a long obituary by Marks's old friend and fellow-member of the St. John's Wood Clique, G.D. Leslie.

As an Academy artist Marks enjoyed considerable and steady success but Marks himself (*Mag. of Art* 1890, p345) ascribed his public fame and his critical reputation to his adoption of bird-painting. His taste for the grotesque or simply odd lead him to the zoo, and in all his pictures, ordinary British birds are only occasionally used as a humorous note of contrast beside a pelican or flamingo.

Secretary Bird, blue and orange Macaw, Avocet, the Eaton Hall panel now exhibited, is one of the most successful of the twelve in terms of colour and composition; it is typical of the clear, strong colour and high finish to be found in the whole set and, according to Arthur Griffiths, was 'the most popular with visitors to Mr. Agnew's gallery'. Marks's relationship with his patron, reputed to be the richest man in England, was not only aesthetically productive but must also have been lucrative: no records of the commission survive in the Grosvenor papers, but a receipt from Marks for £800 for three lunettes forming part of a ceiling decoration suggest that his fees for the bird panels would have been equally generous. The panels hung in Waterhouse's immense new

Gothic Eaton Hall until, in the last twenty years, the house fell into such disrepair that it was demolished in the 1960s. A new house now stands on the site and the panels are again hanging.

Grosvenor Estates

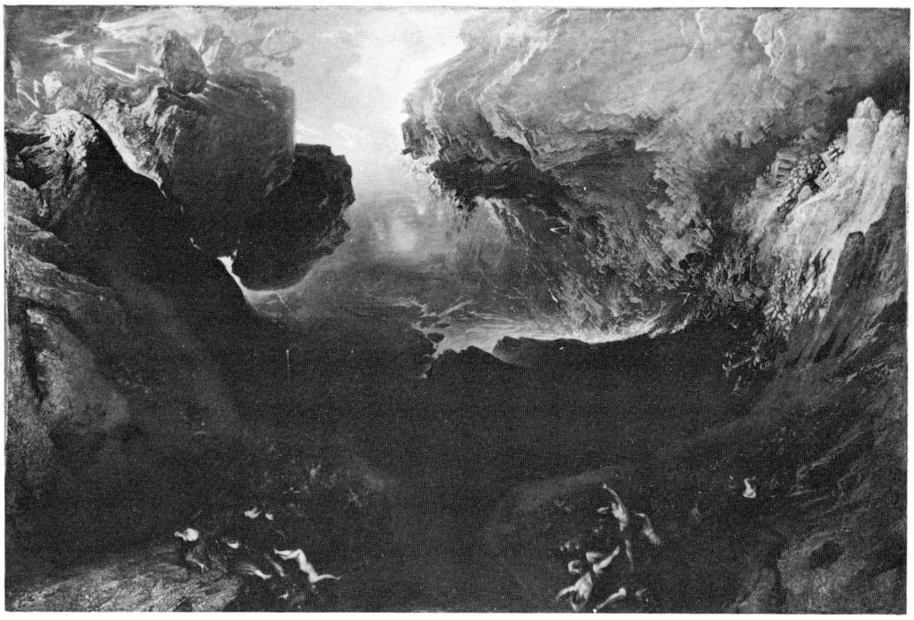

The Great Day of his Wrath *Courtesy: Tate Gallery, London*

JOHN MARTIN, 1789–1854

34 The Great Day of His Wrath

mixed mezzotint by Charles Mottram
28¼ × 40¾ in

Publ. Thomas Maclean, 1857.
LIT: (all references to the three Judgment subjects; for further lit., see bibliographies in Feaver, Balston, etc.) obit., *AJ*, Apr 1854, p119; 'The Pictures of the late John Martin', *AJ*, June 1855, p195; *DNB*; Thomas Balston, *John Martin, 1789–1854, His Life and Works*, 1947, pp233–49; William Feaver, *The Art of John Martin*, 1975, pp188–204 (& see index), pls.147–9, 153–5, 157, colour VII, VIII; cat., *John Martin 1789–1854*, Hazlitt, Gooden & Fox, 1975, pp5, 18–19, pls. III, IV.

The great trilogy of the Judgment paintings occupied much of the last four years of Martin's life and, on his death in 1854, embarked on two decades of touring round Britain even, in 1857, going to America. It is known from various sources that they were seen in Newcastle, Birmingham, Leicester, Chester, Oxford, Bristol, Manchester and in the City and West End of London; their last recorded showing outside London was at Hexham in 1872. One of the more extraordinary aspects of the touring was the sheer logistics of moving the paintings themselves: *The Great Day of His Wrath* (of which the engraving is shown here) measures 77⅝ × 119⅝ in, *The Last Judgment* is 77½ × 128¼ in, and *The Plains of Heaven* is 78¼ × 120¾ in. Some idea of the impact they had on the audiences of the 1850s and 1860s can be gained from a pamphlet written by a later owner of the paintings (quoted Feaver, p200):

> "The rising generation will hardly understand the *furore* these extraordinary Pictures created when they were first exhibited in 1854. I remember the crowd of visitors waiting to be admitted to the Exhibition, and when I at length entered the darkened chamber, and noted the effect produced upon the multitude, and how all seemed to be carried away from worldly thoughts, and, as it were, intoxicated by the solemn, the lofty, and the majestic inspirations of the master mind of the great Artist, youth that I was, I would have rather been John Martin than King of England."

Metropolitan reviewers tended to be more critical and the *Art Journal*, for instance, compared them with the Sistine Ceiling and found that where Michelangelo

> "approached the subject with the most profound awe, Martin [seems] to have allowed his imagination to revel amid its wildest fancies till it extended into the region of burlesque, and almost into that of profanity."

Martin could be partially excused by the fact, according to the *Art Journal*, that he ended his days mentally disturbed; it went on:

> "But what can be said of a public who follow eagerly after such things? . . . Surely there is something most unhealthy in this exhibition of the public taste, this craving after novelty of the most extravagant kind, when works in every way an honour to the country meet with little or no patronage. If this matter is to be accepted as evidence, and it cannot well be rejected, we are retrograding rather than advancing in the knowledge of what true Art is, and of the end it is intended to subserve."

The engravings after the pictures may have been more acceptable to such critics as they were at least denied the colour which contributed largely to the unhealthy qualities so disapproved of by the *Art Journal*. The engraving contracts were signed with Thomas Maclean in June 1851, for *The Last Judgment*, and in June 1852, for *The Great Day of His Wrath* and *The Plains of Heaven;* the paintings were originally intended to be cartoons for the engravings and were not themselves meant for exhibition. They became, however, the consummation of all of Martin's previous work, encompassing the whole range from the Apocalyptic panoramas with memories of the coalmines of his childhood to the ecstatic mirages of the limitless horizons of Heaven. Martin was a lifelong outsider to the Academy, and his spectacular paintings have, as Feaver points out (pp68–70), most in common with the contemporary commercial panoramas. The greatest success of his earlier career had been with *Belshazzar's Feast*, shown at the British Institution in 1821.

The later history of the Judgment paintings is notorious: towards the end of the century they hung, ignored when they were not ridiculed, in Alexandra Palace and for a while in the Dore Gallery; probably after the turn of the century the canvases were removed from their stretchers, rolled and stored until all three were sold in 1935 for less than £7 – the nadir of Martin's reputation and probably the most spectacular example of the decline of an artist's reputation in the history of recent art. The three paintings now hang in the Tate.

The literature on Martin is extensive and William Feaver's recently published volume is now the standard work on the artist.

Leeds City Art Gallery

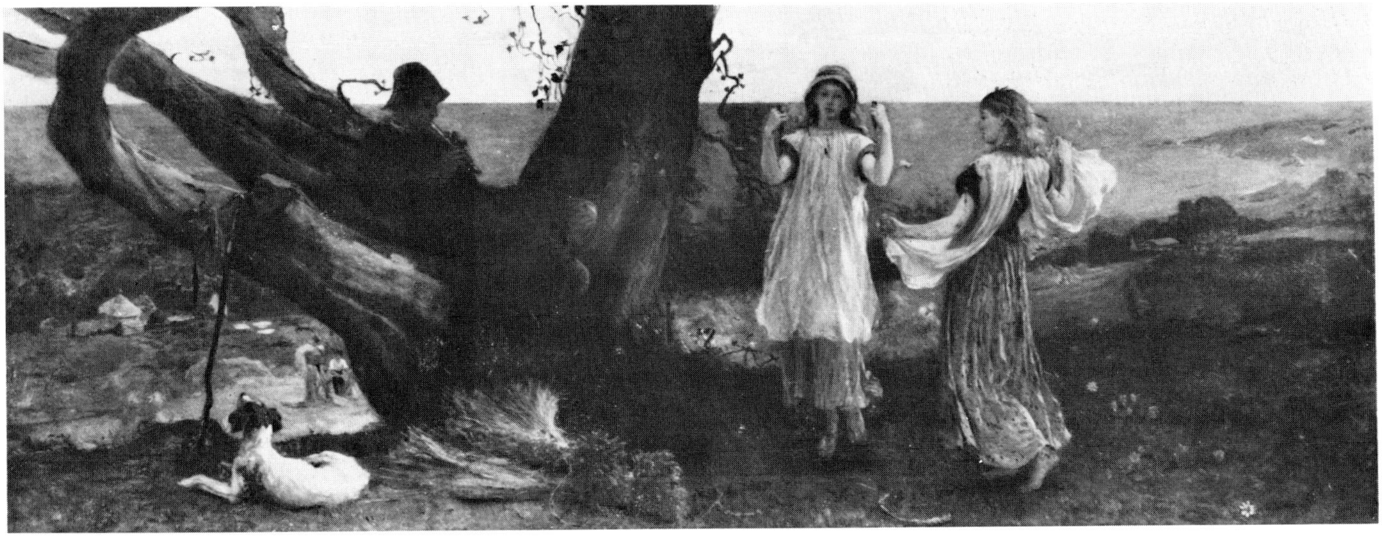

George Heming Mason, 1818–1872, ARA 1869

35 Girls dancing: A Pastoral Symphony 1869

oil on canvas, 27×71 in

PROV: commissioned by Ernst L.S. Benzon, Kensington Palace Gardens; his sale, Christie's, 13 June 1874 (38) bt. Agnew (£892 10s), sold 1875 to Lord Overstone, Carlton Gardens and Overstone Park; Lord and Lady Wantage; A. Loyd; presented to the present owner, *c.*1939.
EXH: RA 1869 (438); *Collected Works of the late George Mason, ARA*, Burlington Fine Arts Club 1873 (13); Manchester Jubilee 1887 (656); Guildhall 1890 (124) Chicago World's Fair 1893 (319); *Fair Children*, Grafton Gallery 1895 (282); RA Winter 1901 (60).
LIT: *AJ*, 1 July 1869, p199; *Athenaeum*, 1 May 1869, pp610–11; *GdBA*, July 1869, p56; *ILN*, 22 May 1869, p526; *Pall Mall*, 19 May 1869, p10; *Times*, 15 May 1869, p12; Sidney Colvin, 'English Artists of the Present Day XXVIII: George Mason, ARA', *Portfolio*, 1871, p117; obit., *AJ*, 1 Dec 1872, p300; obit., *Athenaeum*, 26 Oct 1872, pp534–5; BFAC review, *AJ*, Mar 1873, p68; G.A. Simcox, 'Mr. Mason's Collected Works', *Portfolio*, 1873, pp42–3; Frederick Wedmore, *Studies in English Art*, London, 1876, pp218–19; George Aitchison, 'George Hemmings (sic) Mason', *The Architect*, 1879, p379; Alice Meynell, 'George Mason: A Biographical Sketch, III', *AJ*, June 1883, p188; Temple, 1897, pp244–5; *Catalogue of Pictures forming the Collection of Lord and Lady Wantage*, 1905 (149); Rosalind M. Billingham, *The Life and Work of George Heming Mason, ARA*, Leicester University M.Phil. thesis, 1975 (unpublished).
ENGR: Robert W. Macbeth, ARA, etching; 13×34 in; publ. Thos. Agnew & Sons, 1886; exh. RA 1886 (1422).
STUDIES: Studies for the figures are in the British Museum and at Stoke-on-Trent; another was sold at Christie's, 16 June 1972 (60).

Mason was always a painter's painter, known to what Alice Meynell called 'the little public' of fellow-artists, critics and collectors, who 'hailed with peculiar pleasure a painter whose poetry was at once obvious and delicate'. *Girls dancing* (now known by its later title of *A Pastoral Symphony*) was considered one of Mason's three major paintings: the others were his first great success, *Evening Hymn* (RA 1868, Wyndham Coll. to *c.*1946, untraced), and *The Harvest Moon* (RA 1872, Tate). The success of the *Evening Hymn* had indeed been so great that Stephens was moved to comment in his 1869 review for the *Athenaeum* on its reception;

> "which unexpectedly revealed progress in popular knowledge of and feeling for Art of the higher kind."

He went on to describe *Girls dancing* as

> "a pastoral of the sweetest poetry, of exquisite beauty in colour, and with such abundance in delicate tones as we expect from him. Here is a subject supplemented to Art, not art merely applied to the illustration of a subject. The music, so to say, of Mr. Mason's work is in his intense feeling for low-toned harmonies of subtle colour – in the 'air' of grace which pervades all parts of his picture. This is distinct in the figures of him who, resting at the tree on the left, breathes old-world melodies on his pipe, and pours out his soul at ease, – in that of the vigorous dancer who springs before us with moving robes, – in those of the more subdued companions, – in the lines of the landscape and the halycon grey of the dimmed sky which overhangs all, like peace itself."

The *Pall Mall Gazette* drew an analogy between Hook's elevation of

> "the common life and character of Devon fishermen into a region of high poetry by the sympathetic intelligence of a refined imagination . . . [and Mason who] idealises for us the pastoral rudeness of English peasant life . . . this work is almost majestic by its rendering of free, unreflecting, natural joy. 'The Muses in a Ring' do not move with more harmonious grace than these nymphs of the Sunday-school in their patched cotton gowns and clumsy shoes. When picture-seers shall have got used to Mr. Mason, as they have got used to Mr. Hook, the homeliness of his imaginative world will reveal the ideal aspect of simple modes of life to as large and as mixed a public."

Staffordshire-born, Mason lived and painted in Rome for twelve years, returning to England finally in 1857 to marry; though he settled at first back at his family home, Wetley Abbey, he moved to London in 1864 to be closer to the circle of artist friends he had first met in Italy. His years in Rome had been improvident and, after his father's financial ruin, near-penniless but latterly he found patrons and made many friends in the expatriate artistic community who were later instrumental in salvaging his ever-flagging fortunes. The most significant of these was Leighton, whom he had met in 1853 and who, on Mason's return to England, frequently helped him with professional advice, introductions for commissions, and, most often, simply with cash (see Ormonds, *Leighton*, 1975, pp17–18 etc.). Together with another Roman friend, Giovanni Costa, Mason initiated the method of monochrome underpainting which was later taken up by younger artists also in Leighton's circle like George Howard, William Blake Richmond and Matthew Ridley Corbet, who became known as the Etruscan School (see exh., Fine Art Society, Nov–Dec 1976).

Mason's major paintings moved both contemporary and posthumous critics to comparisons with not only the French nineteenth century – Jules Breton, Millet, Daubigny and Corot – but also with Giorgione, Raphael and Poussin. His work was already being extensively discussed in special articles and lengthy reviews before his early death at the age of fifty-four, and he was afterwards acknowledged as one of the leaders of a whole new group of idyllic landscapists; his younger rival was Fred Walker – their names were almost always bracketed together, though in fact Walker's work tended to be less lyrical and idyllic and more heavily symbolic than Mason's. In the year after Mason's death a large exhibition of his work was shown at the Burlington Fine Arts Club, a rare tribute. Mason maintained throughout his work what the *Art Journal* in 1869 called an 'intensity of sentiment' and 'a sustained rhapsody of colour' with, in Colvin's phrase 'a singular sweetness of imagination'. Colvin, writing in 1871, thought that *Girls dancing*

> "has more firmness of definition, a greater strength and certainty as well as perhaps an intenser beauty, than anything its painter has so far done."

Two years later, Simcox, in his *Portfolio* review of the retrospective, considered that the *Evening Hymn* surpassed all of Mason's other work and that only in it and in the *Harvest Moon* does

> "the passion of the figures rise to a level with the passion of the landscape . . . so far as English country life still has a spiritual side at all, we have the realised ideal of it here."

Simcox interpreted Mason's art as essentially religious, but Frederick Wedmore arrived at a more secular and what was probably a more accurate estimation:

> "His pictures are a musical *suite*. Well-nigh from the beginning to the end they are the vision and presentment of pastoral beauty and rest."

Anonymous loan

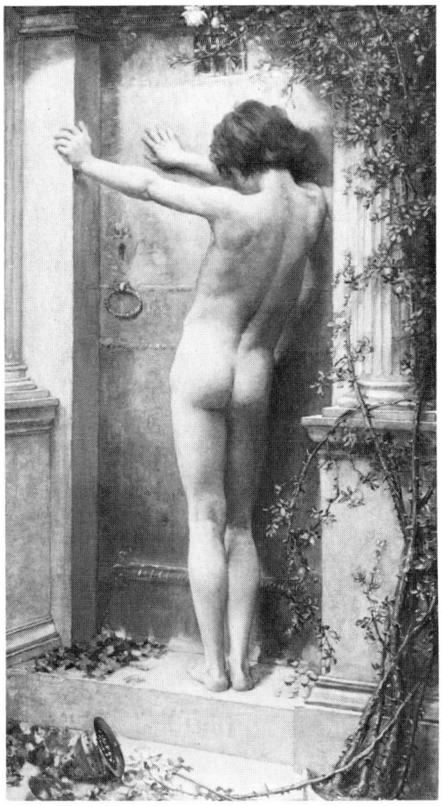

Anna Lea Merritt, 1844–1930, RBA 1902–6

36 Love Locked Out 1890

oil on canvas, $45\frac{1}{2} \times 25\frac{1}{4}$ in
INSCR: ALM (monogram) / 89

PROV: Chantrey Purchase (£150), 1890
EXH: RA 1890 (32); *Chantrey Collection*, RA Winter 1949 (35); recently on loan to Leighton House.
LIT: Blackburn, *RA Notes*, 1890, p6, repr. p31; *Times*, 3 May 1890, p12; Walter Shaw Sparrow, *Women Painters of the World*, 1905, pp77–8, repr. p139; Sir Wyke Bayliss, *Olives: the reminiscences of a president*, 1906, pp48–52; Frederick Wedmore, *Memories*, 1912, pp90–1; Anna Lea Merritt, *My Journey through Life from 1844 to 1924*, typescript, V & A, pp237–8; cat. of *American Artists in Europe*, Liverpool 1976–7 (42).

Love Locked Out was the first painting by a woman artist to be bought with the Chantrey Bequest and, though the fact that it had a low price on it may have influenced the decision, it was nevertheless recognised as a milestone by Anna Lea Merritt's contemporaries. Wyke Bayliss, then President of the Royal Society of British Artists, was unreserved in his admiration of both artist and painting:

> "One of the loveliest of the Landmarks in the realms of Art has been discovered within the lifetime of most of us. I mean the formal, authoritative recognition of the fact that women can paint pictures. It seems strange that the men of our generation should have been so slow to find it out . . . Perhaps the women have themselves been a little to blame – in raising the question whether the most beautiful of the creations of God should go out of their way to improve the loveliness of the world – when they are in themselves all-sufficient. I do not know. I can only be glad that the discovery has been made not too late for me to have seen the painting . . . of 'Love Locked Out' . . . [here a tongue-in-cheek version of the contest between Minerva (Athene) and Arachne, ending in a fight in which Bayliss has Minerva, the loser, attacking her challenger with a mahl-stick] . . . When our Mrs. Merritt has completed her picture . . . she was not beaten over the head with a mahl-stick. She simply sent it to the Royal Academy, and the authorities, recognising it as a work of genius, purchased it . . . thus adding a new loveliness to the National Collection."

Flippant though it sounds, Bayliss was entirely sincere. Though *Love Locked Out* was barely noticed in the reviews of the 1890 RA, it rapidly established itself as one of the chief popular favourites of the Chantrey pictures and remained so, being repeatedly reproduced well into this century. It was even to the sophisticated taste of the critic and writer on matters aesthetic, Frederick Wedmore, who in 1912 called Merritt

> "the author of one of the most acceptable and gracious of the pictorial allegories now visible at the Tate Gallery."

Unfortunately for the artist, the allegory was often misunderstood. Her manuscript autobiography explains her intentions.

> "The thought had been inspired years before [1889] as a monument to my husband. In my thought the closed door is the door of the tomb. Therefore I showed the dead leaves blowing against the doorway and the lamp shattered. 'The light in the dust lies dead', another broken lute. I could not afford to have it done in bronze, as I desired for a monument, so it became only a painting . . . for years I refused to have it copied for which entreaties were innumerable. I feared people liked it as a symbol of forbidden love, while my Love was waiting for the door of death to open and the reunion of the lonely pair."

Her husband was the critic and restorer Henry Merritt, whom she married in 1877; sadly, he died within the year. Anna Lea was born in Philadelphia and, according to the detailed biographical form completed by the artist for the Tate's records, came to Europe in 1866 with her family. Though she never went to an art school she received a classical education and painted and drew on her own from an early age, studying the *Art Journal* as 'her chief art stimulus' (Tate form). Her family's travels around Europe between 1866 and 1870 took her to Florence and Dresden where, in the winter of 1869–70 she had her first studio. They moved on to Paris where she was allowed to enter Cogniet's studio as a student, but the outbreak of the Franco-Prussian War drove her to London. She showed her first painting, a portrait, in the 1871 RA and continued to exhibit regularly from then on a mixture of portraits and subject pictures.

According to a letter dated August 7th 1911, also in the Tate files, that accompanied the return of her completed form, *Love Locked Out* was 'the third of that kind' of subject: the first was *Camilla*, a large full length nude, 'undertaken as a study with no idea of exhibition' which she was persuaded to show at the RA 1883 (it won an Honourable Mention at the 1889 Paris Exposition Universelle), and this was followed by *Eve* hung on the line in the 1885 RA. Her later successes included three large decorative panels for the vestibule of the Women's Exhibition at the Chicago World Exhibition of 1893.

The mis-reading in recent years of the date on *Love Locked Out* as 1884 has lead to the suggestion that Watts was influenced by Merritt's picture in his piece of whimsy called *The Cowl Maketh not the Monk* (RA 1889, Bournemouth, see Watts exh. cat., Whitechapel 1974 (44)). As the date on *Love Locked Out* is in fact 1889, it is clear that the situation was entirely reversed, as would indeed be far more likely in view of Watts's already giant reputation and his position in British art. Wildly inappropriate though the subjects may have been, both Watts and Merritt were clearly much indebted originally to both the composition and the elaborate iconography of Holman Hunt's *The Light of the World* (RA 1854, Keble College), one of the best-known images of the nineteenth century.

The Trustees of the Tate Gallery

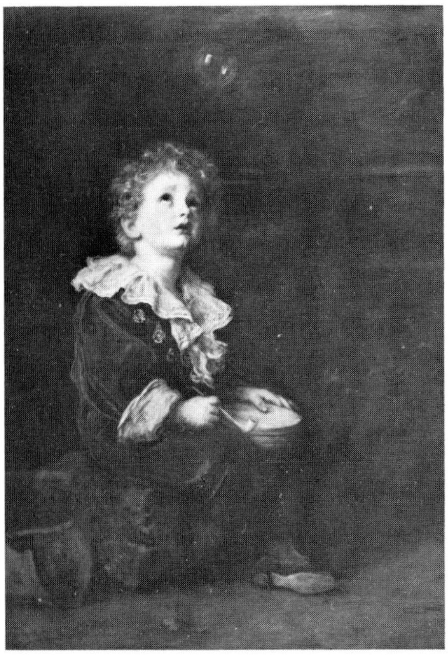

John Everett Millais, 1829–1896,
ARA 1853, RA 1863, PRA 1896

37 Bubbles 1885–6

oil on canvas, 43 × 31in
INSCR: JEM (monogram) 1886.

PROV: Bt. from the artist, early in 1886, by William Ingram for the *ILN*, from whom bt. Thomas J. Barratt, 6 Apr 1886, for A. & F. Pears Ltd. (£2200).
EXH: A. Tooth & Sons' Galleries, Spring 1886 (118); Expo. Univ., Paris 1889 (103); *World's Fair*, Chicago 1893; *Fair Children*, Grafton Galleries 1895 (209); *Exposition Internationale*, Brussels 1897 (54); *Works by the late Sir John Everett Millais, Bart., PRA*, RA 1898 (157); *Millais*, Walker Art Gallery, Liverpool, and RA 1967 (109).
LIT: *Beatrix Potter's Journal, 1881–1897*, transcribed from her code writing by L. Linder, with an appreciation by H.L. Cox, 1966, p154 (15 Nov 1885); *Academy*, 13 Mar 1886, p189; *Athenaeum*, 23 Jan 1886, p145, 3 Apr, p462; *The Builder*, 20 Feb 1886, p296; *Mag. of Art*, Apr 1886, pxxvii; *Times*, 29 Mar 1886, p10; M.H. Spielmann, *Millais and His Works*, 1898, pp136–7, 176, 179; J.G. Millais, *The Life and Letters of Sir John Everett Millais*, 1899, vol.ii, pp186, 187 (repr. of engr.), 189–91, 483, 495; *Times*, 17 Nov 1899, p14, 21 Nov, p11, 22 Nov, p7, 23 Nov, p15, 24 Nov, p7, 28 Nov, p4; Mary Bennett, *Millais* exh. cat., 1967, pp12, 59, repr. pl.39; G.H. Fleming, *That Ne'er Shall Meet Again*, 1971, pp347–9.
ENGR: G.H. Every, publ. Tooth, 1887 (mezzotint).
REPR *ILN*, Christmas Number, 1887 (chromolithograph).

At the time of painting *Bubbles*, Millais was unquestionably the most popular painter in England. One measure of his success was his enormous income. At a dinner party in 1885, he fell into a discussion about money with the Prince of Wales, in which the doctor, Sir Henry Thompson and the barrister, Sir Henry James also took part. These two said that the most eminent men in their professions could earn £15,000 and £20,000 respectively. Millais claimed that a painter could expect £25,000, and continued:

> "For the last ten years I should have made £40,000 had I not given myself a holiday of four months in the year: what I did actually make was £30,000, so that I gave an estimate considerably under the fact!" (recounted by Mrs. Oliphant, in a letter of 21st July 1885, quoted in *The Autobiography and Letters of Mrs. Oliphant*, ed. Mrs. Harry Coghill, 1899, pp325–6).

Also in 1885, he became the first artist to be created a baronet, and in the following year, concurrently with the first exhibition of *Bubbles*, a large retrospective of his work was held at the Grosvenor Gallery.

The model for *Bubbles* was Millais' grandson, Willie James. Children blowing bubbles are traditionally symbolic of Vanitas. The original title of Millais' picture, *A Child's World*, suggests, however, that he intended to convey the charm and wonder of childhood rather than any profounder meaning. *Bubbles* is reminiscent of child portraits by Reynolds; both the painterly technique and the boy's costume have a vaguely eighteenth century quality.

The work received fairly appreciative reviews when it was shown at Tooth's, although the *Magazine of Art* struck an ambiguous and rather weary note:

> "Sir J.E. Millais, in *Bubbles*, is more vulgarly robust and sloppily effective than usual."

It seemed that *Bubbles* was not destined for quite the huge success of the other pictures of children by Millais – *Cherry Ripe*, for example – which had been reproduced in recent years in *The Graphic* and the *Illustrated London News*. When he bought it for the latter journal, William Ingram felt

> ". . . under some apprehension as to its popularity, as from many years' experience of the public taste in these coloured pictures I had found out that 'boy' subjects were not nearly so saleable as those introducing the opposite sex. For this reason, *Bubbles* was given away on a smaller scale than usual – one of four coloured supplements."

The position held by *Bubbles* as Millais' best-known work and one of the most familiar Victorian images is due to its use as an advertisement for Pears' soap. The Chairman of Pears, T.J. Barratt, had long since realised the benefits of widespread advertising. An example in use about the time of his purchase of *Bubbles* showed a healthy-looking baby boy washing his feet with the company's product (see *ILN*, 27 Mar 1886, p321). Barratt saw that *Bubbles* could be effective in a similar way, with the additional advantage of being a work of art. He bought it from the *Illustrated London News* for £2,200. Copyright was included, but Barratt was nevertheless obliged by law to obtain the artist's permission before making the alterations to the design which would be incorporated in the advertisement (notably the addition of a bar of soap). He visited Millais with proofs of the reproduction and seems to have secured his approval. Barratt later claimed to have spent £30,000 on the *Bubbles* advertising campaign.

The appropriation of works of art for advertising was a subject of debate. Certain artists, such as W.P. Frith, whose *The New Frock* appeared in an advertisement for Sunlight soap, protested against the inadequacy of the Copyright Laws in not protecting their pictures from misuse. On the other hand, it was clear that advertising might in the long run be of considerable benefit. M.H. Spielmann wrote prophetically that

> ". . . we may find that commerce of today will, pecuniarily speaking, fill, in some sense and more or less satisfactorily, the empty seat of patronage which was once occupied by the Church." (*Mag. of Art*, 1889, p427).

The view that art was inevitably sullied by being used for such a purpose was expressed by Marie Corelli through a character in her novel *The Sorrows of Satan* (1895):

> "I am one of those who think the fame of Millais as an artist was marred when he degraded himself to the level of painting the little green boy blowing bubbles of Pears' soap. *That was an advertisement*, and that very incident in his career, trifling as it seems, will prevent his ever standing on the dignified height of distinction with such masters in Art as Romney, Sir Peter Lely, Gainsborough and Reynolds."

Miss Corelli made the common assumption that Millais had painted *Bubbles* expressly for Pears. Millais objected to her that he had not, and the passage was changed in later editions of the novel.

The question of whether or not Millais approved of Pears' use of his picture was argued heatedly in a series of letters to *The Times* in November 1899. In the biography of his father, published that year, J.G. Millais said that the artist had been 'furious' when Barratt had shown him the specimens of the advertisement. Barratt denied this vehemently. According to him, Millais had spontaneously exclaimed, "That's magnificent!":

> "Encouraged by his generous words, I spoke of the advantage which it was possible for the large advertiser to lend to art – he could give a very much greater publicity to a good picture than it could receive by being hung on the walls of the Royal Academy. Sir John Millais, with alacrity, appreciated that idea, and when I stated the extreme difficulty experienced by those desirous of advertising by means of the graphic art, to induce good men to paint pictures, owing to the artist's fear for his reputation, Sir John, taking his pipe from his mouth, said, "What . . . nonsense! I will paint as many pictures for advertising as you like to give me commissions for . . ."

William Ingram and Charles Deschamps wrote in support of Barratt, confirming that Millais had also spoken to them of his satisfaction with the *Bubbles* advertisements.

J.G. Millais' reply emphasised that his sources of information were much closer to the artist himself, and indeed included Millais' own remarks on the subject in conversation. The strongest assertion that Millais had disapproved came, however, from Richardson Evans, Honorary Secretary of the National Society for Checking the Abuses of Public Advertising, who claimed that:

> "He was one of the first members of our council . . . I understood him to be half amused and half annoyed at the – How shall I put it inoffensively? – the calmness of those who while practising systematically – without scruple or apparent remorse – wholesale and gross disfigurement, canted about encouraging art."

Millais probably thought in rather less fervent terms. His opinion perhaps went no further than the brief statement he had made some years before to the writer of an article on 'The Artist and the Advertiser':

> "I don't think I have any feeling about advertising; if done badly, I would object." (*Pall Mall Gazette*, 19 July 1889).

M.W.

A. & F. Pears, Ltd.

Henry Moore, 1831–1895, ARWS 1876, RWS 1880, ARA 1885, RA 1893

38 The Clearness after Rain 1887

oil on canvas, 48 × 72 in

PROV: Louis Huth of Hawkhurst, Sussex, and Mayfair, by 1888; his sale, Christie's 20 May 1905 (62) bt. Agnew for Thomas Pilkington; by descent to his grandson.
EXH: RA 1887 (659); Glasgow 1888 (80); Expo. Univ. Paris 1889 (108); *Loan Collection of Works by the "Moore" Family of York*, York 1912 (135).
LIT: *AJ*, Aug 1887, p278, sketch repr. p277; *Academy*, 7 May 1887, p384; *Athenaeum*, 11 June 1887, p773; *GdBA*, 1 July 1887, p86; *Mag. of Art*, 1887, p275; *Portfolio*, May 1887, p104; *Times*, 30 Apr, p10, 21 May, p8, 3 June 1887, p4; *Mag. of Art*, July 1889, p. 37; *GdBA*, 1 Sept 1889, p239, repr. p231; *Portfolio*, Sept 1889, p174; P. G. Hamerton, 'A Modern Marine Painter', *Portfolio*, Apr 1890, p88; obit. *Athenaeum*, 29 June 1895, p844; M. H. Spielmann, 'In Memoriam: Henry Moore, RA', *Mag. of Art*, 1895, pp379–80; Frank Maclean, *Henry Moore RA*, in series 'The Makers of British Art', 1905, pp86–9, 160; R.C. Trafford, 'The Art of Henry Moore, RA', *Windsor Mag.*, May 1911, p702; *Moore Family Exh. Cat.*, York, 1912, p15; Andrew Ferguson, 'Henry Moore, RA, RWS', *The Old Water-colour Society's Club Annual Vol*, 1976, p28.
REPR: Blackburn, *RA Notes*, 1887, p94; *Blackburn, British Fine Art Section, Paris Univ. Exh.*, 1889, p39.
STUDY: oil on canvas; 22 × 31 in, coll. of the marine artist, Luker; F.M. Luker sale, Sotheby's 23 Nov 1938 (63) bt. Malcolm. Lit: Maclean, *op. cit.* p89.

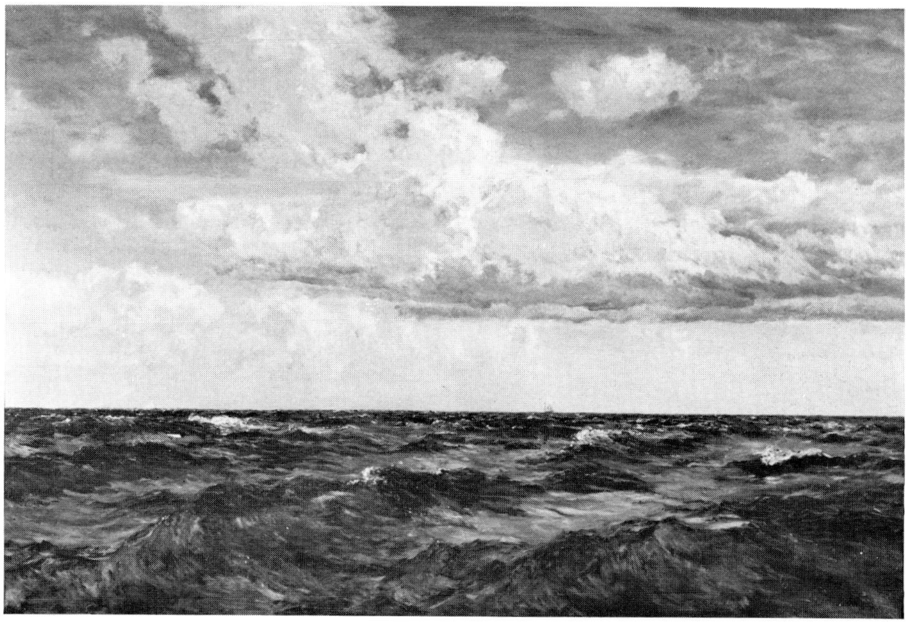

The Clearness after Rain was regarded by Moore's critics, contemporary and posthumous, English and French, friendly and hostile, as one of his two or three masterpieces. The reviewers acclaimed it when it was shown at the 1887 RA and, when it was lent to the Paris Exposition Universelle two years later, French admiration was unbounded: Moore was not only awarded one of the only two Médailles d'honneur given to English artists (the other went to Alma-Tadema, while Leighton's *Captive Andromache*, Burne-Jones's *King Cophetua*, and Orchardson's *Mariage de Convenance – After* were amongst those who only won First-class medals) but Moore was also made a Chevalier of the Légion d'honneur. The reaction of the *Athenaeum* in 1887 is a good example of the heights of praise to which *The Clearness after Rain* moved its viewers:

> "Mr. H. Moore's Titianesque sea-scape . . . is not only a masterpiece comparable with the superb *Mount's Bay* now at Manchester, but the finest piece of sentiment and truest representation of nature on these walls. We have not merely an atmosphere of intense purity, saturated with sunlight and crowned with a firmament of the deepest blue, but a fresh breeze stirs the surface, so that its billows are flecked with foam and constitute an ever-shifting wilderness of blues, clear, opaque, and semi-transparent as the light allows. All the movements and variations of the colour of the waves and the true quality of the firmament and its island-like clouds are given with consummate knowledge, massively, broadly, and intensely, and they form a perfect harmony which is as full of expression as of beauty and dignity. The vastness and loneliness of the 'waste of waters wide and deep' are emphasised by the few sails which, separated from each other by leagues of sea, pass on the horizon. Mr. Moore's other contribution . . . (254) . . . is fine enough to prove that, taking a noble revenge on that Academy which excluded him from its ranks for thirty years (as to the end it excluded Linnell), he sends his finest works to its exhibition . . . masculine and energetic in every touch, and so homogeneous that Titian himself would admire the noble application of the lessons he has taught posterity (evidenced in) Mr. Moore's abundance of resource and noble views of nature."

Reportedly a difficult and individualistic man, Moore had been excluded from the Academy until finally, at the age of 54, the sheer quality of his pictures and the reputation he had acquired as the leading marine painter of the day, rivalled only by John Brett, compelled his election to the RA.

The son of a York artist, the brother of four more (including Albert, the friend of Leighton and Whistler), Moore studied briefly at York School of Design and then at the RA Schools, where he early displayed his inability to get on with authority and, despite the expectations of his fellow-students, failed to win the first Turner Gold Medal in 1857. Henry Stacy Marks records in his autobiography a verse he wrote in support of his friend at the time:

Epigram.
In grave debate the R.A.'s meet; –
'Invention, feeling, we ignore.
Colour and nature – nonsense! stuff!
For Heaven's sake let's have no Moore!'

Since the turn of the century, Moore's name has tended to be linked with that of John Brett, Ruskin's protégé and the painter of *The Stonebreaker* and the *Val d'Aosta*, but this is misleading and was certainly not accepted by either artist. Moore always emphasised that his large paintings were based on the most careful studies and sketches made from nature and many of the smaller ones were done at sea. Maclean tells us, for instance, that the study for *Clearness after Rain* was done aboard one Mr. Burnett's yacht, sailing from Cherbourg to the Isle of Wight and was "especially brilliant and atmospheric". However, apart from his earliest Pre-Raphaelite influenced landscapes, he never espoused hard-line Ruskinian dogma and, as he matured, evolved an entirely original breadth and power that was being paralleled only in France. P.G. Hamerton was forced to print a correction to his article in *The Portfolio* in 1890, when Moore took exception to Hamerton's suggestion that he used photographs, but Hamerton's article was otherwise very favourable and noted that many French artists, including Meissonier, had been delighted with Moore's pictures shown at Paris in 1889, as had the French critics, and went on,

> "(it) only shows what wonderful progress has been made in the understanding of nature and in the breadth of judgment that can tolerate freshness and originality in art."

The intense blue of many of his paintings is instantly recognisable – to the French it was 'la note bleue de Moore' – and can be seen at its highest pitch in *Mount's Bay* (RA 1886, Manchester) and, to a lesser extent, in *The Newhaven packet* (RA 1885, Birmingham), though he could also paint seascapes of the most subdued, silvery tones, as in *Calm before a storm* (RA 1883, York). Moore's dedication to the study of the sea in its every aspect resulted in a lifetime of paintings in which the chief incident was always the sea itself – no anecdotal content, rarely a literary allusion in the title, and always a total absorption with the search for an understanding of the colour and movement of great masses of water; as Maclean, his biographer in 1905 wrote,

> ". . . if we look into these blues of his, into the blue of the *Newhaven Packet* or *Clearness after Rain*, the impression received is primarily that of overpowering blueness and saltness."

T.D. Pilkington, Esq., J.P.

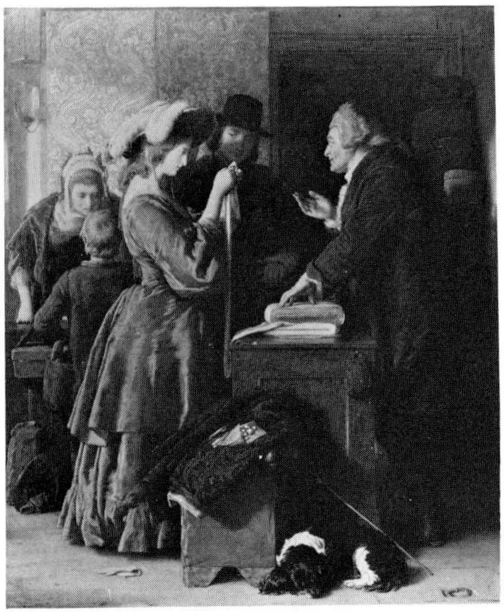

William Mulready, 1786–1863, ARA 1815, RA 1816

39 Choosing the Wedding Gown 1846

oil on panel, 21 × 17¾ in

PROV: commissioned by John Sheepshanks, £1050, by whom presented to the South Kensington Museum in 1857.
EXH: RA 1846 (140); Society of Arts 1848 (XXX); Expo. Univ. Paris 1855; *Mulready Exh.*, South Kensington Museum 1864 (93); Guildhall 1904 (88).
LIT: (selected) *Art Union*, June 1846, p175; *Athenaeum*, 16 May 1846, p503; *Examiner*, 1846, p293; *ILN*, 23 May 1846, p337; *Literary Gazette*, 9 May 1846, p433; Ruskin, *Modern Painters*, II, *Works*, IV, p336 and see XIV, pp300–1; *Times*, 6 May 1846, p5; Théophile Gautier, *Les Beaux-Arts en Europe*, 1855, pp27–9; 'The Sheepshanks Collection', *Athenaeum*, 1857, p857; 'William Mulready, RA', *Fine Arts Quarterly Review*, 1863, I, p382; James Dafforne, 'British Artists LXX: William Mulready, RA', *AJ*, Mar 1864, p67 & repr; F.G. Stephens, *Masterpieces of Mulready*, 1867, pp113–14, 118; 'Selected Pictures: From the Picture in the Sheepshanks Collection. *Choosing the Wedding Gown*', *AJ*, Jan 1869, p4, engr. frontisp; *A Gallery of British Art*, 1873, pp55–6; Redgrave, 1890, p326; Reynolds, 1966, p14.
STUDIES: A study for the whole composition in red chalk (with pencil and white heightening), 20 × 18 in, was coll. Thomas Baring (later Lord Northbrook); exh. RA 1844 (958), Society of Arts 1848 (LXIX), South Kensington 1864 (229), Guildhall 1904 (356). Other drawings were 1848 (LIX) and 1864 (89, 219).
ENGR AND REPR: numerous.

> "A gem!! – a perfect gem in character, in colour, and in treatment. . . . one of the most gorgeous little spectacles of bright colouring that can be conceived . . .
> This inimitable picture . . . To praise this production in the ordinary terms of eulogy would be a derogation from its unique excellence . . ."

The exclamations of the *Literary Gazette*, *Times* and *Art Union* were echoed throughout the press and the crowds were so great around the little picture that, according to Lord Ronald Gower, its place of honour in the principal room had to be railed off in the Wilkie fashion. The subject is from Goldsmith's *The Vicar of Wakefield* (1766), so popular with painters in recent years that the *Art Union* called it 'a very hackneyed source'; Mulready has embroidered the lines Goldsmith gives to the Rev. Dr. Primrose recounting his engagement to Deborah:

> "I had scarcely taken orders a year before I began to think seriously of matrimony, and chose my wife as she did her wedding gown, not for a fine glossy surface, but such qualities as would wear well."

The first idea for the composition, as the *Art Union* points out, appears in the 1843 edition of *The Vicar*, illustrated by Mulready (p1).

Almost all the reviewers, after discoursing on the truth and character of the treatment of the figures found that it was his use of colour that most distinguished the painting:

> "The pitch of colour to which it is brought strikes, as extraordinary, even the uninitiated; but they little dream by what careful anxious self-criticism, acting under the dictates of the most fastidious sense of the beautiful and the harmonious, that charming creation has been wrought . . . It is delightful to trace the unobtrusive skill which the pocket-handkerchief, the heel of the shoe, the bag on the counterside, and other trifling adjuncts are made the most valuable auxiliaries in spreading the different shades of colour." (*Athenaeum*).

This reviewer went on to equate Mulready with the Dutch and Italian masters, as did Ruskin in 1875; the *ILN* was more specific:

> "[it] must be judged as a piece of elaborate finish and richly harmonious colour, with natural every-day expression, like the works of Terburg or Gerard Douw. So judged, it may be classed in the first rank, and deserves the place of honour among the cabinet works of any school . . . [for its] combination of only the richest and most positive colours . . . so judiciously managed, as to leave no impression of garishness."

The *Art Union* review, its hyperbole exceeded only by that it bestowed on Eastlake's *Christ lamenting over Jerusalem* (cat. 9), concluded that Mulready's use of colour:

> "exalts the work to the rank of the finest productions of the greatest masters, and beyond many of their most highly-esteemed works. It is rare to find, even in the greatest men, the union of colour, form, and expression; the reputations of many of the greatest have often grown out of only one of these . . . The qualities of execution displayed . . . are astonishing. If finish be a commendable quality, it is worked up to the parallel of the most exquisite miniature; if its breadth be questioned, it possesses that quality in the highest degree: in short, it is a production which has never yet been equalled in its kind, and never can be excelled."

The painting was considered one of the masterpieces of the Sheepshanks collection presented to the nation in 1857, and when the *Art Journal* engraved it in 1869, it explained that it was impossible to find anything new to say about "this very popular picture", so minutely had it been examined and discussed in the past.

> ". . . where men have not read, they have seen; for it may be safely asserted that, among all the pictures contained in our National Gallery, both in Trafalgar Square and at South Kensington, not one has attracted more universal attention from all classes, high and low, rich and poor, the learned and unlearned in Art-knowledge, than the famous *Choosing the Wedding Gown.*"

From the late eighteenth century to the middle of the nineteenth, many hundreds of paintings with subjects taken from literature were exhibited: Shakespeare, Sterne, Goldsmith, Scott (see Catherine Gordon, *Apollo*, July 1973, pp36–9) and, later, Dickens, were the most popular English authors and Cervantes and Molière the most favoured foreigners. They provided anecdotal subjects that were already conveniently familiar to the public and an artist who used such texts could generally rely at least on approval for his choice of seemly subject-matter if not for his treatment.

Mulready made his name with genre scenes in the manner of Wilkie and with William Collins established a type of small-scale, sentimental genre painting that remained hugely popular throughout the century; its most successful followers were the artists of the Cranbrook Colony, led by Thomas Webster, and including F.D. Hardy, A.E. Mulready, G.B. O'Neill, and John Callcott ('Clothes') Horsley (see cat. of Cranbrook Colony exh., Wolverhampton 1977). Though many of Mulready's paintings, like *The Fight Interrupted* (RA 1816, V & A) were immensely popular, very few pictures by any artist in the nineteenth century achieved the critical and popular success of *Choosing the Wedding Gown.*

Victoria and Albert Museum

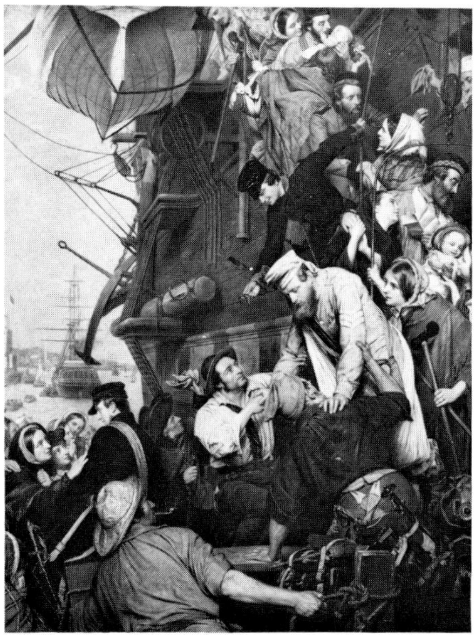

Home Again *Private Collection*

Henry Nelson O'Neil, 1817–1880, ARA 1860

40 Eastward ho! August 1857 1858

oil on canvas, 53½ × 42½ in

PROV: Edward Aldam Leatham, MP, Heath House, Wakefield, & subseq. Misarden Park, Glos. (by 1862); his sale, Christie's, 18 May 1901 (134) bt. Lister for William Proby, 5th Earl of Carysfort; by descent to the present owner.
EXH: RA 1858 (384); London Internat. 1862 (607); Expo. Univ. Paris 1867 (88); Guildhall 1895 (16); 1st 100 Years RA 1951–52 (356).
LIT: *AJ*, 1 June 1858, p168; *Athenaeum*, 8 May 1858, p596; *Critic*, 29 May 1858, p258; *Times*, 1 May, p5, 22 May 1858, p9; *AJ*, July 1862, p151, February 1864, p40; *GdBA*, 1 September 1867, pp214–215; Chesneau, 1885, pp273–276; obits: *Academy*, 20 March 1880, pp220–221; *AJ*, June 1880, p171; *Athenaeum*, 20 March 1880, p384; *Times*, 15 March 1880, p6; *DNB*, 1909, p1072; *A Catalogue of the Pictures at Elton Hall*, London, 1924, p99, repr.; Reynolds, 1953, p86, fig. 69; Reynolds, 1966, p29; *Beck*, 1973, pp36, 60; *Forbes RA Revisited*, p114; Wood, *Panorama*, 1976, pp224–225.
REPR: *Souvenir RA 1951–52*, p67; Wood, *Dictionary*, 1971, p341.
ENGR: W.T. Davey, mixed mezzotint, Lloyd

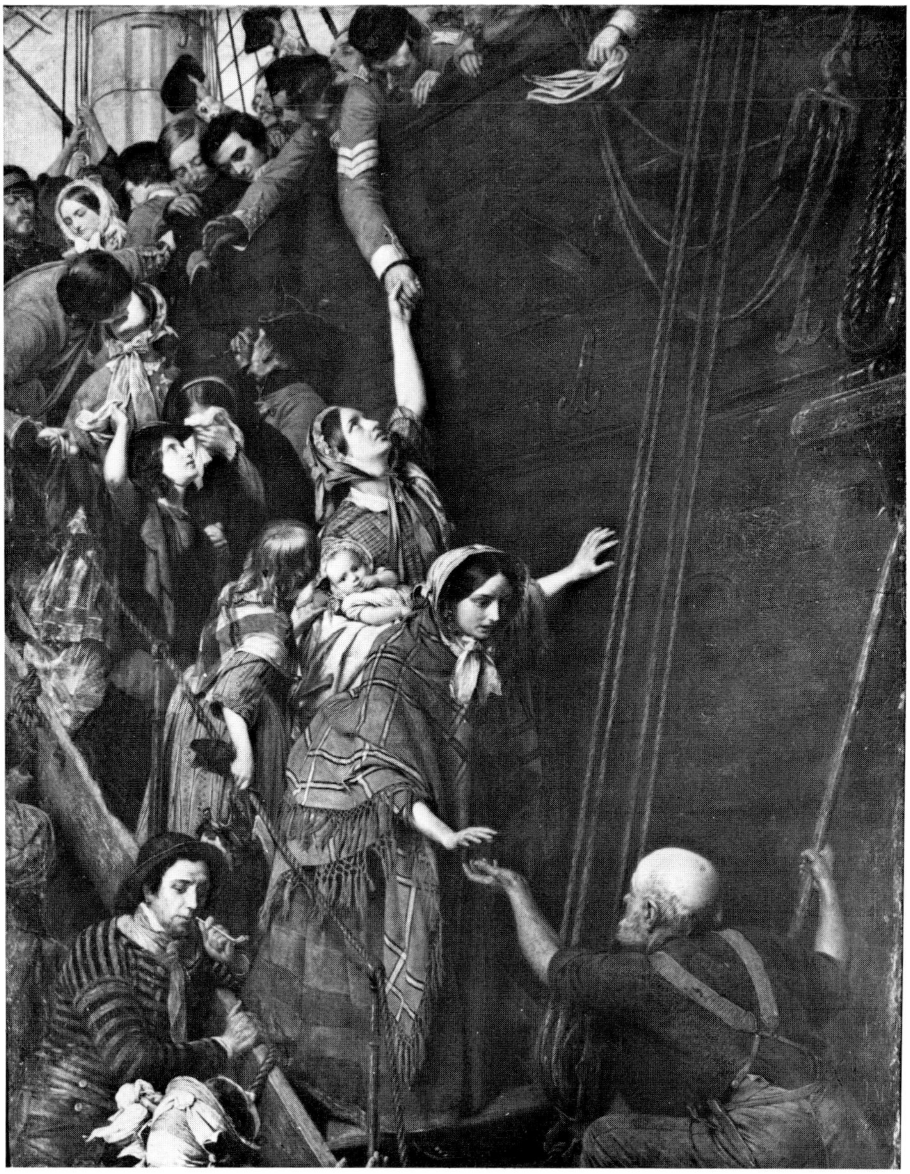

Brothers & Co., 1860 (Beck no. 29).
VERSIONS: 1 reduced version; oil on canvas, $35\frac{1}{2} \times 27\frac{1}{2}$ in; s & d 1858. Prov: James Hamilton Houldsworth, by 1878; Sotheby's Belgravia, 22 Feb 1972 (88) bt. A. Glass. Exh: Glasgow 1878 (2) and Internat. 1901 (199); Whitechapel Winter 1901 (111); Guildhall 1915 (139).
2. pair of reduced versions of *Eastward ho!* and *Home Again*; oil on panel; each $20\frac{3}{4} \times 16\frac{1}{2}$ in; s & d 1861. Prov: probably Sir Charles Booth, Bt., sold Christie's, 13 Mar 1897 (53, 54) bt. Webster (£110 5s); Brigadier Sir Ralph Rayner. Exh: Agnew's 1961 (72, 76).
3. details of central figures, considerably modified, from *Eastward ho!* and *Home Again;* oil on canvas, framed to appear as a pair; $20\frac{3}{4} \times 35$ in. Prov: Sotheby's, 20 May 1970 (48); Forbes Magazine Collection.
4. Forbes catalogue states that a pair of details similar to no. 3 is in a private collection in England.

The Indian Mutiny began in May 1857 and that summer and autumn saw the bitter fighting over Delhi, Cawnpore and Lucknow: August, to which the title specifically points, saw perhaps the greatest number of British troops sent to reinforce those already struggling to suppress the mutinying Bengal army and relieve the three cities. When the Academy opened in May 1858, the Mutiny had a further twelve terrible months to run, news of the massacres and reprisals had been dominating the newspapers and the British public responded with patriotic fervour to O'Neil's touching scene of soldiers parting from their families. Its success was immediate and exceeded in that year's RA only by Frith's *Derby Day*. Other artists' responses to the Mutiny included Abraham Solomon's *The Flight* (from Lucknow) (RA 1858, Leicester), Noel Paton's *In Memoriam* (RA 1858, coll. Alexander Whitelaw in 1911) and Frederick Goodall's *The Campbells are coming: Lucknow, September 1857* (BI 1858, Sheffield). Feelings had been inflamed by the publication in cheap prints and pamphlets (see Boase, 1959, p291) of luridly sensationalised details of the massacres and it was these sentiments to which O'Neil appealed while skilfully avoiding the charges made against Paton of over-taxing the emotions, by using a dockside farewell scene – already familiar in emigration subjects – and making the reference to the Mutiny specific only in the title.

O'Neil's brilliant orchestration of individual types and emotions in his picture found in the *Athenaeum* a fascinated and minutely-detailed chronicler: calling it "a triumph" and "a picture of simple pathos and truth", the review continues:

> "The classes of life, the ages, and the stations of the different leave-takers are admirably expressed and contrasted. The centre of all is a poor soldier's widowed mother, whose foot is just on the last step, and who is gazing with vacant, wet eyes, quite abstracted, on the rough boatman with the blue shirt and red braces, who is holding out to her his strong-knotted hand; . . . next up the steps comes a soldier's wife, a poor woman, but decent enough in her red-chequered trailing shawl, neat straw bonnet and blue ribbons, – she carries in her arms heedlessly (for her eyes are strained upward to catch a last look of the dear fellow's face) a child quite unconcerned, much amused by a soldier doll her elder sister is shaking before her eyes . . ."

and so on, through every figure in the drama, concluding:

> "The grief is wonderfully varied, and is always concentrated, deep, and without self-consciousness. The straining, longing eye of the poor wife and the entranced, heedless sorrow of the widow will live with us many a day."

Other reviewers were only slightly less fulsome: the *Art Journal*, as did *The Times* and the *Critic*, commended O'Neil's achievement of a newly "more robust and healthy style of art" and the originality of the composition, quibbling only with the placing of the gangway too near the bows of the ship. The chorus of praise subsided when O'Neil tried to follow up his success with a pendant, *Home Again* (coll. Major William Spowers, repr. Wood, *Panorama*, 1976, p225), but *Eastward ho!* increased its fame with the publication of the hugely successful engraving in 1860 and, when the picture was shown at the 1862 London International Exhibition, it was a member already of the pantheon of great British paintings.

Christie's 1901 sale catalogue misprinted its Paris exhibition date as 1857 and this has caused confusion ever since: *Eastward ho!* went in fact to the Exposition Universelle of 1867, giving the French critics their first opportunity to voice misgivings over its lack of academically correct composition with its unorthodox diagonal emphasis. Paul Mantz in the *Gazette des Beaux-Arts* was echoed in this by Chesneau nearly twenty years later, but both critics agreed it was an affecting work:

> "Rien n'est plus touchant que ce tableau, rien n'est plus anglais." (*GdBA*, 1867).

A rebellious student at the RA Schools, O'Neil had been a founder member of The Clique but his success at the Academy in 1858 made him a convinced opponent of younger movements: his pamphlet *Modern Art in England and France*, 1869, attacked Pre-Raphaelitism (as represented by Rossetti), the influence of photography on art, the decline of respect for such artists as Delaroche, and the low quality of French art in the Salon of 1869 (revenge, perhaps for French criticisms of him in 1867). He continued these attacks in 1870 and 1871. On his death in 1880 the general opinion had so far swung round from the euphoric patriotism of 1858 as to consider *The Last Moments of Raffaele* (RA 1866, Bristol) "his work of the highest character" (*AJ* 1880). O'Neil's Third Lecture on Painting delivered at the RA and published in 1866, declared his belief that Raphael's *Sistine Madonna* was the greatest painting in the world and concludes with his obviously profoundly-held conviction in the artist's need to rely on his individuality:

> ". . . all imitation . . . *is but a partial abandonment of reason* (O'Neil's italics); for it shows an utter forgetfulness of the special gift imparted to each living soul, and to learn how to make the best use of that divine gift your school must be living Nature, and not dead Art."

A footnote in Lecture IV is a wry conclusion on his own work:

> "It is a very common error to mistake popularity for real greatness."

Private collection

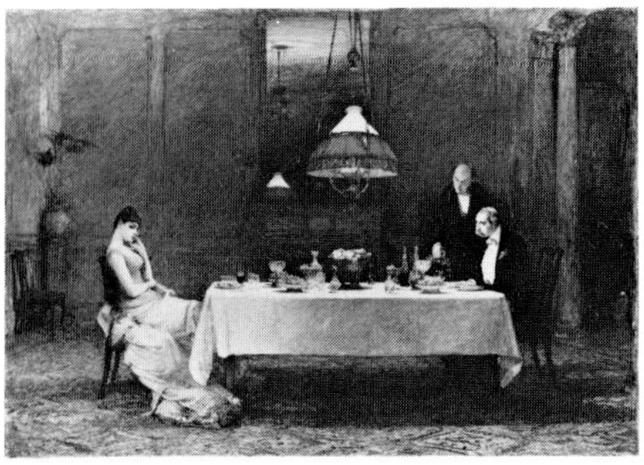

Mariage de Convenance
Courtesy: Glasgow City Art Gallery

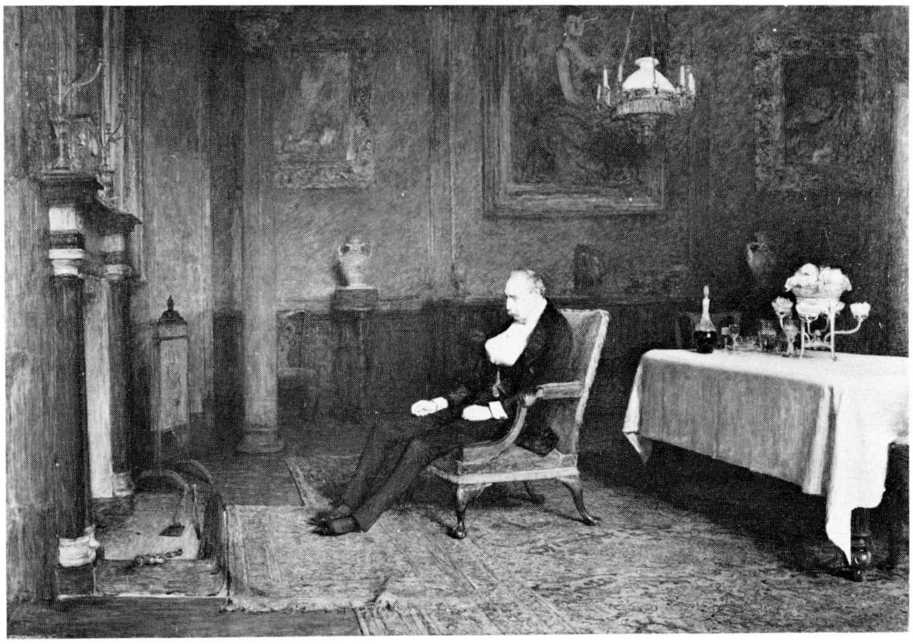

Sir William Quiller Orchardson, 1832–1910, ARA 1868, HRSA 1871, RA 1877, Kt. 1907

41 "Mariage de convenance" – After! 1886

oil on canvas, $44 \times 66\frac{1}{2}$ in
INSCR: W.Q. Orchardson 1886.

PROV: John M. Keiller, Dundee, from 1886; David Croal Thomson; purchased by Aberdeen, 1919.
EXH: RA 1886 (136); Dundee 1886 (45); Manchester Jubilee 1887 (387); Expo. Univ. Paris 1889 (114); RSA 1890 (190); Bradford 1925 (81); RA Winter 1939 (283); *Sir William Quiller Orchardson RA*, Scottish Arts Council 1972 (47).
LIT: *AJ*, June 1886, p185; *Academy*, 8 May 1886, p334; *Athenaeum*, 8 May 1886, p621; *ILN*, 1 May 1886, p449; *Portfolio*, June 1886, p123; *Spectator*, 1 May 1886, p580; *Times*, 1 May 1886, p10; Walter Armstrong, 'Note on Mr. Orchardson as a Dramatist', *AJ*, Feb 1894, pp33–4; Walter Armstrong, *The Art of William Quiller Orchardson*, 1895, pp56, 60; Cosmo Monkhouse, *British Contemporary Artists*, 1899, p183; James Stanley Little, 'The Life and Work of William Q. Orchardson, RA', *Art Annual*, 1897, p23, repr p30; J.B. Manson, 'The Aberdeen Art Gallery, *Studio*, Dec 1921, p252, repr p255; Hilda Orchardson Gray, *The Life of Sir William Quiller Orchardson*, 1930, pp267, 273; Reynolds, 1953, p96, fig. 88; Irwins, 1975, pp340–1, pl.173; Hardie, 1976, p53.
REPR: Blackburn, *RA Notes*, 1886, p28; Blackburn, *Paris Expo. Univ. Illustrated*, 1889, p45.
STUDY: for the figure, charcoal on paper; $22\frac{3}{4} \times 27\frac{1}{2}$ in; National Gallery of Scotland; *Orchardson exh.*, 1972 (46).

Orchardson aimed to be, and was recognised as, a painter of drama. His daughter once asked him, "if Art should be didactic, and if subject were important", and he replied,

> "that fine art must be fine in subject as well as in manner, that a purposeless picture could not be fine in the full sense of the word; and that what most appealed to him personally was the dramatic moment." (Gray, 1930, p273).

All his most popular pictures exploited a moment of dramatic and psychological tension. The first episode in the *Mariage de convenance* (Glasgow) was shown in 1884 and achieved an immediate success: an elderly, balding, but clearly very rich man sits gazing the length of a dining table at his beautiful but bored young wife. The counterpoint of age and youth, disappointment and boredom, decay and beauty is emphasised by the figure of the butler, which adds a dark weight to the age at one end against the light froth of youth at the other. The whole is suffused in Orchardson's characteristic yellow glow of lamplight. He at first thought of calling its sequel 'Ichabod', in allusion to the phrase from the first book of Samuel where it is used as a name to signify 'The glory that is departed from Israel'. In the event, it was exhibited as – *After!* and was, most reviewers thought, the subject picture of the year.

> "The young wife has gone, probably with a sullied name, and the husband who bought her in the sacred name of marriage sits alone and miserable, perhaps remorseful, by his splendid but deserted hearth. The strength of expression concentrated into this single figure of the man of the world off guard, away from curious eyes, in his torture of regret, is remarkable. The whole picture abounds in reticent force and truly artistic management." (*Portfolio*).

The *ILN* considered its technical quality superior to that of the first picture:

> "[it] shows even higher finish and more subtle power . . . Mr. Orchardson's colours are, moreover, losing much of that 'sour unripeness' which formerly marred the effect of some of his most effective compositions. Here the tones are ripe and warm, and the contrast between the steady light of the lamp and the flickering flame of the fire is represented with admirable effect."

The Times felt its success was assured because of the fame of the first picture:

> "Of Mr. Orchardson's talent we have spoken very often, and there is nothing new to say about an art which, within its peculiar limits, is certainly very distinguished and very complete . . . a great power of dramatic characterisation, and a like power of producing a striking effect by means of painting which is intentionally thin in texture."

In the *Mariage de convenance*, 'he comes before the world as a moral teacher', according to *The Times*, but Orchardson was too sophisticated in his treatment of social and moral subjects to fall into the Hogarthian trap. Its most ambitious, and disastrously unsuccessful, Victorian victim was Frith; his attempts at updating Hogarth's *Rake's Progress* appear in two sets of five pictures each – *The Road to Ruin* (RA 1878, Sotheby's 14 Nov 1962 (126)) and *The Race for Wealth* (King Street 1880, ex Baroda Coll., bt. Agnew). The third essay on the theme of marriage was *The First Cloud* (RA 1887, Melbourne), a replica of which was painted for Sir Henry Tate; it cannot, strictly, be included in the *Mariage de convenance* series as the husband is clearly a younger figure, but it equalled the success of its predecessors and went on to become one of the most popular engravings of the next fifty years.

Orchardson's other concern was with history: the first, and most popular, of his historical scenes was his vision of Napoleon standing alone on deck on his way to exile on Elba, *On board HMS 'Bellerophon'* (RA 1880, Tate). It was bought from the Chantrey Fund for £2000, twice the price paid the same year for Poynter's prestigious *Visit to Aesculapius*.

Orchardson left Scotland for London in 1862 in the company of his fellow-Lauder pupil John Pettie and showed at the RA from 1863; he made his first popular success with *The Challenge* shown in Wallis's Gallery in 1863, which was later well-received at Paris in 1867. The *Art Journal* acknowledged his already considerable stature in 1870 by making him the ninety-third subject of their series on British artists. The great expansion of Orchardson literature, always of course the sign of an artist's arrival in the pantheon, occurred in the 1890s, with lengthy articles and books by writers like Armstrong and Monkhouse, the chief propagandists of the grand art of Leighton and the classicists.

Aberdeen Art Gallery

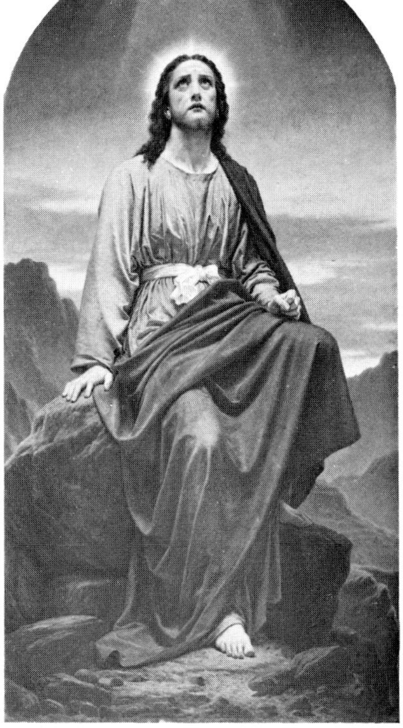

The Man of Sorrows
Courtesy: Tyne and Wear County Museums Service

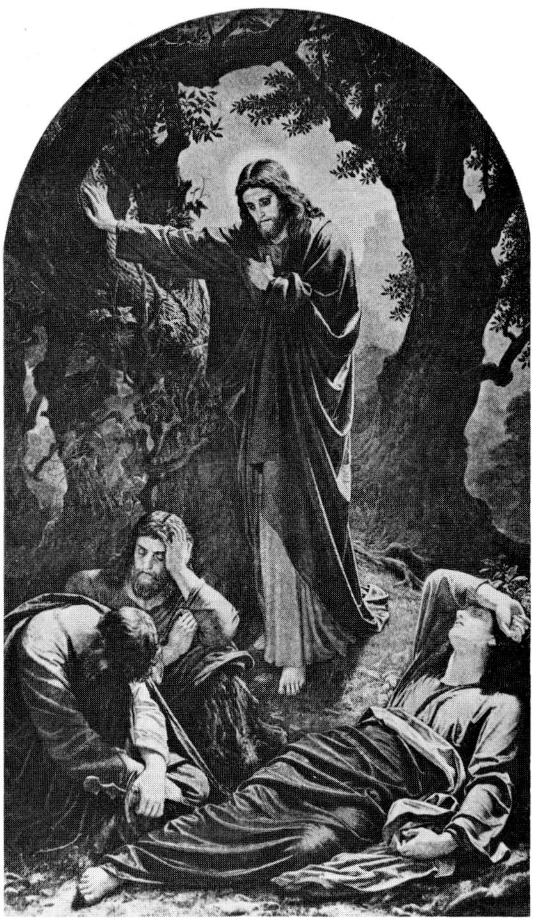

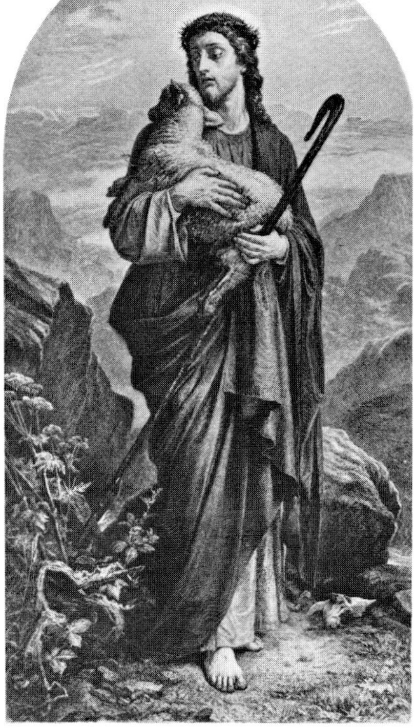

engraving after The Great Shepherd

SIR JOSEPH NOEL PATON, 1821–1901, ARSA 1847, RSA 1850, HM Limner for Scotland 1866, KT. 1867

42 Vigilate et Orate 1884

oil on canvas, arched top, $12 \times 7\frac{1}{2}$ in
INSCR: JNP (monogram) 1884

PROV: Maas Gallery, 1970.
EXH: *Pre-Raphaelitism*, Maas Gallery 1970 (14).
LIT: (references are to his later religious works in general). George R. Halkett, 'Sir Joseph Noel Paton, RSA, LL.D', *Mag. of Art*, 1880, pp4, 6; J.M. Gray, 'Sir Noel Paton, RSA. LL.D', *AJ*, Mar 1881, pp79–80; Alfred T. Story, 'Sir Noel Paton: His Life and Work', *AJ*, Apr 1895, pp112–15, engr. and pls.; Caw, 1908, pp169–70; Alasdair Auld, exh. *Fact & Fancy: Drawings and paintings by Sir Joseph Noel Paton, RSA*, Scottish Arts Council, 1967, pp7, 28–30; M.H. Noel-Paton, *Tales of a Grand-daughter*, privately printed, 1970, pp38ff; Irwins, 1975, pp293–5.
STUDIES 1. *Design for 'Watch and Pray'*; pen and ink; exh. *Pictures, Drawings and Designs by the late Sir Noel Paton*, Fine Art Society 1902 (93).
2. *Design for 'Watch and Pray'*; pencil; exh. 1902 (95).

Noel Paton was rapidly established as one of Queen Victoria's favourite artists when, following the success of his picture of a Crimean veteran, *Home* at the 1856 RA, the Queen commissioned a replica for the Prince Consort's Christmas present in 1859. In December 1861, Albert died and the Queen commissioned from Paton a portrait of herself and her children as a memorial; the artist duly spent much time at Windsor during 1863 (see journal entries, M.H. Noel-Paton, pp33–4ff) making drawings of the Royal Family (exh. 1967 (33)), but, though Paton completed a small painting of Victoria kneeling by the Prince Consort's deathbed, the large portrait was never completed. This seems not to have been held against him, for Victoria appointed him the Queen's Limner for Scotland in 1866 and knighted him the following year. Paton was at this time beginning the religious subjects which were to occupy most of the rest of his career and in 1876 received the first royal commission for a replica of one of these large paintings, *The Good Shepherd* (untraced) which he was then completing, and which, according to the *Art Journal* (1895, p113), was dedicated by special command to the Queen. The Queen later commissioned a replica of *The Man of Sorrows* (1875, Newcastle) and finally the *Vigilate et Orate*; according to Paton's journal he was summoned to Balmoral in 1889 to discuss a triptych, presumably consisting of these three pictures, for the Prayer Room at Osborne House, the Royal Family's summer residence on the Isle of Wight.

They were certainly installed there, with *Vigilate et Orate* forming the centre of the triptych, when the *Art Journal* described it at length in 1895 (pp114–15). They are next recorded in the Osborne inventory of 1913 in the Pages' Waiting Room. Their measurements were given as *The Good Shepherd*, on panel, 42×22 in; *The Man of Sorrows*, on canvas, also 42×22 in; and *Vigilate et Orate*, on panel, $59 \times 35\frac{5}{8}$ in. A 1900 Osborne inventory records a pair of very small replicas of *The Good Shepherd* and *The Man of Sorrows*, both on panel, $10\frac{1}{2} \times 5\frac{7}{8}$ in, in the Queen's Bedroom; neither the three medium-sized pictures forming the triptych, nor the pair of small replicas have been traced and it is assumed that they were dispersed from the Royal Collection probably in the years immediately after the First World War. The small replica of *Vigilate et Orate* exhibited here and the large version of *The Man of Sorrows* are the only versions of the Osborne subjects currently traced.

Queen Victoria's taste for Paton's religious art endorsed that of great numbers of her subjects; in the 1870s and 1880s

> ". . . his large pictures were enormously popular in Scotland, and, sent on tour with footlights and a lecturer, attracted great audiences, and secured a long list of subscribers for reproductions. They were a solace to many serious-minded people, and afforded the popular preacher many a coloured text." (Caw, pp169–70).

The Irwins quote details of two such sermons delivered in Glasgow in 1888 on Paton's *The Choice*, one by a minister and another by the District Superintendent of the Scottish Permissive Bill and Temperance Association, using the picture to reinforce exhortations to temperance and chastity. Even without sermons the pictures attracted crowds, as the *Magazine of Art* noted in 1880 (1881 vol., p.vi) when *Lux in Tenebris* (Sheffield, destroyed 1939/45) had been on exhibition in Edinburgh for two months; an engraving was shortly to be published by the firm run by Hugh Paton. The magazine thought it

> "one of the most successful of the painter's recent works, and . . . a fine example of his earnestness of thought and graceful imagination."

By the turn of the century commentators were critical and Bryan's Dictionary, recording that many of his religious works were engraved and sold in great quantity, 'especially amongst Nonconformists', considered 'his paintings were of a very sentimental and religious character, but attained to extraordinary popularity', and Caw's criticisms in 1908 are stringent. He compared Paton with Holman

Hunt in his desire to elevate moral purpose above aesthetic quality,

> "Yet admirable as they are in intention, his religious pictures are illumined by no fresh and vivid light of thought, and place one in no unexpected and moving relationship to life. Correct and chaste but cold in feeling, high in aspiration but unimpassioned in conception, elegant in form and design, but lacking in spontaneous grace and compelling charm, his religious and allegorical creations are very kindred to those of the Nazarenes . . . Cornelius . . . Overbeck . . . and the rest . . .; and, though he is understood to have disliked their work, he possessed sets of the elaborate outline engravings published in Germany during the forties." (Caw, p169).

Paton's other major religious works included *Beati Mundo Corde* (now Dundee) which with the Sheffield and Newcastle pictures were sold from the James Paton collection at Christie's on 5 March 1910. It also included *The Pursuit of Pleasure* (Durban) of 1855, Paton's first large allegorical subject and the forerunner of his religious pictures. His first great successes had been with *The Quarrel* and *The Reconciliation of Oberon and Titania* (both Edinburgh), the latter shown at the RSA in 1847 and containing much of the sharpness of definition and minute literalism (albeit of a fantasy subject) associated immediately afterwards with the Pre-Raphaelites. He was a close friend and disciple of Millais from student days at the RA Schools in 1843, but his later works owe a greater debt to the religious sentiment of Holman Hunt.

Hon. Ranald Noel-Paton

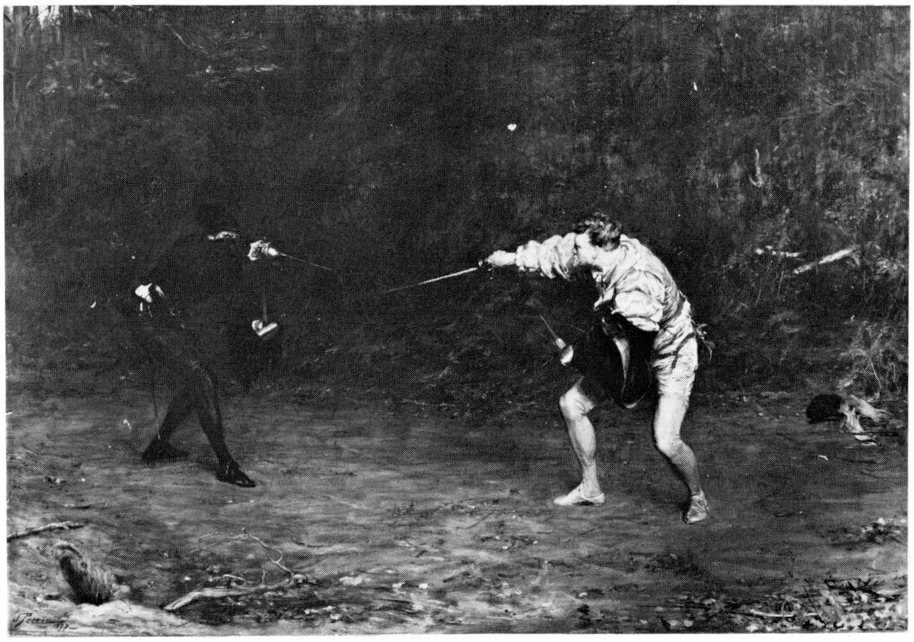

John Pettie, 1839–1893, ARA 1866, HRSA 1871, RA 1873

43 A Sword and Dagger Fight (or To the Death) 1877

oil on canvas, 35 × 55 in
INSCR: J. Pettie 1877

PROV: John Newton Mappin; bequeathed to Sheffield, 1884.
EXH: RA 1877 (203); RA Winter 1894 (201); Whitechapel 1894 (78); *Special Centenary Exh.*, RSA 1926; *Canadian National Exh.*, Toronto 1935.
LIT: *AJ*, June 1877, pp186, 200; *Academy*, 19 May 1877, p444; *Athenaeum*, 12 May 1877, p614; Blackburn, *RA Notes*, 1877, p24; *ILN*, 5 May, p419, 19 May 1877, p474; *Times*, 5 May 1877, p12; Wilfrid Meynell, 'John Pettie, RA', *Mag. of Art*, 1881, p15; obit. *Athenaeum*, 25 Feb 1893, p255; W. Matthews Gilbert, 'The late John Pettie, RA, HRSA', *AJ*, July 1893, p209; RA Winter, *Athenaeum*, 3 Feb 1894, p153; Elijah Howarth, 'The Art Treasures of Sheffield: The Mappin Gallery', *Windsor Mag.*, Sept 1895, p261; Temple, 1897, p280; Martin Hardie, 'John Pettie, RA, HRSA', *AJ*, Apr 1907; Caw, 1908, pp242–3; Martin Hardie, *John Pettie, RA, HRSA*, 1908, pp70, 104, 172, 231; *Sheffield Cat.*, *c.*1930 (58) repr.; Stanley Cursiter, *Scottish Art*, 1949, p122; Hardie, 1976, p51.
ENGR: Arthur Turrell, mezzotint; 16¼ × 24 in, publ. Arthur Lucas, 31 New Bond St., 1891.
STUDIES: finished sketch, *A Sword and Dagger Fight* (also known as *The Duel*), oil on canvas; 19½ × 30½ in; inscr. J. Pettie; James Donald bequest to Glasgow, 1905. Exh: RSA 1878; Glasgow Institute 1882; Glasgow Internat. Exhs. 1888, 1901; *Scottish Nat. Exh.*, Edinburgh 1908. Lit: Hardie, 1908, p231, repr. facing p106. Finished study for one of the figures; 15½ × 21 in. Prov: Christie's 1900.

John Newton Mappin's favourite artist was Pettie and Pettie's single most important patron was undoubtedly Mappin. Of the 153 paintings he bequeathed to Sheffield and which formed the nucleus of the Mappin Art Gallery, there are nine Petties – his nearest rival in Mappin's favour was Frederick Goodall, of whose work there are six representatives, including several small and unimportant pictures. *A Sword and Dagger Fight* was very well received at the 1877 RA – as Pettie's dramatic historical pictures generally were – but it was not until ten years later that it appeared again in public, in the newly built Mappin Art Gallery. It immediately became one of the gallery favourites, so much so that five years later, when it was lent to the Pettie room at the RA Old Masters exhibition of 1894, the winter after Pettie's death, the *Athenaeum* was able to comment:

> "There is *melodrama* of the most energetic sort in the famous *Sword and Dagger Fight* . . . The tale is told with such verve that no one wonders that the picture is the most popular of the painter's achievements."

The rest of the notice demonstrates vividly how quickly Pettie's pictures had become unfashionable:

> "The treatment of the background is extremely clever, and although the sharpness of the contrasts between the intense blackness of the one fighter's dress and the equally intense whiteness of his rival's clothing is a piece of artistic claptrap of the tritest sort, there is no denying the *chic* of the thing. Apart from this, the figures are painted with unusual care and admirable dexterity."

Lionel Cust, the art historian and critic, observed from the Leighton stronghold of the *Magazine of Art* that Pettie's pictures

> "reveal the deceased Academician as a man of strong, if somewhat limited ideas, who had something to say and knew how to say it. There are a life and vigour about his pictures which prove him worthy of his academical honours; and these qualities have procured, and will probably maintain, for him a considerable popularity with the British public." (1894, p112).

Thirteen years earlier, Wilfrid Meynell had concluded his *Magazine of Art* biography of Pettie,

> "Even when Mr. Pettie is not at his brilliant best, he is strongly and strikingly attractive; no cruder colour and no more ignorant touch can stand near his work; his pictures have the peculiar quality of being most killing neighbours in an exhibition. But such killing is of good service; it must inevitably have the effect of modifying and at last of banishing the cold, raw, grating tones which have so long prevailed on the walls of London galleries. Mr. Pettie is now in the very zenith of his powers and in the perfection of his years; our list of his canvases . . . shows how hard, as well as how successfully, he has worked hitherto; but we may

expect that the catalogue will be doubled before his artistic strength is abated."

Pettie's use of colour and the bravura with which it was applied was, in the opinion of the *DNB*, the key to his success. Reviewers of his paintings were often upset by what the *Athenaeum* obituary called 'the glare and coarseness' of his brushwork and, while they were happy to recognise his debt to continental masters in subject matter and composition, remained prejudiced against the evidently French technique to which his Scottish background had predisposed him.

Meissonier was the influence most often detected by his contemporaries and, in the case of the *Sword and Dagger Fight*, his hugely popular painting *La Rixe* (1855) in the Royal Collection. The painting had been a resounding success when it was first shown at the 1855 Paris Exposition Universelle, and was presented to the Queen and Prince Albert on their visit to Paris by Napoleon III. The Irwins point out that it was lent the following year to the RSA in Edinburgh, where Pettie was studying under Lauder, and it is likely that he would have seen it there. A measure of its popularity in this country is the fact that it kept its French title and needed no translation (see Lucas, cat. 31 for further discussion of Meissonier and England). The scene, a violent guardroom brawl, features the same contrast of light and dark-clothed protagonists against a stark background (a wall in *La Rixe*, an earth bank in Pettie's picture), and was clearly Pettie's inspiration, though he has pared away the figures restraining the fighters, leaving them isolated, as it were on a stage. Martin Hardie, Pettie's biographer, discussed the artist's debt to Scott's novels and, though it has not been suggested that this is an illustration to a specific scene from one of the novels, it is a vivid evocation of a typical Scott theme. Harry Furniss, the painter of the famous parody on the RA and its artists, 'The Joke Academy' shown at the Gainsborough Gallery in 1887 (see *Connoisseur*, 1973, pp22–8), drew 'The "Sword and Dagger" Fight' for the *Magazine of Art*, clearly intended as a recognisable reference to Pettie's picture.

Pettie's best known paintings today are probably Glasgow's *Two strings to her Bow* (RA 1887) and *A State Secret* (RA 1874, Royal Holloway College).

Sheffield City Art Galleries

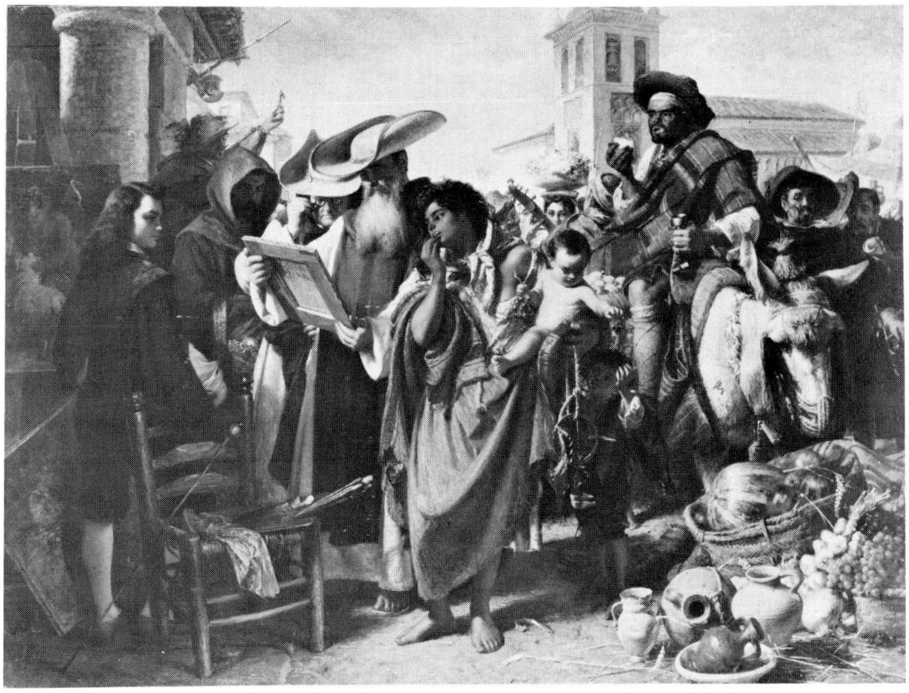

JOHN PHILLIP, 1817–1867, ARA and HRSA 1857, RA 1859

44 The early career of Murillo, 1634 1865

oil on canvas, 72 × 100 in
INSCR: JP (monogram) 1865; B.E. Murillo 1634

PROV: Mr. and Mrs. Henry McConnel, by 1873; his sale, Christie's, 27 Mar 1886 (80) bt. Silva White (£3990); James M. Keiller, Dundee; his sale, Christie's 25 May 1895 (94) bt. Davis (£3990); Sir Joseph Robinson, of London and South Africa; his sale, Christie's, 6 July 1923 (116) bt. Sabary, subseq. bt. back; to his daughter, Princess Labia; her sale, Sotheby's, 20 Nov 1963 (110) bt. Goldstein; anon. sale, Sotheby's, 21 Oct 1970 (53) bt. Agnew for Forbes.
EXH: RA 1865 (156); *Phillip Exh.*, London Internat. 1873 (1329); Manchester Jubilee 1887 (595); RA Winter 1894 (11); *Robinson Coll.*, RA 1958 (82), and Cape Town 1959 (100).
LIT: *AJ*, June 1865, p165; *Athenaeum*, 29 Apr 1865, p591; *Blackwood's*, Aug 1865, pp239–40; *Fraser's*, June 1865, p751; *ILN*, 6 May 1865, p439; *Punch*, 13 May 1865, pp196–7; *Reader*, 20 May 1865, pp579–80; *Times*, 29 Apr 1865, p12; Palgrave, *Essays*, 1866, pp105–6; James Dafforne, *Pictures by John Phillip* with descriptions and biographical sketch of the painter, 1877, pp48–51; Cunningham, 1880, III, pp442–3; reviews of the Manchester Jubilee Exh. 1887; Walter Armstrong, 'Scottish Painters VII', *Portfolio*, Sept 1887, p176; RA Winter Exh., *Athenaeum*, 3 Feb 1894, p153; R.A.M. Stevenson, 'Mr. Keiller's Collection in Dundee', *AJ*, Feb 1894, p58; Caw, 1908, p181; Francina Irwin, 'The Scots Discover Spain', *Apollo*, May 1974, p357; *Forbes RA Revisited*, pp118, 150 (incl. further refs), repr. p119, 179 (colour); Irwins, 1975, pp327, 330; Hardie, 1976, p45.
VERSION: reduced replica dated 1866; oil on canvas; 16 × 19¾ in. Prov: Charles P. Matthews, of Mayfair and Havering-Atte-Bower, Essex, by 1873; his sale, Christie's, 6 June 1891 (104), bt. Agnew (£320 5s) purchaser not recorded at Agnew's. Exh: London Internat. 1873 (1218).
STUDY: *Study for the Picture of Murillo*, sepia, Phillip sale, Christie's, 31 May 1867 (199). Lot 294 was a study for *Velasquez exhibiting his Portrait of the King before the Church*, intended as a companion to the *Murillo*.

'Phillip of Spain's' RA picture of 1865 'out-topped his highest triumph' (*AJ*) – 'the most manly, and masterly work in the exhibition' said the *ILN* and *Blackwood's* stated unequivocally that it

"is a picture which could command a master position in any gallery in Europe, ancient or modern. A work of this signal power and resource might serve as a landmark to show the goal whereunto contemporary art had reached; it also might be used as the measure of the progress made under recent revivals, and will probably stand as a point of departure whence future developments may date . . . This, the master-work of Mr. Phillip, is indeed on many accounts noteworthy: specially is it to be commended for the bold breadth of its handling, which stands out as a protest against that littleness of manner, that niggling detail in execution, which some years ago threatened to sink our English School into contempt. Likewise this picture will be remembered as one of the decisive triumphs of realism, strong throughout in graphic character, emphatic in local circumstance, truthful in all essential features of time and place, and thus actual to the last degree, and, because actual and real, impressive even as truth and nature. In the presence of such a work we have the less cause to regret that 'high art' is extinct, and that ideal treatments are at a discount."

John Phillip's nickname had been earned after his first visit to Spain in 1851. He lived for a time in Seville and the experience both of Spanish art and of Spanish life transformed his work; it had till then been Scottish genre in the manner of Wilkie, but he painted almost exclusively Spanish subjects for the rest of his sadly short life. Most of his first thirty years had been spent in Aberdeen, though three years' study in London introduced him to the members of the Clique, of which he became a member. In 1846 he moved permanently to London, visiting Spain twice more, in 1856 and 1860. He was the acknowledged head of the mid-century school of British artists whose visits to variously exotic countries transformed their work; his followers include Burgess, Long and Storey, but he himself had followed in the steps of Wilkie, Roberts and Lewis. Phillip enjoyed royal patronage from the mid-1850s, but his contemporaries and biographers rated most highly the paintings that followed his last visit to Spain. Of these, *La Bomba* (1863, Aberdeen), *La Gloria* (1864, Edinburgh) and *A Chat round the Brasero* (1866, Guildhall), together with the *Murillo* picture, were always cited as the most important. Phillip thought that *La Gloria* was his greatest painting; it was the one by which he wished to be remembered but, with the exhibition of the *Murillo*, critical and public opinion contradicted the artist's.

The picture was an illustration of a passage in William Stirling's (later Sir William Stirling-Maxwell) *Annals of the Artists of Spain*, 1848, II, p829, describing how the young Murillo 'was reduced to earn his daily bread by painting coarse and hasty pictures for the Feria', the weekly fair of Seville. Phillip edited out of the description of the market items like 'indifferent meat, ill-savoured fish' and 'old mats', which presumably did not suit his lavish Murillo still-life composition in the lower right-hand corner. The rest of the painting is remarkable not only for its faithfulness to Stirling's text but most of all for the way in which elements from Murillo's paintings have been exploited in order to reconstruct a Victorian idea of a seventeenth century Spanish market scene. It is also crammed with its quota of references to Murillo, typical of such paintings, and meant for spotting by the connoisseurs amongst his audience. For instance, the young artist, the figure at the extreme left, gazes at the girl and her baby in the centre who, according to the *Athenaeum*, inspired the pose of *La Servilleta*, Murillo's Virgin and Child at Seville (the resemblance, in fact, is minimal). The painting on Murillo's easel was referred incorrectly to the artist's *St. John and the Lamb* in the National Gallery – it is not in fact identifiable with any of the well-known versions of the subject, though they are nearly as numerous as the forgeries after them. Stirling's book was the first modern history of Spanish art and was of the greatest importance to British artists' understanding of the work of Murillo and Velasquez. Dafforne points out that Phillip probably also used Richard Ford's *A Hand-book for Travellers in Spain, and Readers at Home*, 1845, while in Spain and on his return.

Phillip was considered an artist of such stature than an entire section of the 1873 London International Exhibition was devoted to 329 of his works; this extraordinary accolade was succeeded by a memorial exhibition at Aberdeen in 1880. However, despite the fact that prices for major Phillip paintings continued to be high for the rest of the century (the *Murillo* twice fetched £3990 and *La Gloria* was bought by the National Gallery of Scotland in 1897 for the record Phillip price of £5250, the artist's critical reputation declined from the 1880s. In 1887 Walter Amstrong wrote of the *Murillo*

> "Although, perhaps, his most ambitious picture, it is deficient as a creation. The subject was scarcely suited to his genius, which was its best with themes that gave a chance for style, for balanced arrangement, and for simple arabesque."

Five years later the picture was heavily criticised when it appeared at the RA Winter Exhibition, and Caw's conclusion in 1908 was that Phillip's final place would be as a popular translator of Spain:

> "His art as a whole reveals no philosophy of life, but he saw simply and well, and expressed what he saw brilliantly and with consummate ease; and while his technique gained the applause of his fellow craftsmen, the obviously 'picturesque' character of his subjects gave his pictures a popularity which is likely to be permanent. The hold his Spanish scenes took of the popular mind is attested by the name 'Phillip of Spain' they earned him, and by the fact that most of our ideas of Spanish life, custom and costume are derived from them."

Recent reassessments of 'Spanish' Phillip (his modern nickname) can be found in Charles Carter's catalogue of the Phillip exhibition at Aberdeen in 1967 and related articles, and in the histories of Scottish painting by the Irwins and Hardie.

The Forbes Magazine Collection, New York

PAUL FALCONER POOLE, 1807–1879, ARA 1846, RA 1861–79, RI 1878

45 Solomon Eagle exhorting the people to repentance, during the plague of the year 1665 1843

oil on canvas, 60¾ × 88 in
INSCR: PF Poole 1843

PROV: Henry Wallis; Christie's, 27 Apr 1860 (43) bt. in (£819); Henry Wallis sale, Foster's, 6 Feb 1861 (88) bt. Patterson (£430 10s); E.M. Perkins, by 1862; Charles P. Matthews of Mayfair and Havering-atte-Bower, Essex, by 1884; his sale, Christie's, 6 June 1891 (108) bt. Mappin (£330 15s); Sir Frederick Thorpe Mappin, by whom presented to Sheffield before 1910.

EXH: RA 1843 (423); BI 1844 (407); Royal Manchester Institution 1845 (227, Heywood Gold Medal); London Internat. 1862 (578); *Old Masters and Poole*, RA Winter 1884 (289); Sheffield 1968 (6); RA Bicentenary 1968–9 (226).

LIT: *Art Union*, June 1843, p171; *Athenaeum*, 20 May 1843, p492; *Blackwood's*, Aug 1843, p189–91; *ILN*, 13 May, p328, 10 June 1843, p400, engr. p399; *Times*, 11 May 1843, p8; 'British Artists XLII: Paul Falconer Poole, ARA', *AJ*, Feb 1859, p41, engr. p41; Sandby, 1862, p312; obit., *Athenaeum*, 27 Sept 1879, p408; *ILN*, 12 Jan 1884, p30; *Portfolio*, Feb 1884, p43; *Times*, 7 Jan 1884, p7; Redgrave, 1890, p403; Temple, 1897, p58; A.G. Temple, *England's History as pictured by famous painters*, 1897, p171 & repr.; *DNB*, XVI, p101; Boase, 1959, p214, pl.66b; Reynolds, 1966, p142; Maas, 1969, p38.

ENGR: 1. S. Sly, wood engraving, publ. *ILN*, 10 June 1843, p399.
2. J. and G.P. Nicholls, wood engraving, publ. *AJ*, Feb 1859, p41.

STUDIES: *Head of Solomon Eagle* and *Solomon Eagle*, pictures and studies in oil, Poole sale, Christie's, 8 May 1880 (130 and 160) bt. Macbeth (£2 2s) and Knowles (£2 12s).

Solomon Eagle was received not only as *the* picture of the 1843 RA but as the greatest history painting in English art to date; it was compared favourably with Reynolds' *Ugolino* (Knole), with Poussin's *The Plague at Ashdod* (copy in National Gallery) and even with Géricault's *The Raft of the Medusa*. The much-quoted review in *Blackwood's* is the longest and most fulsome; the *Athenaeum's* praises are briefer and reflect the same astonishment at the impact of the picture:

> ". . . [a] picture which has agreeably surprised us; not that the subject is agreeable, but, on the contrary, so full of horror, pain, and pity, that we should not wish to inhabit the room in which it hung; but in point of power and painting it is admirable: and no subject so full of physical horror was ever more finely treated; it appears to us one of the very best pictures in the Exhibition. The great number of figures, grouped without confusion or perplexity, and the concentration of the interest and effect, round the crazed prophet in the centre; the beautiful girl looking up in front; the ruffian, the reckless gamblers, the delirious patient who has escaped from his bed, the ominous looking masked robbers, armed with aromatic essences, one of those horrid women who we are told went about strangling and rifling the dying wretches, and who looks as if arrested by the denunciations of judgment – all these, and a great variety of accessories, render this picture very dramatic and striking without too far outraging the feelings. There is something, too, very effective in the ghastly glare of light shed over the scene, which is also in accordance with all the descriptions of that hideous period, when in the sultry,

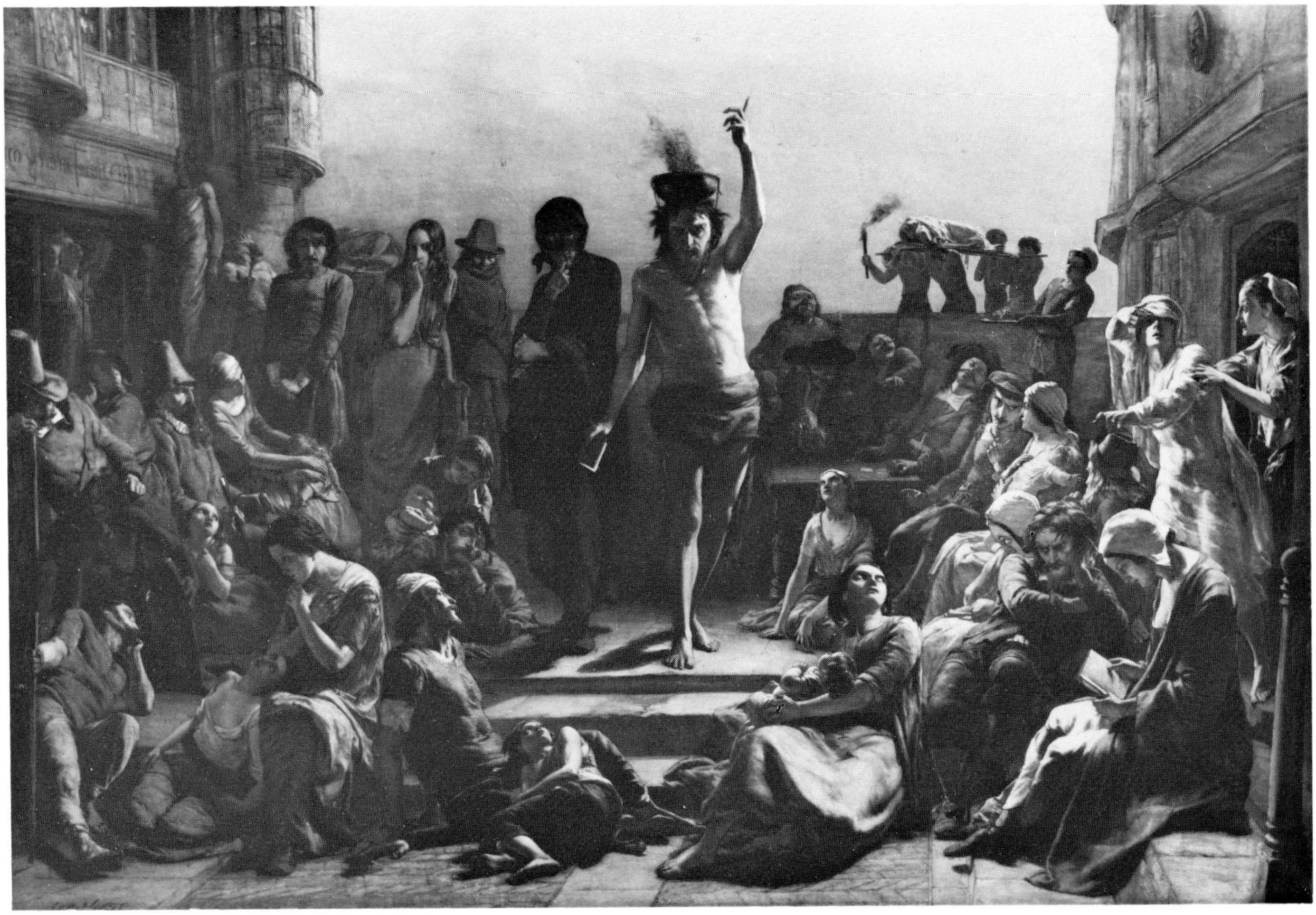

vapoury noon-tide sun, there was a supernatural ominous glare."

Poole showed the picture with a quotation from Defoe's *A Journal of the Plague Year*, first published in 1722 but written as a dramatic eyewitness account of the Great Plague of London of 1664–5. Harrison Ainsworth's *Old St. Paul's* his third and very successful historical novel, which dealt with the Plague, was probably dependent on Defoe, and as Ainsworth's book was published in 1841, it seems likely that Poole was first prompted to his subject by his contemporary's novel but probably then decided to improve its literary pedigree by returning to the earlier and more intellectually respectable source.

Blackwood's commented that it was curious Poole's painting remained unsold at the cheap price of £400. This makes it more likely that the picture of the same title shown the following year at the British Institution is the same painting as that at the 1843 RA. *Solomon Eagle* won the Heywood Gold Medal at Manchester in 1845 and there is no reference in the Poole literature to the existence of a reduced replica or second version of the subject. Similarly all the recorded saleroom and exhibition appearances of the picture include measurements or references that clearly identify the Sheffield picture.

The *Art Union's* reviewer wrote:

". . . The exhibition of this work forms, indeed, an epoch in the Arts. It is not too much to say that no work, produced in our time, has so *suddenly* arrested our admiration – so suddenly elevated its producer from a comparatively humble station to the very foremost rank in his profession. The picture is one for which we challenge competition, among all the schools of Europe. Mr. Poole must be hereafter classed among the great artists of the age and country."

The Times, the *Athenaeum* and the *ILN* joined it in acclaiming Poole as a rising young genius whose future was assured of great brilliance. Poole did his best to vindicate the judgments of his supporters by continuing to produce large subject pictures on the lines of *Solomon Eagle* with similarly dramatic subjects and compositions: amongst these were *The Messenger announcing to Job the irruption of the Sabeans, and the slaughter of his servants* (RA 1850, now in a Methodist church in Minneapolis), *The Goths in Italy* (RA 1851, Manchester), and *The seventh day of the Decameron* (RA 1855, coll. Lord Joicey in 1908). He departed from this style once in *The Visitation and Surrender of Syon Nunnery* of 1846 (Bristol) which gained him his ARA and (see the Bristol catalogue of 1975), anticipates many of the technical and visual characteristics of major Pre-Raphaelite painting of 1849 and 1850. Poole made his living with smaller pictures of pretty rustics such as *The Gleaner* engraved in the *Art Journal*, November 1864; these were popular with collectors but his critical reputation declined. Five years after his death the RA included twenty-eight Pooles in the 1884 Winter Exhibition; these were greeted with undoubted respect for the artist's past reputation but the criticisms made it clear that the euphoria of 1843 was considered evidence of a taste for the sensational in early Victorians. Reviews in the *Portfolio*, *Times*, *ILN* and *Magazine of Art* all commented on his bad draughtsmanship, the result of being self-taught, and the mannered contortions of his compositions. The *Magazine of Art* wrote:

"Their interest – to us at least – is rather literary than artistic. They aim high; they are careful and conscientious in everything – here and there . . . they are touched with real poetry. But they have, as a rule, the great defect of being more or less lifeless. They are elaborate; but, save as expressions of academical romance, they have very little real existence. They prove their author to have been earnest and high-minded, but, as it appears to us, to have had too loose a hold upon the real to excel in the romantic – too incomplete a mastery of fact to go far and fare well in the realms of the ideal."

The obituary in the *Athenaeum* contained probably the most acute analysis of Poole's appeal to his contemporaries:

"Before these pictures the most exacting critics gladly abandoned the academical canons on which their ordinary judgments were founded, and all the world delighted in a new development of design, or rather a new combination of art and poetry. It taught men of letters that art has an existence distinct from that of books. No one can have forgotten the intense force of the impression he received when seeing *Solomon Eagle* or *Syon House* for the first time . . ."

Sheffield City Art Galleries

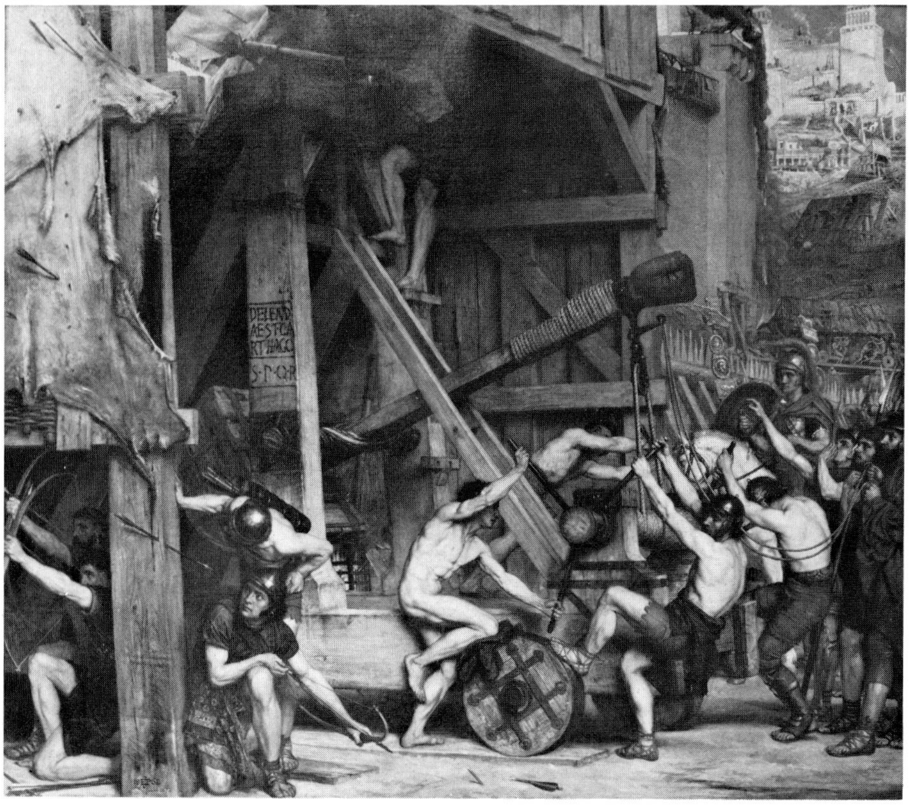

Sir Edward John Poynter, 1836–1919, ARA 1864, RA 1876, PRA 1896–1918, KT. 1896, BT. 1902

46 The Catapult 1868

oil on canvas, $61 \times 72\frac{1}{4}$ in

INSCR: 18 EJP 68 (monogram); DELEND/A EST CA/RTHAGO / S.P.Q.R. (on side of catapult).

PROV: Purch. fr. artist by Sir Joseph Whitwell Pease, Bt., MP; his sale, Christie's, 28 March 1903 (147) bt. Ford; by 1904, Sir Christopher Furness, MP, later 1st Baron Furness of Grantley; anon. (incl. in Poynter sale), Christie's, 19 January 1920 (88) bt. Rt.Hon. W. Runciman, later Lord Runciman of Chathill, by whom presented to the gallery, 1945.

EXH: RA 1868 (402); Internat. Exh. London 1873 (758a); Expo. Univ. Paris 1878 (218); Guildhall 1895 (75); Internat. Exh. St Louis 1904 (213); RA Winter 1922 (208); *Albert Moore & his Contemporaries*, Laing, Newcastle, 1972 (116).

LIT: *AJ*, June 1868, p108; *Athenaeum*, 9 May 1868, pp666–667; *GdBA*, 1 July 1868, p67; Rosetti & Swinburne, *RA Notes* 1868, pp15, 41; *Times*, 21 May 1868, p10; James Dafforne, 'The Works of Edward J. Poynter, RA', *AJ*, Jan 1877, p18, engr. p17; Emilia F.S. Pattison, 'Edward J. Poynter, RA', *Mag. of Art*, 1888, pp248, 250, xxv, repr. p245; Herbert Sharp, 'A Short Account of the Work of Edward John Poynter, RA', *Studio*, Feb 1896, p7, repr. p13; M.H. Spielmann, 'Edward J. Poynter, PRA', *Mag. of Art*, 1897, pp116, 118, repr. p112; Cosmo Monkhouse, 'The Life & Work of Sir Edward J. Poynter, PRA', *Art Annual*, Easter 1897, pp12, 14 repr. p7; Monkhouse, 1897, pp244, 247; Adrian Margaux, 'The Art of Sir Edward J. Poynter, Bt., PRA', *Windsor Mag.*, Jan 1905, pp76–78; obit., *Connoisseur*, Sept 1919, p52; *DNB*, 1927, p439; Gaunt, *Victorian Olympus*, 1952, p82; Bell, 1967, p50, pl.48.

STUDIES: for the central nude figure, repr. *Mag. of Art*, May 1897, p2; unspecified studies, Poynter sale, Christie's, 19 January 1920 (incl. in lot 6).

The success of *The Catapult* at the '68 RA secured Poynter's Associateship. Though opinion was divided over whether it exceeded or fell slightly short of his previous year's triumph, *Israel in Egypt* (Guildhall), praise for Poynter's archaeological and anatomical precision was universal. The only misgivings expressed both by the RA reviewers and Poynter's later biographers concerned the brutal ugliness of the monstrous siege-engine itself, being primed by the Roman soldiers for a renewed attack on the walls of Carthage during the siege which ended in the destruction of the city in 146 BC. 'Delenda est Carthago' – Carthage must be destroyed – (Cato the Elder, quoted in Plutarch's *Life of Cato*) is cut into the wood of the catapult itself.

Poynter was considered the greatest academic draughtsman of his day and *The Catapult* was his greatest single opportunity to display his mastery of the male nude study in what Pattison called these:

> "groups of the strong servants of Rome, stripped to the sun and wind, toiling with an energy which brought up their starting muscles and their splendid thews till the flesh rippled before our eyes like swelling waves beneath the breeze, only with something of a far nobler beauty of playing and changeful line."

Ruskin, the opponent of everything Poynter stood for, attacked precisely this element in Poynter's 1875 RA pictures, claiming:

> "Mr. Poynter's object . . . is to show us, like Michael Angelo, the adaptability of limbs to awkward positions. But he can only, by this anatomical science, interest his surgical spectators; . . ."
> (Ruskin XIV p273).

This so incensed Poynter that he devoted his ninth Slade lecture to a reply in which his commitment to Michelangelesque principles was given in three rules:

> ". . . the action of a figure must be true to itself. The neglect of this rule, wilful or unconsidered, has been the cause of all the odius mannerisms of the later Italian and French schools; . . . the action must be true to the idea to be expressed in the general composition or conception of the subject . . . partly because many positions may be equally expressive, so that no one can be said to be truer than another; partly because in some forms of composition intended to be decorative, a certain licence may be allowed . . . This freedom must however be used with caution, and as a rule the *most probable* action is the one to be adopted . . . The third condition, that which distinguishes the true artist from the mere painter possessed of poetic conceptions, is that the action of the figure shall be expressed in the most beautiful manner, and shall be studied so as to give the artist an opportunity for the display of the highest beauty of the form, whether it be nude or draped.
>
> . . . All these conditions Michelangelo fulfilled in a higher degree than any artist that has lived since the best Greek period."
> (Poynter, *Ten Lectures on Art*, 1879, (pp236–237)).

His devotion to Michelangelo was lifelong: Poynter was painted by Sir Philip Burne-Jones in 1909 (NPG), sitting at his easel – behind him on the wall of his studio is a very large reproduction of the *Creation of the Sun and the Moon* from the Sistine Ceiling.

The son of an architect, Poynter had a conventional training followed by a stay in Rome in 1853 and three years in the rigorously academic Paris studio of Gleyre where he was one of the gang including Whistler, Armstrong, Lamont and Du Maurier immortalised in the latter's novel *Trilby* (1894). This Parisian training was known to his French reviewers who detected the influence not only of Gleyre but of Gérôme in his RA work like *The Catapult*. From the late 1860s Poynter was much occupied first with decorative schemes for the Houses of Parliament, the South Kensington Museum (later the Victoria & Albert), and Wortley Hall, and then increasingly with administrative work as he was successively appointed first Slade Professor at University College (1871–1875), director for art of the South Kensington Museum and principal of the National Art Training School (1875–1881), director of the National Gallery (1894–1904) and PRA (1896–1918). This heavy load of public offices reduced his output to smaller cabinet pictures of classical subjects, but two major paintings were produced: *A Visit to Aesculapius* (RA 1880, Tate), a greatly admired Chantrey purchase, and *The Visit of the Queen of Sheba to King Solomon* (McLean's Gallery 1890, Sydney) for which Poynter is reputed to have received £6000.

Laing Art Gallery, Tyne & Wear County Council Museums Service

RICHARD REDGRAVE, 1804–1888, ARA 1840, RA 1851–81, CB 1880

47 The Sempstress 1846

oil on canvas, 25 × 30 in
INSCR. R. Redgrave 1846

PROV: P. Horthewick; Sotheby's Belgravia, 27 Mar 1973 (49) bt. Fine Art Society Ltd. for Forbes.
EXH: *The Pre-Raphaelite Era: 1848–1914*, Delaware 1976 (1–14).
LIT: (all refs are to the exhibited picture), *Art Union*, 1 June 1844, p158; *Athenaeum*, 18 May 1844, p459; *Fraser's*, June 1844, pp 703–4; *ILN*, 11 May 1844, p227; *Times*, 8 May 1844, p7, 6 May 1845, p6; 'Autobiography of Richard Redgrave, ARA', *AJ*, 1 Feb 1850, p49; James Dafforne, 'British Artists XLV: Richard Redgrave', *AJ*, July 1859, p206; Sandby, 1862, p292; obit., *Athenaeum*, 22 Dec 1888, p855; F.M. Redgrave, *Richard Redgrave, CB, RA, A Memoir, compiled from his diary*, 1891, pp43–5; Wood, *Panorama*, 1976, pp126–8, repr. p126.
ENGR: R. Staines, steel engraving, 8⅜ × 10⅛ in; unidentified publisher, n.d.
VERSIONS: 1. Exhibited picture, RA 1844 (227), oil; prov. unknown.
2. *The Song of the Shirt*, 12 × 9 in (sic); coll. John Clow, sold Winstanley, 21 Apr 1852 (50) as 'Engraved', 15gns. Lot 51, also Clow, was 'The Poor Teacher. Engraved. 12 × 9 15 gns.'
RELATED WORK: *Song of the Shirt*; etching; 5 × 6¼ in, V & A E.49–1889. A squared-up watercolour sketch for this, 4½ × 5½ in, is V & A 220–1889.

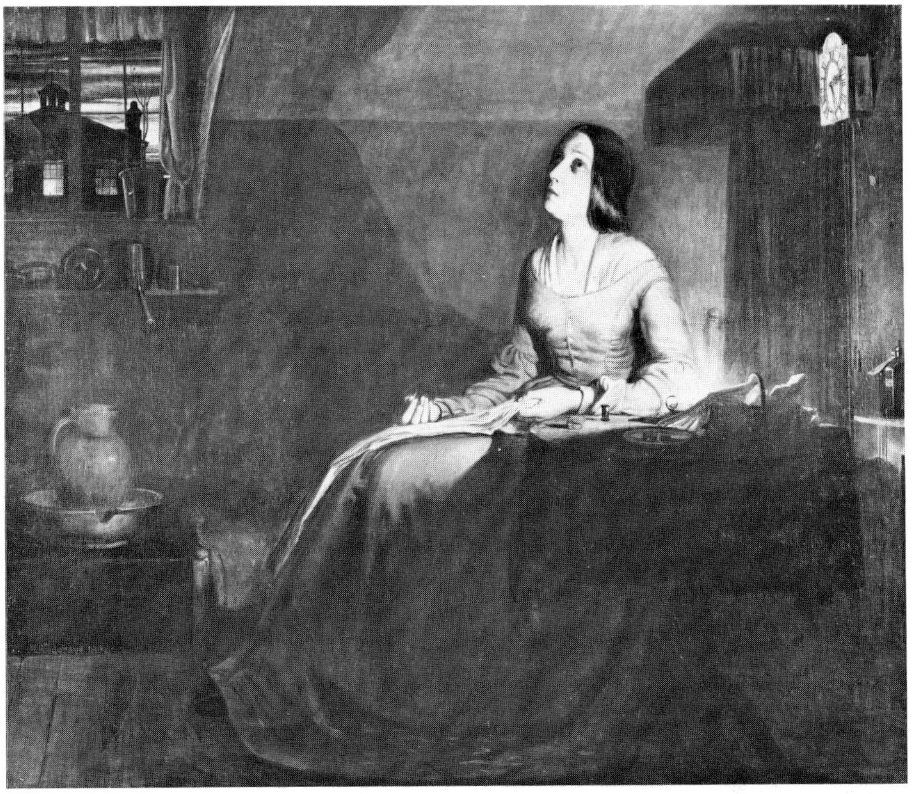

> ". . . It is one of my most gratifying feelings, that many of my best efforts in art have aimed at calling attention to the trials and struggles of the poor and the oppressed. In the 'Reduced Gentleman's Daughter', 'The Poor Teacher', 'The Sempstress', 'Fashion's Slaves', and other works, I have had in view the 'helping them to right that suffer wrong' at the hands of their fellow men. If this has been done feebly, it has at least been done from the heart, and I trust when I shall have finished my labours, I shall never have occasion to regret that I have debased the art I love, by making it subservient to any unworthy end."

Redgrave's modest and sincere conclusion to his autobiographical letter in the 1850 *Art Journal* conceals how very successful his socially didactic pictures were. The *Athenaeum* obituary, though written at the end of the 1880s when Redgrave's early pictures had long been unfashionable and his reputation as an arts administrator and teacher had eclipsed that of him as a painter, commented:

> ". . . his popular pictures are not to be disdained because their themes are somewhat obviously virtuous and goody. Their perfect sincerity gave dignity to the sentiment of (the pictures) which have a reputation that has been extended by engravings and reproductions of other sorts, made and copied abroad as well as at home."

When the original version of *The Sempstress* was shown at the 1844 RA, critics and public alike, with the exception of Thackeray and the *Athenaeum*, were moved by the subject and its treatment of the fourth verse of 'The Song of the Shirt'. Hood's poem on the exploitation of the sweated labour of impoverished women paid pittances for their sewing had made an extraordinary impression on its publication in the 1843 Christmas number of *Punch* (p260); Spielmann's *History of 'Punch'* (p333) recounts how

> "this song, which, in spite of its defects, still thrills you as you read, achieved such a popularity that for sudden and enthusiastic applause its reception has rarely been equalled. It was soon translated into every language of Europe . . .; it was printed and sold as catchpennies, printed on cotton pocket-handkerchiefs, it was illustrated and parodied in a thousand ways; and the greatest triumph of all, which brought tears of joy to Hood's eyes, before a week was out a poor beggar-woman came singing it down the street, the words set to a simple air of her own."

It became not only the poet's most famous work but also one of the best-known poems of the century and the subject of many more paintings by, amongst others, Watts, Millais and Holl. When he wrote the poem, Hood was already suffering from the illness which finally killed him in 1845, asked for his tombstone to be inscribed simply:

> "He sang the 'Song of the Shirt'."

Oddly enough, despite the specific reference in the poem, 'Work! work! work. / While the cock is crowing aloof!' and the fact that the painting, as observed both by *The Times* and the *Literary Gazette*, shows dawn breaking in the sky visible through the garret window, the critics of both the *Art Union* and the confused *Literary Gazette* read the clock on the wall behind the sempstress as 2.30 am. A more likely reading for a dawn sky would be 5.10 and it seems probable that Redgrave's unskilled attempt at foreshortening in the drawing of the clockface has misled some of his contemporaries as well as more recent commentators. Such details were considered of the greatest importance in the interpretations of the nuances an artist had managed to incorporate in his painting, and Redgrave undoubtedly intended the time to be visible to make the point that the sempstress had been working all night.

Redgrave's success of the previous year had been *The Poor Teacher* (RA 1843, Gateshead), showing a young and pretty governess, seated dejectedly in a bare schoolroom, eyes sadly downcast and a letter from her far-away home in her hand. So upsetting did Sheepshanks find this image that, when he commissioned a replica (now V & A), he insisted that Redgrave alleviate the gloom by adding the teacher's pupils playing in the background.

The *Memoir* records a letter to Redgrave from Paul Falconer Poole, then still an ARA, which expresses vividly the sentiments inspired by *The Sempstress*:

> "Will you allow me, although unknown to you, to offer you my small tribute of praise for the picture of 'The Sempstress'? Believe me, *I* think it is the most powerful for truth and touching from its pathos of any picture I have ever seen. Who can help exclaiming, 'Poor soul! God help her'? If any circumstance could make me wage war against the present social arrangements, and make us go down shirtless to our graves, it is the contemplation of this truthful and wonderful picture. Knowing you will receive this honest attestation of the effect your work has caused on my mind, in the spirit with which it is offered, and in admiration of your *heart* as well as talent, I remain, Dear Sir, your well-wisher, P.F. Poole."

From 1847, Redgrave became increasingly involved in public art administration, first as a lecturer in the Government School of Design, then inspector-general of art in the Science and Art Department, art director of the South Kensington Museum, surveyor of the Queen's Pictures, together with innumerable memberships of committees, and published important catalogues of the Royal Collection and the Sheepshanks Bequest, as well as influential manuals on colour and design and, with his brother Samuel, the invaluable *Century of Painters of the English School* (1865). His selfless and industrious public work left him time only for summer-holiday landscape painting, much of it done in the company of his close friend Hook.

The Forbes Magazine Collection, New York

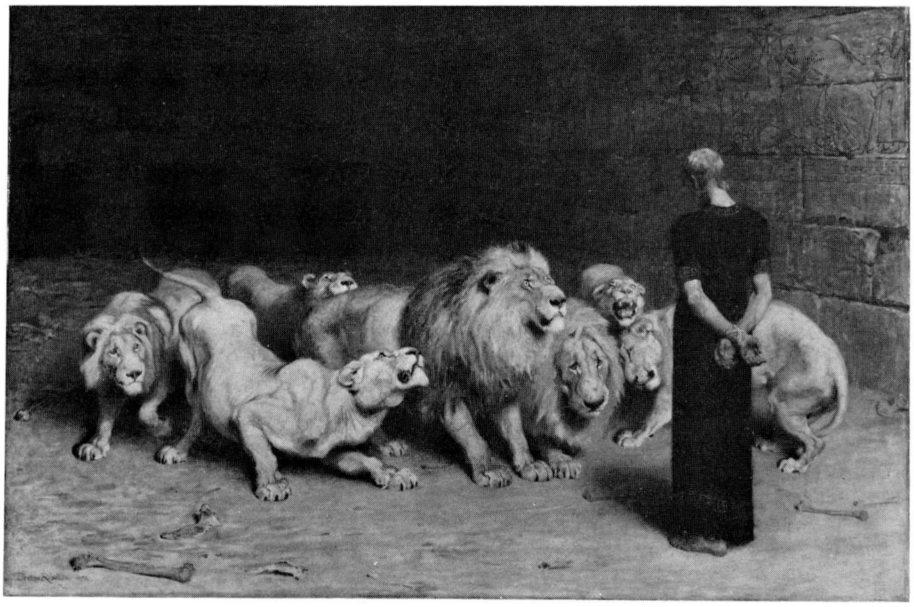

Briton Riviere, 1840–1920, ARA 1878, RA 1880, HON DCL (OXF) 1891

48 Daniel in the Lions' Den 1872

oil on canvas, 38¾ × 60 in
INSCR: Briton Riviere 1872

PROV: Agnew 1872; sold to John Heugh, Feb 1872 (£1000); bt. back by Agnew's, May 1874, sold to Edmund Crompton Potter, Rusholme House, Manchester (£1732 10s); his sale, Christie's, 22 Mar 1884 (51) bt. Agnew (£2625) for T.H. Ismay; by whom presented to Liverpool, 1900.
EXH: RA 1872 (539 as *Daniel*); Expo. Univ. Paris 1878 (232); Liverpool 1886 (29); Manchester Jubilee 1887 (364); Guildhall 1890 (121) and 1900 (6); *Canadian National Exh.*, Toronto 1908; Hampstead 1928; Leamington Spa 1928; Blackburn 1931.
LIT: *AJ*, July 1872, pp182–3; *Athenaeum*, 4 May 1872, p565; *ILN*, 18 May 1872, p486; *Times*, 4 May 1872, p5; W.W. Fenn, 'Briton Riviere, ARA', *Mag. of Art*, 1879, p254, engr facing p255; Chesneau, 1885, p269 & repr; Walter Armstrong, *Fine Art at the Royal Jubilee Exh.*, Manchester, 1887, p28; J.E. Hodgson, *Fifty Years of British Art*, 1887, pp81–2; Walter Armstrong, 'Briton Riviere, RA', *Art Annual*, 1891, p15, repr p7; F.G. Stephens, 'Briton Riviere, RA, DCL: II', *Portfolio*, 1892, pp80–1; obit., *Connoisseur*, June 1920, p119; *Liverpool Catalogue*, 1927, p157; Reitlinger, 1961, p156.
ENGR: Charles G. Lewis: mixed engraving; 19⅝ × 31¼ in; publ. Thos Agnew & Sons, decl. Dec 1874.

VERSION: *Daniel in the Lions' Den*, watercolour, coll. Ed. Cross, Esq; exh. Manchester Jubilee 1887 (1304).

The showing of *Daniel* at the 1872 RA confirmed Briton Riviere as Landseer's heir, a position for which he had been a candidate since the mid-1860s when he forsook his youthful Pre-Raphaelite experiments for the animal subjects which occupied the rest of his life. He proved himself a faithful disciple with *Prisoners* (RA 1869, Port Sunlight, later known as *Fidelity*), a direct tribute to Landseer's *Old Shepherd's Chief Mourner* (cat. 25).

His first important picture in the eyes of contemporary critics was *Circe and the friends of Ulysses* (RA 1871, Cross coll., sold Tooth & Tooth, 21 Nov 1911 (149) bt. Sampson). Circe sits, three-quarters turned away from the viewer, regarding the erstwhile sailors transformed into a herd of swine (painted from his own pigs kept expressly for the purpose) as they scramble towards her in their mud pen. The dramatic device of involving the spectator by making us face the onrush of animals with Circe, so that the spectator too is a protagonist in the drama, was so successful that Riviere applied it again in *Daniel*, shifting figure and direction of movement to the right. The *ILN* considered *Daniel* even better in composition, appropriateness of subject, and in the originality of treatment of a hackneyed subject while *The Times* placed it second only to Fred Walker's *Harbour of Refuge* (Tate) as the most impressive picture of the year. *The Times* pointed out that Riviere had been faced with the always difficult task of surpassing his previous year's acclaimed achievement and had risen successfully to the challenge. Although the *Daniel* lacked 'that element of humour which is always so attractive to a British public', *The Times* went on,

> "it has elements of far higher reach and deeper impressiveness in the unshaken faith of the prophet, the suddenly subdued fury and terror of the lions."

It described the confrontation:

> ". . . the prophet's eye is upon them, and the power of the God of Israel is over him, and the lions crouch or writhe before it. One huge brute, with lambent eyes and jaws that thirst for blood, already feels the invisible but irresistible might bowing his hinder limbs. Others are already completely overcome, and can only grovel in the bloody sand of the den, with impotent roaring. The picture is not one to be forgotten, and will assuredly raise the reputation of the painter, already carried so high by his *Circe*."

F.G. Stephens went considerably further in 1892, interpreting the lions as representative of the forces of human evil ranged against Daniel:

> "One great lion in the centre of the group glares at the prophet with eyes that seem to contract and dilate rapidly, and in the depths of which is steadfast carnivorous fire . . . a less ferocious, but more treacherous brute, crouching before she leaps, fawns and snarls like a mean man before his better, whom he envies, hates and fears . . .; behind the group, a cruel beast, more cunning but not less charged with malice and eager to destroy what he envies, seems to be skulking, while he waits a chance to get out of reach of the controlling human eye."

This passage is an extended and more exaggeratedly worded version of his 1872 RA review for the *Athenaeum*, when he was already much impressed by the picture:

> "Old, greyheaded, weak, and without mortal armour, the man seems helpless, and yet the beasts stare at him and recoil. One knows not which is the most impressive, the gathered savages, or the man; . . ."

Though such praise was obviously welcome, the artist had no need of it to sell his picture; according to Agnew's stockbooks, *Daniel* had already been handled by them at least once before the RA show: they sold it to John Heugh in February 1872 for £1000. Its price almost doubled in the next two years: in May 1874 Agnew's transferred it from Heugh to E.C. Potter for £1732 10s; the picture went through Agnew's again in 1884, when the firm bought it on behalf of T.H. Ismay for £2625. Thomas Holloway had paid the same sum the previous year when he bought *Sympathy* (RA 1875) at Christie's (28 Apr 1883) from Tom Taylor's Aston Rowant Gallery and the price remained the record paid for a Riviere.

When the newly-established *Magazine of Art* featured Riviere in its series 'Our Living Artists' in its second year, *Daniel* was given the place of honour in a full-page wood engraved reproduction. At the great Manchester Jubilee exhibition of 1887, *Daniel* was one of nine oils by Riviere and was acknowledged by reviewers including Walter Armstrong and the artist John Hodgson as the best and most successful of his paintings.

Over the years Riviere was most closely identified in the public mind with his dog pictures; these include *The Last of the Garrison* (RA 1875, Manchester) and *Sympathy* of which Armstrong writes:

> "None of Riviere's pictures have been more popular . . . The small girl, banished to the staircase in disgrace, with the sympathetic terrier deprecating her tears, has found her way into hundreds of homes, both humble and luxurious." (*Art Annual*, p17).

Riviere continued from time to time, impelled perhaps by the possession of an Oxford degree, to attempt grand subjects with classical or allegorical themes but tended to be less successful with these than with his dogs and geese: they include *In manus tuas, Domine* (RA 1879, Manchester), and *An old world wanderer* (RA 1887, Nottingham). In 1890, eighteen years on from his first *Daniel*, he showed at Agnew's *Daniel's Answer to the King* (now Manchester); Daniel's back is turned to the lions, who prowl behind him powerless and cowed, and he gazes up triumphantly through the dungeon window at the unseen king. Armstrong attributed Riviere's success to his resistance to anthropomorphism, 'the besetting sin of the English *animalier*', and to his determination to portray 'the animal's real self'. To this end Riviere spent many years working on a flayed figure of a lion (probably the bronze *Anatomical Lion* shown at the 1897 RA). His use of colour was always attributed to his friendship with the London Circle of Scottish Artists – Pettie, Orchardson, Graham and MacWhirter, a friendship dating from his earliest days in London where he lived from 1871.

Walker Art Gallery, Liverpool

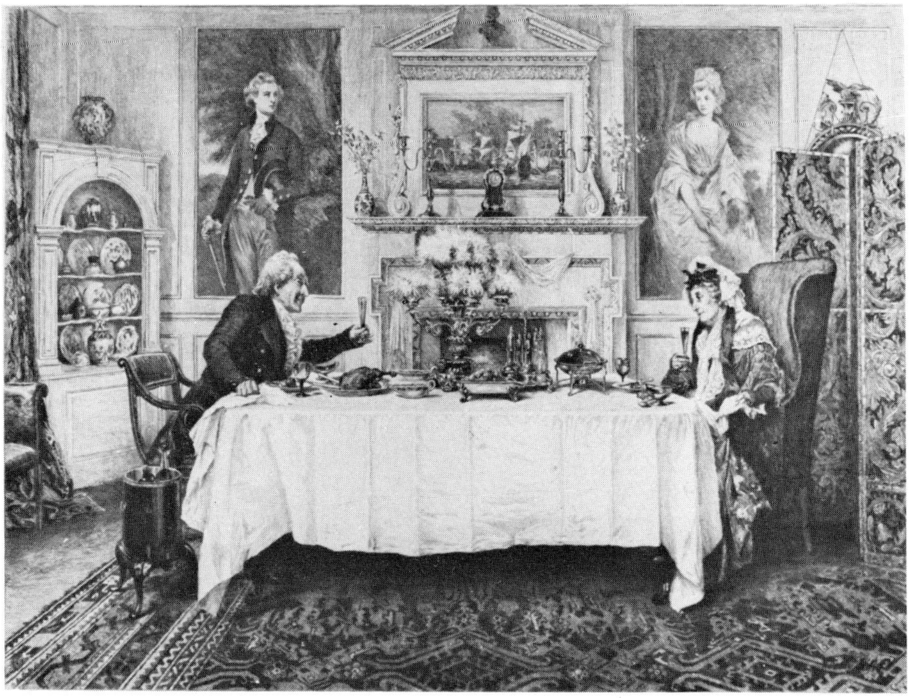

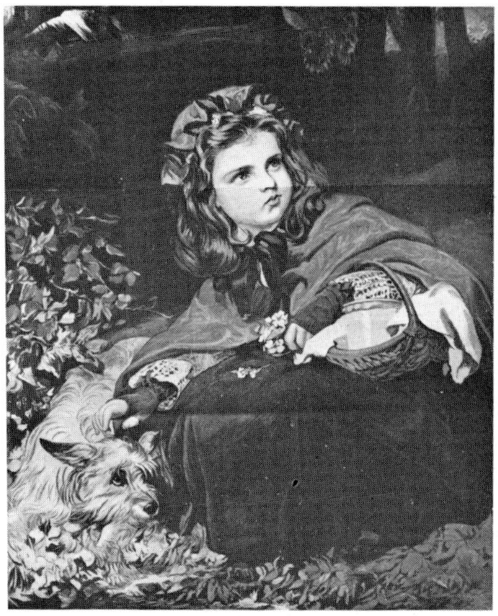

Walter Dendy Sadler, 1854-1923, RI, RBA

49 Darby and Joan 1890

etching by W.H. Boucher, 29½ × 34½ in
INSCR: W. Dendy Sadler / Selected for Mr. E.W. Jackson's collection of proofs / after my works. WDS. / W. Boucher.

Publ. L.H. Lefevre, 1890.
LIT: Harry Quilter, *Preferences in Art, Life, and Literature*, 1892, repr facing p354; F.G. Stephens, 'Walter Dendy Sadler, Humorist and Genre Painter', *AJ*, July 1895, pp197–9, repr p194.

The only important source of information for Dendy Sadler is F.G. Stephens' long article in the *Art Journal* of 1895, perhaps because he was never taken seriously by the RA.

Sadler began exhibiting at the RA in 1873 and his first important successes combined what Stephens defined as his 'piscatorial' subjects with his jolly monks which 'marked his true and original sense of the domestic side of conventual life during the Middle Ages'. Stacy Marks had found his earliest popularity with comic mediaeval subjects like *Toothache in the Middle Ages* (RA 1856), but Dendy Sadler made the period his own with *Steady, brother, steady!* (RA 1875), *Thursday* (RA 1880, Tate) and *Friday* (RA 1882, Liverpool), the monks first catching and then feasting on their weekly fish. The *Darby and Joan*, of 1889, one of a series of sentimental subjects set in the eighteenth century, 'including interiors of extraordinary richness of character and opulent in accessories of furniture, *bric-à-brac*, and what-not', was thought by Stephens to be

> "one of the most tender of the artist's pathetic and anecdotic designs."

He dwells on the touching detail of the portraits of the old couple

> "when they were (it was about 1760) young enough to sit to Mr. Gainsborough at his fine house in Pall Mall. Ever pathetic, the ideas of Mr. Dendy Sadler recall by such means as these the days when Darby was a young bridegroom and Joan a fair and blooming bride. There are sympathetic touches, too, of the subtler sort in making the likeness of the young lover look tenderly and ardently towards the portrait of his charming mistress. She, all compact of happiness, and hardly conscious of her charms, looks down because he gazes at her. The very dog leaping at her knee is significant of their faithful and happy loves, while the still blossoming winter of their lives is aptly alluded to by the chrysanthemums piled in a silver vase upon the table."

Stephens was impressed not only with the trouble Sadler took with his detailing but also with his finish;

> ". . . as only a precise, crisp and very firm touch, brilliant and searching handling and the utmost attention to the effect of light could succeed in treating multitudinous details of the kind in question, it speaks for itself that our artist must needs work with (such) touches though he found that they could also result in a hard and metallic look to the final work."

Sadler made a number of variations on the Darby and Joan theme in pictures like '*Sweethearts Yet*' (RA 1892; *AJ*, 1895, p196), '*'Tis Fifty Years Since*' (RA 1894; *AJ*, 1895, p197), and *The End of the Skein* (Port Sunlight), and in the series of etchings published by Lefevre, of which one is here exhibited, Sadler also did versions of the old couple as they might have seen each other from each end of the table.

Sadler also catered to a more masculine market with scenes, still in full eighteenth century get-up, of card-players, toddy-drinkers in inns, stag dinners and similar hearty camaraderie. The fourth category Stephens defined in 1895 as his latest type dealt 'with the follies and weaknesses of men and women'; it included scenes of comic dilemmas in legal offices over the readings of wills, breach of promise cases, and meetings of creditors.

Lefevre published a number of large etchings apparently during the 1890s after a selection from all Sadler's types and Doncaster has a set of nine, all proof copies inscribed by Sadler for E.W. Jackson.

Sadler seems to have been perhaps the most successful artist of the latter part of the century who was unable to achieve Academy honours. He was a member of the Society of British Artists and of the Royal Institute of Painters in Oil, but never achieved even ARA, perhaps because his work, though extremely popular with the public and noticed in the press, was too dependent on the model of Marcus Stone, Stacy Marks and other earlier Academy stalwarts.

Doncaster Museum and Art Gallery

James Sant, 1820–1916, ARA 1861, RA 1869–1914, CVO 1914

50 Little Red Riding Hood 1863 (1860)

chromotype, 21½ × 17¾ in

PUBL: *ILN*, 19 Dec 1863, facing p644.
LIT: *ILN*, 19 Dec 1863, p642; Mason Jackson, *The Pictorial Press: Its Origin and Progress*, 1885, p304.
After Sant's painting of the same title, RA 1860 (552); coll. Charles Prater by 1862, his sale, Christie's, 4 Mar 1882 (39) bt. in, untraced; exh. London Internat. 1862 (592).

For their Christmas 1863 special supplement the *Illustrated London News* published the largest colour print they had so far attempted: a chromotype reproduction of Sant's *Little Red Riding Hood*. The original painting had been at the 1860 RA; though it was barely noticed by the critics, either then or in 1862, it was made a popular favourite by the *ILN* and continued so throughout the century. The *ILN* had published its first colour supplement in 1855 to celebrate its achievement of sales of 200,000, the result of the abolition of the penny Newspaper Stamp and a record the *ILN* held for twenty-five years, but, as Mason Jackson wrote, the early work was crude:

> ". . . the coloured pictures were little more than ordinary woodcuts with tints printed over them, but their imperfections were principally owing to the breakdown of machinery and the great hurry in which they were produced. In after years much better things were done, and the coloured Christmas pictures which have been for many years produced at the chromatic press of Leighton Bros. take rank among the best work of the kind. They have proved exceedingly popular, and always sold well. That of 'Little Red Riding Hood', after J. Sant, R.A. . . . was reprinted again and again, until the blocks were utterly worn out. They were then re-engraved, and again reprinted."

Sant's picture was indeed evidently so popular that it has proved extremely difficult to find a volume of the *ILN* that had not had the print removed – even the *ILN's* own archive has no copy of it, and, of the few volumes that do still contain one, the print is usually falling to pieces from wear.

While Sant's *Little Red Riding Hood* was probably the most widely distributed and publicly-known treatment of the nursery rhyme character, a great many Victorian artists painted Little Red Riding Hood subjects. A representative sample of these, from the most famous to the rather obscure, indicates that (apart from the early Landseer), Sant's 1860 picture probably set a much-imitated fashion. Landseer showed a *Little Red Riding Hood* at the 1831 RA (a Baxter print of a Landseer *Little Red Riding Hood* was published in 1856), and then Sant was followed by Millais in 1864 (exhibited French Gallery 1865, Roy Miles 1975), William Oliver in 1866 (Sheffield, destroyed 1939/45; a smaller version was at Bonham's 17 Nov 1968 (127)), Sophie Anderson at the Royal Society of British Artists, Suffolk Street 1868 (196 – untraced), several by Watts including one of 1890 (now Birmingham), and Thomas Mostyn at the RA 1896 (repr. *Mag. of Art*, 1899, p130). Another and quite different *Little Red Riding Hood* (oil on canvas $16\frac{1}{2} \times 13$ in) is in the Ingram family; a family story has it that Sir Bruce Ingram (grandson of the founder of the *ILN*, Herbert Ingram, and himself editor 1900–63) and his brothers and sisters were painted as nursery rhyme characters and this may be one of the children painted by Sant.

Sant had already had considerable success with a picture at the RA of 1853 (now at Bury) which as *The Infant Samuel* achieved great popularity through its engraving by Samuel Cousins; *The Times* obituary commented,

> "It was a very English Samuel, and we can imagine that Holman Hunt and the other Pre-Raphaelites who were endeavouring at that time to give a minute archaeological accuracy to their Biblical pictures must have thought very little of it; but it satisfied the British middle-class, and was in perfect harmony with the Low Church sermons they were in the habit of hearing every Sunday." (13 Sept 1916).

This success was repeated late in the century with *The Soul's Awakening* (RA 1888, coll. Mrs. Mount Batten, when shown at the RA Winter 1922); *The Times* called it

> "The other picture by which Sant is still known in hundreds of homes . . . a picture of which the sentimentality delighted the public. Sant was also an extremely successful society portrait painter."

His twenty-two portraits of the friends and relatives of the Countess of Waldegrave, known as the Strawberry Hill collection, was shown at the French Gallery in 1861; it secured his ARA and established his reputation. He was appointed Painter to the Queen in 1871 and continued working up until the last year of his very long life. W.W. Fenn's conclusion to his biography of Sant in the *Magazine of Art* for 1880 identified accurately the secret of Sant's success:

> "He has gauged his own powers most completely, and has not perilled his reputation by attempts at sensational domestic scenes or grand historical groups. He may fairly rest content with the knowledge that the young generations to come will point with delight and pleasure to the portraits of their mothers and grandmothers which he has limned, and with a little smile of secret self-complacency will hope that they have inherited a share of that beauty and grace so pleasantly handed down to them by the dexterous and brilliant brush of James Sant, RA." (p133).

Mary Evans Picture Library

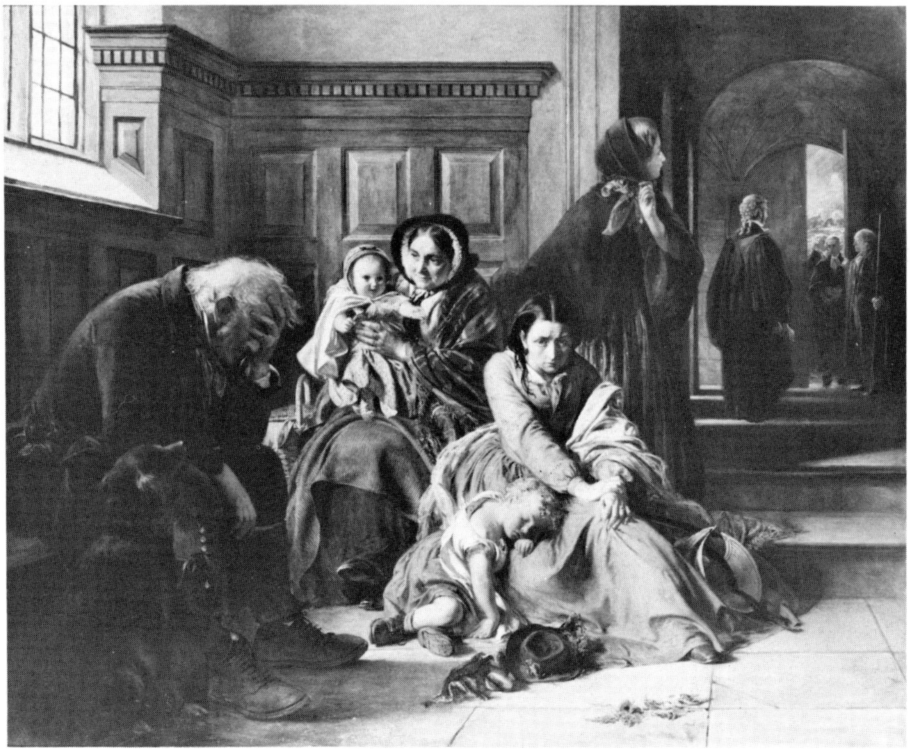

ABRAHAM SOLOMON, 1823–1862, ARA 1862

51 Waiting for the Verdict 1857

oil on canvas, $39\frac{1}{2} \times 49$ in
INSCR: A. Solomon '57

PROV: anon. sale (executors), Sotheby's Belgravia, 9 April 1974 (104).
EXH: RA 1857 (562); Liverpool Academy 1857 (193).
LIT: *AJ* 1 June 1857, p174; *Athenaeum* 16 May 1857, p633; *Critic* 15 May, p232, 1 June 1857, p255; *Punch* 16 May 1857, p200; Ruskin *RA Notes 1857*, *Works* XIV, p114; *Times* 18 May 1857, p9; James Dafforne, 'Abraham Solomon', *AJ*, 1 Mar 1862, pp74–5; *AJ* 1 July 1862, p151; obit. *Athenaeum* 27 Dec 1862, p848; obit. *AJ* 1 Feb 1863, p29; *Millais* 1899, I p240; *DNB* 1909, XVIII, p625; G.C. Williamson, *Murray Marks and His Friends*, London, 1919, p156; David Fincham, 'Three Painters of the Victorian Scene', *Apollo*, May 1936, p244; Reynolds 1953, p3; Reynolds, 1966, pp115, 179; Lionel Lambourne, 'Abraham Solomon, Painter of Fashion, and Simeon Solomon, Decadent Artist', *Jewish Historical Society of England Transactions* 1968, XXI, pp276–7.

52 "Not Guilty" (also known as The Acquittal) 1859

oil on canvas, $39\frac{1}{2} \times 49$ in

PROV: Sotheby's Belgravia, 9 April 1974 (105).
EXH: RA 1859 (557) (as "Not Guilty", companion picture to "Waiting for the Verdict", exhibited 1857).
LIT: *AJ* 1 June 1859, p170; *Athenaeum* 30 Apr 1859, p586; *Blackwood's* Aug 1859, p137; *Critic* 28 May 1859, p520; *GdBA* 15 May 1859, p243; *Times*, 18 May 1859, p12; and see refs for *Waiting for the Verdict*.
ENGR: *The Acquittal* and *Waiting for the Verdict;* W.H. Simmons; mezzotints; each $22 \times 27\frac{1}{2}$ in; publ. H. Graves & Co, 1866 (BM).
VERSIONS: 1. pair of reduced replicas; oil on canvas; $24 \times 29\frac{1}{2}$ in; s & d 1859. Prov: Charles Thomas Lucas, by 1862; his sale, Christie's, 16 May 1896 (121) bt. George; Sotheby's, 9 Dec 1964 (166); M. Newman Ltd; Christie's, 15 Dec 1972 (135, 136) bt. Frost & Reed; Christie's, 3 Feb 1978. Exh: London Internat. 1862 (720, 734); Earls Court 1897 (316, 323); *C19th Life*, M. Newman 1964 (41 a & b). Repr: Lambourne, *op. cit.* pl. XXII.
2. pair of reduced replicas, Tunbridge Wells Museum & Art Gallery; oil on board/panel; 14×16 in. Prov: Alfred Ashton (coll. formed 1852–63), beq. his son & daughter 1952. Exh: Arts Council 1962 (58– *Waiting for the Verdict* only); RA Bicentenary 1968–9 (382, 385). Lit: Rupert Gunnis, *Pictures in the Ashton Bequest*, Tunbridge Wells, n.d. (13, 14). Repr: (*Waiting for the Verdict* only): Reynolds 1966 pl. 66; Wood, *Dictionary*, 1971, p379.
3. pair of reduced replicas, coll. R.R. Hyatt (in 1884). Exh: St. Jude's Whitechapel 1884 (98, 99 as 'copies of larger pictures in the South Kensington Museum (sic).').
STUDIES: for *Waiting for the Verdict*, 40×50 in (with 'Studies in Chalks, &c'), and *The Acquittal*, 40×50 in (with 'Cartoons') and another for *The Acquittal*, Solomon sale, Christie's, 14 Mar 1863 (1, 46, 14).

> ". . . the picture which has served more than any other, perhaps, to raise Mr. Solomon's reputation as an earnest, thoughtful painter, was . . . *Waiting for the*

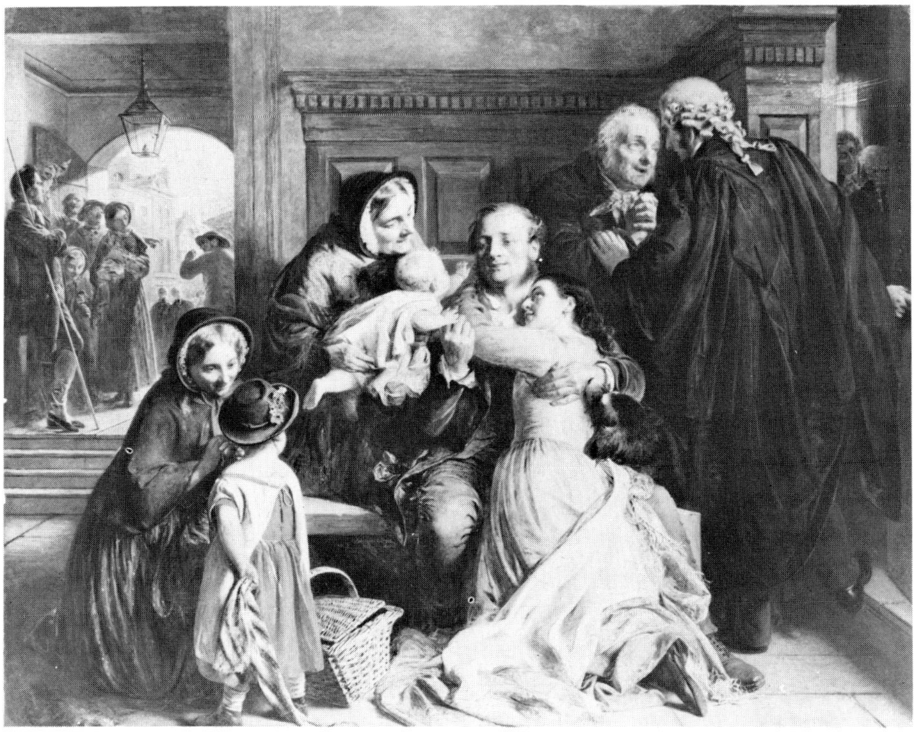

Verdict, a work that forced itself on the attention of the visitors to the gallery quite as much as any in the rooms. So full of suggestive material for description is it, that . . . both it and its companion, *Not Guilty* . . . though the latter is in some respects inferior to the former – are not mere vapid sentimentalities, but works that touch the feelings by their honest, natural expression . . ." (Dafforne).

1862, a year that began triumphantly for Solomon with the *Art Journal* biography in March, ended tragically when news of his election to ARA reached him on the day of his death in Biarritz where he had gone seeking a cure for the heart condition which killed him. The obituaries recognised that these two paintings surpassed all his previous work and were "decidedly of a progressive character as studies of human nature, and for technical qualities of painting" (*AJ*), and most remarkably demonstrated that:

"In this artist we lose one who had shown a really grave feeling of the true purposes and objects of Art." (*Athenaeum*).

Unanimous praise greeted the first showing of *Waiting for the Verdict* in 1857:

"This is an earnest and profoundly pathetic passage of Art . . . The despair of the father, the bitter grief of the wife, the unspeakable distress of the mother, are set forth in terms the most touching. Every portion of the canvas teems with expression contributive to the theme." (*AJ*).

This was echoed by the *Athenaeum*, which emphasised the poignant contrasts of feeling in the prisoner's family waiting for the outcome of the trial:

"An old countryman, the father, bows and sways with grief, while the wife weeps in the pangs and agony of despairing suspense. The unconscious child playing at her side heightens the pathos by an old but never exhausted contrast."

The picture was one of ten noticed by *Punch's* 'John Trot at the Royal Academy' along with Millais' *Sir Isumbras* (Port Sunlight) and Maclise's *Peter the Great at Deptford Dockyard* (Royal Holloway College); the country bumpkin's rhyme went:

"A pictur o' the 'Sizes did also take my
mind,
The jury a consider'n their verdict for
to find,
The pris'ner's poor old veather, his
mother, and his wife,
He beun, as I took it, on trial vor his life."

It was, in fact, the nature of the accusation faced by the absent hero of the painting that provoked what reservations there were about the picture. *The Times* expressed the reactions shared especially by the *Critic* that the subject was so painful that, without something to relieve suspense, to point to hope, it was unsuitable to be hung in a house. It would, on the other hand, be ideal as a morally didactic picture for the Law Courts for, *The Times* concluded:

"Heroic grief exalts and purifies, but domestic misery only pains."

Unfortunately for Solomon, when he responded to these objections, by painting "*Not Guilty*" for the RA two years later, the general opinion was that he had fallen into the sequel-maker's trap:

"This picture, sufficiently vigorous and telling, shares, however, the proverbial fate attendant on the continuation of a once-told story. The mind wrought into the threatening fear of a tragic doom, the plot once marshalled for effect, each repeated echo palls upon the ear, and what ought to end in climax necessarily falls into an expiring decadence. The same fate has likewise befallen Mr. O'Neils 'Home Again' " (see cat. no. 40). (*Blackwood's*).

There is no doubt, however, that both pictures, as the *Art Journal* review of 1859 says, were an enormous success with the public. Millais' *Life* by his son testifies that when *Waiting for the Verdict* was sent to the Liverpool Academy, it was the picture favoured by the public for the annual prize, though Millais' *The Blind Girl*, favoured by the Pre-Raphaelite partisans on the Academy jury, won. Ruskin's brief notice of the picture, peremptory though it was, showed a keen understanding of the nature of popular painting:

"Very full of power; but rather a subject for engraving than painting. It is too painful to be invested with the charm of colour."

In the opinion of Dr. G.C. Williamson, a frequent writer on Victorian artists from the end of the century, in his biography of Murray Marks in 1919, *Waiting for the Verdict* was his only hugely successful picture. It

". . . gained him great renown as it was engraved and sold by the hundred. Copies of the print may often still be seen in cottage homes and in inns, although it was painted as long ago as 1857."

Solomon had already had considerable success with a pair of pictures called *First class – the meeting* (Ottawa) and *Second class – the parting* (Marquess of Lansdowne), shown at the 1854 RA. Both are set in railway carriages – the first shows a girl demurely accepting the attentions of a young man while her father sleeps in the corner seat; the outcry that ensued at the unchaperoned flirtation caused Solomon to paint another version of *First Class* (Roy Miles Fine Paintings Ltd, 1977) to appease the voices of outraged convention – perhaps the same pressures that caused Collinson to retitle his 1857 paintings (see cat. no. 5, 6). These, too, were engraved and became widely known.

Solomon was the elder brother of two other talented though ill-fated painters, Rebecca and Simeon (see Lambourne, *op. cit.*) and followed the usual path through Sass's and the RA schools, exhibiting literary and historical genre subjects from 1840 until he achieved his great successes in the 1850s. The great number of versions he was commissioned to paint of these has caused considerable confusion ever since.

Private Collection

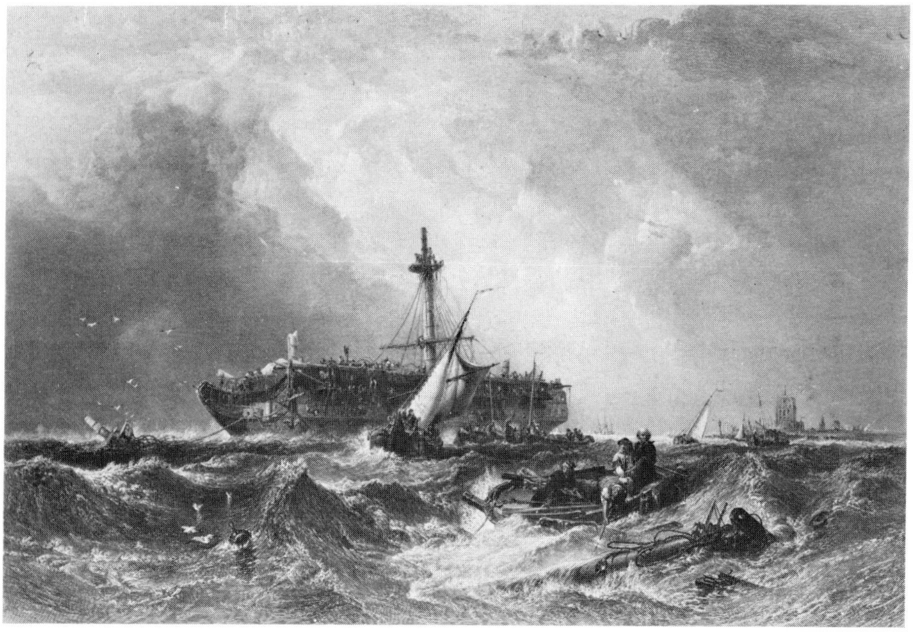

engraving after The Day after the Wreck

CLARKSON STANFIELD, 1793–1867,
ARA 1832, RA 1835

53 The Day after the Wreck. A Dutch East Indiaman on shore in the Ooster Schelde; Zierikzee in the distance. 1844

oil on canvas, 60¼ × 91½ in

PROV: commissioned by E. Bicknell; (?) Hogarth sale, 13 June 1851 (96) bt. Grundy (£924); (?) John Naylor, Town Hall, Liverpool 1854 (31); John Brooks sale, Christie's, 25 May 1872 (40) bt. Agnew (£2940) for Baron Albert Grant; sale of contents of his Kensington House Gallery, Christie's, 27 Apr 1877 (91) bt. Agnew (£2677.10s), sold to Octavius E. Coope, Brentwood; Mrs. Coope; Hon. E. Ponsonby (their son-in-law); Coope sale, Christie's, 6 May 1910 (35) bt. W. Permain (£514.10s); Paul K. Kuehnrich, by whom pres. to Sheffield, 1929.

EXH: RA 1844 (187); Guildhall 1899 (189) and 1904 (107).

LIT: *Art Union*, June 1844, p157; *Athenaeum*, 11 May 1844, p433; *ILN*, 11 May 1844, p306; *Literary Gazette*, 11 May 1844, p307; *Times*, 8 May 1844, p7; 'British Artists XXIV: Clarkson Stanfield', *AJ*, May 1857, p138; Ruskin, *Modern Painters, I, Works*, III, p227; Sandby, 1862, p151; obit., *AJ*, July 1867, p171; obit., *Athenaeum*, 25 May 1867, p694; James Dafforne, *Pictures by Clarkson Stanfield*, with Historical and Critical Descriptions and a Short Biographical Sketch of the Painter, 1873, pp48–9; Cunningham, 1880, pp333, 335; *British Painters of the 18th & 19th Centuries*, c.1880, p45; Temple, 1897, p20; *Sheffield Catalogue*, 8th edn, c.1930 (473), repr.

ENGR: 1. J. Cousen; steel engraving; 14½ × 19⅝ in; dedicated to His Majesty the King of the Netherlands; publ. J. Hogarth, 1847. V & A E.102–1971. Four proofs, in different states, were lot 1122 in the Stanfield sale, Christie's, 8–12 May 1868.
2. Finden; in 'The Royal Gallery of British Art' (quoted in Christie's cats.).

VERSIONS: 1. *Morning of the Wreck*; watercolour; 13 × 18½ in; commissioned by Ralph Bernal; Charles Suthers sale, Christie's, 29 Apr 1876 (27) bt. Agnew; Sir John Fowler, Bt., sale Christie's, 6 May 1899 (27) bt. Agnew.
2. *Morning after the Wreck*; Hogarth sale, Christie's, 13 June 1851 (96) bt. Grundy (£924) – included in the provenance of the exhibited picture on the evidence of Dafforne, 1873, p49, but it may be a reduced replica made for Hogarth, the publisher of the Cousens engraving.
3. *Morning after a Wreck*; coll. John Naylor, Town Hall, Liverpool 1854 (31) – see Graves *Sales*; identifiable with Sheffield picture or version 2?

When in *Modern Painters* Ruskin proclaimed Stanfield 'the leader of the English Realists', he was for once joining in the critical and public acclaim for a contemporary artist. He went on:

> "... perhaps among the more remarkable of his characteristics is the look of common sense and rationality which his compositions will always bear, when opposed to any kind of affectation. He appears to think of no other artist. What he has learned, has been from his own acquaintance with, and affection for, the steep hills and the deep sea; and his modes of treatment are alike removed from sketchiness or incompletion, and from exaggeration or effort."

Going on to discuss *The Day after the Wreck*, Ruskin found fault with its 'morbid purple' and the unwrecked appearance of the ship, though he deferred to Stanfield's professional seaman's eye, and concluded:

> "At all events, this healthy and rational regard of things is incomparably preferable to the dramatic absurdities which weaker artists commit in matters marine; and from copper-coloured sunsets on green waves sixty feet high, with cauliflower breakers, and ninepin rocks; from drowning on planks, and starving on rafts, and lying naked on beaches, it is really refreshing to turn to a surge of Stanfield's true salt, serviceable, unsentimental sea."

Other critics did not qualify their praise – the *Literary Gazette*:

> "Great as is his fame, Mr. Stanfield may now throw down his easel, and proclaim that he has executed his greatest work ..."

The Times thought it 'remarkable for its high finish, the distinctness of the objects, and the transparency of the waters', but the *Art Union* surpassed everyone and devoted half a column of ecstatic prose to the picture:

> "The author of this wonderful picture accomplishes in it the *ne plus* of Art; as long as painting shall be valued for its unison with the divine melody of mysterious nature, so long must the work hold a foremost place among productions of its class."

It particularly admired Stanfield's treatment of the shallow water, still turbulent from the previous night's storm:

> "*Water can have no shadow*: any deep tone it may yield is the result of reflection. This grand and manifest truth is the principle whereon we see all Mr. Stanfield's seas painted; and this, together with an unshrinkingly just appreciation of form, wins unbounded admiration of the philosophical demonstrations of his works."

The Day after the Wreck drew successfully on all of Stanfield's talents – he was a sailor for eight years, retiring from the sea in 1816, when he became a theatrical scene-painter. He had considerable success with large moving panoramas and could work extraordinarily fast; this may account for his ability to combine scene-painting with easel-painting from 1820, when his first pictures were shown at the RA and the British Institution, until 1834 when he ceased regular theatre work, continuing however to paint scenery for friends, especially for his close friend Charles Dickens' famous amateur theatricals. His reputation steadily increased and, by 1863, four years before his death, his major pictures had begun fetching large prices of well over £2000 in the salerooms; this continued until the turn of the century when prices suddenly dropped steeply. So great was his fame that the Royal Academy devoted to Stanfield, with C.R. Leslie, a considerable portion of its first Old Masters exhibition in 1870, though, as Cunningham commented in 1880, some of his greatest paintings (including the *Day after the Wreck*) were not shown. Virtue published Dafforne's volume on Stanfield in 1873: largely a re-editing of previous *Art Union* and *Art Journal* pieces on the artist, it contributed little that was new but was a fittingly handsome memorial tome.

A major Stanfield exhibition is planned by Sunderland Museum in co-operation with the Rheinisches Landesmuseum, Bonn, and a biography of the artist by Pieter van der Merwe is in preparation.

Sheffield City Art Galleries

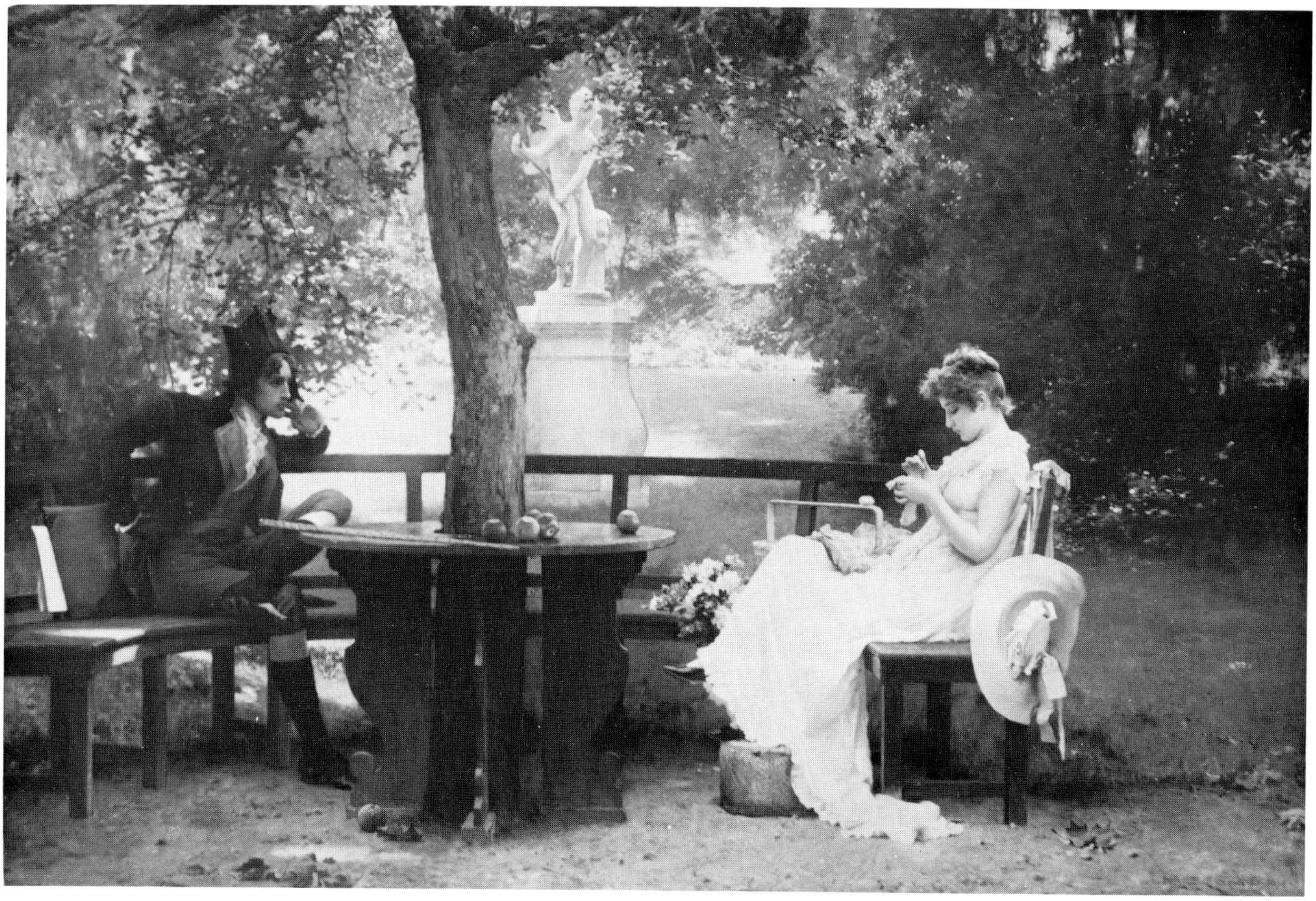

MARCUS STONE, 1840–1921, ARA 1877, RA 1887

54 In Love 1888

oil on canvas, 44×66 in
INSCR: Marcus Stone 1888

PROV: T.E. Beaumont, Kenwood Park, Sheffield, 1888, bequeathed to Castle Museum, Nottingham, 1899.
EXH: RA 1888 (236); Guildhall 1900 (9); Franco-British 1908 (158).
LIT: *AJ*, June 1888, p183; *Athenaeum*, 26 May, p669, 9 June 1888, p731; Blackburn, *RA Notes*, 1888, p6, repr. p40; *Graphic*, 19 May 1888, p530; *ILN*, 5 May, p473, 12 May 1888, p524, repr. frontisp.; *Times*, 16 May 1888, p4; *Mag. of Art*, March 1889, p.xxiv; Alfred Lys Baldry, 'Marcus Stone, RA', *Art Annual* 1896, pp22, 32, repr. facing p22; *Athenaeum*, 14 April 1900, p472; *Graphic*, 21 April 1900, p579; *Nottingham Catalogue*, 1926 (215).
REPR: *Souvenir*, Franco-British 1908, repr. betw. pp142–143.
ENGR: photogravure, publ. Berlin Photographic Co., 1889; one was part of lot 29 in the sale of the artist's minor effects, Robinson Fisher, 23 June 1921.
STUDIES AND VERSIONS: Watercolour sketch for the whole composition, repr. Baldry p8; sketch for the figure of the girl, repr. Baldry p2. *June: A Study*, exh. RA 1911 (103) is identical with the latter, with the addition of a hat and some details, and may be a reworking of the original 1888 study or a fresh, but very closely copied version. Unidentified study for *In Love* included in the Stone sale, Christie's, 24 June 1921 (133, as 'a picture' – usually an oil); *In Love – a design on glass* was lot 148.

"The prettiest of the pretty pictures painted by Mr. Stone", declared the *Magazine of Art* in 1889, a view shared by most commentators of the day and by Stone himself. In a letter to T.E. Beaumont, the picture's owner (dated 12 January 1889, coll. Castle Museum, Nottingham), Stone asked for the loan of *In Love* for the Paris Exposition Universelle later that year; the organising committee had requested a list of his preferred pictures:

> "At the head of that list I have placed 'In Love' as the picture I should prefer to stand by, as I know it to be my best . . . it will be a bitter disappointment to me if you say No! . . . [though] I shall have a sneaking sympathy with your refusal. It is a great deal to ask and I have been unfortunate enough to become used to such refusals.
>
> But at the same time, I must tell you, what a great boon it would be to me. It would also assist a cause which is a material one, that our school should endeavour to hold its own amongst others, and lastly, it would add somewhat to the value of the picture that it should be shown in what I believe will be the greatest gathering of the world's modern art, as the work the painter has selected as his best . . ."

Despite the marshalling of such astute arguments, Stone's plea was unsuccessful and he was represented in Paris by *A Gambler's Wife* (RA 1885).

Stone had no formal training and was taught by his father, the painter Frank Stone, working with him and his friends who included many of the members of the original Clique – Frith, Mulready, Egg, Phillip and Elmore. He was also helped in his early struggles to earn a living as an illustrator in the 1860s by his father's literary friends like Dickens, Thackeray, Lytton, Reade and Wilkie Collins. Stone's early paintings were historical tableaux in the spirit of E.M. Ward; *On the road from Waterloo to Paris* (RA 1863, Guildhall), showing Napoleon sheltering in a peasant cottage after his defeat, was his first major success, but he found his metier in 1876, deciding

> ". . . to limit himself to the one [human passion] which makes the widest appeal to all sorts and conditions of men and women, and to produce idyllic compositions full of tender expression, subtle domestic dramas in which Love would always be found playing the leading part . . . His lovers have undergone numberless vicissitudes and have suffered their full share of the rubs that make the course of true affection proverbially uneven. Quarrels, reconciliations, disappointments, the pleasure of perfect accord, and the thousand and one lights and shades of courtship and recent matrimony have in turn provided him with material . . ." (Baldry, p20)

Stone rapidly evolved his formula, his figures in costumes:

> "of a date when something of the older picturesqueness still remained to them, associated, however, with sufficient of the modern fashion to make them intelligible and attractive to present-day observers. The frills and flounces, the cocked hats and long-skirted coats of the time of the French Revolution, are not so unfamiliar to us to-day that we have to draw seriously upon our imaginations to accept as credible the scenes in which they appear, and yet they have about them an atmosphere of picturesqueness which assorts more pleasantly than our own daily dress with love passages and moments of tender ecstasy." (Baldry, p21)

and his gardens equipped with prettily-rustic furnishings that crop up over and over again. *In Love* features a statue of Eros which had already appeared in *In the Shade* (RA 1879, Parke-Bernet, Los Angeles, 27 May 1974, lot 25), with a simpler pedestal, while the elaborate pedestal alone, crowned with an urn, appears in *Two's Company, Three's None* (RA 1892, Blackburn). The statue itself is apparently a Victorian reconstruction of a Hellenistic figure of Eros in the Vatican, but its use in this fashion owes most to Fragonard's *The Swing* (1766/7, Wallace Collection). The symbolic content is completed by the ripe apples fallen from the tree under which the lovers sit.

Stone controlled his output carefully, generally restricting himself to one major picture a year; as each of these was almost invariably engraved, his pictures were amongst the most widely known in the latter part of the century. Although, in common with many long-lived Victorian artists like Dicksee and Linton, Stone lived to see his work eclipsed and ridiculed, the obituary in *The Connoisseur* (admittedly always the kindest of the post-Fry commentators on the relics of Victorian art) was still able to conclude, with generosity:

"Practically every work he produced was engraved, and his pictures were always among the most popular attractions at Burlington House. If not creations of the highest art, they were always simply and unaffectedly painted, characterised by happily expressed and pleasant sentiment, and thoroughly English in their inspiration."

However, his success in the '80s gave him the financial means to join that select band of artists able to commission a Norman Shaw house, in Melbury Road, Kensington, with Leighton, Watts, Hamo Thornycroft and Luke Fildes for neighbours.

Castle Museum, Nottingham

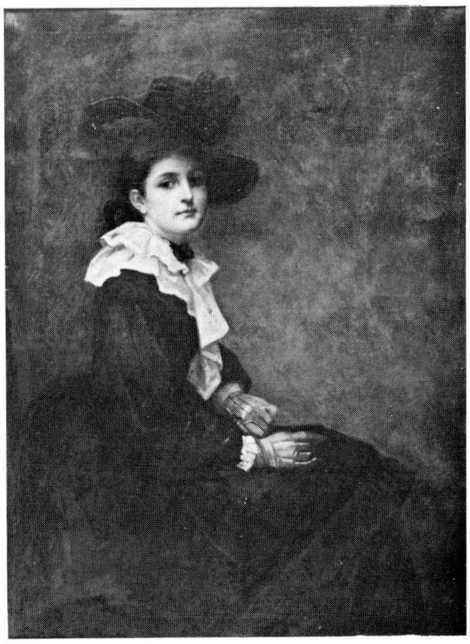

George Adolphus Storey, 1834–1919, ARA 1876, RA 1914

55 Mistress Dorothy 1873

oil on canvas, 43 × 34 in

PROV: Alfred de Rothschild, Halton, Bucks.; Lionel de Rothschild, Exbury House, Hants.; by descent to the present owner.
EXH: RA 1873 (893).
LIT: *AJ* August 1873, p238; *Athenaeum*, 3 May, p569, 17 May, p636, 31 May 1873, p700; *Graphic*, 7 June 1873, p539; James Dafforne, 'The Works of George Adolphus Storey', *AJ*, June 1875, p176, engr. p174; W.W. Fenn, 'A Painter of Prettiness', *Mag. of Art*, 1883, p355; F.G. Stephens, *Artists at Home*, London, 1884, p90; G.A. Storey, *Sketches from Memory*, London, 1899, pp277–286; 'Beautiful Women I have Painted – An Interview with G.A. Storey, A.R.A.', *The Tatler*, 22 July 1908, pp92–93, repr. p93.

Although Storey, a member with Stacy Marks, Yeames, and Walker, of the St. John's Wood Clique, is most often identified as the painter of anecdotal themes in what a contemporary critic called his 'capital De Hooghish Dutch interior' style, *Mistress Dorothy* is the product of his earlier love of Spain. As a young Academy exhibitor of briefly Pre-Raphaelite works from 1852, with Leigh's (1852) and the RA Schools (1854) behind him, Storey spent six months in Madrid and Toledo during 1862–63; he copied assidously in the Prado and the lessons of Velasquez' portraits are here evident.

Comments in the reviews of the 1873 RA were brief though complimentary:

"... we are quickly attracted by the refined and sweetly expressive *Mistress Dorothy* ... There is a quiet steadfastness of gaze about this sweet face that raises it above mere prettiness; and the grave tones of dress and background are arranged with graceful, artistic feeling." (*AJ*)

"... a charming portrait of a young lady in a broad-brimmed hat and black riding-dress. The painter's improvement is marked, his colour brightens and refines, while in the rendering of sweet and pure expression he is quite unsurpassed." (*Graphic*)

With hindsight, Storey's biographers of 1875 and 1883 were able to observe that *Mistress Dorothy* made Storey's reputation as a portrait painter and resulted in many commissions as did, for example, the portrait of Samuel Cousins for Holl in 1879. Storey accorded the saga of the painting, exhibition and sale of the picture nearly ten pages in his autobiography, far more than to any of his other pictures, and clearly regarded it with great affection. He relates how, on each of three successive visits, he upped its price to Tom Agnew from 100 to 300 guineas to avoid having to part with it and when she was sent to the Academy:

"Sir Francis Grant was then President, and he too was taken with 'Dorothy'. When she came up before the Council of Ten, over which he presided, he exclaimed – 'My God what a fine woman! what a splendid creature! Who's the painter?' and on being informed, said, 'Bravo! Storey!'

"It so happened that that same evening Sir Francis Grant dined with Baron Rothschild, and ... spoke of her in high terms ... the very next day after that dinner in Piccadilly, a splendid equipage, with a pair of prancing and snorting steeds, drove up to my modest dwelling in St. Mary's Terrace, Paddington, and a handsome young gentleman presented himself to the modest artist to ask if his picture ... was for sale and for how much? I named the same price that I had asked Tom Agnew, namely three hundred guineas, sent a small sketch of the work, and the next day received a cheque for the amount. And, furthermore, after 'Dorothy' returned from the Academy, the Baron sent me an invitation to call and see him in Piccadilly, where I found him and 'Dorothy' *en tête-à-tête*: He was on the sofa and she on a chair not far off.

"'There she is,' said he. 'I like her to keep me company, and you must come and see her and me whenever you feel inclined ...' ... I paid many visits to ... Baron de Rothschild, and was always amiably received – and all through 'Dorothy'."

The painting was hung as a pendant to Millais's *Vanessa* at the RA, and Storey continues:

"Millais said of her in his jovial-hearted way, 'If I hadn't a wife already I would have married that girl.' Fred Walker was quite angry with me for not letting him know about her; he bit his nails and said she was just the sort of wife he was looking for, and when I told him she was another's he stamped his foot and said – never mind what he said."

Most remarkable about the painting's reception was the fashion it set that summer:

"Nearly every day after this picture was seen ... I had letters from ladies asking me about the hat worn by Mistress Dorothy. Large hats were not then in vogue; the pork-pie was all the rage, so I suppose there was a novelty in this one, which, after all, was only an old Chelsea pensioner's head-gear twisted into a different shape, and ornamented with a ribbon and a big bow ... One of my sisters, on going to her milliner's to choose a costume for the Ascot week, was shown the last new thing in hats, taken from a picture in the Royal Academy, namely, 'Dorothy'."

Mistress Dorothy's most important antecedent was Gainsborough's portrait of *Mrs. Siddons* (1785, National Gallery from 1862), though the pose is of course reversed. The fashion for eighteenth century revivalism had been set earlier in the century by artists like Leslie and Mulready, painting scenes from the novels of Goldsmith and Sterne and it was led in the 1860s and 1870s by Millais with pictures like *Stella* (RA 1868, Manchester), culminating in his most overt expression of homage in *Clarissa: A Recollection of Gainsborough* (1887), Storey's picture seems to have continued to influence artists as late as the 1890s: James Sant's *A Portrait* in the 1892 RA and even Fantin-Latour's *Portrait of Sonia* (1890, Washington) share identically posed girls, three-quarter length, in what could be called variously eighteenth century style and sporting swashbuckling black hats.

The sitter was Miss Ellen Edgcumbe Score, the daughter of a naval lieutenant; she lived until 1938, latterly in Bedford, and her grand-daughter owns a fine pastel portrait of her by John Bagnold Burgess.

Edmund de Rothschild, Esq., T.D.

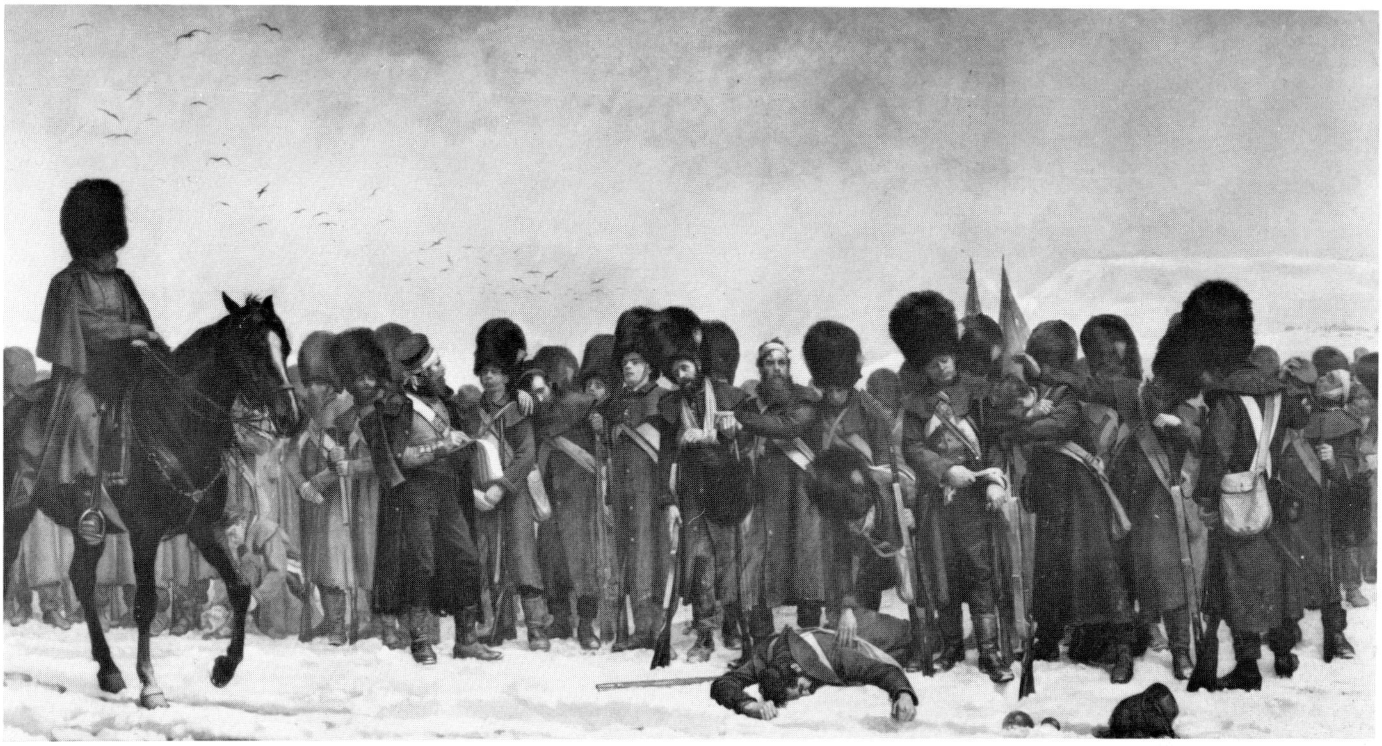

Elizabeth Thompson, later Lady Butler, 1846–1933

56 Calling the roll after an engagement, Crimea (The Roll Call) 1874

oil on canvas, 36 × 72 in

PROV: commissioned in 1873 by Charles J. Galloway of Manchester and Knutsford, Cheshire, for £126; ceded to Queen Victoria, May 1874.

EXH: RA 1874 (142); Oxford 1875; *Miss E. Thompson's New Picture Inkerman, and her other Battle Pieces, The Roll Call, Quatre Bras, and Balaclava*, Fine Art Society 1877; *City Art Gallery Inaugural Exh.*, Leeds 1888; Guildhall 1897 (11); Franco-British 1908 (259); "*The Roll Call" and Water-colour Drawings by Lady Butler*, Leicester Galleries 1912 (7).

LIT (selected): *AJ*, June 1874, pp163–4; *Academy*, 23 May 1874, p584; *Athenaeum*, 16 May 1874, p670; *Graphic*, 9 May 1874, p455; *ILN*, 9 May 1874, p446; *Punch*, 16 May 1874, p206; *Times*, 2 May, p12, 4 May, p8, 26 May 1874, p6; and see cat. Fine Art Society 1877, pp6–10, for further reviews from *The Pall Mall Gazette, The Morning Post, The Standard,* and *The Saturday Review;* John Oldcastle, 'Elizabeth Butler (née Thompson)', *Mag. of Art*, 1879, p260, part engr. p261; Henry Stacy Marks, *Pen and Pencil Sketches*, 1894, pp216–19; Wilfrid Meynell, 'The Life and Work of Lady Butler', *Art Annual*, 1898, pp1, 4, 6–7ff, sketch p32; obit. Charles J. Galloway, *Times*, 16 Mar 1904, p10; Elizabeth Butler, *An Autobiography*, 1922, pp98–9, 101–18, 126; Viola Meynell, *Alice Meynell: A Memoir*, 1929, p40; Russell Ash, 'English Paintings of 1874', *Connoisseur*, Jan 1974, p33, repr. p34; Wood, *Panorama*, 1976, pp228–31, repr. p228.

ENGR: 1. Frederic Stacpoole, line and stipple engraving, 20⅝ × 40¼ in, declared by J. Dickinson & Co., 1874, publ. Fine Art Society Ltd, 1877. 2. W.T. Hullard, mixed engraving, 15 × 30 in, publ. Fine Art Society Ltd, 1882.

The Roll Call was one of the three most sensationally successful Academy pictures of the century. Wilkie's *Chelsea Pensioners reading the Gazette of the Battle of Waterloo*, shown at the RA in 1822, was the first painting ever to be railed off from its mob of admirers; *The Derby Day* was the first of Frith's great paintings to need similar protection thirty-six years later. The jealousy caused by this accolade had been so great that when similar crowds gathered around Elizabeth Thompson's painting in 1874 it was thought more diplomatic to instal a policeman rather than a railing.

"... one stands and waits one's turn for the *Calling of the Roll*, the chorus of 'Wonderful!' rising all day around this work ..."

wrote F.T. Palgrave in the *Academy*, and the "Wonderful!" only echoed the cheers in which J.R. Herbert had led the Academy Selection Committee when the picture was brought before them. On Varnishing Day, three days before the Private View, Elizabeth Thompson wrote in her dairy of her arrival:

> "I soon espied my dark battalion ... *on the line*, with a knot of artists before it. Then began my ovation ... I never expected anything so perfectly satisfactory and so like the realisation of a castle in the air as the events of this day." (*Autobiography*, p106).

Millais, Calderon, Prinsep, Herbert, Du Maurier, Tom Taylor showered congratulations on her and, at the Private View for members of the Royal Family, the Prince of Wales wanted to buy the picture. On 1 May came 'the to-me-glorious private view of 1874' and she wrote to her father of:

> "this most memorable day. I don't suppose I ever can have another such day, because, however great my future successes may be, they can never partake of the character of this one ... You know that 'the *elite* of London Society' goes to the Private View. Well, the greater part of the elite have been presented to me this day, all with the same hearty words of congratulation on their lips and the same warm shake of the hand ready to follow the introductory bow. I was not at all disconcerted by all these bigwigs ..." (*Autobiography*, p108).

She was required to recount every detail of the elaborate preparations and study made for the painting and was to be lionised by Society for the rest of the summer.

The Prince of Wales, at the Academy Banquet on the 2nd, pronounced the picture 'deserving of the highest admiration' and predicted a great future ahead of the young woman artist; the Queen sent for the picture to be shown at Buckingham Palace and immediately expressed her wish to buy it. Unfortunately, it had been commissioned for £100 by Charles Galloway, who had raised this to 120 guineas (£126) on the favourable report of his agent and paid before the Academy opened. Galloway was an important Manchester industrialist, a manufacturer of boilers and heavy engineering equipment, and typical of the more discerning new patrons of contemporary art. He was understandably reluctant to part with the picture and drove a hard bargain, but was finally persuaded to cede *The Roll Call* to his sovereign:

> "on condition that I should paint him my next Academy picture for the same price as he had given for the one he was ceding, and that the Queen should sign with her own hand six of the artist's proofs when the engraving of her picture came out." (*Autobiography*, p111).

Fortunately for the artist he did not hold her to this agreement and finally agreed to take *Quatre Bras*, painted for the 1875 RA, for £1,126 complete with copyright. He died in 1904 and his considerable collection was sold at Christie's (24/26/27 June 1905): there were 422 lots, a majority of which were contemporary British paintings and drawings, with a number of continental paintings by, amongst others, Corot, Troyon and Fantin. His British pictures included the work of Gilbert, Linton, Charles Green, E.J. Brewtnall – all of whom had originally made their name as illustrators in the 1870s, but the greatest number were by E.J. Gregory whose chief patron he had clearly been, and whose masterpiece *Boulter's Lock*, now at Port Sunlight, was lot 69 in the sale. Galloway sold *Quatre Bras* and it went to Melbourne in 1884, but lot 8 in his sale was a watercolour copy of the picture and lot 289 was a watercolour by the artist herself, '*Gallop!*': *A reminiscence of Woolwich*.

The public and critical reaction fully confirmed the opinion of Elizabeth Thompson's patrons and fellow-artists: her diary entry for the public opening day records:

> "A dense crowd before my grenadiers. I fear that fully half of that crowd have been sent there by the royal speeches on

Saturday. I may say that I awoke this morning and found myself famous. . . . Overwhelmed with congratulations on all sides; and as to the papers, it is impossible to copy their magnificent critiques, from *The Times* downwards." (*Autobiography*, p110).

Tom Taylor's piece in *The Times* contains most of the elements which made up the picture's success – the Crimean subject matter, still a highly-charged and emotional memory for the nation though twenty years past, the sober and almost photographic realism of the treatment, the suffering of the individual soldiers, shown after the battle so that the violence and heroism of the actual battle is rendered the more potent by being implied but not shown, and finally, the most sensational of all, that such a brilliantly realised scene of war should have been by a woman at all, let alone such a young one. In fact, so overcome were most commentators by this fact that her age was persistently quoted as twenty-three though she was actually twenty-eight. *The Times* wrote:

> ". . . a picture from the battle-field, neither ridiculous, nor offensive, nor improbable, nor exaggerated, in which there is neither swagger nor sentimentalism, but plain, manly, pathetic, heroic truth, and all this the work of a young woman . . . Her picture . . . promises to be one of the sensations of the year, and unlike most sensations, one with nothing unwholesome about it . . ."

Each reviewer detailed the characterisations and the words which recur are 'earnest', 'truth' and 'honesty'. The *Art Journal*:

> ". . . In this line of soldiers worn out with conflict, some wounded, others fallen with their dying faces cleaving to the snow, there is the terrible quietude and passionless severity of absolute fact. The supreme merit of the work, in an artistic sense, lies in this very quality of perfect self-control that refuses to emphasise the misery that is already great enough, and is content with the reserve and silence proper to reality. And this is a gift, it must be noted, very rare among English painters . . . Each wound might have been turned into an occasion for the display of sentiment, and the canvas might have been filled with a number of pathetic incidents – very 'pretty', perhaps, but without the force of truth. It is the modesty and seriousness of Miss Thompson's work that entitle it to be ranked as a genuine expression of Art, as well as a popular picture."

The other episodes in the picture's triumph have been much repeated: how the Queen sent for it again to Windsor to show the Czar, and how it was taken to Florence Nightingale's bedside when the exhibition was closed. Oldcastle's 1879 article on Thompson in the *Magazine of Art* summarised the main events of her career:

> "First year, rejected with a rent in the canvas; second year, rejected without a rent; third year, skyed; fourth year, 'The Roll Call' on the line . . ."

and went on:

> "It is not given to many, even among great geniuses, to move the heart of the million. Masters in literature, in painting, in music. have been fain to content themselves with an audience 'fit though few'. But an audience of the whole people listened to this young girl's story . . . Wild stories were set afloat as to her origin and history; a quarter of a million of her photographs were sold within a few weeks . . ."

The last, staggering, statistic, putting her on a par with a twentieth century Hollywood or pop star, makes the final point: Elizabeth Thompson had been adopted as a public property, her likeness was identified with her work and the patriotism manifested in her painting made of her a national heroine with a fame surpassed only by that of Florence Nightingale. When *Quatre Bras* was shown the following year, Ruskin, in a famous passage in his 1875 RA Notes, handsomely withdrew from two entrenched positions:

> "I never approached a picture with more iniquitous prejudice against it than I did Miss Thompson's: partly because I have always said that no woman could paint; and secondly, because I thought what the public made such a fuss about must be good for nothing. But it is amazon's work this; no doubt of it, and the first fine Pre-Raphaelite picture of battle we have had . . . it remains only for me to make my tardy genuflexion . . . before this Pallas of Pall Mall . ." (*Works*, XIV, p308).

The Roll Call had a number of further showings, notably in 1875 at Oxford in aid of the flood victims of the French Midi and in 1877 at the Fine Art Society's gathering of the artist's four great pictures to date. The engraving rights were bought by J. Dickinson & Co. for the very large sum of £1200 who subsequently sold the rights to the Fine Art Society, the eventual publishers of both the large and small engravings of the painting.

Her Majesty Queen Elizabeth

Shown at Leeds and Leicester only, replaced at other showings by 56a, the Fine Art Society engraving after *The Roll Call*, lent by the Fine Art Society Ltd.

Elizabeth Thompson (Lady Butler)

57 **Scotland for Ever!** 1881

oil on canvas, 40 × 76½ in
INSCR: EB / Plymouth 1881

PROV: Colonel T. Walter Harding purchased and presented to Leeds, 1888.
EXH: S. Hildesheimer & Co. at the Egyptian Hall, Piccadilly, 1881; *City Art Gallery Inaugural Exh.*, Leeds 1888 (46); Guildhall 1894 (33); *The Waterloo Centenary, 1815–1915: An Exhibition of Pictures by Lady Butler* (in aid of the Officers' Families Fund), Leicester Galleries 1915 (7); *Early Days*, Leeds 1974 (20).
LIT: *AJ*, May 1881, pp157–8; *Athenaeum*, 16 Apr 1881, p534; *Graphic*, 11 June 1881, p571, engr. (see below); *ILN*, 16 Apr 1881, p379; *Mag. of Art*, 1881, p304; *Punch*, 16 Apr 1881, p169; *Times*, 13 Apr 1881, p9; Meynell, *op. cit.*, 1898, p12, repr. facing; Butler, *Autobiography*, 1922, pp186–7, 191; *Country Life*, 21 Nov 1952, repr. p1640; John Sunderland, *Painting in Britain 1525 to 1975*, 1976, pp40, 220, pls. 169, 171 (colour detail); Linda Nochlin, introduction, cat. *Women Artists: 1550–1950*, Los Angeles 1976, pp53–4, 249, repr. p53.
ENGR: central figures, wood engraving, *Graphic*, 11 June 1881, pp580–1.

The Roll Call had been a sombre memorial to the soldiers of the Grenadier Guards at the Crimea; the dramatically scarlet and white *Scotland for Ever!* was born in a moment of Academic exasperation at the greenery yallery of Sir Coutts Lindsay's Grosvenor Gallery. The artist, Mrs. Butler since 1877, recalled the episode in her autobiography:

> "At little Edenbridge [in 1879] I was busy making studies of any grey horses I could find, as I had already begun my charge of the Scots Greys at Waterloo at my studio. That charge I called 'Scotland for Ever', and I owe the subject to an impulse I received that season from the Private View at the Grosvenor Gallery, now extinct. The Grosvenor was the home of the 'Aesthetes' of the period, whose sometimes unwholesome productions preceded those of our modern 'Impressionists'. I felt myself

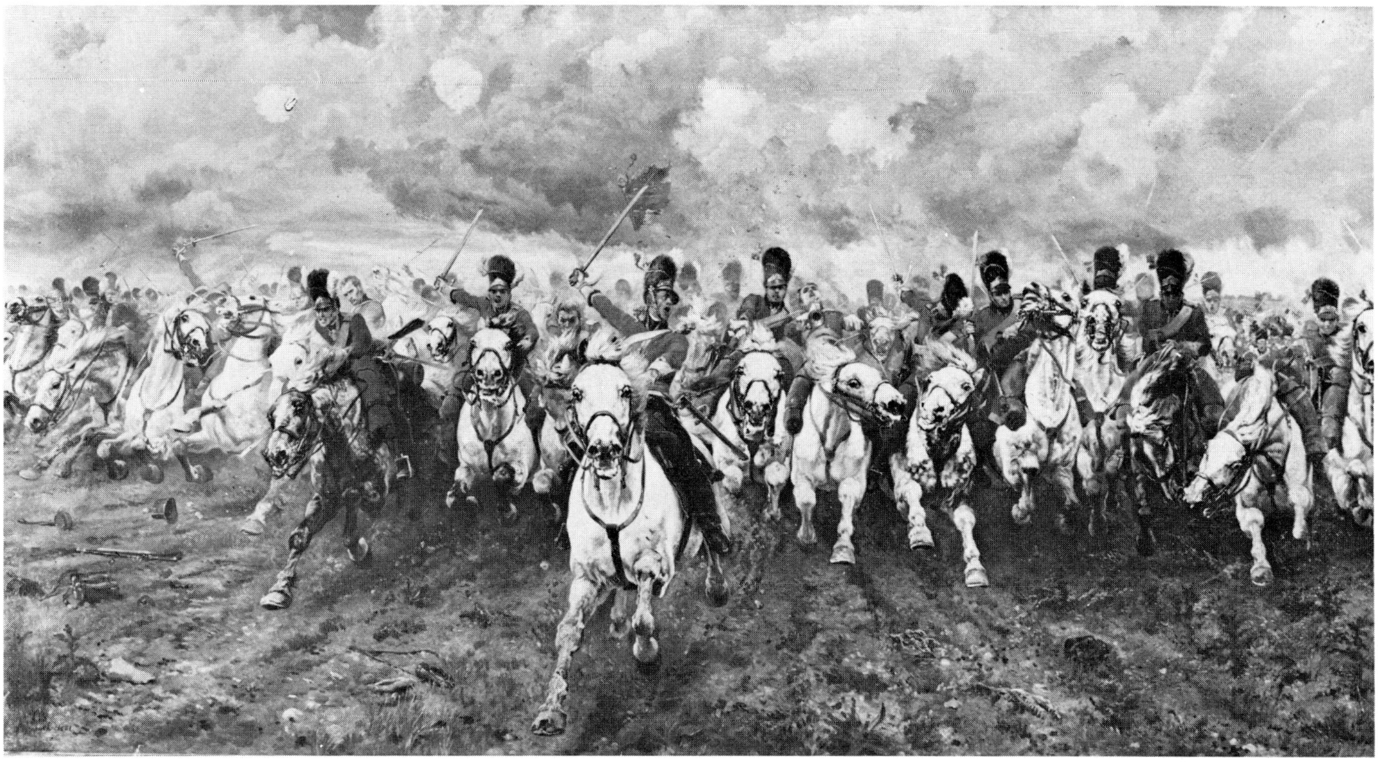

getting more and more annoyed while perambulating those rooms, and to such a point of exasperation was I impelled that I fairly fled and, breathing the honest air of Bond Street, took a hansom to my studio. There I pinned a 7-foot sheet of brown paper on an old canvas and, with a piece of charcoal and a piece of white chalk, flung the charge of 'The Greys' upon it." (p186).

It was not at all uncommon for such anger to be caused by the contents of an early Grosvenor Gallery exhibition: it had been open since 1877, showing the work of Burne-Jones, Whistler, Tissot, Legros, Albert Moore, Holman Hunt, and Walter Crane, all readily identifiable as dangerously modern or at least dangerously foreign. It also, however, showed many works by such pillars of the Academy as Millais, Leighton, Watts, Poynter, Alma-Tadema and even the then PRA, Sir Francis Grant, and was not quite the revolutionary outpost it represented in the aesthetic polarisation that had occurred in London during the previous twenty years. The exhibition of *Scotland for Ever!* opened at the Egyptian Hall in Piccadilly at the beginning of April 1881; on 23 April, Gilbert and Sullivan's *Patience* received its first performance at the Opera Comique: the Aesthetes were very thoroughly trounced that year in the eyes of the public.

It is curious that Elizabeth Butler should have felt so aggressive towards the Grosvenor Gallery in view of her own rather Bohemian childhood spent wandering around Italy, educated by her father, a man of private means, and her mother, a talented amateur musician and artist; her younger sister Alice, a poet and reviewer, was married to Wilfrid Meynell, also a reviewer. The Meynells' first house was 'exquisitely arranged with Morris papers and good colour everywhere' (Meynell, 1929, p61) and Elizabeth, though married to a soldier whose rapid promotion and knighthood in 1886 indicated great proficiency at his job (see *DNB*), had met him because he had determined to be introduced to the painter of *The Roll Call;* however, Mrs. Butler was clearly the more conventional of the two sisters.

She had always painted military subjects and the artists she admired were all academic; in her autobiography, for instance, she recounts a visit to Paris at the end of 1874 when she visited the studios or exhibitions of Bonnat and Carolus Duran, neither of whom she liked, and De Neuville and Gérôme, both of whom she admired. Of Gérôme she wrote:

"it was an epoch in my life when I saw him . . . He talked a great deal and knew me by name and '*l'Appel*', which he politely said he heard was '*digne*' of the celebrity it had gained." (p127).

The influence of French painters of military subjects was recognised by many contemporary commentators: reviewing *Quatre Bras*, *L'Art* pointed to Vernet, Bellanger and Protais, and Chesneau too was critical of her dependence on Vernet, while de Neuville was frequently cited. Alphonse de Neuville was particularly successful in England; the French Gallery showed his battle pictures regularly and *Le Bourget*, for instance, at their Winter Exhibition of 1878, stole the show from the English artists and received most of the space in the reviews.

Scotland for Ever! had a mixed reception: *The Times* and the *Magazine of Art* praised it at length, while the *Athenaeum* lead the criticism of its technical shortcomings, particularly in the foreshortening and the finish. The painting had been intended to follow her other successes at the RA, but the *Autobiography* speaks darkly of a law suit that forced her to show the picture separately while the Queen's commission, *The Defence of Rorke's Drift*, appeared alone at the RA.

"I was very sorry, as I expected rather a bright effect with all those white and grey galloping hippogriffes bounding out of the Academy walls . . . By a happy chance I had a supply of very brilliant Spanish white (*blanco de plata*) for those horses, and . . . I don't think [it] has a rival." (p191).

The favourable reviews of the picture spoke of 'her extraordinary mastery of movement' and her 'well-known powers of grouping', together with the individuality of each man and horse.

Her biographer in 1898, Wilfrid Meynell, concluded that Lady Butler's enduring place was as a humaniser of the individual in battle:

"Lady Butler has done for the soldier in Art what Mr. Rudyard Kipling has done for him in Literature – she has taken the individual, separated him, seen him close, and let the world so see him." (p31).

He saw her work as the artistic expression of the century's Humanitarianism (as voiced most expressively by Ruskin and Carlyle) and of the horror of slaughter in war; though as her brother-in-law it seems safe to assume that he would not have written anything that was contrary to her actual principles, it seems more likely that her ambitions were slightly less morally elevated and that (p31):

"to find her draughtsmanship quoted by Millais as a glory of the British school, and to know that Meissonier, almost on his deathbed, offered homage to her name."

would have had the greater importance to her.

Leeds City Art Gallery

Shown at Leeds, Bristol and the Royal Academy only.

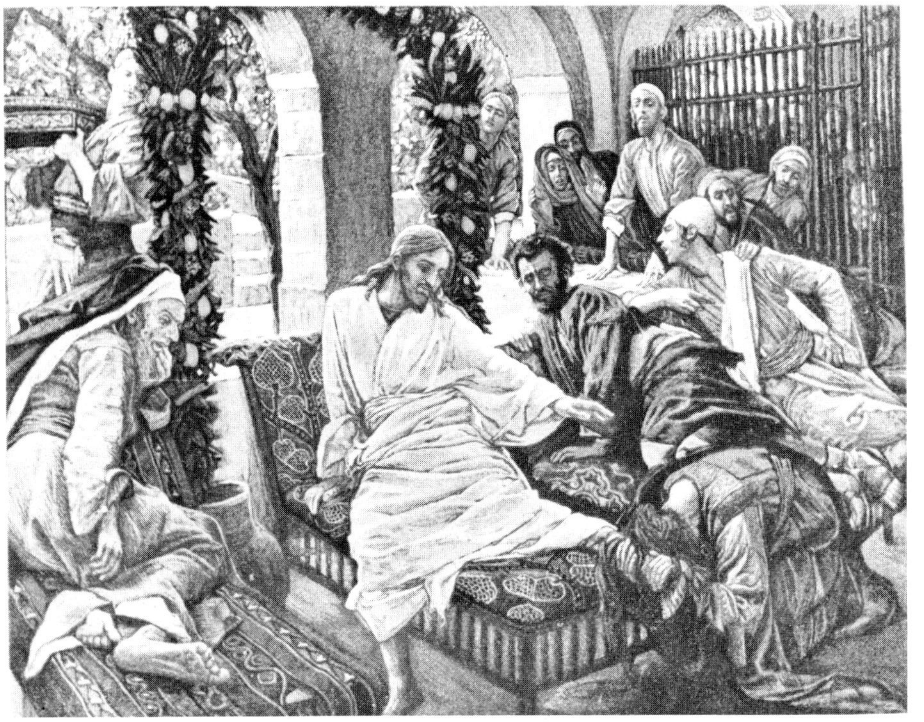

Mary Magdalene's box of precious ointment

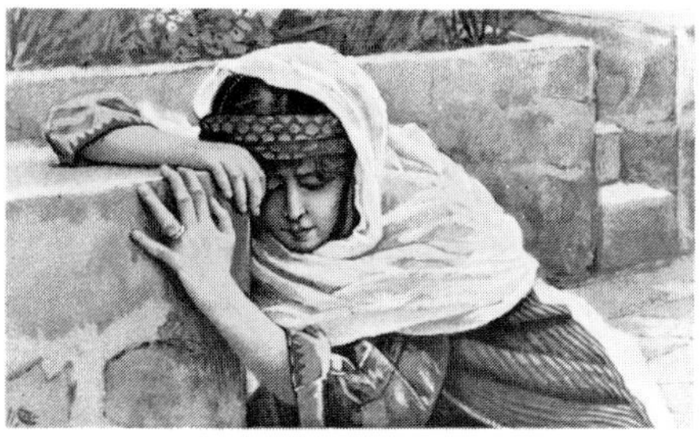

The Canaanite woman

James Jacques Joseph Tissot, 1836–1902

58 The Life of Our Lord Jesus Christ 1897–8

349 lithographs, 16 copper-plate engravings, approx. 150 wood engravings, 2 vols, each $15\frac{3}{4} \times 12\frac{3}{4} \times 2$ in; in wood cases.

Publ. Lemercier et Cie, Paris, and Sampson Low, Marston & Co, London, 1897–8, with notes translated by Mrs. Arthur Bell; dedicated to Gladstone.

LIT: (references are to the Lemercier Gallery exh. of the original drawings and to the published vols) *Athenaeum*, 5 Oct 1895, p461, 28 Mar 1896, p418, 27 Nov 1897, p754, 26 Feb 1898, p284, 6 Aug 1898, pp199–200; *ILN*, 11 Apr 1896, pp474, 476; Robert H. Sherard, 'James Tissot and his "Life of Christ" ', *Mag. of Art*, 1895, pp1–8; *Times*, 26 Mar 1896, p8, 13 Nov 1897, p9; cat. of *The Life of Our Lord Jesus Christ. 365 Pictures taken from the Four Gospels. Supplemented by Paintings & Pen & Ink Drawings. Landscape & Figures. Studies made in Palestine by J. James Tissot*, Lemercier Gallery, 1896, incl. further reviews from *Daily Telegraph, Daily News, Daily Chronicle, Morning Post, Standard, Westminster Gazette, Western Morning News;* James Laver, "*Vulgar Society" The Romantic Career of James Tissot 1836–1902*, 1936, pp54–63; cat. by Henri Zerner, David S. Brooke, Michael Wentworth, *James Jacques Tissot 1836–1902 A Retrospective Exhibition*, Rhode Island and Toronto, 1968, intro. and (56–9); Willard E. Misfeldt, *James Jacques Joseph Tissot: A Bio-critical Study*, Washington University Ph.D thesis, 1971 (unpubl., see microfilm print publ. University Microfilms Ltd), pp246–278.

La Vie de Notre Seigneur Jesus Christ was published in the original French by Mame et fils of Tours in 1896–7 and was an exceptional and heavily-publicised undertaking. It was illustrated with 349 lithographs and sixteen copper-plate engravings after his finished gouaches, and over 150 wood engravings of small sketches and ornamental designs, reproduced with an extraordinary degree of technical expertise. Many of them had already been exhibited at the Salon du Champ de Mars during the summer of 1894 where they had excited reverential admiration – many women even knelt to pray before them. When the original designs were brought to London in 1896 and shown at the Lemercier Gallery in Bond Street (a subsidiary of the Parisian printing firm responsible for the colour plates), English reactions were slightly more restrained but no less admiring.

> "M. Tissot's wonderful series of pictures illustrative of the Four Gospels have already made a great stir as I expected they would. Every day the Lemercier Gallery is crowded, and the procession of the solemn-visaged who go through the rooms is almost devotional. At first you hear criticisms of the art: but presently that in a sense is forgotten, and at length, when the Passion is reached, nobody speaks above a whisper, and as the last scene of the Divine Tragedy is approached, you see the tender-hearted trying to hide their emotion." (*Western Morning News*).

When the publication of the English version of the *Life of Christ* was completed in 1898 the critical reception was eulogistic: the *Athenaeum* wrote:

> "The entire body of these brilliant versions is now in our hands, and also the harmony of the Gospels which, with Mr. Tissot's connecting comments, forms the text, so that nothing remains but to pronounce this wonderful 'Life of our Lord' one of the greatest artistic achievements of that illustrious French School from all the traditions of which it is so complete and successful a departure. These drawings are full of individuality and energy, animated with the racial spirit and idiosyncrasies of the nation to which they belong. Nor are the veracity and vigour confined to the figures. The landscape of the Holy Land, the architecture of its cities, the climatic peculiarities of the country, the rich hues of its lucid night effects, and even the glow within the silver of the Eastern moonlight – each of these elements, so precious to the realistic painter, and so valuable as illustrating the text, has its place in these searching and comprehensive studies. M. Tissot has illustrated the life and acts of Christ and His followers on a scale and in a way which no painter had attempted before."

Tissot concluded the volumes with a plea for the reader's prayer for God's blessing on the artist and his work and the *Athenaeum* went on,

> "About the devoutness of this appeal, the profound veneration and freedom from any debasing element of the 'modern' sort, from the impulse of *chic* and self-satisfaction in the designs before us, there can be no question . . ."

Reviewers drew analogies between Tissot and the Pre-Raphaelites, Blake, and the Early Renaissance, finding that he surpassed Holman Hunt for precision of details as well as in sheer quantity, that he had much of Blake's visionary quality as well as some of his mannerisms, and that with the literal reality of his drawings he had achieved much of the spiritual purity to be found in quattrocento representations of the same scenes.

After Paris and London the original designs were toured around North America: New York in 1898, Chicago, Philadelphia, Toronto and Boston in 1899, and St. Louis in 1900; everywhere the reception was ecstatic. The American editions of the *Life of Christ* had begun in 1896 and continued (from various publishers) until at least 1905. The astutely-organised exhibitions, combined with the superbly-produced volumes themselves, made a great deal of money for Tissot and his publishers, enabling him to carry out his next treasured project of illustrating the Old Testament in the same fashion. This he completed just before his death, and the two volumes were published in Paris in 1904.

The whole extraordinary venture was recognised by Tissot's contemporaries as a radical departure from his previous image as the sophisticated painter of the London and Parisian Society and demi-monde, and his late career was summarised by the *ILN* in 1896:

> "The fashionable artist, who had but little dash of the Bohemian in him, gave place to the recluse. A strong religious revival was operated in him, and he set himself to follow the footsteps of the great Founder of his faith and to study with that patient exactitude he had thrown into his earlier works the country and people which he had made sacred in His life and teaching."

Tissot spent months in Palestine during at least two, and probably more, visits, though the only documented trips for the *Life of Christ* were in 1887 and 1889. The extreme literalism of his representation of the life of Christ (based on elaborate sketches and photographs) had a novelty and impact which, combined with the sheer quantity of his output and the industry it represented, probably account largely for the great popularity of the illustrations. The Catholic revival in France and the conventional reaction against Wildean decadence of the 1890s in England provided the ideal audience and Tissot was able finally to achieve that great popular success which had eluded him earlier, though the intimate and highly finished oils of his mistress and their life together in London are today sought after at high prices. Tissot had received 1,000,000 francs for the reproduction rights of *The Life of Christ*, and the North American tour alone brought him $100,000; the seal was finally set on a colossal financial success when in 1900 the Brooklyn Museum, New York, bought the entire set of original drawings for *The Life of Christ* for $60,000.

The Courtauld Institute of Art

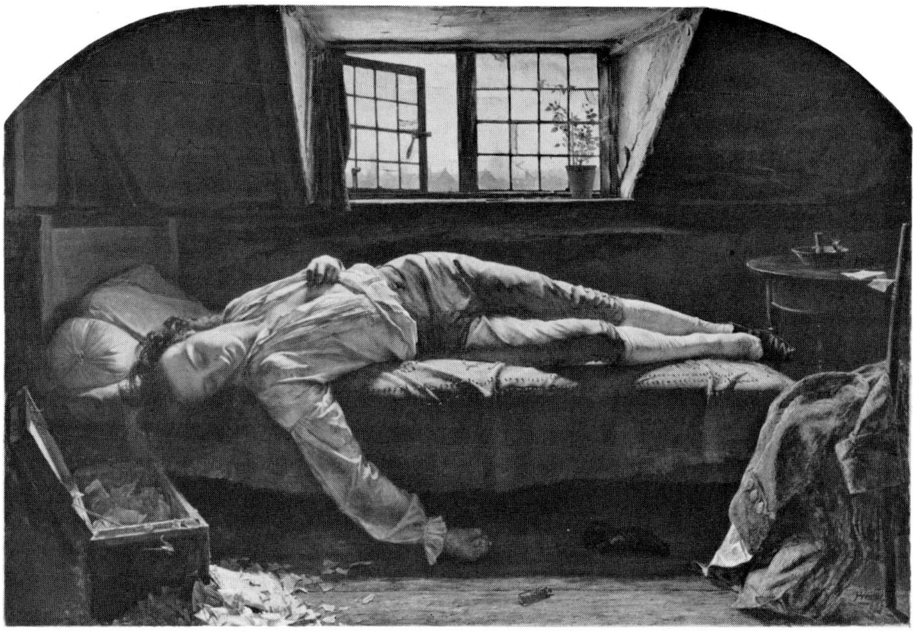

HENRY WALLIS, 1830–1916

59 The Death of Chatterton 1856

oil on canvas, 24½ × 36¾ in
INSCR: H. Wallis, 1856

PROV: Augustus Egg; his sale, Christie's, 18 May 1863 (146) bt. Agnew (£813 15s), sold to Samuel Withers, Liverpool; (?)his sale, Foster's 25 Mar 1868; A.W. MacDougall, Bath, by 1868; his sale, Christie's, 13 Mar 1869 (91) bt. in (£430 10s); Charles Gent Clement, by 1886, by whom presented to the nation, 1899.

EXH: RA 1856 (352, as *Chatterton*); Manchester Art Treasures 1857 (371); Expo. Univ. Paris 1867 (114); Leeds 1868 (1391); Whitechapel 1886 (150); Birmingham 1891 (200); Guildhall 1895 (86); *Pre-Raphaelite Brotherhood*, Tate 1948 (22); *Le Livre Anglais*, Bibliothèque Nationale, Paris 1951 (497); *Art Treasures Centenary*, Manchester 1957 (212).

LIT: *AJ*, June 1856, p169, engr. facing; *Athenaeum*, 10 May 1856, p590; *Literary Gazette*, 17 May 1856, p284; Ruskin, *RA Notes 1856*, *Works*, XIV, p60; *Times*, 12 May 1856, p12; Holman Hunt, *Pre-Raphaelitism and the Pre-Raphaelite Brotherhood*, 1905, II, p88; Phythian, 1908, p162; obit., *Burlington*, Mar 1917, p124; Ironside and Gere, *Pre-Raphaelite Painters*, 1943, p44, pl.71; Gert Schiff, 'The Death of Chatterton', *Neue Zürcher Zeitung*, 5 Feb 1966 (transl., Tate file); Reynolds, 1966, pp68–9; Bell, 1967, p44, pl.34; Anne d'Harnoncourt, *The Awakening Conscience*, Courtauld Institute MA Report, 1967 (unpublished), pp40–3 & cat.; Linda Kelly, *The Marvellous Boy: The Life and Myth of Thomas Chatterton*, 1971, pp116–19, detail repr cover.

REPR: *The Nation's Pictures*, 1901, IV, pl.17; Wood, *Dictionary*, 1971, p398; etc.

VERSIONS: 1. oil on panel, 6⅝ × 10 in. Prov: Sam Mendel sale, Christie's, 24 Apr 1875 (384) bt. Agnew; Baron Albert Grant sale, Christie's, 28 Apr 1877 (129) bt. Vokins; Rt. Hon. William Kenrick, PC, by whom presented to Birmingham, 1918.
2. oil on panel, 8 × 11¾ in, Sotheby's Belgravia, 28 Nov 1972 (50); Yale Center for British Art.
3. replica (no further details); coll. Joseph Dixon; exh. Whitechapel Spring 1908 (34), identifiable with 1 or 2?

Henry Wallis exhibited in London for almost twenty-five years, from 1854 to 1877: while most of his work received little attention, two pictures, *The Death of Chatterton* and *The Stonebreaker* achieved immortality. *Chatterton*, shown at the 1856 RA was acclaimed as 'a brilliant opening' (*Literary Gazette*), in which the figure drawing was 'admirable . . . and the effect of the London morning light stealing in at the attic window is rendered with great felicity.' (*Times*). For the *Athenaeum* it was:

> "One of the most thoughtful pictures exhibited this year . . . a sad scene, full of pathos; though, perhaps, too sad for those whose path of life is softly carpeted, and who shut their doors on all unpleasant realities."

It went on to recount a bowdlerized version of Chatterton's life in which the boy genius's forgeries of mediaeval documents and poems are called 'his reckless Grub-Street lampoonings'. It continues:

> "With a little idealisation of face and form, Mr. Wallis represents the dead poet, the poison-phial just slipped from his relaxed hand, stretched cold and stiff on a miserable pallet below a garret window, through whose horny, smoked panes, we see the careless city, crowned by the mountain dome [of St. Paul's] that is for everlasting... the rest of the story being told by a candle just gone out, the blue stifling smoke of which curdles about the ceiling. By the bedside is a chest full of torn poems, for the proud lad, who would rather starve than share his landlady's dinner, spent his last moments in carefully destroying all he had written. In how many garrets have such scenes been enacted with the same great city hushed below, careless of the forms whose shadows fall upon its stones and pass away. Mr. Wallace has flattered Chatterton as to face, without doing him justice, – his great laughing eyes, rich flood of hair, and proud sullen mouth were worthy of the Apollo. The body is well drawn, and the satin coat and violet breeches form a pleasant unison of colour. Idealised as the face is, it is excellently modelled, and its proportions are exquisite, and the effect of poison is conveyed in its blue lividness, without exciting disgust. Well may the spectator exclaim, with a sigh –
>
> Cut is the branch that might have
> grown full straight,
> And burned is Apollo's laurel bough.
>
> [Marlowe, Dr. Faustus, quoted by Wallis in the RA catalogue]
> . . . this, indeed, was one that 'perished in his pride'."

Chatterton's suicide in 1770 at the age of seventeen placed him securely amongst those legendary tragic geniuses who became romantic heroes. There are Chatterton pictures by Flaxman (*c*.1790), Singleton (engraved 1794, and Fourau (1842) and others including, later in the century, Henrietta Ward's picture now at Bristol and his life was the subject of innumerable poems, plays and biographies in England and in France. Wallis's painting crystallised the Chatterton ideal into a brilliantly stage-managed tableau of great intensity and impact and in this his contacts with the Pre-Raphaelites were decisive. He was certainly identified with the Pre-Raphaelite camp by those critics hostile to it, and *Chatterton* was criticised for its exaggerations and consequent loss of truth, though even then any harshness tended to be mitigated by a final admission, as in the *Art Journal*, that:

> "The picture, however, exhibits marvellous power and may be accepted as a safe augury of the artist's fame."

Ruskin urged his public to

> "Examine it well inch by inch: it is one of the pictures which intend, and accomplish, the entire placing before your eyes of an actual fact – and that a solemn one."

Two years later when Wallis exhibited *The Stonebreaker* (now Birmingham) Ruskin continued to support him in print, but it was the last significant painting Wallis produced. His final years were spent writing learned works on Middle Eastern ceramics.

Trustees of the Tate Gallery

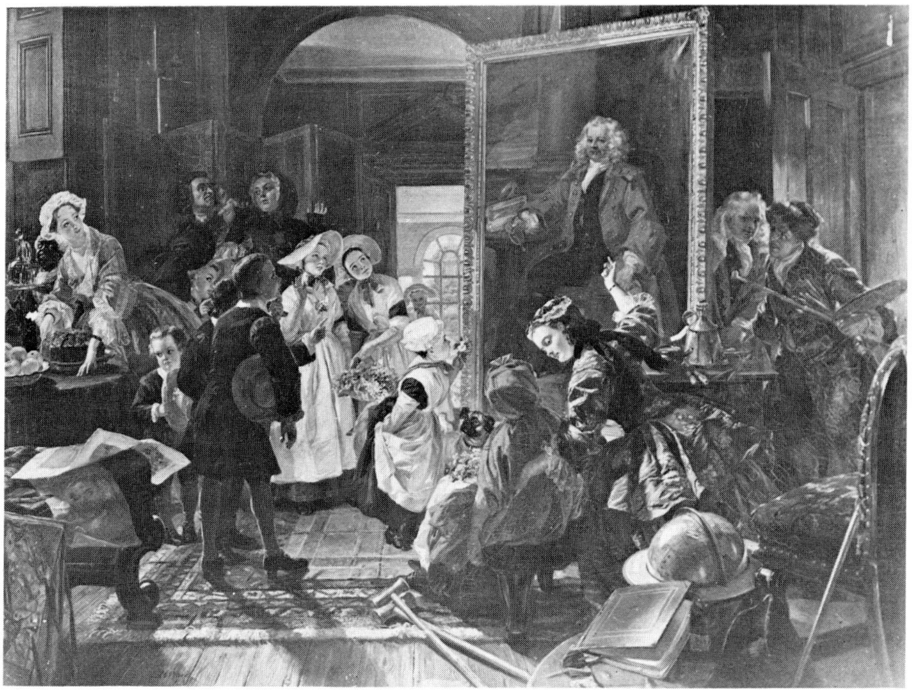

EDWARD MATTHEW WARD, 1816–1879, ARA 1846, RA 1855

60 Hogarth's studio, 1739 – Holiday visit of foundlings to view the portrait of Captain Coram 1863

oil on canvas, 47½ × 65 in
INSCR: E M Ward / R A / 1863

PROV: commissioned by Duncan Dunbar; his sale, Christie's, 30 Apr 1864 (533) bt. in; his executors, Christie's, 19 May 1866 (43) bt, Burton; John Burton, Poppleton Villa, York, by whom bequeathed to the gallery 1882.
EXH: RA 1863 (199); Birmingham Soc. of Artists 1864 (52); York 1879 (167); York (incl. Burton Bequest) 1883 (86); *Burton Collection*, York 1970 (115).
LIT: *AJ*, 1 May, p97, 1 June 1863, p106; *Athenaeum*, 2 May 1863, pp589–90; *ILN*, 2 May, p495, 9 May 1863, p518; *Times*, 2 May 1863, p11; Hugh Willoughby Sweny, 'Edward Matthew Ward, RA', *Mag. of Art*, 1878, p18; obit., *Times*, 17 Jan 1879, p6; James Dafforne, *The Life and Works of Edward Matthew Ward, RA*, 1879, pp48–50; *York Cat.*, 1907 (17) ill. p13; *York Preview* 90, April 1970, pp820, 823, repr. p819, *York Cat.*, 1974, p86, pl.9.
STUDY: Coll. of F.W. Cosens, Queen's Gate, London, in 1872 (*AJ*, 1872, p225).

In the first week of May, just before the 1863 RA opened, the *Art Journal* published a column and a half previewing the pictures being shown in the forthcoming exhibition by Mr. and Mrs. Ward – Edward Matthew and Henrietta. They were close friends of the journal's editor, Samuel Carter Hall, and of its proprietor, James S. Virtue, and this valuable advance publicity provided on other occasions during the 1860s was surpassed only by that given to Frith.

After explaining the subject (Hogarth showing his newly painted portrait of Captain Coram, founder of the Foundling Hospital, to some of the orphans), and commending the charm and expressiveness of the painting, Hall made a particular point of the suitability of the picture for engraving, giving his reasons:

> "A natural and healthy tone of feeling pervades the whole treatment of this scene, in the embodiment of which the artist has been content to rely upon the varied yet simple elements which the story presented... The figures introduced present the varied phases of life, from childhood to extreme old age, and are worked out with remarkable individuality . . . We are particularly impressed with the singular fitness of this subject for engraving; and to a large class of the public we are sanguine it would be specially acceptable. The feelings aroused by the contemplation of such an incident, so treated, are both pleasurable and wholesome." (*AJ* 1863, p97).

The *Athenaeum* took up precisely this point in its first RA review and, after specially approving the little girl in the centre who is peering at the portrait, clutching a posy in her left hand, went on:

> "... Other suggestive incidents are given in this excellent and manly picture, that will be popular, and is one which, being solidly painted and free from all sensational qualities, would not only make a good engraving, but be, in its healthiness, fit for engraving."

The emphasis on healthiness and fitness for engraving sprang from two concerns: the first was with Ward's own predilection for the more morbidly sensational aspects of scenes from the French Revolution: he had painted subjects like *The Royal Family of France in the Prison of the Temple* (RA 1851, Preston), perhaps his biggest single success, and *La Toilette des Morts*, his other '63 RA picture, showing Charlotte Corday preparing for execution. The second sprang from the wider issues of what exactly was considered appropriate for engraving; the publication of an engraving instantly made a picture accessible to a far wider public than it had had on the walls of the Academy and it was this that made the guardians of public morality concerned about content as much as about quality of works that were engraved.

Ward's earliest reputation had been made with scenes from the seventeenth and eighteenth centuries; two of the most famous were in the Vernon bequest to the nation, now in the Tate – *Doctor Johnson in the Ante-room of Lord Chesterfield* (RA 1845) and *The South Sea Bubble* (RA 1847). Ward was the most important of the mid-century artists who, following Mulready and C.R. Leslie, looked to the eighteenth century for subject-matter. In the 1870s and 1880s Reynolds and Gainsborough were to be the most important eighteenth century examples to follow, but for Ward and his contemporaries Hogarth was the truly moral artist. Essays, volumes of engravings and biographies of Hogarth had been published in considerable numbers since the turn of the century by amongst others, Cook (1802–3), Clerk (1810), Hazlitt (1819 and 1843), and Trusler (1833), but it was George Augustus Sala's series of nine essays on Hogarth, published in *The Cornhill Magazine*, February-October 1860 (and in one volume, 1866), that renewed the interest of his artist-contemporaries in Hogarth and Hogarthian subject-matter. Ward's *Hogarth's Studio* was exhibited with a quotation from Sala's fifth essay (*Cornhill*, June 1860, p722) emphasising the benevolence of the old philanthropist as he hides behind his portrait to hear the childrens' reaction. Ward's references to Hogarth's own paintings are not only in the subject but in many specific details: for instance, the pug is Hogarth's own dog, Trump, most familiar in Hogarth's self-portrait of 1845 (Tate); the children, though dressed in Foundling Hospital pinafores, have the cherubic brightness of the Graham children in Hogarth's portrait of 1842 (Tate), and the crutches in the foreground of Ward's picture are used as a compositional device in the same way as the handle of the child's carriage in the foreground of the Graham portrait.

Ward's reputation declined in the late 1860s and during the 1870s as he slid into a depressive illness; despite some late honours, when the *Magazine of Art* in its first issue, devoted the first of its articles on 'Our Living Artists' to Ward (he had been the second only to Constable in the *Art Journal*'s earlier series), he took his own life in January 1879. Virtue published a memorial to his friendship with Ward later in the year in a handsome volume including all thirteen engravings published over the years by the *Art Journal*.

York Art Gallery

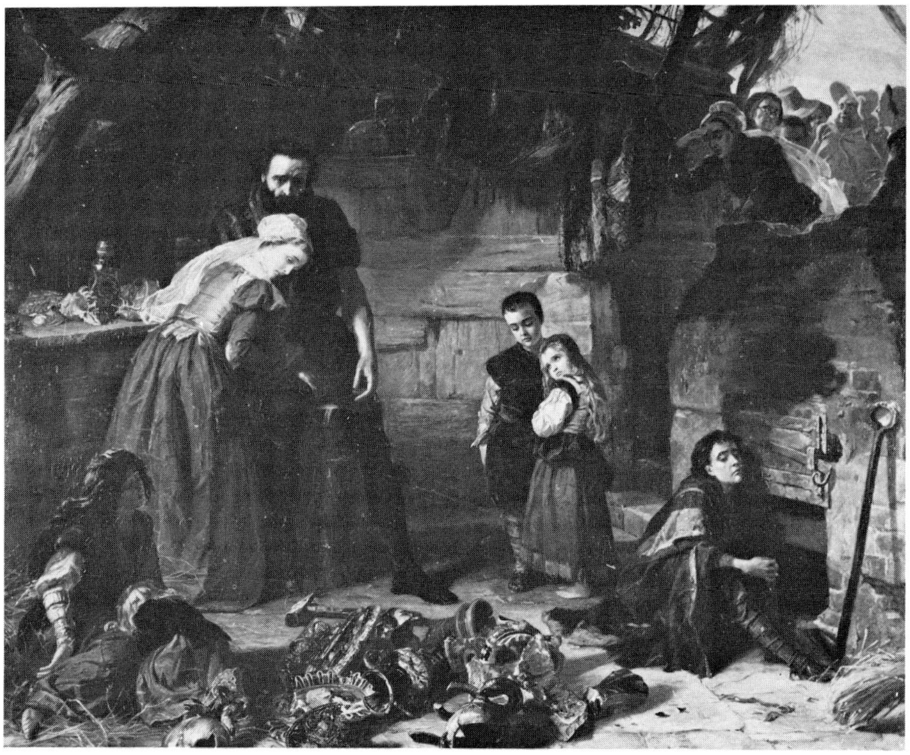

HENRIETTA WARD, 1832–1924

61 Palissy the potter 1866

oil on canvas, 44 × 52 in
INSCR: Henrietta Ward 1866

PROV: Andrew Holtz, by 1867; his sale, Christie's, 6 Feb 1886 (141) bt. in; poss. his sale, Foster's, 23 Feb 1887 (uncat.); purch. fr. Foster's by Leicester, 1887.
EXH: RA 1866 (385); Expo Univ. Paris 1867 (117); London Internat. 1871 (335).
LIT: *AJ*, 1 Apr, p116, 1 June 1866, pp166–7; *Athenaeum*, 5 May, p603, 19 May 1866, p675; *Blackwood's*, Aug 1866, p191; *Times*, 5 May, p9, 22 May 1866, p12; 'Selected Pictures: from the Coll. of Andrew Holtz, Esq. – Palissy the Potter', *AJ*, 1 June 1868, p120; E.C. Clayton, *English Female Artists*, 1876, II, p165; S.J. Viccars, 'The Leicester Corporation Art Gallery – I', *Mag. of Art*, 1893, p19; *Leicester Cat.* 1899 (38); *Illustrated Selection of Pictures in the Leicester Art Gallery*, 1906, p36; ed. Elliott O'Donnell, *Mrs. E.M. Ward's Reminiscences*, 1911, pp160–3; extracts from this repr. as 'Memories of a Long Life', *The Evening News*, 6 May–7 June 1918 (scrapbook, V & A, p31); Mrs. E.M. Ward, ed. Isabel G. McAllister, *Memories of Ninety Years*, 1924, pp119–120; obit., *Connoisseur*, Sept. 1924, p57.
ENGR: C.W. Sharpe, steel engraving, publ. *AJ*, 1 June 1868, facing p120.
VERSION: reduced replica, 25 × 30 in. Prov. James S. Virtue (proprietor of the *Art Journal*) sale, Christie's, 1 Mar 1879 (160) bt. Stannage; A.S. Dixon, by 1883, his sale, Christie's, 26 Apr 1918 (117) bt. Sampson. Exh: Huddersfield 1883 (34).

In April 1866 Hall and Virtue gave Henrietta Ward's *Palissy* two whole columns of advance publicity, surpassing anything they had done for the Wards previously. In their opinion, this 'very remarkable work' raised the granddaughter of James Ward and the daughter of the miniaturist George Raphael Ward to new heights and meant that:

> "we are not . . . called upon to regard her with indulgence as a woman working under disadvantages to which men are not subjected . . . for if hitherto she might claim some consideration on the ground of 'sex', her production this year will, we are sure, be classed among the best efforts of the British School – such as few artists of our time can surpass . . . her pictures are, in all ways, not only far removed from the commonplace, but reach the loftier limits to which Art is capable of attaining."

Her success was ascribed to her thoughtful use of literary sources and, allowing for the hyperbole of loyal friendship, most critics were in agreement with Hall that *Palissy* was Henrietta Ward's best picture to date. *Blackwood's* took the opportunity for some liberal propaganda:

> "Mrs. E.M. Ward . . . exhibits her best work, *Palissy the Potter*, which places her in the foremost rank among ladies who in Europe have used the brush. In the pending reconstitution of the Royal Academy, it is worthy of consideration whether means can be devised by which female talent shall receive fair recognition."

Blackwood's was not alone in its recognition of women artists, but, despite the admission of women students to the RA Schools from 1860 (though under very restricted conditions), Elizabeth Thompson (Lady Butler) was narrowly defeated in the ARA election in 1879 and it was not until 1922 that the first woman ARA was elected. Indeed apart from Angelica Kauffmann and Mary Moser, who were founder members of the RA, there have been only seven women out of a total of 543 members and associates of the RA to 1968, since when there have been a further seven among 45 new members.

It was agreed that Henrietta Ward was no colourist, but her earnest and conscientious attempt to imagine the scene, as the potter stares aghast at the shattered remains of his failed experiment, was much appreciated beside what *The Times* criticised as the 'stagy exaggeration in subjects of sentiment and grimace in subjects of humour [which] are the Scylla and Charybdis of our school.' According to the *Art Journal* the picture attracted 'the public [who] confess to the deep interest of the scene, by thronging to the quarter where poor Palissy is found stricken in grief.' Most of the public had first heard of Bernard Palissy (1510–1589), the French Protestant potter and inventor of the ware to which he gave his name, when Henry Morley published his *Life of Palissy* in 1852.

This drew on the work of two French historians, Dumesnil and Lamartine who had published biographies, in turn based on Palissy's autobiography, in 1851 and 1852. The first edition of Morley's book contained some embroidered incidents and much invented dialogue which, in response to criticisms, were cut from the next, and most successful, edition of 1855; further editions followed in 1869 and 1878, and other writers produced popularised versions well into this century. Palissy ware influenced English seventeenth century pottery and was collected in England in the eighteenth century but it was not until the Great Exhibition of 1851 that modern pottery in the Palissy style, chiefly by Minton, appeared (see John Morley, 'Palissy and the English', *Apollo*, Dec 1962, pp794–6). The potter had spent many years in fruitless experimentation, trying to produce glazes and designs that could rival both Italian maiolica and Chinese pottery, while he and his family starved, until he finally arrived at his own style incorporating snakes and lizards, among a variety of small animals, as decoration on his rustic wares; after achieving royal favour, he was imprisoned as a heretic and died in the Bastille. His dramatic life combined with the intriguingly grotesque nature of his work caught the imagination of artists and public alike and a number of Palissy subjects had already been exhibited by the time Henrietta Ward produced hers: for instance, W.J. Grant's *The last trial of Madame Palissy* (RA 1858) and A. Legget's *Palissy and the King* (RSA 1865). Victorian artists climbed eagerly onto the latest scholarly bandwagons: the spate of Palissy subjects can be paralleled on other occasions, most notably perhaps after the publication of the discoveries at Pompeii which produced paintings like Poynter's *Faithful unto Death* (RA 1865, Liverpool).

Having previewed and then reviewed the painting in 1866, the *Art Journal* crowned its efforts on the artist's behalf by engraving the painting in 1868 and naming her as the leading female artist in England. The great Frith had given his congratulations, writing to her father on 10 May 1866:

> "The only drawback I have to the pleasure the receipt of your note gives me is the regret I feel that your daughter's admirable picture does not belong to a friend of my own, to whom I recommended it as strongly as it deserved. I sincerely congratulate the possessor . . . It would have been a disgrace to the taste and judgment of collectors if such a picture had left the Gallery unsold."
> (*Leicester Cat.* 1899, p14)

Henrietta Ward, in her autobiographies, declared that the picture 'was one of the most popular, and certainly one of my best efforts.'

Leicestershire Museums and Art Gallery

John William Waterhouse, 1849–1917, ARA 1885, RA 1895

62 Hylas and the Nymphs 1896

oil on canvas, $35\frac{5}{8} \times 64\frac{1}{4}$ in
INSCR: J.W. Waterhouse / 1896

PROV: purchased from the artist for £800, 1896.
EXH: Guildhall 1896 (?); RA 1897 (307); Expo. Univ. Paris 1900 (260); Glasgow 1901 (475); St Louis Internat. Exh. 1904 (114); Franco-British 1908 (165); Oldham 1912; RA Winter 1922 (92); *Jubilee Autumn Exh.*, Liverpool 1922 (41); Wembley 1925 (W.12); Hull 1927–8; Huddersfield 1946; Preston 1947; ICA 1951; *Victorian Favourites*, Manchester 1956; *Le Salon Imaginaire*, Akademie der Künste, Berlin 1968 (164); RA Bicentenary 1968–9 (355); *Pre-Raphaelites from Manchester*, Agnew's 1974.
LIT: *Studio*, 1896, p109; *AJ*, June 1897, p178, repr facing p178; *Academy*, 8 May 1897, p502; *Athenaeum*, 1 May 1897, p581; *Mag. of Art*, 1897, pp47, 58; *Times*, 1 May 1897, p16; 'Mr. J.W. Waterhouse's Painting, *Hylas and the Nymphs*', *Studio*, May 1897, pp243–7, repr facing p243; R.E.D. Sketchley, 'The Art of J.W. Waterhouse, RA', *Art Annual*, 1909, pp18, 23, 32, repr facing p16; Phythian, 1908, p308; Reynolds, 1966, pp71, 93, pl.56 (colour); *Manchester Concise Catalogue*, 1976, I, p193 & repr; Anthony Hobson, *J.W. Waterhouse*, forthcoming.
REPR: *RA Pictures*, 1897, p190; and on numerous further occasions.
STUDIES: Study for nymph third from right, lifting her hair from her shoulders; repr *Studio*, May 1897, p244. Study for same figure with waterlilies, repr 'Some Drawings by J.W. Waterhouse, RA', *Studio*, Sept 1908, p252. Study for same figure, with traces of waterlilies; black chalk heightened with white on blue/grey paper; $12\frac{3}{4} \times 15$ in; coll. Dr. Kurt Schnitzer, California. These may be identifiable as the same drawing, first published in its working state in 1897, worked up, perhaps for sale, and published in 1908, finally surviving, though apparently rubbed, to its present state. Studies for other figures were repr *Studio*, May 1897, pp245, 247; and a charcoal study was in the artist's sale, Christie's 23 July 1926 (part of 10) bt. Nicoll (£2. 2s).

In the mid-1880s Waterhouse was at the peak of his career, for he had been elected RA the previous year, and the great collectors of the day and the major municipal and colonial galleries vied with each other for his latest large paintings. *Hylas and the Nymphs* was eagerly anticipated for the 1896 RA but could not be finished in time and was shown later in the year at the Guildhall, finally reaching the Academy walls in 1897, by which time it was already the property of Manchester Corporation.

Conventional voices in the *Times*, *Academy* and *Athenaeum* dismissed it briefly with complaints about the sameness of feature in the nymphs, what the *Academy* called "this particularly modern lack of the variety of nature," observable in his previous work; a close look at Filippino Lippi and the Flemish was recommended as the cure. *The Times* felt that they were "as much alike, indeed, as if they had all been painted from the same model," this spoilt the illusion: "even mythology ought, in a picture, to be made to seem real, and the spectator ought not to be forced, as he is here, to think of the model and the studio." These literalist objections were refuted by the more progressive critics who were unanimous in their praise. *The Magazine of Art*:

> "Mr. Waterhouse has surpassed himself in his exquisite picture . . . and, consciously or otherwise, has approached not only the spirit, but many of the highest qualities of Sir Edward Burne-Jones at his most delightful period. The colour is not so robust as usual, but it is subtler; the drawing

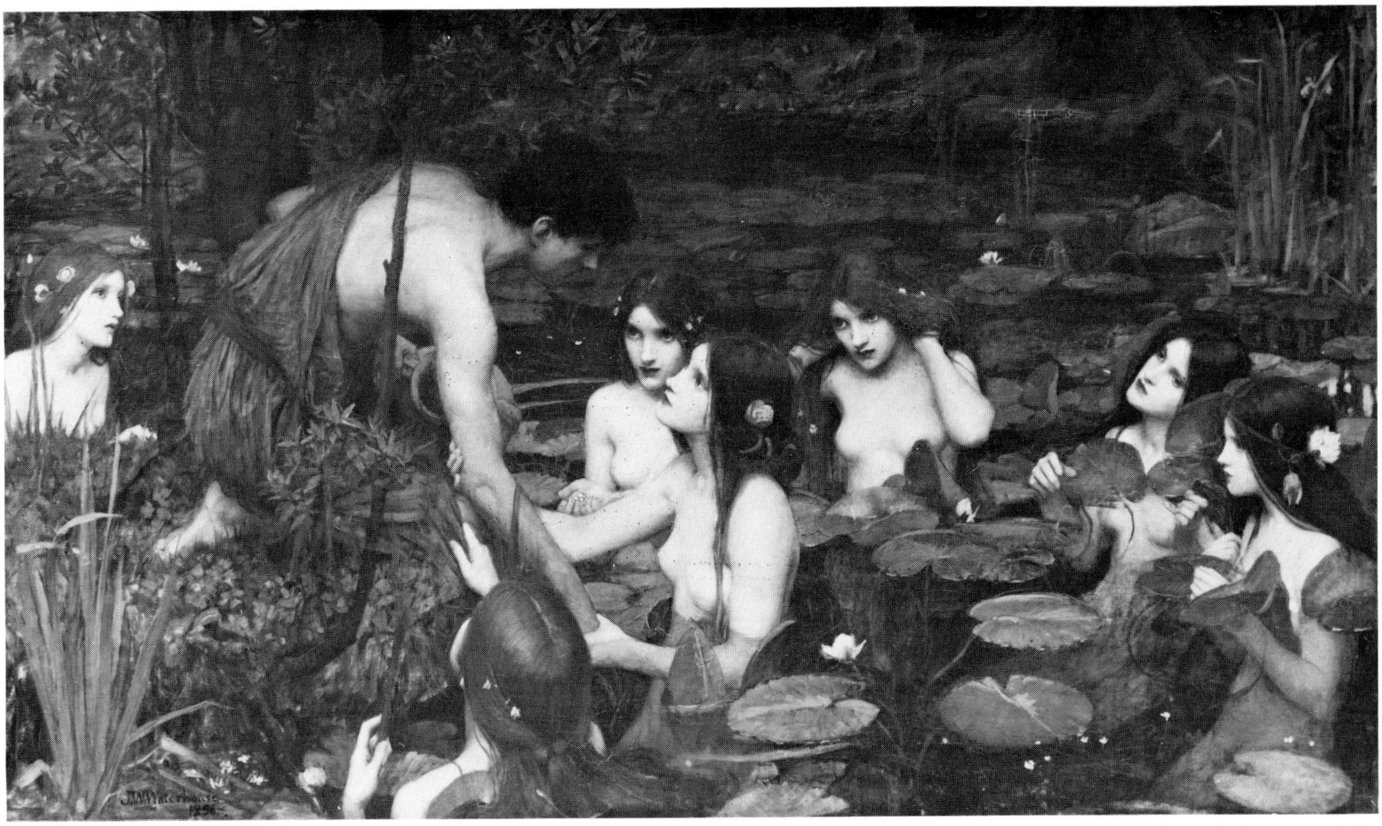

is, perhaps, daintier than ever, and not only daintier but more masterly and more poetical. The grouping of these sweet-eyed nymphs is superb in its apparent accident; their fair forms rise like flowers from among the lily-leaves; the flesh tones are cool and beautiful in colour; and a spirit of real poetry pervades the canvas. The extreme resemblance of all these maidens one to another, and the facts that, first, there is no foreshortening where the bodies enter the green water, and secondly, that the water does not sufficiently lose its translucency in its greater depth, may perhaps be urged against it; but realistic objections hardly hold good when advanced against the artistic reputation of a poetic myth treated with delicious grace."

Waterhouse's greatest supporter in print was *Studio*, which surpassed even its own previous coverage of Waterhouse by devoting an article to the painting, illustrating not only it but three preparatory studies with a eulogistic text. It praised his originality, his determination to maintain a consistent development of his own poetic inspiration:

"He has never given way to the temptation by which modern artists are beset, to gain popularity by concessions to the general demand for triviality of subject and showy cleverness of technical expression . . . *Hylas and the Nymphs* . . . is . . . absolutely free from any taint of that sentimentality which is too often substituted by modern workers for deeper intellectual qualities. Mr. Waterhouse's composition is dramatic, but its drama is a matter of subtle touches rather than an obvious and exact setting forth of a story."

It approved the artist's decision to render the spirit of the myth without "any pretence of classicism in manner" but with a Grecian purity and dignity of expression.

"Mr. Waterhouse becomes in this work an apostle of the delightful Paganism, by the loss of which so much that is beautiful has been taken out of life; and he is so persuaded of the charm of the creed to which he subscribes by every stroke of his brush that he can scarcely fail to make, among the people who incline to his view, hosts of sincere converts."

Hylas, squire to Heracles on the *Argo* was sent to fetch water but was enticed by the nymphs of the stream to abandon his earthly life and join them. The *Art Journal* review considered the artist's treatment of the myth and discussed his artistic masters:

". . . the art of Mr. Waterhouse [is] a combination of the better attributes and intentions of Leighton and Sir Edward Burne-Jones. In the gracefully moulded form of the doomed Argonaut there is all that love of anatomical beauty in which Leighton revelled. The Naiads wear no look of native witchery; theirs is a sad and sympathetic welcome, tinged with that ascetic mournfulness which, in an intenser key, is the dominant note of the art of Sir Edward Burne-Jones. Mr. Waterhouse, then, has interpreted the myth from the solemn view of impending doom to Hylas, and suggests none of that gladness which the classic legend's undercurrent of blissful immortality contains . . . he has conveyed the impression of a great stillness. The gnarled roots of trees form a trellised ceiling – green cactus and pale lilies the floor – of a tomb. It is, indeed, in a picture of this standard that one is compelled to recognize the convincing force and charm of the higher gifts of the imagination when used as the source and mainspring of the painter's craft."

Praise from sympathetic critics, its erotic and symbolic content, its immediate physical accessibility in a major public collection and its frequent loan to important exhibitions combined to make it perhaps the best-known picture of the period. Other Waterhouse paintings which had been almost equally well-received were for the most part out of public sight for much of the time; the chief exception was *The Magic Circle* purchased with the Chantrey Bequest in 1886 for £650. His other major pictures included three belonging to Sir Henry and Lady Tate, *Consulting the Oracle* (RA 1884), *Saint Eulalia* (RA 1885), and Waterhouse's other most famous picture, *The Lady of Shalott* (RA 1888), all now in the Tate Gallery; Sir Cuthbert Quilter's *Mariamne* (RA 1887, Forbes Magazine Collection), and the two pictures owned by George McCulloch which at the sale of his collection in 1913 fetched the highest pre-war prices for Waterhouse, *Flora and the Zephyrs* (RA 1898), £1785, and *Saint Cecilia* (RA 1895, private collection), £2415.

City of Manchester Art Galleries

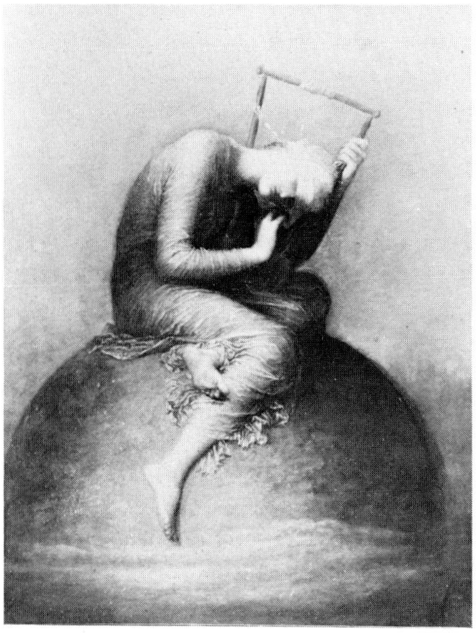

Hope *Courtesy: Tate Gallery, London*

George Frederick Watts, 1817–1904, ARA and RA 1867, OM 1902

63 Hope 1886

coloured mezzotint, 20 × 15½ in

LIT: (references are to all versions of *Hope;* selected) *Academy*, 15 May 1886, p350; *Portfolio*, Apr 1886, p84; *Times*, 3 May 1886, p7; Julia Cartwright, 'The Life and Work of George Frederic Watts, RA', *Art Annual*, Easter 1896, p11, repr facing p8; Monkhouse, 1899, p31, frontisp.; Charles T. Bateman, *G.F. Watts, RA*, Bell's Miniature Series of Painters, 1901, pp25, 35–6, 43, repr frontisp; G.K. Chesterton, *G.F. Watts*, The Popular Library of Art, 1904, pp11, 77, 94–108, 135, repr p99; Mrs. Russell Barrington, *G.F. Watts: Reminiscences*, 1905, pp37, 162; Mary S. Watts, *George Frederic Watts, The Annals of an Artist's Life*, 1912, II, pp57, 106, 150, 163, 270; H.W. Shrewsbury, *The Visions of an Artist: Studies in G.F. Watts, RA, OM, with verse interpretations*, 1918, pp61–70, repr facing p61; Stewart Dick, *Our Favourite Painters*, 1923, pp243–4, repr facing p248; cat., *G.F. Watts*, Arts Council, 1954–5 (65); cat., *G.F. Watts: A Nineteenth Century Phenomenon*, Whitechapel Art Gallery, 1974, foreword, (66); Wilfrid Blunt, *'England's Michelangelo': a biography of George Frederic Watts, OM, RA*, 1975, pp xviii, 62, 155, 212, 220, 237, pl.12, b.c.

> "All my pictures in the Tate Gallery are symbolical and for all time . . . Their symbolism is, however, more suggestive than worked out in any detail. I want to make people think. My idea is really the Book of Ecclesiastes with a higher impulse." (Bateman, p22).

In 1886 Watts publicly announced his long-cherished plan to present a body of his work to the nation; this was finally carried out in 1897, when eighteen paintings entered the newly-completed Tate Gallery; they were followed during the next five years by four more, making a total of twenty-two allegorical, and mostly rather large important paintings, designed for the moral and spiritual instruction of the People. Of these, *Hope* had been his most popular painting since the Watts exhibition at the Grosvenor Gallery in 1881–2 when his allegorical works became known to a wide public for the first time. The painting presented to the Tate is, according to Watts's friend and disciple Mrs. Russell Barrington, a replica by his assistant, Cecil Schott, which Watts worked on. The original completed version from which the Tate version was copied is now owned by a publishing company, but Watts had been working on the idea since about 1865; a number of versions exist including a red chalk drawing almost the full size of the Tate picture, at the Watts Gallery, and an oil sketch on panel, at the Walker Art Gallery, Liverpool.

Julia Cartwright, one of Watts's legion of devoted women followers, and author in 1896 of the first extended study of the artist, wrote of *Hope*:

> "We are all of us familiar with that pathetic form, the saddest, weariest Hope that was ever painted, sitting blindfold on the globe, in the dim twilight of the world. Her pale blue robe gleams white against the darkening sky, her lyre is in her hands, and her fingers strike the chords; but one string alone is left, and, bending down, she tries, with passionate longing, to catch the faint sound of the music for which she yearns. All the trouble and disquiet of modern times is in that picture, all the doubt and questioning of these latter days, when 'men lie down in darkness and sorrow, and know not whether their night has a morrow', or, at best, cling despairingly to the old truths, and 'faintly trust the larger hope' ".

This interpretation is confirmed by a brief note Watts sent asking Briton Riviere, a close friend, to look at the picture in progress in his studio:

> "The new picture is *Hope;* all the strings of her instrument are broken but one, and she is trying to get all possible music out of the poor tinkle." (Mary Watts, II, p150).

The picture's title nevertheless caused confusion and led Chesterton to a long discussion of the painting in which he contrasted Watts's treatment of an allegory of Hope with a:

> "hypothetical picture of *Hope* in conventional flowers and conventional pink robes . . . Suppose that [the spectator] found himself in the presence of a dim canvas with a bowed and stricken figure cowering over a broken lyre in the twilight. What would he think? His first thought, of course, would be that the picture was called *Despair;* his second (when he discovered his error in the catalogue) that it has been entered under the wrong number; his third, that the painter was mad. But if we imagine that he overcame these preliminary feelings and that as he stared at that queer twilight picture, a dim and powerful sense of meaning began to grow upon him – what would he see? He would see something for which there is neither speech nor language, which has been too vast for any eye to see and too secret for any religion to utter, even as an esoteric doctrine. Standing before that picture he finds himself in the presence of a great truth. He perceives that there is something in man which is always apparently on the eve of disappearing, but never disappears, an assurance which is always apparently saying farewell and yet illimitably lingers, a string which is always stretched to snapping and yet never snaps. He perceives that the queerest and most delicate thing in us, the most fragile, the most fantastic, is in truth the backbone and indestructible. He knows a great moral fact: that there never was an age of assurance, that there never was an age of faith."

In the final two years of his life Watts and his wife built a gallery beside their house at Compton in Surrey which housed all of the artist's remaining pictures and which was intended as a lasting memorial to his work; Watts lived to see it opened to the public on Good Friday, 1904. He had begun his allegorical paintings in 1848 with *Time and Oblivion;* amongst the most famous of his later allegorical works were *Love and Death* (versions at Bristol, Tate, Melbourne, Adelaide and elsewhere), *Mammon* (Tate, sketch at Compton), *Love and Life* (Louvre), and *The Sower of the Systems* (Compton).

The Trustees of the Watts Gallery

Henry Clarence Whaite, 1828–1912, ARWS 1872, RWS 1882, 1st PRCambA 1885, PMAFA 1892

64 The Rainbow 1862

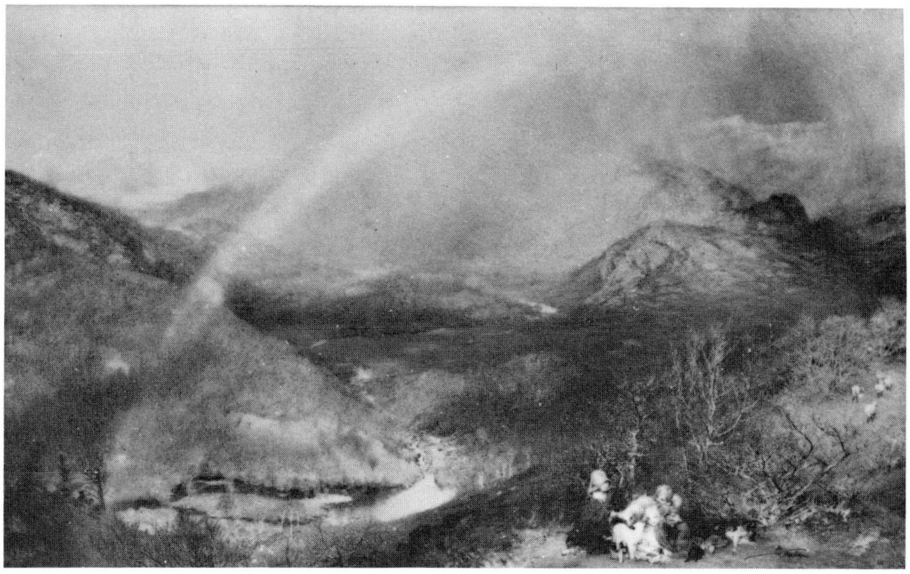

oil on canvas, $54\frac{7}{8} \times 84\frac{1}{2}$ in

PROV: Alderman W.G. Ward, Mayor of Nottingham, on loan to Nottingham by 1878; his sale, Christie's, 18/19 March 1881 (260) bt. Agnew (£183 15s), not entered in stock book; purchased by Nottingham, 1893.
EXH: RA 1862 (596); Academy of Fine Arts, Manchester 1862 (264, Heywood Gold Medal); *The Collected Works of Mr. H. Clarence Whaite, PRCA, RWS*, Manchester 1898 (19); *Loan Exh. of Pictures and Water-Colour Drawings by H. Clarence Whaite, Anderson Hague, Frederick W. Jackson, and Tom Mostyn*, Manchester 1908 (64).
LIT: *AJ*, June 1862, p136; *Athenaeum*, 3 May 1862, p699; *Manchester Courier*, 13 Sept 1862; *Manchester Examiner and Times*, 2 Dec 1862; *Manchester Guardian*, 13 & 22 Sept 1862; *Catalogue of the Pictures and Objects in the Midland Counties Art Museum*, 2nd ed., Nottingham 1878, pp49–52; obits. 1912, *Manchester City News*, 8 June, *Manchester Evening Chronicle*, June, *Manchester Guardian*, 6 June; *Nottingham Catalogue*, 1926 (246) (Manchester reviews and obits. from cuttings-books in Manchester City Reference Library and City Art Gallery).

Whaite was, in the best possible sense, the archetypal successful provincial artist: real London success always eluded him, but in Manchester (his home town), in the North-west and Midlands generally, and in Wales, where he painted most of his pictures and became the first President of the Royal Cambrian Academy, he was a major and influential figure. *The Rainbow* was his first and greatest success: it was well if briefly reviewed by the London press when shown at the 1862 RA, but when it arrived in Manchester immediately afterwards it won the Heywood Gold Medal, the most important single award available to English artists outside London. The *Manchester Examiner and Times* commented that he had yet to gain full recognition from his home town but

> "... Manchester will some day be proud of him ... He goes to nature and puts down on canvas, with a rare facility of hand, regardless of conventional comment, what he there contemplates, so far as the truth is in him ..."

The Rainbow was recognised as the most ambitious of his pictures to date and the result of years of labour which included much study from nature from a hut specially built for Whaite on the way between Capel Curig and Bettws y Coed. The review went on,

> "There is the stamp of enthusiasm impressed upon every portion of this singularly original and striking illustration of nature's beautiful phenomena . . . There is the brilliant imagery of the poet expressed in the minute detail of the worker. Go over the canvas inch by inch, and see how patience has guided the pencil; look at it in its completion, and what a wondrous interpretation of most evanescent radiance – yet revelation infinite ..."

The reviewer objected only to the foreground figures which he felt interrupted the purity of the landscape 'in this daring as well as dazzling piece of work'.

The *Manchester Guardian* was still more enthusiastic; it gave a detailed description of the subject which it saw as the first warm day after spring; the ice and snow are beginning to melt, though the sap is not yet rising in the trees

> "... these dumb eloquent witnesses of a repose like death, which will give place to a glorious life, skirt the brook that came from yonder heights and clothe the hill-side. A thin cloud is passing over the valley, and trails a misty skirt upon the grassy slope. It obscures the top of the nearer mountain with a most witching mystery. Upon the cloud the sun has imprinted a rainbow, clear, bright, ethereal, and evanescent on the canvas as it is in its own pure essence. Some children from a farmhouse in a warm nook on the right beneath the fir trees, have climbed to an eminence behind their home, where they sport with some lambs. The minuteness of some of the details and the care with which they have been treated are wonderful. At the same time this care has been at no expense of freedom. The consequence is that the picture will repay study every way. Look at it from a distance, and one is surprised at the breadth of the subject, and the beautiful tone which pervades it. Examine it closely, and there is no slurring over one portion to throw another into undue prominence; but a painstaking and effective finish of every part. The texture of the cloud is perfect; the forest of trunks and branches is truth itself; and nothing can exceed the beauty of the half clothed rocks on the left, with the patches of young grass creeping over them. The picture as a whole is a finished poem of pastoral beauty."

Technically, the painting is clearly a mixture of Pre-Raphaelite observation in the treatment of the landscape with contemporary sentiment in the Birket Foster group of gambolling children in the foreground. Ruskin had noticed Whaite's oils and watercolours in the 1859 RA and commented first on his oil *Barley Harvest*,

> "Very exquisite in nearly every respect; perhaps, take it all in all, the most covetable bit of landscape of this year, and showing good promise, it seems to me, if the painter does not overwork himself needlessly. The execution of the whole by minute and similar touches is a mistake. Certain textures need to be so produced, and certain complexities of form; but the work is never good unless it varies with every part of the subject, and is different in method, according to the sort of surface or form required. Nothing finished can be done without labour; but a picture can hardly be more injured than by the quantity of labour in it which is lost. Uncontributive toil is one of the forms of ruin."

Ruskin went on to approve Whaite's watercolour *Snowdon*, and compared it with those of A.W. Hunt which he considered were

> "suffering under the same oppression of plethoric labour. I do not often, in the present state of the English school, think it advisable to recommend 'breadth'; but assuredly both ..., if they wish to do themselves justice, ought to give up colour for a little while, and work with nothing but very ill-made charcoal which will not cut to a point." (*Works*, XIV, pp229–30).

As the first idea for the composition of *The Rainbow* appears in Whaite's etching *Autumn* for the Junior Etching Club illustrated edition of Hood's *Poem's* in 1858 (published by Gambart) it seems unlikely that Ruskin's highly technical letter on the reflection of rainbows in water, published in the *London Review* of 16 May 1861 (*Works*, XIV, pp474–5) would have swayed him much, but Ruskin's strictures on his over-minute handling do seem to have had some effect in his 1862 painting, where the handling is soft and full.

Despite the distinction of incurring the criticism of both Ruskin and the more conventional London critics for his minute execution, Whaite went on to show watercolours regularly until the turn of the century: he was still being noticed, for instance, by *Studio* in 1902 (June, p54), and a long article by David Croal Thomson describing Bettws-y-Coed and illustrated with watercolour sketches by Whaite was published by the *Art Journal* in 1894 (September, pp267–71). In the latter part of the last century and at the beginning of this most of the major cities outside London acquired large Whaites: for instance, Manchester bought *The Heart of Cambria* in 1886 and two more in 1898 and 1908, Cardiff was presented with *Snowdon* in 1912, and Nottingham, where he had family connections but probably more because of the enthusiasm of Mayor Ward for Whaite's work, exhibited on loan or bought a number of his oils and watercolours. Whaite was a very active promoter of two Academies of Fine Art: he was a member of the Manchester Academy of Fine Arts in its first formal year of existence, 1859 and its third President, from 1892 until his death (see *A Short History of the Academy*, Manchester, 1959, revised 1973). Appropriately enough, as most of his work was done in Wales, Whaite was also a founder member and first President of the Royal Cambrian Academy of Art at Conwy.

Castle Museum, Nottingham

William Lionel Wyllie, 1851–1931, ARA 1889, RA 1907

65 Commerce and Sea Power 1898

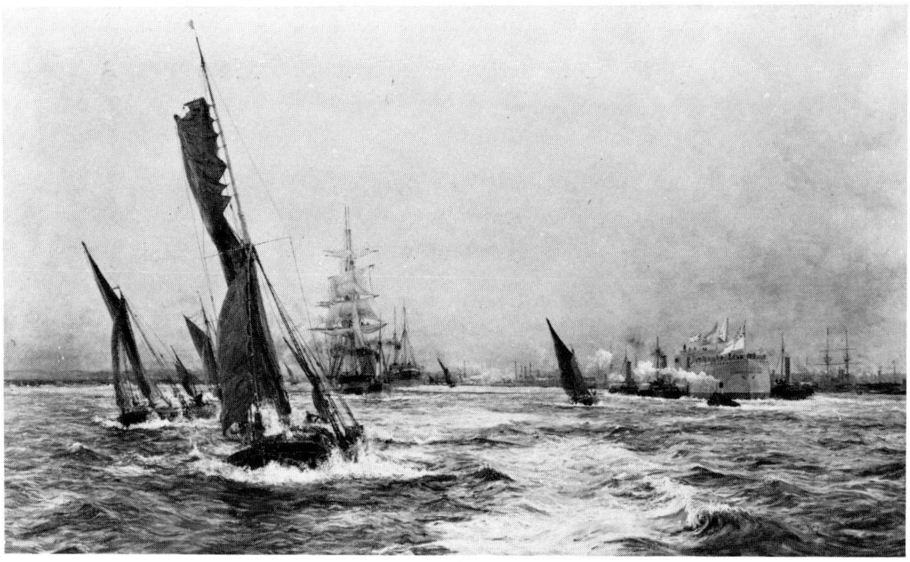

oil on canvas, 36 × 60 in
INSCR: W.L. Wyllie

PROV: Deputy Charles T. Harris, JP, by whom presented to the Corporation of London, 1900.
EXH: RA 1898 (210); Guildhall 1900 (60); Whitechapel Spring 1901 (33); RA Winter 1933 (600), South London Art Gallery 1973.
LIT: *AJ*, June 1898, p177, repr p174; *Graphic*, 30 Apr, p531, 2 May 1898, p46; *Times*, 14 May 1898, p16; Marian A. Wylie, *We Were One: A Life of W.L. Wylie, RA, RE, RI*, 1935, p163.
REPR: Blackburn, *RA Notes*, 1898, p53 (sketch); *RA Pictures*, 1898, p154; Admiral Sir Cyprian Bridge, GCB, 'William Lionel Wyllie, RA', *Art Annual*, 1907, p20.

Wyllie made his name with his great success *Toil, glitter, grime, and wealth on a flowing tide* (Tate, on loan to National Maritime Museum), the Chantrey Purchase for 1883, and rapidly became established as the country's leading painter of shipping and the sea, a position he occupied for most of the rest of his life. The following year Wyllie, who had shown regularly at Dunthorne's since 1883, was given the first of four one-man exhibitions at the Fine Art Society (1884, 1889, 1892 and 1907) and later two at the Leicester Galleries (1904 and 1911), a remarkable and possibly unique total for a Victorian artist. All the works were watercolours, Wyllie's favourite and brilliantly used medium; he meanwhile maintained a steady output of oils, almost all of which were well-received, though a trough occurred in his fortunes in the mid-1890s from which *Commerce and Sea Power* helped to lift him in 1898. *The Times*:

> "This is a good year for Mr. Wyllie; we lately saw in a Bond St. gallery a large collection of his sketches, and now at the Academy we have no less than five pictures from his hands, of which two, *Commerce and Sea Power* and *The Harbour Bar*, are the best and most complete that he has shown for many a day. In the former the grey hull of the newly-launched battleship with the tugs around her, and, in a parallel line, the merchant steamer and the river barges, all at home in the tossing water, and in the distance tall chimneys and the smoky cloud, make a picture full of reality and animation which must appeal to every Englishman. The weak point of Mr. Wyllie is that in his pictures the water, though alive with movement, is not liquid enough; it has too much substance, a fault into which Turner, in such a picture as the great "*Spithead*" in the National Gallery, never fell. But for communicating a sense that the ship is actually being driven before the wind or by its own steam power, Mr. Wyllie has no equal among the living painters of shipping and the sea."

The *Graphic* and the *Art Journal* also saw the picture as a return to some of the quality of *Toil, glitter, . . .* but the latter noted that his brushwork had lately tightened and become more laboured:

> "at the expense of breadth. This may perhaps be accounted for by Mr. Wyllie's great marine knowledge, and undoubtedly his pictures appeal to a wide circle of nautical enthusiasts."

The extent of Wyllie's popularity with mariners can be gauged by the fact that the publishers commissioned the text for the 1907 *Art Annual* on Wyllie from an admiral, Sir Cyprian Bridge, who confessed himself a stranger to art criticism but wrote of his unbounded admiration for Wyllie's skill as a painter of ships and the sea. Bridge admired Wyllie's ability to paint, very accurately, unglamorous steamships in a way that assuaged the sailor's longing for the purity of sail, and liked the frequent evidence in Wyllie's pictures of a close knowledge and love of his subject. Wyllie did indeed spend much time at sea: for instance, the introduction to his 1889 Fine Art Society catalogue testifies to several weeks spent as correspondent for the *Graphic* on board a ship in the thick of a tough naval exercise off Bantry Bay. Bridge also recognised the value of Wyllie's pictures as propaganda: the pictures of battleships reminded any potential enemies of the Empire's invincibility at sea, and the views of commercial shipping demonstrated the extent of Britain's trading ties. Wyllie was so accurate in his detailing that he was also indispensable to the naval historian, and Bridge concluded:

> "Sailors brought up in the older ships and long accustomed to the sight of them, also heartily in love with them as they were, can yet see beauty in the newer types. The designs of many of our great battleships show that our naval architects can produce a construction that pleases the eye as well as conveys to the spectator an impression of stupendous power. In making this evident to the thousands who see his pictures, Mr. Wyllie has done justice to a great profession, the members of which have often been signally successful in imparting to their productions a sightliness which wins admiration as sincere as that given to their solidity and force."

In 1899 a second Chantrey Purchase was made- *The Battle of the Nile* (Tate) and in 1901, Wyllie painted one of the principal pictures commemorating the death of Victoria, *The Passing of a Great Queen* (Liverpool), showing the transporting of her body across the Solent. An enthusiastic yachtsman, Wyllie also made innumerable watercolours and some oils of sailing boats, including perhaps his most successful, *Butterflies and Working Bees* (RA 1894, Royal Corinthian Yacht Club). Much of his income in the later part of his career came from the publication of some two hundred etchings, in carefully regulated limited editions; many of these were of Thames subjects and inevitably invite comparison with Whistler's, a test they survive with credit. The largest recent showing of Wyllie's work was in 1972 at the Malcolm Henderson Gallery; information on the artist is currently being compiled by the artist's descendants and by Roger Quarm at the National Maritime Museum (see R. Quarm, 'The Waves in Watercolours', *Country Life*, 4 Aug 1977, pp296–7).

Guildhall Art Gallery

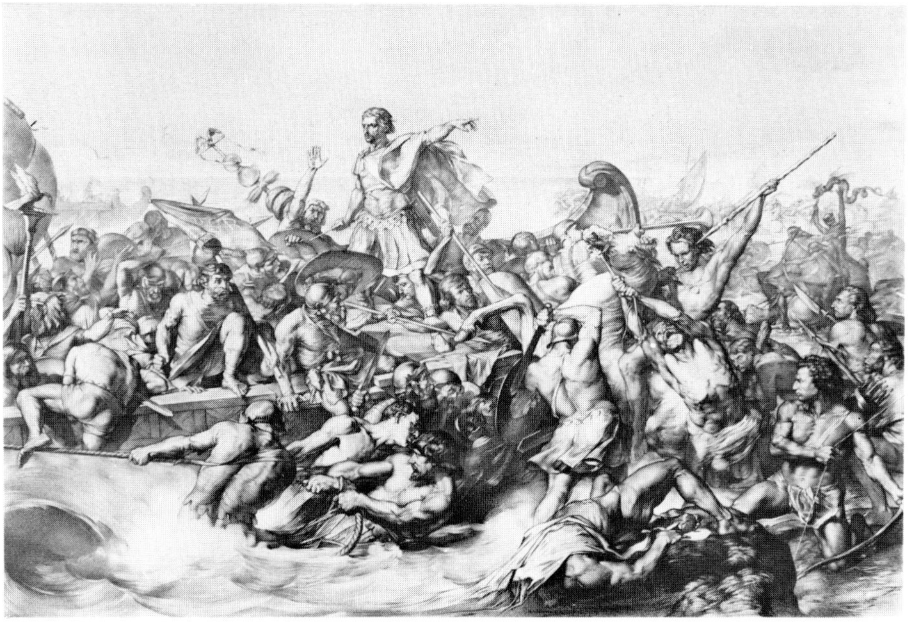

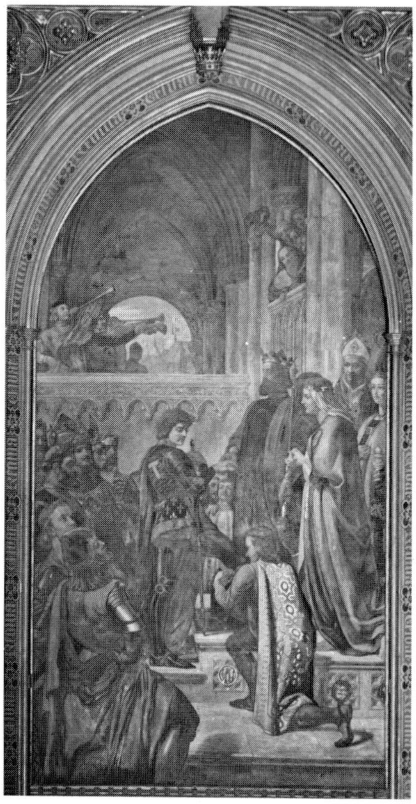

C. W. C. Cope
Edward III conferring the Order of the Garter on the Black Prince – fresco
Courtesy: Department of the Environment

EDWARD ARMITAGE, 1817–1896, ARA 1867, RA 1872–94

66 Caesar's First Invasion of Britain 1843

lithograph by William Linnell after the cartoon exh. Westminster Hall 1843.
winner of a £300 premium.
$16\frac{7}{8} \times 22\frac{1}{2}$ in
Publ. Longman, Brown, Green & Longmans, London, 1847.
Victoria & Albert Museum

CHARLES WEST COPE, 1811–1890, ARA 1843, RA 1848–83

67 Sketch for Edward III conferring the Order of the Garter on the Black Prince 1845

oil on canvas, $38\frac{1}{2} \times 23$ in
INSCR: C. W. Cope 1845
EXH: Westminster Hall 1845 (59); RA 1850 (73); Liverpool 1850; Glasgow 1851.
Lent by permission of the Speaker of the House of Commons

WILLIAM DYCE, 1806–1864, ARA 1844, RA 1848

68 Spectators at the Baptism of Ethelbert 1845

fragment of a cartoon on paper, lined with canvas and backed with hardboard, 37 × 103 in.
EXH: (The complete cartoon, approx. 16 × 9 ft) Westminster Hall 1845.
Lent by permission of the Speaker of the House of Commons

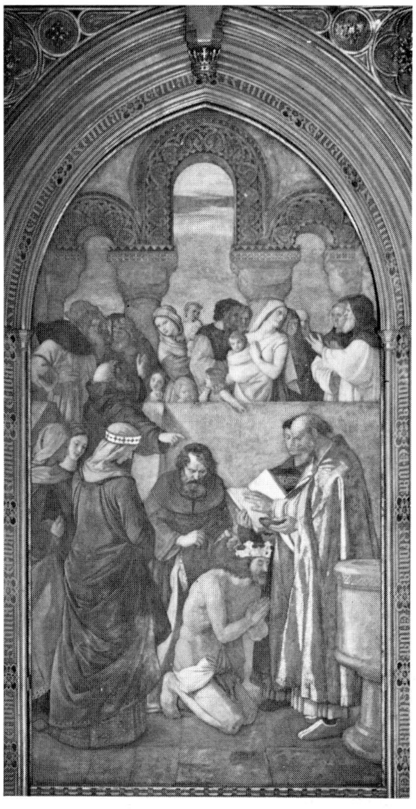

W. Dyce
Spectators at the Baptism of Ethelbert – fresco
Courtesy: Department of the Environment

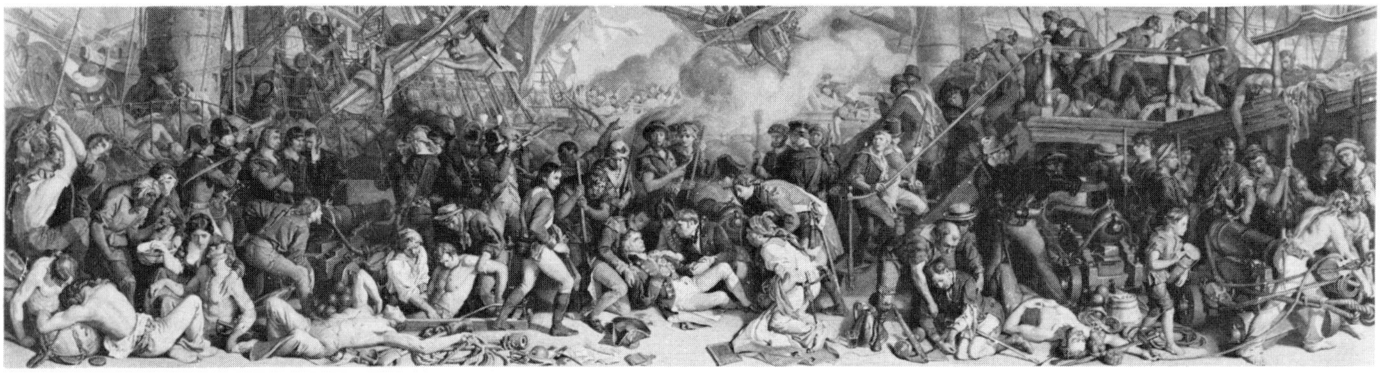

The Death of Nelson – fresco *Courtesy: Department of the Environment*

DANIEL MACLISE, 1806–1870, ARA 1835, RA 1840

69 The Death of Nelson 1861–6

engraving by Charles W. Sharpe after Maclise's oil version (now Liverpool) of the fresco on the north wall of the Royal Gallery, House of Lords, $16\frac{5}{8} \times 48\frac{1}{4}$ in
Publ. Art Union of London, 1874.
Victoria & Albert Museum

THE PALACE OF WESTMINSTER DECORATIONS

LIT: For a complete discussion of the decorations see T.S.R. Boase, 'The Decoration of the New Palace of Westminster, 1841–1863', *JWCI*, XVII, 1954, pp319–358, abridged and recast for M.H. Port, Ed., *The Houses of Parliament*, 1976, pp268–281; and the indispensable and exhaustive catalogue by R.J.B. Walker, *A Catalogue of paintings, drawings, sculpture and engravings in The Palace of Westminster* – Part IV. Paintings and drawings, excluding portraits, 1962. For Maclise, see the Arts Council exhibition catalogue by Richard Ormond and John Turpin, *Daniel Maclise 1806–1870*, 1972.

The old Houses of Parliament burned to a shell in 1834; at the beginning of 1836 Charles Barry won the competition for a design for the rebuilding and the new Palace of Westminster was begun in 1837. In 1841 a Select Committee was appointed to study 'the promotion of the fine arts of this Country in connexion with the rebuilding of the Houses of Parliament'; its president was the Queen's new Consort, Prince Albert, and its secretary was Eastlake. It was decided to hold a competition for fresco designs in chalk or charcoal, between 10 and 15 feet long with life-size figures and illustrating subjects from British history or from Spenser, Shakespeare or Milton, all this for three prizes of £300, three of £200 and five of £100. There were 140 entries, the winners were young and relatively unknown artists, and all but one had chosen subjects from early British history. The £300 premiums were won by Armitage for *Caesar's Invasion of Britain* (see lithograph now exhibited), Watt's *Caractacus led in triumph through Rome*, and Cope's *The First Trial by Jury*; £200 premiums went to J.C. Horsley for *St. Augustine Preaching*, J.Z. Bell for *Cardinal Bourchier urging the Dowager Queen of Edward IV to give up from Sanctuary the Duke of York*, and H.J. Townsend for *The Fight for the Beacon;* the third prizes went to Frost's *Una alarmed at the Fauns and Satyrs*, E.T. Parris's *Joseph of Arimathea converting the Britons*, H.C. Selous's *Boadicea haranguing the Iceni*, John Bridge's *Alfred submitting his laws to the Witan*, and Joseph Severn's *Queen Eleanor*.

The huge cartoons were shown in the Westminster Hall during the summer of 1843 and the greatest excitement was generated. Lady Eastlake gave a vivid account of it, with quotations from her husband's diary:

> "The *éclat* given to the occasion by Her Majesty's visit, by the Prince's participation, and by its intrinsically novel and interesting character, rendered this exhibition, opened at first for a shilling, a very fashionable resort. At the expiration of a fortnight, the public were admitted gratis, except on Saturdays, when the attendance exceeded all expectations both in numbers and intelligence. 'July 22nd, 1843. The daily throng is immense; the public takes great interest, and the strongest proof is thus given of the love of the lower orders for *pictures*, when they represent an event. I abridged the catalogue to a penny size for the million, but many of the most wretchedly dressed people prefer the sixpenny one with the quotations, and it is a very gratifying sight to witness the attention and earnestness with which they follow the subjects with the books in their hands. Ten thousand of the sixpenny catalogues have been sold.' (It had then been open to the public for a week). 'The higher classes complained that the Exhibition was not open longer for a shilling, but the Commissioners have wisely determined to let it remain for the public as at present, and for several weeks to come. Clerks of counting-houses have petitioned to be let in on Sundays, but this cannot be granted. The gates are closed from time to time when the Hall is full, and the people are let out through the Law Courts. Meanwhile the newcomers collect in crowds, waiting for admission, and carriages draw up, subject to the same necessary delay. No possible arrangement, and no number of hands, could regulate the delivery of umbrellas and sticks, and the unclaimed ones have accumulated in consequence. I have therefore directed the doorkeepers to use their discretion, and let in many with their umbrellas. The question of dress I have settled, of course, without any line of demarcation; only children are not let in under a certain apparent age. They are nevertheless carried in with the throng, and as the policemen collect them they are walked out again in droves, and packed up for a time in the vestibule till there is, room to get out. All the workmen from the Houses of Parliament go in, but chiefly in the evening, because, being as white as millers (the masons), they have the discretion to time their visits.
>
> "You will see by the Catalogue that the references and quotations are good of their kind, being indeed from the highest sources. I stated to the Commissioners yesterday, in reporting about the Exhibition, that the Catalogues in the hands of so many thousands would be the first introduction of many to an acquaintance with our best poets and writers.' "
>
> Between twenty and thirty thousand a day visited this Exhibition, which was kept open for two months. (*Contributions to the Literature of the Fine Arts* by Sir Charles Lock Eastlake, with a Memoir compiled by Lady Eastlake, Second Series, 1870, pp172–4).

According to Boase (*JWCI*, p326) Lady Eastlake's figures are greatly exaggerated and only an average of 1800 people a day visited the exhibition with 4000 on the final day, but it was nevertheless a staggering response from the public and evidence of a thirst for cultural and moral uplift that was everything – and more – that Prince Albert and his fellow-Commissioners could have desired. The copyright on the first eleven prizewinners was bought ten days after the exhibition had opened; they were lithographed by the Linnell family and were published in 1847, a complete set is in the V & A, from which the one by Armitage is here exhibited.

Both Cope and Dyce were commissioned in 1844 to prepare a cartoon, coloured sketch and a specimen of fresco painting for the first frescoes in the House of Lords; both showed their work, along with Armitage, Horsley, Maclise, Noel Paton and Tenniel, at the Westminster Hall in 1845, but this exhibition did not receive the rapt attention of the public, though the critical reception of the work of Dyce and Horsley in particular was enthusiastic. Dyce's fresco, for which he made a cartoon that measured some 16×9 ft, took as a subject *The Baptism of King Ethelbert;* Ethelbert the seventh century King of Kent, draped only in a loincloth, is baptised by St. Augustine in St. Martin's Church, Canterbury, watched by his Queen and the crowd of courtiers who appear in the cartoon fragment now exhibited. Ethelbert was one of the founders of English law and was therefore an entirely appropriate subject for the Palace of Westminster. Dyce, Cope and Horsley had spent some time in Italy studying fresco technique; Dyce was already a disciple of the German Nazarene school and Cope and Horsley followed his example, visiting Munich to discuss modern methods already in use by Cornelius (who had been brought to England as an adviser on the decorations in 1841) and

Hess. Dyce's *Ethelbert* was the first fresco to be painted in the new Palace of Westminster and was completed in the summer of 1847. Cope's *Edward III* was begun as Dyce finished, and was completed the following year. A small, finished, oil version, dated 1847 was purchased by Sheffield in 1971, together with a watercolour study, $12\frac{3}{8} \times 6\frac{7}{8}$ in. Cope was to spend the next twenty years working on a further ten frescoes and Dyce was occupied for much of the time until his early death in 1864 on the frescoes for the Queen's Robing Room. The time and energy this work took dominated the lives of all the artists involved in the Palace of Westminster decorations and, effectively, killed several. As the novelty and grandeur of the scheme wore off, criticism mounted in the press and in Parliament of the lack of coordination in planning, of the subjects chosen by the artists and, above all, of the almost immediate physical deterioration of the frescoes themselves. Most of the artists were totally inexperienced in fresco techniques and the application of what they had learned abroad, combined with the instructions of Cornelius, Eastlake and Prince Albert, when applied to the walls of the new building in the dank and polluted Northern city air proved hopelessly inadequate. Much of the time following the completion of each fresco was spent in repeated attempts to repair the damage that rapidly appeared, but the attempts were doomed to failure.

Maclise, who had been involved in the decorations since 1844, took on the frescoes for the Royal Gallery in 1857: he was to have decorated the entire, vast chamber, but the two central paintings – *The Meeting of Wellington and Blucher after the Battle of Waterloo*, completed in 1861, and *The Death of Nelson*, completed in 1865 – broke his health and spirits and he was unable to continue, dying five years later. The cartoon for *Wellington* had been received with great admiration, but Maclise was quickly discouraged by the problems of fresco, resigned, but was persuaded to visit Germany where he learnt the waterglass technique of painting and returned to resume the *Wellington* which he painted in two years. It was over 12 ft high and 45 ft long; the *Nelson* was made a foot longer. The engraving shown here was made from Maclise's finished oil painting of the subject (now in Liverpool), which he squared up and transferred to the full size. The colours were brilliant, but sadly for Maclise, the equally vivid colours in the *Wellington* were already deteriorating and it became obvious that the *Nelson* would share its fate. The paintings are now virtually monochrome, despite restoration and cleaning over the years, but their massive and extraordinary orchestration of innumerable figures, and their enshrining of the two great national heroes ensured that the engravings of them published by the Art Union entered that group of nineteenth century images whose ubiquity and dramatic intensity ensured them an enduring place in the nation's visual memory.

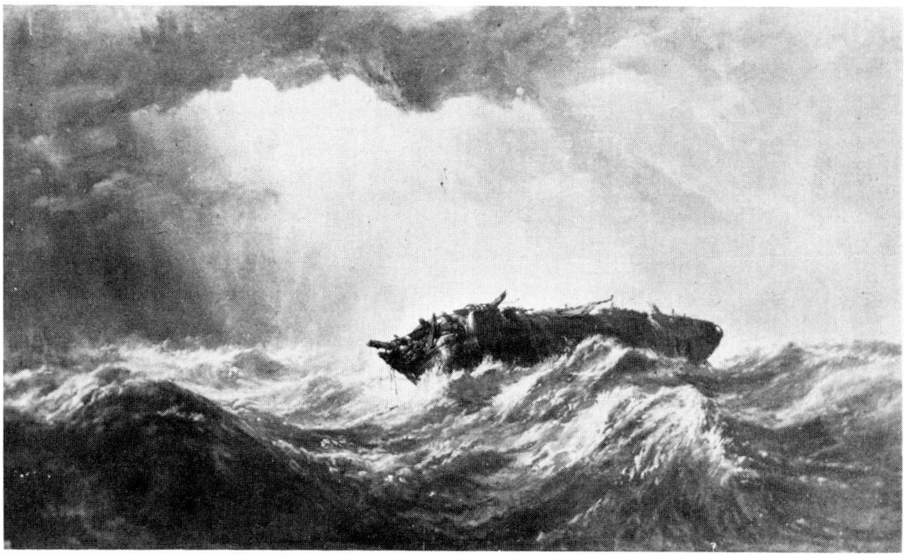

CLARKSON STANFIELD (see cat. no. 53)

The Abandoned 1856

oil on canvas, 35×60 in

PROV: purchased from the artist by Thomas Baring, later 1st Earl of Northbrook (for £525); by descent to Francis, 2nd Earl of Northbrook, d. 1929; sold, Sotheby's 16 July 1930 (100), bt. Ingram (£7), see *Art Prices Current*, 1929–30; untraced.
EXH: RA 1856 (94); Manchester Art Treasures 1857 (504); London Internat. 1862 (377); RA Winter 1870 (171); Manchester Jubilee 1887 (576); Guildhall 1890 (4) and 1897 (80).
LIT: *AJ*, June 1856, p164; *Athenaeum*, 17 May 1856, p620; *Critic*, 16 June 1856, p308; *Literary Gazette*, 10 May 1856, pp259–61; *Times*, 3 May 1856, p9; extensively noticed in reviews of subsequent exhibitions, Stanfield obituaries and dictionary entries; Dafforne, *op. cit.*, 1873, pp19–20; Dr. J. Macaulay, *Sea Pictures*, Religious Tract Society, 1883, frontisp.; *Temple*, 1897, p20, repr.; Ruskin, *Works*, XIII, pp29–30, XIV, p52, XXXIV, p564. T.S.R. Boase, 'Shipwrecks in English Romantic Painting', *JWCI*, 1959, p346, pl.34e; Boase, 1959, p126, pl.66a.
STUDY: small sketch in coll. T.S.R. Boase, 1959.
VERSIONS: several copies are known: a particularly good copy (32×48 in) attributed to Samuel Walters is in a private collection in Cheshire. A small copy is in a private collection in Essex.

The Abandoned was generally considered to be Stanfield's greatest work achieving previously untouched heights of poetic expressiveness. It was accompanied in the RA 1856 catalogue entry by a long quotation from the essay 'The Voyage' in the *Sketch Book* (1820), by Washington Irving (whom Stanfield met when the American visited England), describing the drifting hulk covered in barnacles and seaweed, its crew long dead. Wrecks were of the greatest and most poignant interest to Victorians; many lives were lost at sea each year, and scenes of wrecks and rescues – most notably those painted after the famous Grace Darling rescue – appeared frequently at the exhibitions and were often considerable successes. Stanfield's picture excited great admiration because it achieved its effect completely without the presence of figures:

> "It may be questioned whether anyone who saw this picture when exhibited could ever forget the appalling scene represented. Lifted on the crest of a mighty wave, the vast hulk rises from the deep trough of the sea, with lines of broken cordage hanging over her sides, and her riven copper visible as she heels over, yet standing out in bold relief against an angry leaden-coloured sky. Signs of human life are nowhere to be seen; no other ship along that waste of waters meets the eye of the spectator – dark, dreary, and desolate, that once trim and gallant vessel is dashed hither and thither, the sport of the waves, without a hand to direct her motion or to keep her from being engulphed (sic) in the deep ocean. The picture is a poem as pathetic in its painted language as the eloquent words of the American writer." (Dafforne, p20).

The inclusion of the painting at so many of the century's major exhibitions indicates the importance attached to it; indeed, so famous did it become that only two years after it was shown at the 1856 RA, Egg was able to rely on the audience's recognition of the picture and consequent understanding of its symbolic use, when he placed a print of *The Abandoned* on the right hand wall of the room in the first scene of *Past and Present* (RA 1858, cat. no. 10a). Sadly, since its sale at Sotheby's in 1930, all efforts to trace it have failed.

Stanfield was tagged the 'English Vandevelde' and received the ultimate accolade from Ruskin of being placed second only to Turner and this because he painted man-made ships more than God-made Nature: in the year of the triumph of *The Abandoned*, Ruskin wrote:

> ". . . Stanfield's chief dignity is his being a painter less of shipping than of the seal of time or decay upon shipping (as in the very beautiful picture of this year's academy . . .). For a wrecked ship, or shattered boat, is a noble subject, while a ship in full sail, or a perfect boat, is an ignoble one; not merely because the one is by reason of its ruin more picturesque than the other, but because it is a nobler act in man to meditate upon Fate as it conquers his work, than upon that work itself." (*The Harbours of England*, 1856).

Perhaps even Ruskin overreached himself when he wrote, "One work of Stanfield alone presents us with as much concentrated knowledge of sea and sky, as, diluted, would have lasted one of the masters his life." It was, however, an entirely accurate measure of Stanfield's stature in the eyes of his contemporaries.

Untraced: sepia photograph of *The Abandoned* exhibited, publ. Manchester Art Treasures 1857. *Witt Library*.

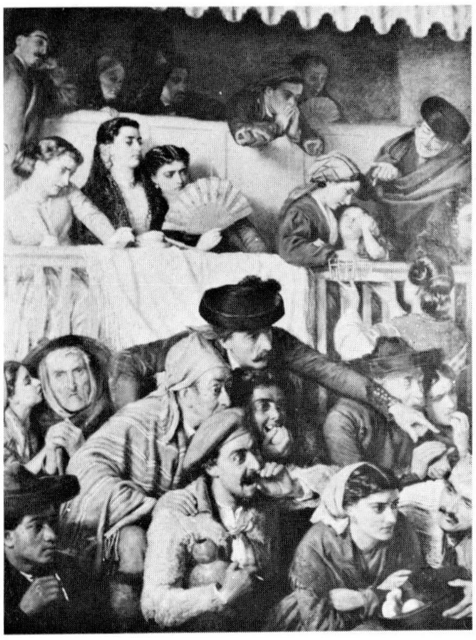

John Bagnold Burgess, 1830–1897, ARA 1877, RA 1888

"Bravo, Toro!" 1865

oil on canvas, 43 × 33 in

PROV: Sir David Salomons, Bart.; Sir David Lionel Salomons, Bart.; Christie's, 21 May 1943 (1) bt. Mitchell Galleries Ltd.; B. Welch, Charlwood Park, Horley, Surrey, sold Christie's 27 November 1953 (5) bt. Hallsborough Gallery; M. Newman Ltd.; Oscar Herner, Mexico City, mid-1950s; present whereabouts unknown.
EXH: RA 1865 (304); Exposition Universelle, Paris, 1867 (11).
LIT: *Art Journal*, 1 June 1865, p170; *Athenaeum*, 6 May 1865, p627; *ILN*, 13 May 1865, p451; Hippolyte Gautier, *Les Curiosites de l'Exposition*, Universelle de 1867, Paris, 1867, p153; 'Works of John Bagnold Burgess, ARA', *Art Journal*, October 1880, pp298–299 repr.; 'John Bagnold Burgess, ARA', *Magazine of Art*, 1882, p134; Chesneau, London, 1885, p277; *DNB* XXII, 1909, p334.
VERSION: (?) reduced version 32 × 23 in; Christie's, 6 Feb 1948 (131) bt. Mitchell Galleries.

In the year of 'Spanish' Phillip's *Murillo* (cat. no. 44) remarks on "*Bravo, Toro!*" at the 1865 RA were kind though brief or qualified. "A capital picture . . . [it] must be accepted as a great success", wrote the *Art Journal*, near the end of its section SCENES DOMESTIC AND SUBJECTS MISCELLANEOUS, while the *Athenaeum* gave it a paragraph of description concluding,

> "The work is full of expression, and, in its way, capitally painted . . . Although not without vulgarity of manner, and in need of refinement of colour . . . this is, within its proper limits, a very good picture."

The painting established Burgess as Phillip's best-known follower and he consolidated his reputation with pictures like *Stolen by Gipsies* (1868, Bonham's 1966), *Licencing the Beggars: Spain* (1877, Royal Holloway College), and *An artist's almsgiving* (1886, Reading), and with these the reputation of "*Bravo, Toro!*" seems also to have increased. By 1880 when Burgess received the accolade of a biographical article from *The Art Journal* the picture was regarded as a masterpiece:

> ". . . the *chef d'oeuvre* of the artist at this period, and upon which so much of his reputation has been founded, was one of the most popular pictures of the exhibition of 1865, "*Bravo, Toro!*" a Spanish bull-fight. The encounter itself is not seen, but the spectators of it are grouped together on the canvas with striking and vivid reality. [In] this clever and characteristic work . . . terrible excitement, amounting to savageness, is depicted on the faces of the male sightseers; and horrible eagerness adds to the repulsiveness of features which, at least under these circumstances are scarcely human. The contrast between these and the women occupying the box above is great; coldly, and almost calmly, they await the issue of the barbarous contest, caring nothing for the life of the man or the suffering of the beast. That this is the result of habit and custom by no means reconciles us to the strange loss of all the tenderness and kindness which are woman's proudest qualities. But the artist is true and skilful in his delineation of this phase of Spanish life, and we cordially commend the talent which represents it so faithfully. The rich costumes and natural grouping are most admirable."

Two years later the *Magazine of Art* ignored its rival's concern with the moral issues of the bullfight:

> ". . . there has been, for any time these fifteen years past, enough and to spare of individuality and originality in his work to have warranted much earlier than he received it the award of an Associateship in the Royal Academy. So long ago as 1865 he established himself in the estimation of the public, as well as in the opinion of the best judges, as a painter of no mean power, by the exhibition of a picture at the Royal Academy which, from its nature, has been hard for him to surpass. It is not often that an artist can hit upon a subject that lends itself so entirely to pictorial treatment as did that of "*Bravo Toro!*". To describe it or dwell on it here would be gratuitous, well known and associated as the work is with the name of Burgess. Full of beauty and fine in colour, powerful in drawing, expression and execution, it deservedly claimed, and has retained, a large meed of public favour; and if its painter has not always seemed to keep up to the high standard of excellence which it promised, the shortcoming may readily be attributed, as we have said, to the fact that equally telling subjects are not easy to find. If those, upon Dr. Johnson's principle, who paint the manners, tone, and temper of Spain with the veracity which is conspicuous in this artist, should themselves be Spanish in feeling and character, then assuredly Mr. Burgess is by right the very man for the work."

The only voice of dissent was Ernest Chesneau's; "*Bravo Toro!*" was used as a typical example of a particular kind of English artistic vice:

> "What we complain of in most of these English pictures is, that a too great importance is paid to facial expression. Look at that group of persons, standing apart in a Spanish circus, during a bullfight; how savagely they yell and roll their eyes! Leaving the object of all this wild uproar to the spectator's imagination, the artist, Mr. Burgess, who is nevertheless decidedly talented, has thrown all his skill into representing a collection of inflamed countenances hideously distorted by blood-thirsty excitement . . . As a study it may be remarkable, but as a picture it is horrible."

Its offensiveness to French taste may partially be explained by the fact that Burgess's composition was eminently English, based (as the *DNB* pointed out) on Hogarth's *The Laughing Audience*.

"*Bravo, Toro!*" was bought by Sir David Salomons (1797–1873), a liberal MP, Lord Mayor of London in 1855–6 and an influential figure in the struggle for Jewish emancipation. His interesting collection of paintings passed to his nephew and heir; they were dispersed after the latter's death in 1925.

Untraced: photograph exhibited

Henrietta Rae, 1859–1928

Psyche before the throne of Venus 1894

oil on canvas, 76 × 120 in

PROV: purchased from the artist by George McCulloch; his sale, Christie's, 23 May 1913 (86) bt. Tooth (£304 10s), by whom sold to an unrecorded buyer.
EXH: RA 1894 (564); Liverpool Autumn 1894 (1002); Dore Gallery 1895 (30); McCulloch Coll., RA Winter 1909 (156).
LIT: Blackburn, *RA Notes*, 1894, p19, repr. p118; *ILN*, 14 Apr, p462, 12 May, pp571, 595, 11 Aug 1894, p175; *Mag. of Art*, 1894, p274, 1895, pp396, 37; *RA Pictures*, 1894, piii, repr. p13; *Times*, 5 May 1894, p16; Frank Rinder, " 'Henrietta Rae' Mrs. Ernest Normand", *AJ*, Oct 1901, p307; Clara Erskine Clement, *Women in the Fine Arts*, 1904, pp253–4; Arthur Fish, *Henrietta Rae (Mrs. Ernest Normand)*, 1905, pp79–85, repr. facing p80; obit., *Times*, 28 Mar 1928, p11; Maas, 1969, p232.
STUDY: an oil sketch for the whole composition, 18 × 29½ in, was sold Sotheby's Belgravia, 11 July 1972 (116) bt. Maas Gallery; private coll.
ENGR: photogravure, publ. Arthur Tooth & Sons Ltd.

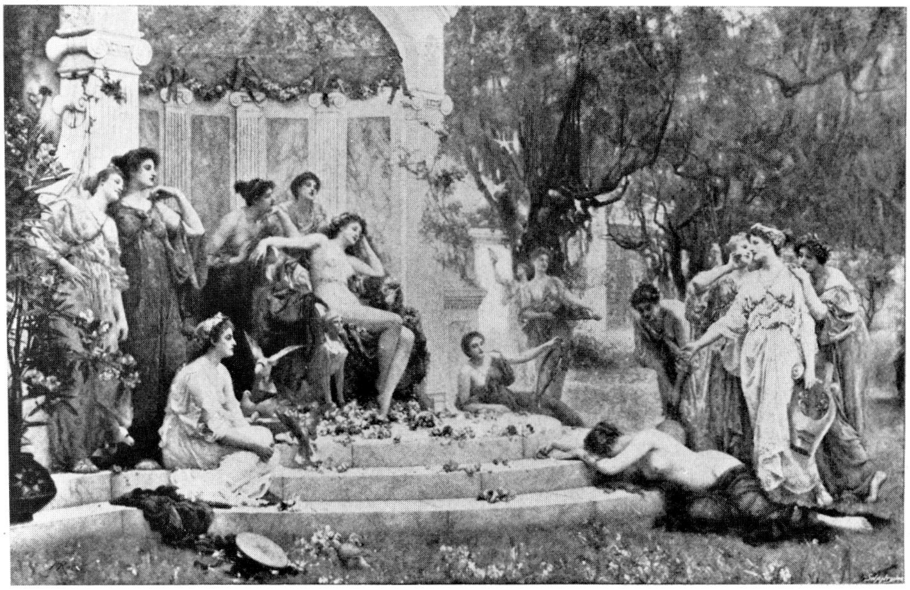

Henrietta Rae began what critics, biographers and friends alike were to call her *chef d'oeuvre* while she and her husband, the painter Ernest Normand, were still living in Holland Park Road, round the corner from her mentor Lord Leighton. The painting, *Psyche before the throne of Venus*, was so large that the early work had to be done in Sir William Richmond's studio nearby, until a new studio was built especially at Norwood. When finally shown at the Academy in 1894 its reception was, in Fish's words, 'triumphant'. *The Times* grouped the paintings of nudes together:

> "The picture of this class which will be most discussed and probably most admired is the very ambitious performance of Mrs. Normand . . . Hung in one of the most important positions, this large [picture] takes every eye, and attracts by its clever composition, its good drawing and pleasant colour. The artist has avowedly illustrated Mr. William Morris's setting of the famous story, but one looks in vain, in this comely and amiable Venus, sitting enthroned before her victim, for any of that ferocity which is of the essence of her character in the poem and in the ancient tale. In fact, Mrs. Normand's whole picture errs on the side of over-prettiness; there is little emotion even in the prostrate figure of Psyche, and none anywhere else. Still, the picture marks a great advance upon any former achievement of the artist, and many an Academician might be well pleased to have painted it."

The objections to its prettiness were shared by Spielmann in the *Magazine of Art* and had already been made by Leighton when he saw the painting on Show Sunday (when the RA exhibitors opened their studios to show their pictures for the forthcoming exhibition). Though he praised it greatly, Leighton concluded "that it had a tendency to prettiness of which he could not approve"; the artist naively repeated this to McCulloch, who had already bought the painting, and Leighton, well aware of the importance vested in his opinion, immediately wrote to the collector:

> "Let me seize this opportunity of saying how sincerely pleased I am to hear that you have bought Mrs. Normand's charming picture. Mrs. N. is *full* of talent, and a most enthusiastic artist – but she is given to self-depreciation (a very rare attribute) – and the purchase of so important an effort is a great and merited encouragement to her."

Leighton's intervention indicates not only his characteristic generosity towards a younger artist but perhaps an awareness that his follower's work was recognisably identifiable with his own; Rae's *Psyche* evidently shared much of the limpid voluptuousness of Leighton's paintings of the nude and the subject was taken from Morris's poem *The Earthly Paradise* of 1868–70, another part of which had at least helped to provide Leighton with the subject of one of his major paintings, *Hercules Wrestling with Death for the Body of Alcestis* of 1870 (see Ormonds, *Leighton*, 1975, pp77–8). Rinder confirms the contemporary recognition of the picture's great debt to Leighton and goes on to describe the subject:

> ". . . (here) we have the first clear testimony to the advantages which accrued from the study of classic beauty and of the influence of Lord Leighton, a lyre belonging to whom, by the way, is reproduced in the picture. After many wanderings in search of her lover, it is to the precincts of a glorious palace that Psyche, the personification of the human soul, has come. The throne of Venus is beneath a dome of gold, and, flanked by pure Ionic pillars, is a garden bright with roses and oleanders, where, too, are ilexes; it is sweet, one is assured, with the fragrance of the honeysuckle . . ."

Blackburn gave exact details of the colours. Rae painted at least two and possibly three separate versions of the central figure of Venus seated on her throne; one of these, commissioned by Athol Thorne in 1902 for a decorative panel in his house, is reproduced in Fish, facing p112, and gives some idea of the colouring of the original picture. Either this panel or another, slightly modified, version of *Venus* is in a private collection in Scotland (34 × 49 in). The Witt Library contains a process reproduction of a wood engraving after the figure in a vertical format and with considerable modifications.

The artist has achieved a considerable measure of success before 1894 with pictures like *Ophelia* (RA 1890, Liverpool) and variations on the style of Marcus Stone, Dicksee and Watts, but by 1893 she was considered of sufficient stature to serve on the Hanging Committee at the Liverpool Autumn Exhibition, the first time a woman had achieved the distinction at a major public exhibition. Extra sophistication was gleaned from a period in Paris in 1890, when Rae not only saw the work of the great French Academics like Cabanel and Bouguereau but was briefly tempted from Academic paths by the later landscapes of Monet and the other Impressionists and

> "produced many sketches in their methods, with purple and violet shadows that ranked with the best of them. Her less impressionable husband was almost proof against such influences, and did not hesitate to discuss the exaggerated tendencies of the theorists with them after the evening meal. That such discussions were by no means dull can readily be imagined." (Fish, p70).

The subject pictures continued into the new century but she also began showing portraits and in 1901 carried out with her husband important decorative paintings in the Royal Exchange. Rae is the subject of current research by Mr. William Dubin of California, to whom the writer is indebted for valuable references.

Untraced: photograph exhibited